THE SILENT GI

Whether or not Henry Sinclair Horne was the 'silent' General he might certainly, if he were still alive, lay claim to being the 'forgotten' General of the Western Front. His self-effacement in a profession not renowned for shrinking violets undoubtedly made its contribution to his relative anonymity – he wrote no memoirs nor kept more than sketchy diaries – but it is still surprising that such an important contributor to the defeat of the German army in the Great War has not until now received the attentions of a biographer.

After a customary slow start in the late Victorian army, Henry Horne first made an impact during the Boer War, fortuitously as it was to turn out, under the eyes of a Colonel Douglas Haig. By the outbreak of the Great War, Henry Horne was a Brigadier General. Two years later he was a full General in command of the BEF's First Army. His was one of the most rapid elevations to top rank recorded in the war. In the two years he spent as an army commander he commanded the brilliant capture of Vimy Ridge, the desperate defensive Battle of the Lys, the successful assault on the Drocourt-Quéant Switch, the outstanding crossing of the Canal du Nord and the liberation of Douai, Cambrai, Lens, Valenciennes and Mons.

Napoleon always sought to ensure that his generals were lucky. In that respect Henry Horne would have suited him. He was lucky in having a long-standing close professional relationship with the Commander-in-Chief, F.M. Haig; in having under his command at First Army the elite Canadian Corps and some distinguished British divisions; and in having as his Chief of Staff one of the outstanding staff officers of the war. But there was more to Henry Horne than just luck.

This belated biography assesses Henry Horne's relationship with Haig and the Canadian Corps. It also evaluates his contribution to the technical advances of the artillery during the war and describes the battles which he conducted. It attempts to accord to Henry Horne the recognition and credit that he deserves but which has for so long been withheld.

Don Farr was born and raised in southwest London. He was educated at Emanuel School, Wandsworth, where his lifelong interest in the First World War was kindled.

The peripatetic nature of his career in the Diplomatic Service curbed somewhat his ability to pursue this interest but since retirement he has been able to make frequent visits to the battlefields of the Western Front and carry out the research for, and writing of, this book. Don Farr is married with three grown-up children. He and his wife live in Wokingham, Berkshire.

General Sir Henry Horne

THE SILENT GENERAL

Horne of the First Army

A Biography of Haig's Trusted
Great War Comrade-in-Arms

Don Farr

Helion & Company Ltd

Helion & Company Limited
26 Willow Road
Solihull
West Midlands
B91 1UE
England
Tel. 0121 705 3393
Fax 0121 711 4075
Email: info@helion.co.uk
Website: http://www.helion.co.uk

Published by Helion & Company 2007
Designed and typeset by Helion & Company Limited, Solihull, West Midlands
Cover designed by Bookcraft Limited, Stroud, Gloucestershire
Printed by Lightning Source

Cover: Portrait of General Lord Horne by Oswald Birley (courtesy of Mrs Maive Impey)

© Helion & Company Ltd 2006
This paperback reprint 2009

ISBN 978-1-906033-47-7

British Library Cataloguing-in-Publication Data.
A catalogue record for this book is available from the British Library.

For details of other military history titles published by Helion & Company Limited contact the above address, or visit our website: http://www.helion.co.uk.

We always welcome receiving book proposals from prospective authors.

For Ann,
with love and thanks,
and for
Gerald, Julian and Nicola,
with love.

Contents

List of Illustrations

List of Maps

Acknowledgements

I must first of all acknowledge my debt to the distinguished military historian, the late Robin Neillands. It was he who, in a talk given to the Thames Valley Branch of the Western Front Association in the 1999–2000 season, mentioned that no biography of Henry Horne had ever been published, thus stirring me into action!

Most of my research has been undertaken at the Imperial War Museum, the Liddell Hart Centre for Military Archives at King's College, London and the Public Record Office (now National Archive) at Kew. At the IWM I have, over the course of many visits, been well looked after and advised by the staff of the Departments of Documents and Printed Books. In the former case my special thanks are due to Dr Simon Robbins, the 'guardian' of the Horne papers, Rod Suddaby and Anthony Richards. In the latter case, Christopher Hunt has usually been my mentor and been particularly helpful in advising on suitable maps and clearing their use. I should also acknowledge the great help I received from Alan Wakefield of the IWM's Photo Archive in identifying and providing copies of most of the prints used in this volume. Permission to use these prints was promptly and generously given by Yvonne Oliver of Photographs Licensing. I must also thank Dil Banerjee of the Museum's Department of Art for permitting the inclusion of the Francis Dodd portrait of General Horne. The artist's legatee, Julia Rushbury, kindly raised no objection.

At the Liddell Hart Centre for Military Archives, Patricia Methven and her colleagues, Katie Mooney and Kate O'Brien, were unfailingly helpful in solving the mechanical mysteries of microfilm readers and also advising on copyright clearance for the collections I consulted. For permission to quote from the collection of Field Marshal Sir Wm Robertson I am indebted to The Trustees of the Liddell Hart Centre for Military Archives. For permission to quote from the published works of Captain Sir Basil Liddell Hart I am indebted to the Literary Executor of the Liddell Hart Estate. It was at the Liddell Hart Centre that I read the First World War diaries of Field Marshal Earl Haig. Permission to quote from them, as I have extensively, has been kindly granted by The Trustees of the National Library of Scotland, acting on behalf of the present Earl Haig. I am grateful to Colm McLaughlin of the National Library of Scotland for arranging this. Kate O'Brien of the Liddell Hart Centre was instrumental in putting me in touch with Dr William Sanders Marble, who readily gave permission for me to quote from his doctoral thesis, *The Infantry Cannot Do with a Gun Less*.

I must also record my grateful thanks to Becky Thomas, the Permissions Controller of Faber & Faber Ltd for permission to quote from Siegfried Sassoon's *Memoirs of an Infantry Officer*. I should also mention the help I received from Marian Sweet of the Barbara Levy Literary Agency in trying to fathom where the Siegfried Sassoon rights repose.

I would like to thank Ian Cull, a fellow member of the WFA's Thames Valley Branch, for permission to quote from *The China Dragon's Tales: the 1st Battalion of the Royal Berkshire Regiment in the Great War*.

During my research I visited the Royal Artillery Museum and Library at Woolwich and am indebted for the help I received there from Messrs P. Evans and Les Smith. The latter spent much time researching the 'gun-arc' for me. I also spent a fascinating day with the Archivist of Harrow School, Mrs Rita Gibbs. She very kindly dug out for me all references to Henry Horne in the School Archive and also provided me with photographs of the School's portrait of him by Sir Oswald Birley.

A very enjoyable part of my research was the brief period my wife and I spent in Wick, County Caithness, where Henry Horne began and ended his days. We based ourselves at the North Highland Archive where Archive Assistant Gail Inglis proved invaluable in tracking down relevant material and putting us in touch with local residents who could help further. Among these were Alistair F. Sinclair, the current owner of the Stirkoke Estate, and his lady, who were most generous in their hospitality; Mrs W.B. Ironside of Haster, who readily shared the fruits of her research into the history of the Stirkoke Estate; Mrs Marion Owen of Thurso, who put at our disposal the facilities of the Caithness Field Club and the local Family History Association; David More, who recalled for us some family stories of Stirkoke House when the Hornes were in residence, and provided a photograph of the memorial to Henry Horne erected by his tenantry; Douglas Woodall, who trustingly gave us the key to St John's, Wick's Episcopalian church to enable us to view its Horne memorabilia; and Mrs Alison Young of the solicitors, Georgeson.

(An uncovenanted bonus for the visitor to Wick is an excellent French restaurant, Bord de l'Eau, run by the Franco-Scottish team of Daniel and Janice Chrétien. Not to be missed!)

Regrettably it was only after our return home from Wick that I made contact with Noel Edmonson whose column 'Wicker's World' is one of the adornments of the widely-read John O'Groat Journal. Noel very readily offered to publicise my project in his column and gave me many column inches. This led to a most gratifying response from the Wick area and the Caithness diaspora, from whom I received a hatful of family recollections and other useful information. Gordon Johnson, a specialist researcher in pre-1700 Scotland, was very helpful in providing detailed information on the early days of the Episcopalian community and church in Caithness. Others who came up with useful information were Mr William Coghill of Birmingham, Mr Andrew Guttridge of Thurso, Mr Bill Mowat, MBE, JP of Wick, Mrs Catherine M. Wilson of Thrapston, Northamptonshire, Mr Don Shepherd of Leighton Buzzard, Mr W.D.G. Chalmers of Elgin, and Mrs Pat Hall of Swindon, who very generously provided some Horne family photographs extracted from her grandmother's photo album.

It was as a result of the Wick visit that I finally made contact with Henry Horne's three granddaughters, Mrs Maive Impey, Mrs Eve Horner and the Countess Deirdre de Roany. I have to say that since doing so, they have given me their unstinting support and encouragement as well as complete freedom to quote from the Horne archive they lodged with the Imperial War Museum in 1997 and subsequently. Mrs Impey has been most generous in her hospitality, in showing me such Horne memorabilia as she retains and in allowing my wife and me to photograph her portrait of her grandfather by Sir Oswald Birley. Countess de Roany has also loaned me certain material including some papers which only turned up a couple of years ago. In addition I received copies of the hand-written entries in two family Bibles at her behest. These copies were very kindly provided by Simon A. Leslie of Edinburgh, a grandnephew of Henry Horne. Mr Leslie has been very patient in responding to several questions I have put to him, as has Mrs Louise Scott, a step-granddaughter of Lt Colonel Henry Hildreth, Lady Kitten Horne's late second husband. I am grateful to them both. One other member of the Horne family, Lt. Colonel Roger Horne, very kindly loaned me a copy of his granduncle's South African diary, which had been proving very elusive.

During the writing and preparation for publication of The Silent General I sought advice and help from many sources which were almost invariably readily forthcoming. The well-known military historian, Ian Passingham, was particularly generous with his time, and his advice on the preparation of my text for publication was invaluable. I am also indebted to Dr John Bourne, Professor Peter Simpkins, Tony Morris, John Lee and Niall Cherry, familiar names all in military history circles, for their advice and encouragement so readily given. Closer to home, so to speak, I owe an immense debt of gratitude to a military history buff and personal friend, Vic Sayer. He very kindly offered to be the first reader of my typescript and came up with many valuable suggestions for improving it and restraining any tendency on my part towards hyperbole and over-imaginative interpretations. Major James Nairne has also offered support and suggestions for which I am beholden. I am grateful too for the encouragement and advice I have received from fellow members of the WFA Thames Valley Branch, notably Michael Orr, Mike Lawson, Bridgeen Fox, Phil Mills, Barbara Taylor and Jo Legg. Michael Orr has been especially generous in giving me access to all his research into the history of the 55th (West Lancashire) Division, which will one day soon be converted into a book by him on that distinguished division.

I must too record my gratitude to my publishers, Helion and Company Ltd, for enabling The Silent General to reach a wider potential readership. Duncan Rogers of Helion needed no second bidding to take on the task of publishing a completely unknown author when others had declined. I hope his faith in this author and the book does not prove misplaced.

Last but not least I must record my grateful thanks to my wife Ann for her vital part in this project. Not only did she keep me sane and focussed in the face of an Apple Mac which seemed determined to be as perverse as possible, but she has done all that was necessary to put the book into final form for publication, e.g., typesetting, spell checking, mapmaking, photograph setting, and a myriad of other things incomprehensible to a computer illiterate like me. I am forever in her debt.

Abbreviations

AA	Artillery Adviser
ADC	Aide-de-Camp
ANZAC	Australian and New Zealand Army Corps
BEF	British Expeditionary Force
BGRA	Brigadier General Royal Artillery
Bn	Battalion
CGS	Chief of the General Staff
CIGS	Chief of the Imperial General Staff
C-in-C	Commander-in-Chief
CO	Commanding Officer
CRA	Commander Royal Artillery
DAA	Deputy Assistant Adjutant
DCLI	Duke of Cornwall's Light Infantry
FM	Field Marshal
GCB	Knight Grand Cross, Order of the Bath
GHQ	General Headquarters
GOC	General Officer Commanding
GOC-in-C	General Officer Commanding-in-Chief
GQG	Grand Quartier Général (French Supreme Headquarters)
HE	High Explosive
HLI	Highland Light Infantry (Glasgow Regt)
HQ	Headquarters
IWM	Imperial War Museum
JP	Justice of the Peace
KCB	Knight Commander, Order of the Bath
KCMG	Knight Commander, Order of St Michael and St George
Km(s)	Kilometre(s)
KOYLI	King's Own Yorkshire Light Infantry
KRRC	King's Royal Rifle Corps
LHCMA	Liddell Hart Centre for Military Archives
MBE	Member, Order of the British Empire
MC	Military Cross
MGRA	Major General Royal Artillery
MGRE	Major General Royal Engineers
NCO	Non Commissioned Officer
OED	Oxford English Dictionary
QMG	Quartermaster General
RA	Royal (Regiment of) Artillery
RFA	Royal Field Artillery
RFC	Royal Flying Corps
RGA	Royal Garrison Artillery

RHA	Royal Horse Artillery
RUSI	Royal United Services Institute
RWF	Royal Welsh Fusiliers
SLI	Somerset Light Infantry
SWB	South Wales Borderers
WFA	Western Front Association

Introduction

In its obituary of General Lord Horne of Stirkoke, published on 15 August 1929, the day after his death, *The Times* referred to the widely-held contemporary assessment of Henry Horne as 'The Silent Commander of a Stationary Army'. The newspaper's obituarist evidently regarded this phrase as an apposite description of Lord Horne's life and career from the moment he became GOC-in-C of First Army. In endorsing the description, the obituarist was not seeking to disparage his subject; quite the contrary. But nevertheless, the reference to Henry Horne's army as having been 'stationary' does it and him less than justice.

The allusion to Lord Horne's silence arose largely from the fact that, unlike some of his fellow generals whose careers reached their apogees, or nadirs, in the First World War, he did not write his memoirs or publish any diaries he may have kept. One can see in this a reflection of an innate reticence and lack of any urge to self-aggrandisement, and not, as the cynics might suggest, a fear of the critical reception that had greeted one or two of his peers' attempts at self-justification. He reinforced his reputation for silence by not courting publicity and confining his public speaking to occasions when he deemed it unavoidable.

It was long assumed that, in addition to failing to write his memoirs, Lord Horne had also left no private papers and diaries which might shed light on his life and career. It was only in 1997 that this proved not to be the case when his family entrusted several boxes of documents to the Imperial War Museum. These consisted largely of letters written to his wife from the Western Front, and diaries, photographs, maps and press cuttings mainly, but by no means entirely, pertaining to the First World War. Henry Horne wrote to his wife at least once a day, and sometimes more often, while they were apart and Lady Horne kept these letters, although there are significant gaps in those in the possession of the Imperial War Museum. Regrettably, if understandably, the letters are often more preoccupied with domestic matters than the great events in which Henry Horne was participating. The diaries too contain virtually none of the ruminations on great events and personalities for which the biographer might have hoped. Nevertheless the letters especially often describe in some detail the great events he was currently involved in and his hopes and fears for their outcome.

It is a curious fact that alone of the generals who commanded armies on the Western Front, Lord Horne has not attracted a biographer. Nor does he often seem to get his own entry in dictionaries or similar publications on the First World War (an honourable exception being John Bourne's recent *Who's Who in World War One*).[1] One can even scan the indexes of serious works on the Western Front without finding his name. This apparent oversight is hardly merited.

Horne was appointed to the command of the BEF's First Army in late 1916. The First and Second Armies were established at the beginning of 1915 in recognition of the growing size of the BEF. Throughout 1915, while the Second Army stood largely on the defensive around the Ypres Salient, it was the First Army which took the battle to the enemy with the assaults at Neuve Chapelle, Aubers Ridge, Festubert and Loos. Its reputation as the 'stationary' army must derive firstly from its non-participation in the Battle of the Somme (by which time the BEF had acquired Third, Fourth and Reserve (later Fifth) Armies); and secondly from its relative inactivity in 1917, if one overlooks its participation under Horne's command in the Battle of Arras – hard to do given its resounding success at Vimy Ridge. In 1918, after playing a significant role in blunting the German spring offensives, First Army played its full part in the victorious Allied advances which forced the Germans to seek an Armistice.' Stationary' hardly does justice to such a record of achievement.

Although he was not someone whose career generated controversy or excited great passions (another reason perhaps for his relative neglect), there are 3 aspects of Lord Horne's career which merit some detailed examination. The first is his personal and professional relationship with Field Marshal Earl Haig, credited by some with being behind Lord Horne's rapid advancement up the promotion ladder after 1914, especially rapid for someone whose background was neither cavalry nor infantry and who had not completed the Staff College course. The second is his involvement, if any, with technical developments in the artillery, notably the evolution or invention of the creeping barrage, the perfection of which made such a huge contribution to Allied victory in the First World War. The third is his management of non United Kingdom forces under his command. For much of his tenure of First Army, Horne enjoyed the services of the Canadian Corps. Enjoyment is not perhaps the right word to describe his experiences with the Portuguese Corps. But in both cases his tact, sensitivity and professionalism ensured that the relationships largely worked at the personal and professional level.

What follows will seek to shed some light on these issues and help to restore Lord Horne to his proper place and standing in the histories of the Royal Artillery, the British Army and the First World War.

Part One

1861–1914

Chapter I

Early Days

On 19 February 1861 Mrs Constance Mary Horne gave birth to her fourth child and third son, the boy who was to become General Lord Horne of Stirkoke. The birth took place at Bilbster House, about 5 miles west of Wick, Caithness, one of a number of properties in the area owned by Major James Horne, father of the new born child. The infant was given the names Henry Sinclair at his baptism, which was conducted at St John's Episcopal Church, Edinburgh on 20 April 1861 by his father's younger brother, the Rev John Horne, Church of England Vicar of Earley in the county of Berkshire.[1]

The Horne family connections with the area of Caithness surrounding the fishing town of Wick were well established before the beginning of the nineteenth century. There is an early reference to a Jane Horne, who gave birth in 1773 to Alexander Gunn (who was destined to become a distinguished Church minister based at Watten, only a mile or so from Bilbster). Jane had a brother who was to become known as John Horne of Stirkoke. Their father was a William Horne, described as a Tacksman[2] of Scouthill, Watten, who died at the age of 79 on 29 September 1831.[3]

John Horne of Stirkoke had at least two sons, William and Donald. The latter, destined to be Lord Horne's grandfather, was born on 20 May 1787. He was married on 1 June 1821 to a Jane Ogilvie of Chesters, Roxburghshire, who was to leave him a widower after only 13 years of marriage. Donald earned his living as a 'Writer to the Signet' ('WS') an Edinburgh-based lawyers' body which originally dealt with Scottish crown and government matters. Before her early death, Donald's wife produced at least 3 sons, the eldest of whom, James, would become the father of Lord Horne. Donald was to die, aged 83, on 23 June 1870.

The Horne family's close connection to the Stirkoke estate began with John Horne of Stirkoke's purchase of the property in 1822. In 1827 Lord Horne's great uncle, William Horne, succeeded to the property and added others. But he was made bankrupt in 1843 after which the estate was administered by James Brown, an accountant from Edinburgh. In 1853 the estate was purchased by Major James Horne, thus keeping it in the family, if not in the direct line of succession.[4]

Major James Horne appears to have been the first in his family to pursue a military career. Born in 1822, he was commissioned into the 71st (Highland) Regiment of Foot (The Highland Light Infantry) in 1843. During his 12 years with the colours he served with both the 71st and 92nd (Highland) Regiments, spending much of his service in Canada.

The year following his purchase of the Stirkoke estate, he sold his commission and left the army. For a time after his return to civilian life he lived in Cheltenham. It was here that, on 16 August 1855, he married Constance Mary Shewell The announcement of the wedding read:

> August 16, 1855 at St Mary's Church by the Rev John Horne, MA, Balliol College Oxford, brother of the Bridegroom, James Horne Esq of Stirkoke

Caithness, Major Ross-shire etc Rifles, late Captain 92nd Highlanders, to Constance Mary, daughter of Edward Warner Shewell Esq of 18 Royal Crescent, Cheltenham.

Major Horne's father-in-law was a wealthy and prominent citizen of the Gloucestershire spa town. His wealth appears to have derived to a considerable extent from his ownership of a number of properties in the affluent areas of the town. For many years he was Chairman of the Cheltenham Board of Commissioners and when he died in 1878, at the advanced age of 85, he was still in office as Chairman of the Cheltenham Water Company. He and his wife Emma, who died in 1881, raised a very large family. Their children all appear to have lived to maturity, but at least six of them predeceased their father and a further one died between the deaths of his parents. Curiously and tragically, no fewer than 3 sons died in separate incidents at sea, even though only one of them was a naval officer. Three other sons pursued careers in the Indian army. One was carried off by sudden illness; a second died of wounds at Kandahar during the Second Afghan War; only one survived to return to Cheltenham on his retirement. Two daughters also predeceased their father, one of whom, aged only 19, was a further victim to the risks inherent in living in India in the nineteenth century.[5]

Parts of Shewell's life read like a Victorian novel. His will insistently disinherited the children of yet another son who had predeceased him. Could he have disapproved of his late son's choice of wife? He also engaged in an acrimonious and very public dispute with the rector of the parish of St Mary's Cheltenham, where he was a devout communicant, over proposals to raze the church and rebuild it. He opposed this and apparently won the day, for the church is still there. It boasts a stained glass window and several plaques in memory of some of Shewell's children.

Following the death of Mrs Shewell, a large number of the properties belonging to her late husband's estate were sold with the proceeds being divided among the surviving daughters, including Constance Mary. This windfall would almost certainly have been in addition to a generous settlement made on her by her father at the time of her marriage to James Horne.

When he returned to Scotland with his bride, Major James Horne took over the running and development of the Stirkoke estate with an area of 7,117 acres and a rental value of £2,476. As a leading citizen of Caithness he devoted himself actively to public service. With his military background, he was ideally suited to raise and manage the Rifle Volunteers of Caithness in the rank of Major. But he also became a magistrate and the chairman of a board dealing with law and order issues. He was appointed Deputy Lieutenant of Caithness. He even stood, unsuccessfully, as a Conservative candidate in the 1868 general election, which brought Gladstone to power for the first time in a Liberal landslide.

During the brief 19 years of marriage they were to enjoy, Constance presented James Horne with no fewer than 12 children, 6 boys and 6 girls, of whom all but 2 survived to adulthood. James and Constance Horne suffered a double blow in late 1872 when their eldest child, Donald, died at the age of 16, only a few days after the death of their youngest daughter, Gertrude, aged only 11 months. James Horne's premature death, only 2 years later at the age of 51, has been partly put down to his failure to recover from this double tragedy. Constance Horne lived on at Stirkoke House until her own death on 13 July, 1906 at the age of 70.

The record of Henry Sinclair Horne's early life is sketchy, but it would be reasonable to suppose that, as the son of a relatively wealthy landowner and gentleman farmer with a country estate, he would have been an eager devotee of the country pursuits – hunting, shooting and fishing – which he was to pursue and indulge in with great enjoyment throughout his life.

He must also have been drawn in to the worship of the congregation of the Evangelical Church to which his parents belonged. The congregation of Wick/ Thurso had been founded in 1855. As part of the Anglican community, it was the natural haven for James and Constance Horne and they immediately took a leading role. James became one of two lay members of the church building committee – the congregation had no permanent place of worship in the early years – and was eventually responsible for the financial arrangements under which the Church of St John was finally built in Moray street, Wick. The new building was consecrated in 1870 when Henry Sinclair Horne was 10 years old. (It is still there and the Horne family's close connection with it is evidenced by a series of memorial plaques.) Constance Horne appears to have acted as a sort of musical director and organist-in-chief. It must have been within the Evangelical congregation that the foundations were laid for Henry Sinclair's lifelong Christian faith.[6]

The young Henry Sinclair must have received some schooling in these early years prior to preparatory school but there is no indication of where this happened. The national census of 1871 does not show Henry Sinclair in residence at the family home of Stirkoke House, unlike most of his siblings. It is very probable that he was already boarding at his preparatory school, Southlea, in Malvern, Worcestershire; he was certainly in residence there a year later. Southlea Preparatory School no longer exists, apparently having closed down in the 1930s. At the time Henry Sinclair was there it was still a relatively new establishment, having been founded in the 1860s by a distinguished educationalist, W R C Hays. Quite why James and Constance Horne chose the school for their son is not clear. It seems to have had no close connection to his future public school. If it was not the school's burgeoning reputation that attracted them, it may have been something as mundane as Malvern's proximity to Cheltenham, which would have enabled the young boy's maternal grandparents to keep a close eye on things.

Only a month before his father's untimely death, Henry Sinclair entered the famous public school, Harrow. There he was following in the footsteps of his late elder brother, Donald, who had left the School over 2 years previously, only 8 months before his death. Henry Sinclair followed Donald into Mr Bosworth Smith's House, the Knoll. Although but a short time at Harrow, too short to reach and make a mark at the senior levels of the School, Henry Sinclair formed a deep attachment to it which was to remain with him throughout his life. Whilst there he proved to be an above average student, ending in the upper half of the modern upper fifth form. Curiously, however, given his choice of arm for his military career, he showed no particular aptitude for mathematics. On the sporting side, he was a member of his House cricket first XI. At football, on the other hand, his enthusiasm seems to have exceeded his talent.

In the words of the obituary published in the School magazine *The Harrovian* shortly after his death, 'Those who were with him in the Knoll speak of him as a boy who was liked and respected by the House; a typical Scotsman, silent and reserved.[7]

From Harrow, the young Horne moved on to prepare for entry into The Royal Military Academy, Woolwich, the first step in his military career.

Chapter II

The Young Officer

On 20 September 1878, at the age of 17, Henry Horne entered the Royal Military Academy, Woolwich, and set out upon his military career. The Academy, popularly and almost invariably referred to as 'The Shop', was one of the oldest military academies in existence, having been founded in 1741 to train 'Gentlemen of the Ordnance', or aspiring officers of the artillery and engineers.[1]

Quite why Horne had set his sights on a career in the Royal Regiment of Artillery is not clear. The example of his father might have suggested the infantry, his love of horses the cavalry, as more likely career choices. In a lighthearted moment towards the end of his life, he told his listeners that, as a boy, he had been taken by his father to a review of the Caithness volunteers at Wick. So impressed had he been by the busby of the Caithness artillerymen that he there and then decided that the artillery was for him. Even allowing for the strength of childhood impressions, this story smacks of a good yarn.

Horne received his commission into the Royal Artillery on 19 May 1880, rather sooner than would have normally been the case. But during the year 1880, 3 batches of young officers were commissioned instead of the usual 2. As a consequence, the number of young officers gazetted into the Regiment from The Shop that year was the highest (109) in any one year since its foundation. This was unlikely to improve the usual glacial speed of advancement up the ladder of promotion in the Regiment, as was to be borne out by Horne's early experience.[2]

In June 1880 Horne joined the Royal Garrison Artillery. He was posted to the 4th Battery of the 7th Brigade which was quartered at Woolwich. In April 1882 the Battery was redesignated the 3rd Battery Lancashire Division. But only a month later Horne moved on, having been appointed Adjutant of the 1st Brigade Southern Division, Royal Garrison Artillery, based at Portsmouth.

In December 1883 Horne was transferred to the mounted branch of the Regiment and moved to Weedon, Northamptonshire. There he joined N Battery of the 2nd Brigade, which was later redesignated the 71st (Broken Wheel) Field Battery, a Battery with proud traditions and high standards of efficiency. It had recently greatly distinguished itself at the Battle of Tel-el-Kebir in Egypt. Two years after joining N Battery, Horne was appointed Adjutant of the 2nd Brigade. He continued to hold this appointment, although he was still on the strength of N Battery, until he moved on in June 1887. Horne was very proud of his association with the Battery and kept in touch with it for the rest of his life.

The posting to Weedon began a long association with the county of Northamptonshire and the Pytchley Hunt, with which he was to indulge his love of hunting for many years to come.[3] Field Marshal Lord Milne, a fellow Gunner, was to recall, 'Possibly he (Horne) was happiest in the hunting field, where the easy, graceful seat of his soldierly figure could not but attract attention'.

It was almost certainly through the Pytchley at this period that Henry Horne met the lady who, some years later, would become his wife. Mrs Kate Blacklock, as she then was, shared his enthusiasm for hunting, as would their daughter in due time

In 1887 overseas service beckoned and November of that year found him in India where, on 17 August the following year, he was promoted to Captain with 8th Battery, Western Division, Garrison Artillery. Shortly afterwards, he moved to 1st Battery, Northern Division (renamed 7th Mountain Battery in 1889). From there he was posted to the 27th Field Battery in January 1890. In September of the same year he was appointed Staff Captain, Royal Artillery Bengal, based at Meerut.

February 1892 saw him moving to his final appointment in India when he became Adjutant, Royal Horse Artillery, based at Kirkee. It was during this appointment that, for the first time if not the last, Horne demonstrated a knack for becoming associated with technical advance. The 'gun-arc'[4], which was to become an integral part of the equipment of the artillery of the field army, was first evolved and made use of at the Royal Artillery practice camp at Hinjaori in 1895. It all happened under the auspices of the camp Staff Officer, Captain Henry Horne.

Early in his career Horne had been seen as a model subaltern of a battery with a way with an Irish song, which had become a feature of mess nights. In India he was seen as a coming man. While Adjutant at Kirkee he demonstrated his love of sport, predictably, for such a natural horseman, engaging enthusiastically in pig sticking and polo. In the words of Lieutenant General Sir Herbert Uniacke, Colonel Commandant, RA, at the time of Horne's death:

> Not only was he an excellent Adjutant but a leader in many forms of sport. He was Hon Secretary of the Tent Club which could only be kept going when a man could be found with the necessary initiative and energy to run the sport under most difficult conditions. At polo he played Back in the Regimental side.

In 1896 Horne was ordered back to England. There he first joined 53rd Field Battery and then T Battery, Royal Horse Artillery. On 1 July of the following year he married Kate, by now the widow of William James Sinclair Blacklock, of Newnham Hall, Northamptonshire, and the daughter of George McCorquodale of Gladlys, Anglesey and Newton-le-Willows, Lancashire.[5] The friendship the couple had formed during Horne's time at Weedon in the mid-1880s had been kept up by letter during his time in India. In 1891, Mr and Mrs Blacklock under-took a round-the-world tour, during which they passed through India. Horne met them in Delhi and showed them the sights of the future capital of the Raj and Meerut for a few days, before having to return to his military duties.[6] He and Kate continued to maintain touch by letter.

In late 1894, Mr Blacklock died as a result of injuries sustained in a tragic hunting accident. Soon afterwards, Horne, still in India, declared his attachment to Kate by letter.[7] According to a letter he was to write to her from the Front in 1915, he had fallen in love with her nearly 30 years previously.[8] But there could have been no question of pursuing a courtship with her at that time, as she was a married woman. For the next decade Horne was to carry a torch for her. However, in the light of the changed circumstances following Kate's bereavement and her consequent freedom to remarry, Horne was greatly distressed when his advances were rebuffed. But when he returned to England in 1896, he managed to overcome her objections. It was to be a marriage of great happiness.

The relationship of Henry and Kate Horne must have derived much of its great strength from their shared interests. The most important of these would have been their shared steadfast Christianity. They had met through their love of hunting. They were, too, both keen anglers and were to take full advantage of their Scottish connections to pursue the sport. When he was at the Front during the First World War, Henry was to encourage Kate to spend as much time as she could fishing in Scotland. She needed little urging.

Kate's late father and late husband had been partners in the old-established printing firm of McCorquodale and Co, and she had been left very comfortably off financially. It was probably largely her money that would enable the Hornes to live in some style. But until the end of his life, Henry was to remain financially prudent, which perhaps indicates that things might not always have been so easy.

Kate had a son, Jack, and a daughter, Dorothy, from her first marriage. On 24 February 1899 she gave birth to what was to prove to be the only child of her marriage to Horne. Their daughter was also named Kate, but was to be familiarly known as Kitten.

Shortly after their marriage, Henry and Kate purchased Priestwell House in the village of East Haddon, Northamptonshire. This was to be the family home until early in the Second World War, sharing that role from the early 1920s onwards with Stirkoke House.

In 1898, Horne was promoted to Major and ordered to Mauritius to command No 8 Company, Western Division, RA. He did not however join his new Company, but remained in Plymouth, attached to Western Division head-quarters. It was here that the outbreak of the South African War was to find him.[9]

Chapter III

South Africa

The long-standing friction between Great Britain and the Boer republics of the Orange Free State and the Transvaal finally degenerated into all-out war on 11 October 1899. President Kruger of the Transvaal was induced to issue an ultimatum to the British government couched in such terms as to ensure its rejection; it duly was.

Although the crisis in Southern Africa had been building up over a long period, the outbreak of war found Britain, and especially its army, totally unprepared for the sort of conflict it was now called upon to fight. There were far too few troops in place in the region even to ensure the safety of Natal and the Cape Colony from invasion, let alone to carry the fight to the 2 Boer states. The troops that were there were ill-led and inadequately trained to fight a modern war against sophisticated opponents. The Boers were a far cry from the courageous, but hopelessly outgunned, tribesmen the army had largely been accustomed to dealing with in the nineteenth century.

The War Office took immediate steps to address the problems of troop numbers and leadership by mobilising and despatching I Army Corps to South Africa, under General Sir Redvers Buller. Major Henry Horne was one of the many British soldiers caught up in this flurry of activity. He was placed in charge of a small unit of 6 officers, 390 NCOs and men, largely reservists recalled to the colours, and 6 horses, which was mobilised at Woolwich on 9 October. It left Woolwich on 3 November for Chatham from where it sailed the following day. After what was described as an 'unpleasant' voyage the unit arrived at Capetown towards the end of the month and disembarked.[1]

The beginning of 1900 found Horne at Naauwpoort in charge of an ammunition column consisting of 80 horses, 130 mules, 6 oxen and 23 wagons and carts. The column was attached to the Cavalry Division, which was under the command of Major General John French. On 2 January it was ordered to join the division's advanced troops at Colesberg, Cape Colony. Its main role was to keep the division's artillery batteries, which were constantly on the move, plentifully supplied with ammunition. The task led to long days in the saddle for Horne. The climate was benign – hot days and cool nights – and Horne thrived on the work. He rapidly formed a view of how best to deal with the Boers in the light of the total and costly failure of an unsupported infantry attack by the Suffolk Regiment to capture a Boer-held hill near Colesberg. He wrote:

> There is only one way I feel sure of fighting these fellows, and that is to pound them with artillery, and then let the infantry work up in very extended order, firing from behind rocks, etc. When they get near pound away with the guns harder than ever, so that the Boers dare not show themselves to fire, and they will get nervous and run. We can always silence their guns at once, as directly we get a shell near them they leave the gun and go and lie down.[2]

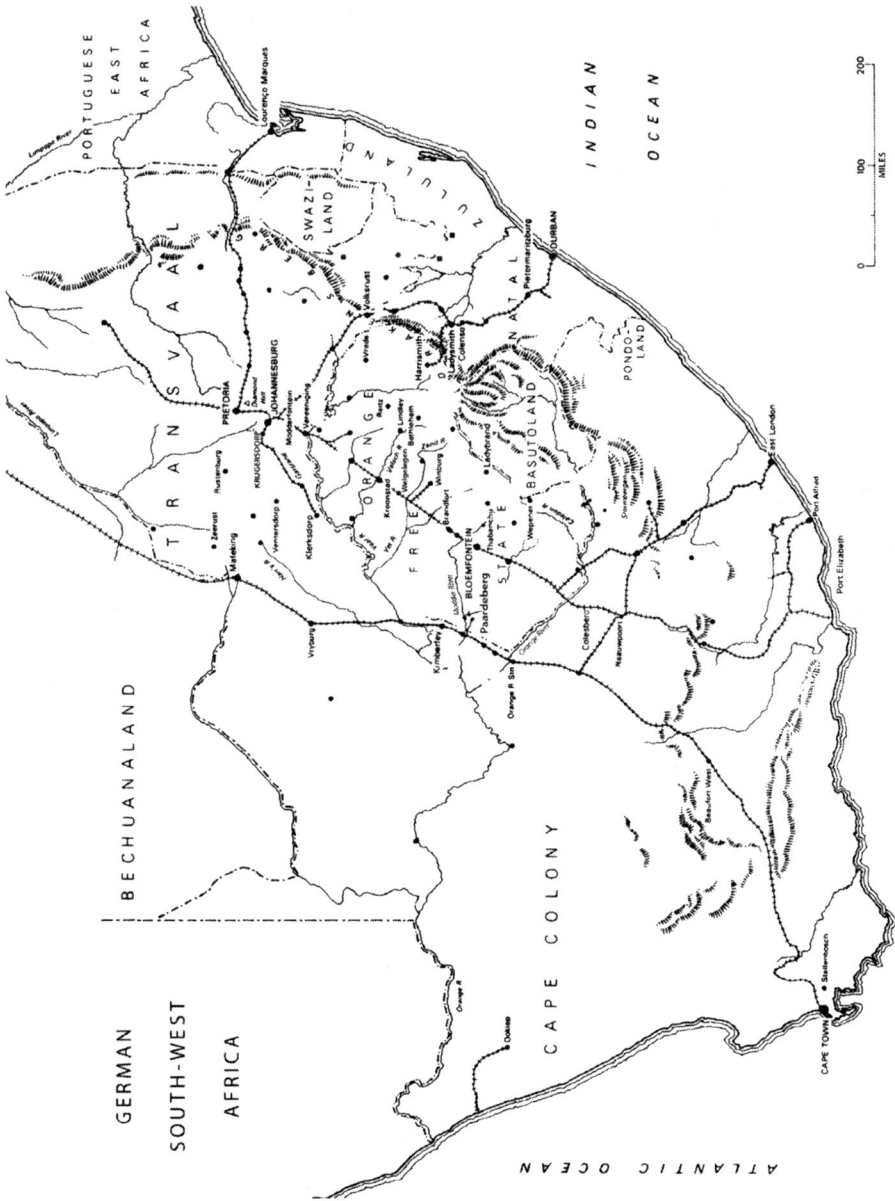

Map 1: Southern Africa

By the time that Horne joined the Cavalry Division, Major General French had already had an exciting war. Along with his chief staff officer, Lt Colonel Douglas Haig, he had been recalled from Ladysmith in Natal just prior to the town being completely surrounded and besieged by the Boers. The two future Commanders-in-Chief of the British Expeditionary Force in France underwent an uncomfortable journey under fire in the last train to leave Ladysmith, but emerged unscathed.[3] Following their early experiences of the fighting, Haig had already reached some conclusions on the tactics that would be required to counter the Boers and the shortcomings the 3 arms of the service had so far displayed. He was critical of the artillery for its over dependence on shrapnel (not to be cured until well into the First World War). This enabled the Boer gunners to take shelter when under fire and return to man their pieces once the fire was lifted, little or no damage having been done to the guns themselves. Haig was also critical of the lack of mobility of the British guns compared to those of their opponents.[4]

By early February 1900 the Cavalry Division had in its sights the relief of the town of Kimberley, under siege by the Boers. The division set off from Modder river in the early hours of 11 February. Horne's ammunition column formed part of the 3rd Brigade of the division. Horne was critical of the arrangements for the division's march over the next 4 days which exhausted men, horses and mules in the effort to effect the relief at the earliest possible moment. He could not see how the cavalry could carry the required 3 days' supplies for man and horse. Horne found himself having to take charge of chaotic situations at river crossings as the support echelons tried to keep up with the cavalry.

By the third day of the advance Horne was obliged to leave the mule portion of his column to follow on, while he pressed ahead with the horse-drawn wagons. The following day, he was to be denied the pleasure of being present at the actual entry into Kimberley on 15 February 1900, as the siege was raised. The ammunition column had been left behind for lack of horses, practically all of which had had to be handed over to replace those that had been lost in the division's horse artillery batteries. The route of the relentless drive to relieve Kimberley was marked by the corpses of the Cavalry Division's horses. Horne deplored their sacrifice to the perceived urgency of raising the siege and liberating Cecil Rhodes, who had managed to get himself trapped in the town. He questioned whether this political consideration had justified the serious damage that had been done to the division as an effective fighting force.[5]

The relief of Kimberley ushered in a period of success for the British as the invasion of the Orange Free State, under the command of the new British Commander-in-Chief, Field Marshal Lord Roberts, and his Chief of Staff, Field Marshal Lord Kitchener, gathered momentum. Kitchener maintained pressure on the army of the Boer General Cronje, eventually bringing it to bay near Paardeberg, the Cavalry Division having successfully cut off its escape route. Horne and his column had followed the cavalry up from Kimberley, forming part of the British Army which was gradually tightening the noose round Cronje. They were however largely passive spectators of the fighting. On 27 February, Cronje surrendered at Paardeberg with nearly 4,000 men. Horne was full of praise of both the planning and execution of what he thought would be a far-reaching success.[6]

Lord Roberts' next major objective was to be the capture of Bloemfontein, the capital of the Orange Free State. After a few days' pause a 3-pronged drive on the city began on 7 March. Enemy resistance was slight to begin with but gradually stiffened. Generally some distance from the fighting, the main problems Horne had to cope with were the difficult terrain for his wagons and the poor condition of his semi-starved horses and mules. For much of the time he was out of touch with his brigade and the division and only heard by chance that Roberts had entered Bloemfontein. Keen to be there on the first day of its capture Horne pressed on, reaching the city outskirts by 18h00 on 13 March. That same evening he rejoined the rest of his brigade 2 miles north of the city.[7]

Horne had joined the Cavalry Division at a time when French and Haig were prepared to welcome a more imaginative and effective approach to the employment of their divisional artillery. Horne was soon in a position to help in the delivery of this. Shortly after the capture of Bloemfontein, he was given command of R Battery, Royal Horse Artillery, like his former command part of 3rd Brigade of the Cavalry Division. Its armament consisted of 6 guns and one pom-pom (Maxim Vickers automatic 1 pounder).

As he moved on, Horne could look back on a job well done. His tenure of command of the ammunition column had been short but he was to leave a permanent mark. He had been one of the first to realise the necessity of handing over draught horses with their neck collars, a practice which was later to be adopted officially.[8]

Horne's first experience of command in the field with his new unit came in late April and early May. The 3rd Brigade were to operate in support of 8th Infantry Division which had been ordered to relieve the town of Wepener, about 60 miles southeast of Bloemfontein. The operation necessitated dislodging the Boers from a strong position at Thaba-Nchu and Horne's guns were to see a great deal of action as they successfully dealt with the Boer artillery. His main problem was less the enemy than the constant long marches, often on reduced rations as the supplies could not keep up. This left both his men and horses exhausted, in the latter case often terminally so. Wepener was duly relieved; the Boers melted away as the British closed in. Horne's battery made its way back to Bloemfontein, arriving on 4 May. Although his guns had performed very well, Horne could not regard the death of 24 of his horses, with another 26 unfit for further use, as anything other than a tragic waste.[9]

R Battery was given very little time to recover before it was on the road once again. Horne was ordered to overtake Lord Roberts' main force, which was advancing on the town of Kroonstad, about 120 miles to the northeast. Before setting off on 7 May, Horne was able to replace his losses in horses but remained well, if not critically, short of men. In 3 days the battery covered the 75 miles to Welgelegan station, where Lord Roberts had established his headquarters. Here Horne learned that the Boers were expected to resist the crossing of the Zand river 8 miles ahead.

In the event little resistance was encountered when the crossing was made on 10 May. But Horne's battery had a busy day, once they were over the river, dealing with a long-range gun and 2 guns and a pom-pom which had tied down the British mounted infantry. With the help of a dramatic gallop in line abreast to shorten the range, Horne engaged the Boer artillery and forced it to retire. He kept up the pressure on the enemy, who were disposed to resume their shelling from every suitable ridge as they retired. By nightfall the battery had marched 21 miles, fighting at intervals.

After a bitterly cold night, the advance was resumed until it came up against Boer entrenchments at Boschrand, about 7 miles south of Kroonstad. These were abandoned by the Boers during the following night, enabling the advance to Kroonstad to resume. The town too was found to have been evacuated and was occupied by Lord Roberts' troops on 12 May. There was to be a two-week pause before the invasion of the Transvaal began.[10]

When Lord Roberts' infantry divisions crossed the Vaal river into the Transvaal on 27 May, R Battery formed the right rearguard. A few rounds sufficed to drive off the Boers who had been collecting in some force and the battery crossed the Vaal in the evening. For the following 2 days R Battery continued to advance on Lord Roberts' right flank encountering no enemy as they passed through grim and deserted mining areas, which reminded Horne of the Black Country of the English Midlands. On 30 May, however, the Boers mounted a determined attack which could have resulted in a severe setback for 3rd Brigade. About 500 Transvaal police, supported by 3 guns and a pom-pom, threatened to give the brigade some serious trouble. Horne distributed his guns well. Two of them, placed on the right, forced the Boers to withdraw by firing over them with short fuses. One of the enemy guns was also put out of action. The fighting lasted less than an hour, with Horne describing it as exciting while it lasted.

The following day, after a further march northwards, the brigade occupied the dynamite factory outside Johannesburg while Lord Roberts' troops took the surrender of Johannesburg fort and paraded through the town. On 3 June the march resumed towards Pretoria. The Boers resisted strongly from the forts and ridges south and west of the town, but Horne's battery was only lightly engaged in the fighting. On the evening of 4 June the Boers withdrew, enabling Lord Roberts to enter the town on the 5th.[11]

A few days prior to the capture of Pretoria Horne had ruminated prophetically on the future development of the war.

> I do hope that peace will be made in the next few days, or that if not, they will stand at Pretoria and let us besiege it. Otherwise I am so afraid that we shall spend ages moving about the country hunting scattered parties of Boers, which will be horrible work, very hard and trying for us, and unsatisfactory in its results.[12]

Horne's fears were soon to begin to be realised. Any hope that the capture of Pretoria would signal the end of Boer resistance, and the start of genuine moves to peace, was quickly dissipated. It became clear that a Boer proposal for peace talks had merely been a stratagem to buy them time to regroup and reorganise, a stratagem which was all too successful. Within 3 days of the occupation of Pretoria, the 3rd Cavalry Brigade was on the move again, with orders to join 'Hamilton's Force' at Diamond Hill, a strongly held Boer position east of Pretoria. Horne's battery was so short of fit horses by this time that he was obliged to return 2 of his guns to Pretoria. After a frustrating day on 11 June, during which 2nd and 3rd Cavalry Brigades made unavailing attempts to outflank the Boer positions, the following day saw infantry and mounted infantry gain the crest of Diamond hill. A secondary Boer position proved impregnable however. Horne's role on both days had been to protect Hamilton's right flank. His guns were kept busy and did their job well. During the night the Boers evacuated their secondary position and, after a day's rest, Hamilton's Force returned to Pretoria, arriving on the 16th.[13]

Three days later, the force left Pretoria and headed south to join moves to entrap the Boer General Christiaan de Wet in the mountains south of the town of Bethlehem about 200 miles from Pretoria. Horne's battery experienced very little opposition as it marched steadily southwards, reaching Reitz on 6 July and Bethlehem a few days later. While on convoy escort duty, which was supposed to take his battery to Winberg by way of Reitz and Kroonstad, Horne learned that de Wet was marching north. The 3rd Cavalry Brigade were ordered to Lindley to intercept him.

On 19 July, just 8 miles from the town, which was now in Boer hands, the brigade came under fire. Horne's battery, now up to full strength, soon found itself engaged by Boer guns. As was their custom, however, they rapidly retreated as soon as Horne's guns had their range, but not before they had suffered some damage. The battery's pom-pom proved its effectiveness in pushing the Boers off a crest from where they would have been able to enfilade the British positions. Horne's guns materially assisted in preventing the Boers, who greatly outnumbered the British, from surrounding and rounding them up.

The Boers broke off the engagement and moved north with 3rd Cavalry moving in parallel with them. They took up positions in the hills north of Vredefort where the depleted and tired British forces tried to draw a cordon around them. In Horne's view, the British attempts until mid-August to hem in de Wet were rendered nugatory by the mistaken decision to allow him to cross the Vaal virtually unhindered, together with the failure to seal off his line of retreat. Horne was particularly critical of the performance of the Cavalry Division, which had not demonstrated sufficient urgency at vital times. This particular campaign ended for 3rd Cavalry Brigade when, attached to Lord Methuen's force, they marched to Zeerust, arriving on 22 August.[14]

Zeerust was to offer no opportunity to rest and re-equip before the brigade was ordered to accompany the Colonial Division on a march of 140 miles through 'disturbed' country to Krugersdorp, just west of Johannesburg. Horne was highly critical of this order. It would expose the brigade and the division, both severely depleted in numbers, to traversing country which would offer the Boers excellent opportunities to set up ambushes. He wondered why the General Staff in Pretoria could not have arranged for the journey to be done by rail.

Horne's fears were not misplaced. It was only the lack of resolution of the Boers, the doughty fighting of the Colonials, and the effective handling of the British guns, that saw the column through. Krugersdorp was reached on 2 September, 8 days after setting out. There had been stiff fighting on most days as well as heavy rain and thunderstorms. The column suffered casualties of about 10%. In Horne's view, these were a fair reflection of the folly of sending a small force marching through disturbed country.[15]

Horne's operational handling of his battery and the great qualities he had shown as a determined fighter with tactical flair, had quickly brought him to the favourable attention of his seniors, notably Field Marshal Lord Kitchener, Major General John French and Lt Colonel Douglas Haig. He was to enhance his reputation as he led his Battery in various driving operations in the Orange river valley and Cape Colony as the British sought to force the Boers to give up the unequal struggle. But, as Horne had feared, the Boers were to continue the fight for a further 2 years after their loss of Pretoria, largely using guerilla methods. Horne and his battery were to be involved for much of this time in the fruitless hunt for the Boer's most successful and elusive commando leader, General Christiaan de Wet.

Horne's experiences over this period reflected the general exasperation felt in the British army at the tactics adopted by the Boers; they were not what the British were accustomed to. Horne however soon adjusted to the Boer habit of temporarily abandoning their guns when under attack. He ascribed this to 'nervousness' (a euphemism for cowardice?) rather than an understandable precaution. He also learned to live with the difficulty of spotting the enemy guns, which were generally well concealed and used smokeless powder. His adaptability and readiness to fight the Boers on their own terms probably also left a lasting favourable impression on his superiors. Horne's strongly held belief that even war should be played by the rules can be exemplified by one incident early on in the campaign. A trooper had been killed by a shot fired from a farm flying the white flag. Horne's strongly expressed view was that the farm should be burned. But the commanding General demurred.

In late 1901 Horne was promoted to Brevet Lieutenant Colonel. He told his wife that he might instead have been awarded the DSO, but on balance he thought the promotion would be better for the furtherance of his career. Shortly afterwards the frustration of his long, absence from home and family was partially alleviated when his wife and daughter sailed out for a family reunion and holiday with him at the end of the year.[16]

From January 1902 until the close of the campaign at the end of May, Horne did duty with remounts at Durban and Bloemfontein successively. When he returned to England later that year he had been away for nearly three years, far longer than even the most pessimistic could have foreseen. Nevertheless, his had not been a bad war. In addition to his promotion, he had been Mentioned in Despatches and held the Queen's Medal with five clasps and the King's Medal with two clasps.[17] As it was to turn out, even more important for his future career was the very favourable impression he had made, for his abilities as an organiser, fighting soldier and gunnery officer, on Lord Kitchener, on Major General John French and, above all, on Colonel Douglas Haig.

Chapter IV
The Inter-War Years

On his return from South Africa, Brevet Lieutenant Colonel Henry Horne was appointed Commanding Officer of Royal Artillery No 3 Depot, a recruit depot at Weedon in Northamptonshire, thus renewing his association with the town and the county. The location suited Horne and his wife very well as they could live at East Haddon and hunt with the Pytchley. His appointment dated from October 1902. Two years later he was certified fit for promotion to Regimental Lieutenant Colonel. In the words of Lt General Sir Herbert Uniacke:

> No one could have been better fitted to command a recruit depot. Combining an inflexible insistence on efficiency with the greatest kindness and courtesy to all ranks, No 3 Depot became essentially a 'happy' unit, and those battery commanders counted themselves fortunate who received drafts of recruits that had passed through Horne's hands.[1]

His promotion duly came through on 14 November 1905. It entailed a move to Ireland, where he took over command of XXXI Brigade, Royal Field Artillery at Fermoy, county Cork. Within 6 months he received a further promotion to Brevet Colonel.[2]

On arrival in Ireland, Horne and his wife took up residence in the small town of Mallow, about 10 miles from Fermoy, where they were able to indulge their passion for hunting, with the Duhallow hounds. So enjoyable was his association with this hunt that Horne came near to resigning from the army in order to become Master of the Duhallow. But something prevented him taking that fateful step and he was saved for the army.[3]

It was while he was based at Fermoy that Henry Horne's mother died at Stirkoke on 13 July 1906 in her seventy first year. This was one of 3 family tragedies that affected an otherwise tranquil interwar period for the Hornes. In 1903 James Kenneth Horne, the son of Horne's eldest surviving brother, had died in a fire at Eton College at the age of 14. But most keenly felt, especially by Kate Horne, who never fully got over the loss, was the death of Jack Blacklock, her son by her first marriage. A Captain in the 8th Hussars based at Lucknow, India, he suffered a riding accident while pig sticking and succumbed to his injuries on 2 May 1912. His body was repatriated and buried in the Blacklock family plot at Newnham Church, Northamptonshire on 19 June.[4]

Despite this tragic loss of her son, and the earlier loss of her first husband, both to riding-related injuries, the devotion of Kate and her husband to their horse riding never wavered. (They were not to know that their beloved daughter Kitten, who had become one of the leading horsewomen in Northern Scotland, would also be killed by being thrown from a horse in 1956.)

In June 1908 Horne took over command of VIII Brigade, Royal Horse Artillery, which was based at Newbridge, just west of Dublin. In October 1910 he gave up this command and left Ireland on transfer to Aldershot. General Sir Horace

Smith-Dorrien had requested Horne for the position of Staff Officer for Horse and Field Artillery, Aldershot Command. Sir Horace also asked for the grading of the job to be raised from Lt Colonel to Colonel rank so as to offer continuity in training and enable the holder to command all RHA brigades when they were concentrated together for annual training, and to command the RHA practice camp. The War Office acquiesced in both requests and Horne was offered, and accepted, the appointment for a term of 4 years with advancement in rank to substantive Colonel.[5]

With their return to England the Hornes once more took up residence in East Haddon. Their relationship followed the accepted norms of the time, with the man very much the master of the house and the wife the dutiful spouse. Kate Horne took few decisions without consulting her husband. This presented few problems when Henry Horne's absences on duty lasted at most a few days. Matters became more complicated when he was away for long periods on the Western Front. His letters reflect this. They contain a plethora of domestic trivia as he seeks to guide and advise Kate on the management of the house, the stables, the servants and, occasionally, their daughter.

In the event Horne served less than 2 years as Staff Officer for Horse and Field Artillery, Aldershot Command. On 1 May 1912 he was appointed Inspector of RHA and RFA under the Inspector General of Home Forces, with the rank of Brigadier General. Lt General Sir Herbert Uniacke later recorded:

> Here he quickly made his influence felt in the Regiment. A model of consci-entiousness and straight as a die himself, he was quick to detect all kinds of humbug and could not endure the scrimshanker, the schemer or anyone who did not 'play the game'. At the same time no one was ever more ready to appreciate sound work and true merit, and those fortunate enough to win his trust could always count on him as a wise counsellor and true friend.[6]

Horne's new position meant that, although based at Horse Guards in London, he spent a great deal of his time travelling round the country inspecting the artillery units for which he was responsible wherever they were based. Inevitably this involved frequent visits to Aldershot where Sir Horace Smith-Dorrien had been succeeded as Commander-in-Chief early in 1912 by Lieutenant General Sir Douglas Haig. The incumbent of this position was designated to command I Corps of the British Expeditionary Force if Britain were to become embroiled in a continental war.

Only 2 years later this was to come about with the outbreak of the Great War when Haig took I Corps to the Western Front. Horne was well placed to play an important role in Haig's plans. From the days of their respective 1912 appoint-ments until the ends of their active careers, Haig's and Horne's fortunes were to be closely linked, probably to their mutual benefit, but indisputably to the latter's.

Part Two

WORLD WAR: AUGUST 1914– APRIL 1916

Chapter V

August–December 1914: BGRA I Corps

On 4 August 1914 Great Britain and its Empire declared war on Germany. Since the start of the twentieth century, if not earlier, the prospect of a belligerent confrontation with Germany had been growing. The perceived threat from this quarter had had the effect of driving France and Britain closer together. Relations between the two countries were put on a new footing by the Entente Cordiale, concluded in 1904. Two years later, Anglo-French military staff talks began. From then onwards, the War Office and military chiefs were to plan on the assumption that there would at some stage be a war with Germany and that Britain would send an expeditionary force to fight alongside France on the European mainland. By 1914 the plans had been refined to provide for six infantry and one cavalry divisions being dispatched to France on the outbreak of hostilities. They would take up position on the left of the French armies. These arrangements were less than a formal commitment, but they nevertheless constituted quite a moral obligation to France.

The British public and the majority of the country's leading politicians were blissfully unaware of the Anglo-French staff talks and where they might lead. It was not until the assassination of the Austro-Hungarian Archduke Franz Ferdinand and his wife, by Serbian nationalists in Sarajevo on 28 June 1914, triggered a Europe-wide crisis that the possible implications for Britain started to emerge. What might have proved to be a serious dilemma for the British government, in the teeth of hostile public opinion, was obligingly solved by the German decision to violate Belgium's neutrality. This had been guaranteed by the 1839 Treaty of London, to which Britain was a signatory. It was the casus belli which enabled the British government to declare war on Germany and retrieve its moral obligation to France with near unanimous popular support.

Despite its contempt for the capabilities of the British Army, derived in large part from its tiny size and less than convincing performance in the Boer War, the last thing Germany needed in 1914, as it set about settling matters with France in the west and Russia in the east, was a belligerent Britain. It was the German strategy for fighting a war on two fronts, embodied in the Schlieffen Plan, that had brought this about.[1] The plan called for the bulk of the German army to march through Belgium on its way west and south of Paris to come round and trap the French between it and the remainder of the German army deployed defensively along the Franco-German border. The former German Army Chief of Staff, Count von Schlieffen, had assumed that the Belgians would allow the Germans to cross their territory, albeit under protest. But the Belgians chose to fight and invoke the Treaty of London. The British mobilised and, on rejection of their ultimatum to the Germans to withdraw, declared war.

Immediately on the outbreak of war Horne was appointed Brigadier General Royal Artillery (BGRA) at the headquarters of Lieutenant General Sir Douglas

Haig's I Corps. He sailed from Southampton and arrived at Le Havre on 15 August, from where he joined Haig's headquarters on its advance into Belgium.

The role of BGRAs at the HQs of the two corps making up the British Expeditionary Force at the start of the war was a rather nebulous one. The corps as such had no artillery of their own; it was allocated to, and the responsibility of, the individual divisions within the corps. The divisions had their own Commanders Royal Artillery (CRAs) and army protocol precluded the possibility of these receiving orders from a BGRA. As William Sanders Marble put it;

> The Artillery Advisors at Corps HQs were still lacking any purpose and tended to be used as spare senior staff officers. Even when several divisions were involved in an attack – when planning might have been expected – AAs were not involved. It was possible for an AA to observe divisions preparing to attack without the slightest conception they should take part even when there was not enough preparation or organisation. Instead artillery support was left to the discretion of the divisional commanders. There was still a great concern that the proprieties of command not be slighted.[2]

Even when Haig changed his Corps' artillery dispositions only a few weeks into the war by establishing a 'Special Artillery Group', comprising a mixture of field artillery, siege howitzers and medium guns, this had to remain under his personal control and command. Direct command of the group could not be delegated to a subordinate.[3]

Horne would not have shared Marble's view of the limitations of his role. In a letter to his wife Horne described his appointment as senior to that of a divisional CRA. He was finding his work at I Corps HQ very interesting as Haig was making great use of him, which suited his appetite for hard work.[4] Horne was right in assessing that there was no danger of him being sidelined; Haig had far too high an opinion of him for that, extending well beyond Horne's professional expertise as a gunnery officer. Haig had already demonstrated his faith in Horne at the outset of the shooting war.

The BEF had been ordered forward into Belgium to take up position to the left of the French Fifth Army with a view to attacking what the French General Staff believed to be the weak right wing of the German advance. The French were fully aware of the Schlieffen Plan but refused to believe, erroneously, that the Germans could have mobilised sufficient reserves to bring their right wing up to the strength foreseen in the Plan. In any case, reasoned the French, the Germans would have to strip out their right wing to strengthen their left to try to stem the irresistible onslaught that the French were making in Alsace-Lorraine under Plan XVII, their equivalent of Schlieffen.[5]

The French General Staff notwithstanding, by the time the BEF arrived near Mons and the French Fifth Army around Charleroi, the evidence was growing that they were faced by vastly superior numbers of Germans. The Allies took up defensive positions. On 23 August the Battle of Mons was fought with General Sir Horace Smith-Dorrien's II Corps bearing the brunt of the German onslaught. Haig's Corps, deployed to the right of Smith-Dorrien's, were only lightly engaged.

Despite the BEF's success in stemming the German tide throughout the day, a BEF retreat had become inevitable given the huge preponderance in German numbers. The danger could only grow of the BEF being outflanked to either side;

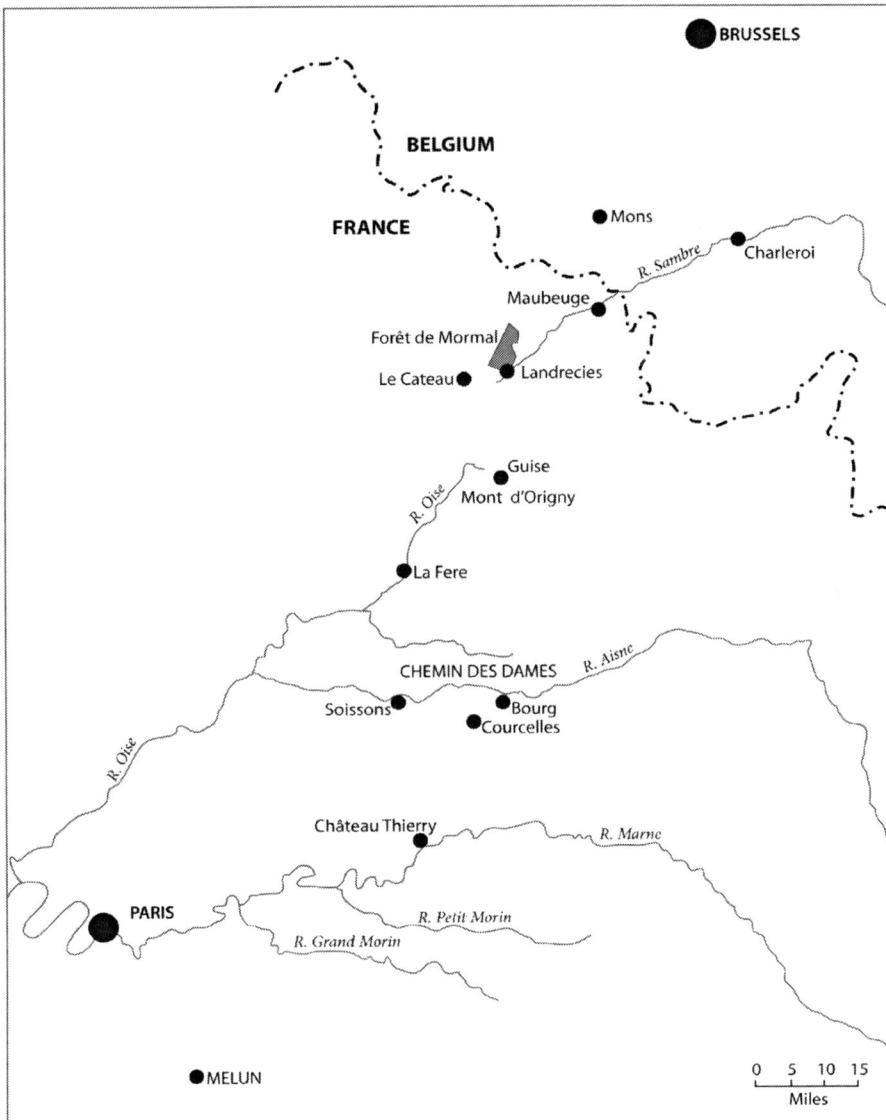

Map 2: The BEF Retirement from Mons 23.8–6.9.14

on the left through still militarily empty and undefended country; and on the right through the gap left by the withdrawal, without warning to the BEF, of the French Fifth Army. It was to cover this retreat that Haig entrusted to Horne the command of a rearguard, consisting of 2 battalions of 4th Guards Brigade, the 5th Cavalry Brigade and two brigades (XXXI and XLI) of the Royal Field Artillery. The rear-guard was to assemble at 02h00[6] on 24 August and make an offensive demonstration at daybreak to enable 1st and 2nd Divisions to disengage and begin their retreat.[7]

Thanks to this offensive demonstration Horne's rearguard never came under serious pressure during the morning of the 24th. By 11h00 he was planning to return his troops to their divisions. But 5th Division of II Corps were finding it difficult to disengage, which obliged 3rd Division (II Corps) to stand fast. Horne's rearguard on 3rd Division's right was directed to conform with them.[8] Again the rearguard was relatively untroubled and was able to begin its own retreat south at 16h30, once 3rd Division had retired.[9]

Over the next few days I Corps' retreat continued, more bothered by fatigue and the extreme heat of the late summer than by the Germans. The II Corps were less fortunate and were forced to stand alone and fight the Battle of Le Cateau on 26 August. The 2 corps had become widely separated as their lines of retreat had diverged to either side of the Forèt de Mormal. There was no opportunity for I Corps to intervene in the battle.

By 28 August, as I Corps continued their retirement on Fère-en-Tardenois in continuing heat, Haig instructed 1st Division to provide the rearguard. Horne was put in charge of a flankguard, consisting of 5th Cavalry Brigade, 4th Guards Brigade and XXXVI Brigade RFA.[10] The rearguard held the heights of Mont d'Origny with the flankguard to its west. The corps' route of retreat took it through Origny. The Germans made ineffectual attempts to work round the right flank of the rearguard but were easily held off. The flankguard's 5th Cavalry Brigade, commanded by Brigadier General Sir Philip Chetwode, came under sharp attack by enemy cavalry. A mixture of effective defence and counterattacks saw them off and severely dampened their ardour for future aggression. The corps' retreat was able to continue relatively untroubled.[11]

The long Allied retreat came to an end on 5 September. The following day the Allies went over to the offensive, during which the Battles of the Marne and the Aisne were fought. On 14 September the Germans in turn ended their retreat and could not be dislodged from their prepared defensive positions on the Chemin des Dames. This signalled the beginning of the end of mobile warfare and the onset of trench warfare.

For the first few days of the allied advance, Horne was with Haig's HQ. But on 10 September Brigadier General Findlay, CRA 1st Division, was killed. Horne was dispatched to replace him until a permanent replacement could be organised.[12] For the first 4 days of his temporary tenure, the division were pursuing the retreating Germans, although Horne found it difficult to understand why they were retiring.[13] On 13 September, Horne crossed the River Aisne at Bourg and the following day came up against the enemy, dug in on the Chemin des Dames.[14] The next 4 days were to be characterised by heavy German shelling and small attacks and counterattacks designed to secure maximum advantage in the now near-static situation. General Finlay's permanent replacement, Brigadier General Fanshawe, arrived at 1st Division HQ on 18 September and relieved Horne, who returned to I Corps HQ at Courcelles.[15]

No sooner was Horne back at HQ than Haig gave him another important duty, this time one which properly came under the remit of a gunnery officer. In the words of Marble:

Haig delegated to Horne the organisation of the artillery fire and the co-operation between artillery and aeroplanes. Horne spent much more time working with the Royal Flying Corps than organising artillery fire. Every day flying was possible he personally went to the aerodrome and took reports from pilots. Orders were then passed to the CsRA as Horne was not a commander.[16]

Horne's diary records these aerodrome visits, and the importance he attached to the subject is evident. He had rapidly realised that long-range artillery was going to be an important factor in the war and, with that, would come a need to see 'over the hill'. The aeroplane's ability to fulfil this role, when coupled with an ability to convey immediately what was being observed to the ground, would greatly enhance the artillery's effectiveness.[17] For his part Haig needed no reminding of the usefulness of aeroplanes in reconnaissance and artillery spotting. He had been humiliated in the Army's 1912 manoeuvres by his opponent, General Grierson[18], who had made very profitable and innovative use of the fledgling air arm to outmanoeuvre Haig. Horne's endeavours were directed towards establishing and improving co-operation between aeroplanes and artillery batteries. By 8 December he was able to see the first practice in which airborne artillery observers were provided with radio for ground communication.[19]

In a letter to his wife Horne described a typical day's work.

Breakfast 5.30. Aeroplane Headquarters to see the reconnaissance reports, and what the Germans are doing in the way of advancing their trenches and where they have their guns. Arrange the distribution of the artillery fire for the day. Visit a certain number of the artillery headquarters for consultation, explanation, etc. Back to see the results of the second air reconnaissance. Further visits to batteries and arrange for the night firing. That with odd jobs regarding changes in position of our troops etc fills in the day and I am glad to get to bed about 9 p.m.[20]

It is clear that Horne did not conceive his role in terms of sitting behind a desk at headquarters. Throughout his time on the Western Front he took every opportunity to get out and about, visiting the HQs of subordinate and neighbouring formations. He also visited the front line whenever he wished to see for himself the lie of the land or the conditions in the trenches. He was very conscious of the sufferings of the front-line troops during bad weather and when the trenches were in poor condition. As far as possible he would make his journeys on horseback, although time and circumstances usually necessitated the use of a staff car. So passionate was he about riding that he would often pre-position a horse at some point on his itinerary to get some time in the saddle.

With the front stabilising north of the Aisne, Field Marshal French began to put pressure on French GHQ to relocate the BEF where it had always been intended it should be, on the left of the French armies. Horne shared the belief of most of his senior colleagues that this would restore the BEF's capacity to manoeuvre as well as put it where it could best defend its main supply ports on the French coast.

General Joffre was agreeable and by 21 October I Corps was in action east of Ypres. Once again the British found themselves up against a huge preponderance of Germans. Their initial attacking ambitions were quickly converted into the desperate, and ultimately only just successful, defensive battle which later earned the name of the First Battle of Ypres.

Horne's diary for the period of First Ypres contains no details of his own activities. It seems probable that he was acting as a senior staff officer, helping out where the pressure was greatest. Haig certainly did use him to liaise with the commanders of neighbouring French army units, an important function given the rather chaotic interspersing of units of the 2 nations brought about by the hole-plugging nature of a desperate defensive battle.[21] (The improvisations called for to keep the line intact were evocatively described as 'putting up'.) Whatever Haig's reasons for using Horne in this role, they can have had nothing to do with the latter's grasp of French; Horne's command of the language at this stage was at best rudimentary. He was to work hard to overcome this deficiency, with some success, but was never to achieve anything approaching fluency.

Horne's rather terse diary recorded the shelling of Hooge Château by the Germans on 31 October and the resultant deaths and injuries among the staffs of 1st and 2nd Divisions. On several days he recorded 'very anxious day' as the BEF teetered on the brink of defeat. But by 21 November the battle was winding down and I Corps were relieved for rest and reequipping. By this time Horne had been a Major General for nearly a month.

Horne owed his promotion, 'For distinguished service in the field',[22] largely, if not entirely, to his competent handling of the rearguard, and subsequently the flankguard, during the Retreat from Mons. Haig had recommended Horne for Mention in Dispatches in the following terms:

> Brigadier General H.S. Horne – A most capable Commander as well as being thoroughly versed in all Artillery matters. He inspires me with such confidence that when the situation required a detachment of all arms to be formed I selected him to command it. Notably on 24th August (first day of the retreat) and on 28th August (March from Mont d'Origny).[23]

Horne was granted his Mention in Dispatches and, by 27 October, was sufficiently confident of his promotion to mention it in a letter to his wife, saying that he thought it more than he deserved.[24] It was confirmed the following day, with effect from 26 October. For the time being, Horne remained at I Corps HQ. He was granted a week's leave on 22 November and, while in London, saw the Secretary of State for War, Field Marshal Lord Kitchener, and the Military Secretary at the War Office, General Robb. Horne pressed the latter for a command but was told there was nothing available at present.[25]

Horne's experiences in the opening weeks of the war had given him some food for thought on the current and future role of artillery. He was impressed by the Royal Artillery's performance up to the Battle of the Aisne. Although often outnumbered most batteries had done well. The German infantry wilted under the British shrapnel fire. At close quarters, both in artillery and musketry, the British were more than a match for the Germans. But the British had little answer to the German long-range guns. Their big guns, called Black Marias by the British soldier, fired 90 lb shells. Their long range made British counter-battery fire difficult. Horne's first experience of static warfare gave him an insight into the role that barbed wire was to play and the importance of inventing some means of cutting it with artillery.[26] Eventually the problem would be contained but not before huge casualties had been sustained.

Horne had also become aware of the artillery's supply shortcomings, which were to reach crisis point and become a national scandal the following year. He met the former Secretary of State for War, the Rt Hon Sir John (Jack) Seeley, who was visiting the Aisne, and whom he described as a, 'Silly creature ... I had the chance of telling him some truths about the neglect to listen to the warnings we Gunners had given about our guns, shells, etc.' He formed a rather more favourable view of Winston Churchill, the First Lord of the Admiralty, who also visited the Aisne, even though he rather cynically thought it was just to, 'get clasp for Aisne'.[27]

On the last day of the year his wait for a command ended when, on Haig's recommendation, he was appointed temporary General Officer Commanding 2nd Division, with immediate effect.

Chapter VI

1915: Divisional Commander

The beginning of 1915 found both sides coming to terms with the new concept of trench warfare and giving urgent thought to how to break the apparent stalemate. On the German side the decision would be taken to adopt a largely defensive posture in the west and focus on defeating the Russians in the east. By contrast, defence was never conceived of as an option by the Allies; for the French C-in-C, General Joffre, it was merely a question of when and where he should mount his offensives to drive the hated invader off the soil of France with, if at all possible, increasing participation from the slowly enlarging BEF. In 1915, France remained incontrovertibly the senior partner of the alliance, a fact which, to a large extent, was to determine where and when the BEF would seek to attack during the year. Even in the one case, Neuve Chapelle, when the British attacked in isolation, a major reason for the decision to do so was to demonstrate to the French that the BEF was attack-minded and keen to play its full part.

Although the BEF had suffered heavy casualties in the first few months of the war, particularly during the First Battle of Ypres, its losses were numerically light compared with those of the French and Germans. Nevertheless, unlike those 2 countries, there was virtually no pool of trained manpower, especially at the junior officer/NCO level, from which to draw replacements. Until the volunteers for Kitchener's New Army could be trained, all that was available were a few divisions made up of regular battalions hastily being returned from garrison duties in the Colonies, the Territorial Army, the Indian Army and the first Canadian division. All of these were to find themselves on the Western Front in 1915. A further major problem which was to bedevil the BEF was the shortage of suitable artillery for static warfare, notably heavy guns and howitzers, and of the shells required for them. Not only were the shells available largely shrapnel, when high explosive was the main requirement, but they were being produced in pitifully inadequate quantities. It has been estimated that in 1915 Britain was producing 22,000 shells per day compared with French production of 100,000 and German of 160,000. To compound the problem, the British shells were proving unreliable, with a high proportion of 'duds'.[1]

By the beginning of February Joffre had settled on his grand design for 1915. He planned 3 large offensives, in northern Lorraine, Champagne and Artois. It was Artois which was to concern and involve the BEF.[2]

Horne arrived at 2nd Division headquarters at Locon, 3 miles northeast of Béthune, on 1 January 1915 and immediately took over temporary command from Brigadier General Fanshawe, who had been acting since the departure of Major General Charles Monro. The following day his appointment was confirmed and made permanent. But things might have been different, as Haig's diary entry for 28 December 1914 records.

> Locke-Elliot [a liaison officer between FM Lord Kitchener and the Indian troops in France] had also arranged to stop the telegram asking for Younghusband to be sent to command the Lahore Division vice Watkis. I

entirely agreed with him as Younghusband is no use. I suggested General Horne for the appointment but I expect an officer of the Indian Army will have to be appointed … [3]

Haig proved correct, but only 3 days later he recommended to the Military Secretary that Horne should be given command of 2nd Division. This time there was no hitch.

The vacancy at 2nd Division had arisen from Field Marshal French's decision, conveyed to Haig and Smith-Dorrien on 18 December, to split the BEF into 2 armies at once. The First, consisting of I, II and III Corps would be commanded by the recently promoted General Haig; the Second, consisting of IV, V and VI Corps, by General Smith-Dorrien.[4] The new armies came into being on 26 December, First Army being constituted of I, IV and Indian Corps and not as originally envisaged. The vacancy at the head of I Corps was filled by the promotion of Major General Monro to Lieutenant General, leaving the gap at 2nd Division into which Horne stepped.

Horne was understandably elated at his appointment. He saw it as a great compliment for a Gunner to be placed in command of an infantry division of over 20,000 men. In a letter to his wife he expressed confidence in his ability to cope with his new responsibilities. He was delighted that his GSO1 (effectively Chief of Staff) was to be Colonel Malcolm of the Argyll & Sutherland Highlanders, writing, 'Such a good soldier, and such a nice man, he has been with I Corps all the time so that he and I are great friends'.[5] Given his controversial performance subsequently as Fifth Army Chief of Staff, it was perhaps fortunate for Horne that Malcolm spent only a few days at 2nd Division in tandem with Horne before moving on. His replacement, Lt Colonel H E Gogarty, lasted only 7 weeks before giving way to one of the outstanding staff officers of the war, Lt Col Louis Vaughan.

The 2nd Division was part of I Corps which found itself on the extreme right, or south, of the BEF section of the line. The BEF front line ran roughly north-south from the Ypres Salient, to the east of St Eloi, then crossed the Béthune-La Bassée road just to the east of Cuinchy. A little south of this the French took over. The I Corps was responsible for the line from the junction with the French, northwards past Festubert. Apart from his brief period on the Somme with XV Corps, this area of northern France, flat, frequently soggy and dotted with pit head mining machinery, slag heaps and mining villages, was to form the background to the rest of Horne's time on the Western Front.

Henry Horne was taking over a division with an excellent reputation which would continue to be rated as one of the BEF's best for the rest of the war. Like all the BEF divisions that had been in France and Flanders since the early days of the war, 2nd Division had suffered severely in the 1914 fighting. Its casualties in the period from the outbreak of war until the end of the First Battle of Ypres amounted to 10,069 officers and men, including 1,456 killed and 2,637 missing.[6] Horne's early preoccupation would be with integrating and training drafts of replacements. He would also seek to make things as tolerable as possible for his troops, faced with the dismal prospect of manning trenches for long periods over the first winter of the war.

Horne paid regular visits to the trenches and found the conditions deplorable. Unsurprisingly the main problem was an excess of water; the trenches were flooded feet deep in many places. Horne feared this would lead to much sickness if it went on. To keep the men out of the water, arrangements were made to minimise digging down and instead build up breastworks, despite their greater vulnerability to shellfire. At the same time the number of troops in the front line was thinned out as much as possible leaving the line held only by small posts. The bulk of the troops were kept in the support trenches.[7]

Horne urged his staff to take advantage of German quiescence during January to strengthen and consolidate the divisional line. Once this was achieved, Horne looked forward to being able to 'bgin to try to attack them a bit.'[8] Commenting on an attack by the Germans on 1st Division near Givenchy and Cuinchy, on 25 January, in which both sides lost heavily, he wrote, 'We cannot fight nowadays without casualties on a large scale!'[9]

The 1st Division's losses resulted in 2nd Division being moved south on 4 February to relieve them. Horne transferred his headquarters to Béthune. His Division was now responsible for the defence of Festubert (assigned to 5th Infantry Brigade), Givenchy (6th Infantry Brigade) and Cuinchy (4th Guards Brigade). But his first move was an aggressive one, the first enterprise of importance for the division since his takeover of command.

The operation's purpose was the modest one of strengthening the British line at the Cuinchy brickstacks where the British and German front lines were in very close proximity. Some of the brickstacks were in British hands, the rest in German. On 6 February, a 15 minute bombardment was followed by assault artillery and machine guns drawing a screen across the enemy's position, so effectively that 4th Guards Brigade were able to dig a new trench by daylight and the Engineers to wire it. As the bombardment lifted, the Irish Guards and 3rd Bn Coldstream Guards rushed in and secured the enemy position.[10] It was held against a counterattack which was largely broken up by artillery fire. Horne was very pleased at the outcome and the congratulatory message received from FM French.[11]

While Horne was bedding down at 2nd Division, General Headquarters (GHQ) were actively planning a major assault. The Battle of Neuve Chapelle was the first set piece battle of the war in which the British took the offensive. Originally conceived as a joint Anglo-French attack, Joffre withdrew the French element (which would have been an attack in the Lens-Vimy Ridge-Arras area), when the BEF declined to take over an area of French-held line north of Ypres.[12] FM French nevertheless decided to go ahead with the British part of the attack. He wished to show the sceptical French that the BEF were keen to play their full part and could be a potent attacking force as well as an effective defensive one. A successful attack would also convince a sceptical Field Marshal Kitchener that the German lines could be breached. Finally, an attack was deemed to be just the thing to get the British troops mobile again after a difficult winter in the trenches. The heavy casualties suffered by the BEF in the early battles of the war, culminating in First Ypres, had been replaced in quantity, if not necessarily always in quality, by Territorial Army and Indian Army units.

Neuve Chapelle is a small farming village about 14 kilometres southwest of Armentières, which passed under the control of the Germans on 27 October 1914. It was a tempting target for the British. The German line at this point formed a salient about 2 kms to the west of the low (about 35 metres above sea level at its

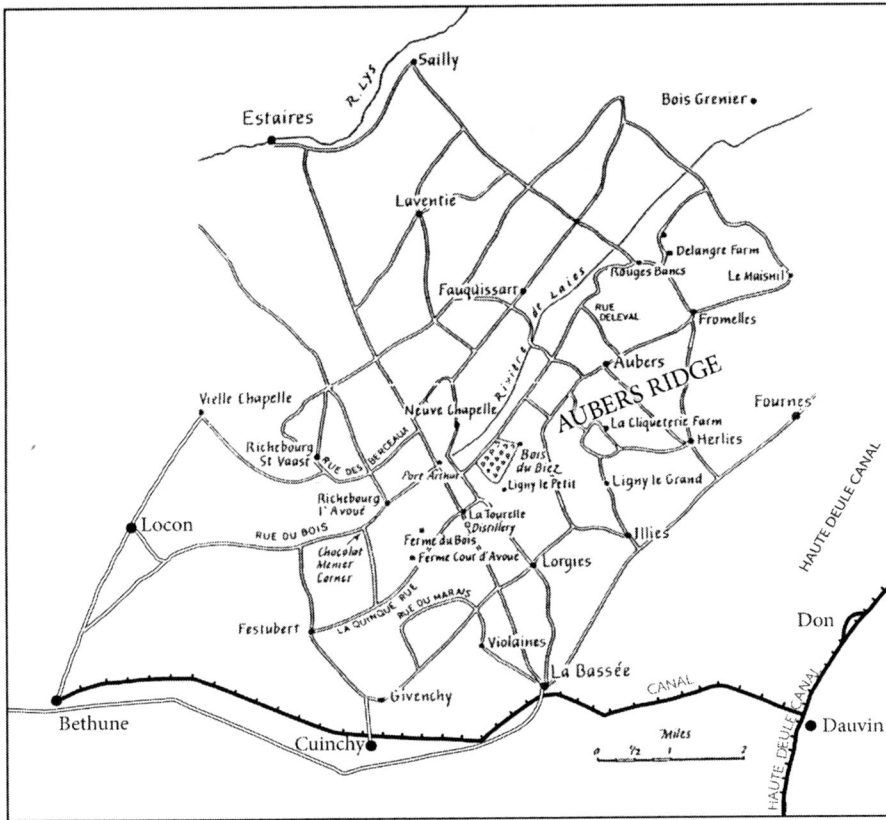

Map 3: Neuve Chapelle, Aubers Ridge and Festubert: battlefields

highest point) but strategically important Aubers Ridge. This 10 kms long feature, the capture of which was to be the focus of British aspirations for many weeks in 1915, gave the Germans an overall view of the British lines and kept them relatively drier. But their strategy of seeking a decision on the Eastern Front in 1915 had led them to reduce their frontline strength in France, especially opposite the BEF; they shared the French scepticism about the offensive ardour of the British.

The offensive was entrusted to Haig's First Army. His plan called for the Indian Corps and IV British Corps to pinch off the German salient, capture Neuve Chapelle and seize Aubers Ridge. Ultimately the cavalry might be released to descend on the huge prize of the city of Lille, 20 kms to the east of the ridge. Following a short, but violent, artillery bombardment lasting 35 minutes the infantry would assault on 10 March, relying on speed and surprise. For the first time use would be made of an artillery timetable which would include a defensive barrage designed to prevent the Germans bringing up reinforcements or supplies. Aerial photography, although still in its infancy, helped the planners prepare accurate maps of the enemy's trenches and defences. The assaulting battalions were thoroughly trained in their tasks.

It transpired that the BEF had indeed achieved significant numerical superiority. Only one and a half German battalions faced the 15 assaulting battalions. Surprise too was achieved and the village of Neuve Chapelle was quickly captured. The chance of a really striking success was however lost when some of the attackers were restrained from pushing on when the opportunity was there to do so. The Germans were consequently given the chance to bring up reserves and strengthen their defences. On the second day, 11 March, little was achieved. On the third, the Germans counterattacked strongly. They were bloodily repulsed, but First Army was in no state to take advantage and the battle came to an end late on 12 March.

The First Army's I Corps had only been assigned a supporting role in Haig's plans for the battle. As part of this, 2nd Division were ordered to attack 750 yards of the enemy's trenches to the northeast of Givenchy. The intention was mainly to hold the enemy in place and prevent them sending reinforcements to help their beleaguered comrades at Neuve Chapelle. But it was also deemed to be a desirable operation in itself.

Synchronising with the main attack, 2nd Division began to shell the enemy trenches at 07h30, stopping ten minutes later and resuming at 07h50. At 08h05 the bombardment became intense. Five minutes later the range was lengthened to encompass the enemy's second line positions and flanks, as the infantry went over the top. According to the Official History, the subsequent misfortunes of the attacking infantry were largely due to the failure of the preliminary bombardment adequately to prepare the position for assault.

> Owing to difficulties in ranging in the mist and to the fact that the enemy's front trench was sited on the reverse side of a slight rise in the ground, neither the wire entanglement nor the front line itself was sufficiently shelled.

Horne's CRA, Brigadier General W. H. Onslow, explained that to allow for the effect of temperature on cordite, fire was opened at increased range and the mist prevented satisfactory correction of the range during the bombardment.[13] Horne himself blamed the artillery's failure to cut the enemy wire on the intervening housing of Givenchy village and trees, forcing on the guns a higher trajectory than desirable for wire cutting. The front attacked was, in addition, too wide for the amount of artillery available – only 22 howitzers for 750 yards.[14]

All these explanations no doubt have validity. But essentially they reflect the inexact science that gunnery against entrenched troops and their entrenchments was at this early stage of the war. It must have been particularly hard to bear for Horne. As was almost inevitably to be the case, it was the infantry who would pay the price.

The infantry attack was entrusted to 6th Brigade. The 5th Brigade were to offer supporting fire against the enemy trenches at Cuinchy, and 4th Guards Brigade were in reserve. At 08h10 the 3 assaulting battalions went over the top. On the right, the leading line of 2nd Bn South Staffs, despite heavy machine gun fire and enemy wire which had hardly been touched, reached the German trenches. Their supporting lines could not however get through to them and a German bombing attack drove them out of their precarious foothold. Repeated attempts to get back in failed. In the centre, 1st Bn King's managed to advance only 150 yards with all their officers becoming casualties. They could not penetrate the uncut German wire and were forced to retire. On the left, some troops of 1st Bn King's

Royal Rifle Corps (KRRC) succeeded in crawling through the German wire and 7 of them established themselves in the German trench. They maintained themselves there until 14h00, even though no support could reach them through the heavy machine gun fire. They then retired to their own lines, by which time only 3 of them were unwounded.

Following the failure of the first assault, Horne decided to attack on a narrower front after a further 30 minute bombardment. At 14h15 the right and centre attacked, but were quickly checked by the enemy's machine guns. Nothing daunted, Horne was ready to try again under cover of darkness. His plan was however vetoed by the Corps Commander, Lieutenant General Monro, who postponed all further operations, effectively ending his corps' participation in the Battle of Neuve Chapelle.[15]

The 2nd Division's casualties had been high, with 26 officers and 582 other ranks killed, wounded and missing. The attack had clearly been a failure but some solace was drawn from the belief that the enemy had been held in position and been unable to withdraw any troops to assist hard-pressed comrades elsewhere. The problems were clearly identifiable; the failure to cut the enemy wire, even in its current relatively undense configurations, and the lack of success in suppressing enemy machine gun fire. Neither problem was to prove soluble for many months to come.

As regards the battle as a whole, the British command felt it could derive some encouragement. The German salient had been more or less eliminated and Neuve Chapelle remained in British hands. Surprise had been achieved through use of a short bombardment, a lesson which was however to be set aside in deference to other considerations. In general the lessons to be drawn were from British failures. Failure of communication, which prevented the initial success from being exploited. Failure of the shell supply to keep up with the demands of a major engagement. And failure to realise in the planning of future operations that the Germans would learn lessons too from their mistakes at Neuve Chapelle and take remedial measures.

In the brief interval between Neuve Chapelle and the next major attack, 2nd Division engaged in mining and countermining warfare with the Germans. On 20 February Major Norton-Griffiths[16] and a number of miners had been attached to the division. The Germans opposite 2nd Division were to regret their initiation of this type of warfare. Norton-Griffiths was the sort of officer who made things happen and he was to prove a more than adequate response to the German miners. A minor underground war took place.[17] Casualties were not heavy, but the underground activity and the new concern that the Germans might use gas in the area, as they had had just done at Ypres, kept the division on a high state of alert and experimenting with crude forms of gas masks.

In Horne's eyes the use of gas was a further proof Germany's descent into barbarism. Already appalled by their bombing of civilian targets from Zeppelins, and their alleged use of bullets with the nose flattened off, in contravention of the Hague Convention, Horne wrote angrily to his wife that the use of poisonous gases was 'a most barbarous thing. They are extraordinary, inhuman brutes, and grow more and more so. I think England is perhaps at last beginning to realise that it is time to take the war seriously'.[18]

For the rest of 1915 the imperatives of the Anglo-French alliance took over, with Britain emphatically the junior partner. If Neuve Chapelle had achieved little else, it had diminished French disdain for the BEF's offensive capabilities. The discussions between the British and French after the battle were the better for it. Joffre's immediate plan called for a major assault by the French Tenth Army on Vimy Ridge, to take place in early May. He wanted the BEF to attack towards Aubers Ridge, 24 hours after the French began their assault, to prevent the German reserves being moved south of the La Bassée Canal to meet the French threat. With reason, FM French feared having to attack German troops alerted to the possibility of a subsidiary attack by Joffre's proposed timings. But he was unable to overcome Joffre's insistence, and it was only two 24-hour delays, enforced on the French Tenth Army's plans by bad weather, which enabled French eventually to get his way of simultaneous attacks. Only one of the two 24 hour delays was extended to the BEF.

Following a 5 day bombardment by 1,200 guns, the French infantry went over the top at 10h00 on 9 May to begin the First Battle of Artois. Despite heavy losses from German machine gun fire which had not been suppressed, XXXIII Corps, commanded by General Philippe Pétain, captured Carency, Neuville St Vaast, La Targette and the Bois de la Folie. The famed Moroccan Division broke through the German line and took Vimy Ridge, having advanced 4 kms in just a few hours. They were exhausted and desperately needed reinforcement but the reserves were too far back to arrive before the following day. Only a few Foreign Légionnaires were on hand to help. Their problems were compounded when they came under heavy fire from their own artillery, and a German counterattack retook the ridge in the evening. In the following days the Germans also retook the villages of Carency and Neuville after bitter house-to-house fighting. Despite these setbacks the offensive continued, with the French seeking to capture Notre Dame de Lorette, Ablain-Saint Nazaire and Souchez. All 3 were eventually taken, Souchez not until June. General Foch, the Army Group Commander, ordered the offensive ended by mid-June, by which time the battle had cost the French 102,533 casualties of whom 42,108 were dead.[19]

The BEF's subsidiary part of the offensive became known as the Battle of Aubers Ridge. Once again it was to fall to Haig's First Army to conduct it. Haig proposed to launch a simultaneous pincer attack against the German defences north and south of Neuve Chapelle, with a gap between the 2 attacks of about 6,000 yards. As at Neuve Chapelle the assaults would be preceded by a short, intensive artillery bombardment lasting 40 minutes, to achieve surprise. The southern prong of the pincer would form the main thrust and involve 1st Division of I Corps and the Meerut Division of the Indian Corps attacking side by side on a front of 2,400 yards north-eastwards to secure the line Rue du Marais-Lorgies-Ligny le Grand-La Cliqueterie Farm. Horne's 2nd Division were placed in corps reserve behind 1st Division 'in readiness to continue the advance'. The northern prong would be headed by 8th Division of IV Corps and would attack south-eastwards to secure the line Rouge Bancs-Fromelles-Aubers-La Cliqueterie Farm. Once these advances were consolidated, the guns would be moved forward and reinforcements brought up. First Army would then be positioned for a second phase of the offensive, an advance of about 5 miles to a line running from Bauvin to Don on the Haute Deule Canal.[20]

Haig's plans took little account of the strenuous efforts the Germans had been making since Neuve Chapelle to strengthen their defences. They had been made more resistant to artillery bombardment. In addition machine guns had been cunningly sited in well concealed positions and the number of troops manning the front line had been increased. As these measures were well beyond the capacity of the available British artillery to deal with, there were the makings of a serious and costly reverse.

The British bombardment began punctually at 05h00 on 9 May and at 05h40 the infantry went over the top. The southern assault was made by 2nd and 3rd Brigades of 1st Division on the right and the Dehra Dun Brigade of Meerut Division on the left. It soon became apparent to the attackers that the British artillery had not only not done its job of cutting the enemy wire and making their frontline trenches unusable, but was also directly damaging them with shot falling short due to worn gun barrels and defective ammunition. The attackers were enfiladed by machine guns and hit by a storm of rifle and artillery fire. Only 2 small parties managed to get into the German lines, but in insufficient strength to maintain a presence. Within 20 minutes the attack had failed all along the line with the survivors either lying out in No Man's Land or struggling back to their own breastworks (which were under heavy German bombardment).

The northern assault was made by 24th and 25th Brigades of 8th Division. The average width of No Man's Land in front of the 5 assaulting battalions was only 100 yards. Again the attackers suffered from friendly fire and once out of their trenches they came under withering machine gun fire. Nevertheless about 30 men of 2nd Bn Northamptons secured a toehold in the German lines and 2nd Bn Rifle Brigade and 1st Bn Royal Irish Rifles, storming into the enemy trenches, secured 250 yards of them. They then regrouped and advanced to seize Rouge Bancs. After 2 mines were exploded under the German front lines, the 1/13th Bn London Regiment (the Kensingtons) charged and occupied the mine craters without loss. They regrouped and overran the enemy's main position and second line and captured Delangre Farm (a German strongpoint). The 2nd Bn Lincolns, in support, succeeded in extending the 250 yards of enemy trench captured to 400 yards. but all attempts to reinforce these breaches of the German defences withered away in the face of heavy machine gun and artillery fire. The first attack came to an end with both brigades in a shattered state.

The southern assault was renewed at 07h00 following a 45 minute bombardment specifically aimed at cutting the German wire, but which almost certainly did more harm to the British wounded and unhurt lying out in No Man's Land since the first attack. The disorganised attackers had virtually no hope against an intact German defence and the attack faded quickly to nothing. Nothing daunted, the GOC of 1st Division, Major General Richard Haking, offered to renew the attack but was stopped by his corps commander. A supporting attack by the Indians was cancelled. Unfortunately the message did not reach a Gurkha unit, which succeeded in reaching the German trenches and doing some damage with their *kukris* before being killed.

Unaware of the scale of the losses that the attacking brigades had suffered, Haig ordered his corps commanders to renew their attacks as soon as possible. In the case of the southern prong this should be at 12h00 after a 40 minute bombardment. However it was soon apparent that the necessary reliefs could never be completed in time and Zero Hour was postponed to 14h40 and later to 16h00. Similar problems were facing the northern prong where objections to renewing the attack were being voiced from battalion CO level upwards. When Haig learned that the attack had been aborted, he ordered IV Corps to launch a more effective assault at 16h00, an order which was not, in the event, carried out.

The southern prong attack was launched on time and men of 1st Bn Black Watch succeeded in getting into the German front line but in insufficient strength to establish themselves there. The rest of the 1st and Meerut Division attacks were repulsed with heavy loss. At 19h00, Horne's 2nd Division were ordered to relieve 1st Division with a view to mounting a Brigade-strength attack at 20h30. The attack was fortunately cancelled because of the chaos in the British trenches caused by wounded men moving, or being moved, back.

Apart from the fighting withdrawals necessary to extricate the troops from their lodgements in the German lines in the northern prong, the Battle of Aubers Ridge was in effect over. Haig tried to get it renewed later that night and on the following day, when it was planned that 2nd Division would participate. But the attacks were cancelled in the light of the state to which the First Army formations had been reduced, and the growing shortage of shells. British casualties amounted to 11,619; the German losses were about 1,550. Precisely no ground had been gained.[21]

There could however be little respite for the British, not that they were seeking any. The French offensive was continuing and there was still a perceived need to tie the Germans down and prevent them moving their reserves south to face the French. On 12 May the Commander of the French Tenth Army urged on Haig his hope that the British attack would resume as soon as possible 'so as to attract some of the reinforcements which the enemy are, it is thought, bringing up.'[22] At a conference later that day Major Generals Horne and Hubert Gough (the Commander of 7th Division, which had been transferred from IV Corps to I Corps on 10 May) outlined their proposals for a new attack. The 2nd Division would mount the first British night attack of the war on a 2 brigade front southwards from their current positions. They would be supported and protected on their left by a simultaneous attack by a brigade of Meerut Division of the Indian Corps. The aim was to gain and consolidate the first 2 lines of German trenches in time to launch a dawn advance on Fermes du Bois and Cour d'Avoué.[23] The 7th Division, which was too unfamiliar with the area to contemplate a night attack, would attack eastwards on a convergent line with 2nd Division, from their new positions south of 2nd Division, at dawn on the same day. Their aim was to capture La Quinque Rue and link up with 2nd Division around La Ferme Cour d'Avoué.

Given that the prime purpose of what was to become known as the Battle of Festubert was to help the French, Haig had set his divisions only limited objectives, advances of 1,000 yards in the 2 separate attacks. The failure of the short preliminary bombardment at Aubers Ridge to achieve any of its objectives, apart from surprise, persuaded Haig and Horne that the time had come to emulate the French and go for a long bombardment to shatter the German defences and demoralise the defenders. It began on 13 May and lasted 2 days. Unfortunately the artillery effort was still hampered by worn and insufficient guns and inadequate and sometimes defective ammunition.

About 10,000 British and Indian infantry went over the top at 23h30 on 15 May. Horne had entrusted the attack to his 5th and 6th Brigades, leaving 4th Guards Brigade in divisional reserve. The 6th Brigade's attack, on the right of the division's line, initially went well with 7th Kings, 1st Royal Berks and 1st KRRC all establishing themselves in the German trenches. By 01h30 they were in possession of the second German line. The fortunes of 5th Brigade were more mixed. The right-hand battalion, 2nd Royal Inniskillings, successfully occupied the German front line, but 2nd Worcesters on their left. and Garhwal Brigade of the Meerut Division, further left still, were less fortunate and ran into alert German defenders. Machine gun and artillery fire were poured into them with the help of flares and rockets which turned night into day.

After conferring with the Commander of 5th Brigade, Horne ordered a further assault by 2nd Worcesters to be synchronised with 7th Division's dawn attack, timed for 03h15. The Worcester's assault would be preceded by a 30 minute bombardment. Meerut Division also agreed to assault again at the same time. In accordance with the original plan, 6th Brigade would also resume their attack at dawn.

About the only success resulting from the renewal of 2nd Division's assault, was the occupation by 2nd Inniskillings of the German second line. The 9th Bn Highland Light Infantry (HLI), which had replaced the Worcesters, made no progress. Nor could 6th Brigade exploit their previous success; enfilade machine gun fire pinned them down and inflicted heavy losses. The Meerut Division attack again failed.

The 7th Division's attack was closely supported by the fire of 6 guns which had been secretly brought forward into the front line. Although the high-explosive shells they rained down on the German trenches wrought some damage, the attacking infantry were nevertheless met with such a hail of machine gun fire that the attack had to be suspended for 15 minutes for more shelling to take place. Some progress was made but the results were patchy. Losses had been heavy.

Midmorning of the 16th found one brigade in the German trenches and the 2 divisions still not having linked up. Attempts to rectify this were thwarted by the intensity of the enemy machine gun and artillery fire. In mid-afternoon Horne ordered his 2 attacking brigades to consolidate the ground gained, dig communication trenches and get some rest. During the night, orders were issued for the resumption of the attacks on the 17th. Their planned timing was disrupted by a sudden surge of Germans seeking to surrender, and they only got underway at 09h30. The 5th Brigade made no progress, which exposed 6th Brigade to enfilade fire and checked their slow advance. Both brigades resumed their attacks in the afternoon following a further 30 minute bombardment, but were once again stopped by enemy fire. The 1st King's of 6th Brigade did however succeed in linking up with 7th Division.

The 4th Guards Brigade had by now been brought up from reserve and went into the line on the right of 6th Brigade. The Germans had meanwhile been preparing a second defensive line and were beginning to pull back to it. This enabled the 2 British divisions to take the German front line and lay siege to the new German second line. The battle had become attritional.

By 18 May, 5th and 6th Brigades were in the process of being relieved. The Guards Brigade were ordered to attack in conjunction with 7th Division at 16h30 after a 2 hour artillery bombardment. The 2nd Bn Grenadier Guards made some progress but the Irish Guards made no progress towards Ferme Cour d'Avoué, suffering heavy casualties. They were ordered to dig in.

By the early hours of 21 May the relief of all 3 brigades of 2nd Division had been completed and the division were in corps reserve. With 7th and Meerut Divisions also relieved the battle was winding down. The Canadian, 51st(Highland) and 47th(London) Divisions, which relieved them, contented themselves with consolidating the ground gained. The battle officially ended on 27 May.[24]

About 1,000 yards of ground had been gained for no apparent tactical advantage. Aubers Ridge was still in German hands and was to remain so until October 1918. The battle had cost the British 16,648 casualties as against about 5,000 German, not even beneficial in attritional terms. The 2nd Division's casualties had been heavy, at 5,446. Horne wrote, 'Casualties very heavy. One must not allow oneself to think of them, but must accept that it is for God and country.' The following day, 'I have lost many of my best officers and personal friends. Such is War!'[25]

Festubert was the first major action since the advent of trench warfare in which Horne had played a leading role. Although, like everyone else, he was at the bottom of a long learning curve, there were signs that he would be very receptive to any ideas that might overcome the lack of tactical flexibility that trench warfare imposed. It was still too soon to look to the BEF's artillery to provide these ideas; indeed, at this stage, it seems to have been almost as much a threat to its own side as to the enemy. But he did opt to attack at night, a courageous and sensible decision. He also readily adopted the suggestion that the first waves of attacking troops should form up and lie down in front of their trenches before Zero Hour, thus putting them that much closer to the enemy and less vulnerable to being picked off by machine guns and artillery firing on set lines.

Horne was very conscious of the losses to his division. He accepted that losses were inevitable but would not be content unless every effort had been made to minimise them. In a by no means untypical departure from the mythical general wringing his hands at his losses, secure in his headquarters well to the rear, Horne personally reviewed and addressed what must have been the fairly dispirited survivors of his much depleted battalions. Typical was his address to 1st Bn Royal Berkshires.

> Major Hill, Officers, NCOs and Men of the 1st Royal Berkshire Regiment. You have had a very hard time for the past ten days. The preparations for the attack which took place on Saturday night were very trying, and necessitated hard night work with a great amount of fatigue. Your courageous rush across the ground to the German trenches was such as to make me feel perfectly

confident that the gallantry, determination and noble sacrifices will always be maintained.

The reputation of the Royal Berkshire Regiment for its hardihood and gallantry is well known throughout the whole war, and I tell you that in no other regiment in the 2nd Division do I place more confidence than in yours, which acts so thoroughly and courageously at all times.

The attack on Saturday was excellently planned and excellently carried out, with such results that the consolidation of the ground gained left no doubt as to your ability to hold the trenches. This was maintained next day under heavy artillery and rifle fire, and you prevented all attempts of the Germans to drive you out.

We shall await still further victories from the Royal Berkshire Regiment which has acquitted itself so nobly in the past. The Army and Corps Commanders have told me to express their sincere appreciation of your work, and I myself feel very proud to be associated with you and to command the 2nd Division.[26]

The end of the Battle of Festubert ushered in a period of 4 months during which there was no major activity on the British front. The 2nd Division spent periods in various parts of the line coupled with time out of the line. At one point they relieved a French division. It was becoming almost a BEF tradition to criticise the state of trenches taken over from the French, but Horne described those his troops took over as 'not quite as we like to have them but not all that bad'.[27] Horne was always to make a great effort to stay on good terms with his French opposite numbers when they found themselves neighbours and his efforts were generally cordially reciprocated.

In early June the division received a large number of replacements which almost restored it to full strength. This ended a period of anxiety for Horne who had been worried at its weakened state. He had been following the debate in Britain about the possibility of introducing a measure of compulsion to military service. He was much in favour; the sooner the better. He welcomed the advent of the new Government[28] and the increasing influence of David Lloyd George in it, as someone who would get things done. After meeting Lloyd George, now Minister of Munitions, when he visited GHQ in July, Horne told his wife that there was considerable friction between the Minister and Lord Kitchener. The latter was generally believed to be to blame and would come off worst. Horne clearly believed it was time for Kitchener to resign as Secretary of State for War.[29]

On a personal level, Horne was greatly disappointed not to have been Mentioned in Dispatches in FM French's April dispatch, even though all his Brigadiers and staff had been. There was much agonising about this and protestations to his wife that he only wanted the recognition for her sake. Horne raised the matter with Haig and FM French's new Chief of Staff, General Sir William Robertson, both of whom expressed mystification. He was only calmed down when FM French explained that he operated a sort of Buggins' turn with Mentions, and Horne had had his turn earlier. Horne was an avid collector of awards and recognitions and invariably, and rather implausibly, claimed that he only sought them for the sake of his wife.[30]

On 15 July Lieutenant General Monro relinquished his command of I Corps to take command of the newly established Third Army. Hubert Gough of 7th

Division succeeded him on promotion to Lieutenant General, and thus became Horne's immediate superior. A month later, 4th Guards Brigade left 2nd Division, to be replaced by 19th Brigade, which contained a mixture of English, Welsh and Scottish battalions. By this time preparations were under way for the next stage in Joffre's 1915 strategy.

Joffre's proposals for an offensive in September 1915 called for a major French effort in Champagne, to be supported by a simultaneous attack in Artois, which would once again aim at capturing Vimy Ridge. In support of this latter operation, Joffre wanted the BEF to attack between the La Bassée Canal and the town of Lens, the area of front covered by Haig's First Army. Both FM French and Haig considered the ground over which the attack would have to be made to be entirely unsuitable for offensive operations and said so forcefully. It was almost devoid of cover and dead flat, with such high ground as there was firmly in German hands. In addition the Germans possessed most of the ideal observation points provided by the slag heaps and winding gear towers of the many coal mines in the area. One of these latter constructions, a double winding gear tower which looked like, and was nicknamed Tower Bridge, was a conspicuous landmark. The British artillery tried in vain to destroy it. But as soon as they were to capture it, it was quickly destroyed by the German artillery.

French's and Haig's objections were overruled by Lord Kitchener. He allowed himself to be persuaded by General Joffre that not only was the ground suitable, but a British attack there was essential if the simultaneous French offensive in Artois was to succeed. Kitchener was fully aware that Joffre's evaluation of the battlefield owed more to French military imperatives than reality. But he felt unable to override him, in the interests of Anglo-French harmony.[31]

Joffre's overall plan called for a 4 day-long bombardment prior to all the assaults going in. The French enjoyed a sufficient density of guns to allow a reasonable hope that their bombardment would successfully cut the German wire, badly damage their fixed defences and destroy their morale. No such hope could be entertained by the British, with only half the gun density of the French and a chronic shell shortage. Unsurprisingly Haig and his IV Corps Commander, Lieutenant General Sir Henry Rawlinson, assigned the major role in the battle, were gloomy at the prospects for success. In the event, the Battle of Loos came close in its early stages to being a British success, against all the odds. But the seemingly ineluctable verities of the Western Front reasserted themselves and the battle ended as a costly disappointment.

At the start of the battle the British front line ran north-south from just north of the La Bassée Canal to the town of Grenay. The southern sector, between Grenay and the Vermelles-Hulluch road, was assigned to IV Corps which would attack with, from right to left, 47th (London), 15th (Scottish) and 1st Divisions. The northern sector, from the Vermelles-Hulluch road to the La Bassée Canal, would fall to 3 divisions of Gough's I Corps, from right to left, 7th, 9th (Scottish) and Horne's 2nd. The Indian Corps would make 2 feint attacks north of the La Bassée Canal.

The main reserve would consist of XI Corps (Lt Gen Sir Richard Haking), comprising the Guards Division and 2 Kitchener New Army divisions, the 21st and 24th, only recently arrived in France. FM French's decision to constitute a

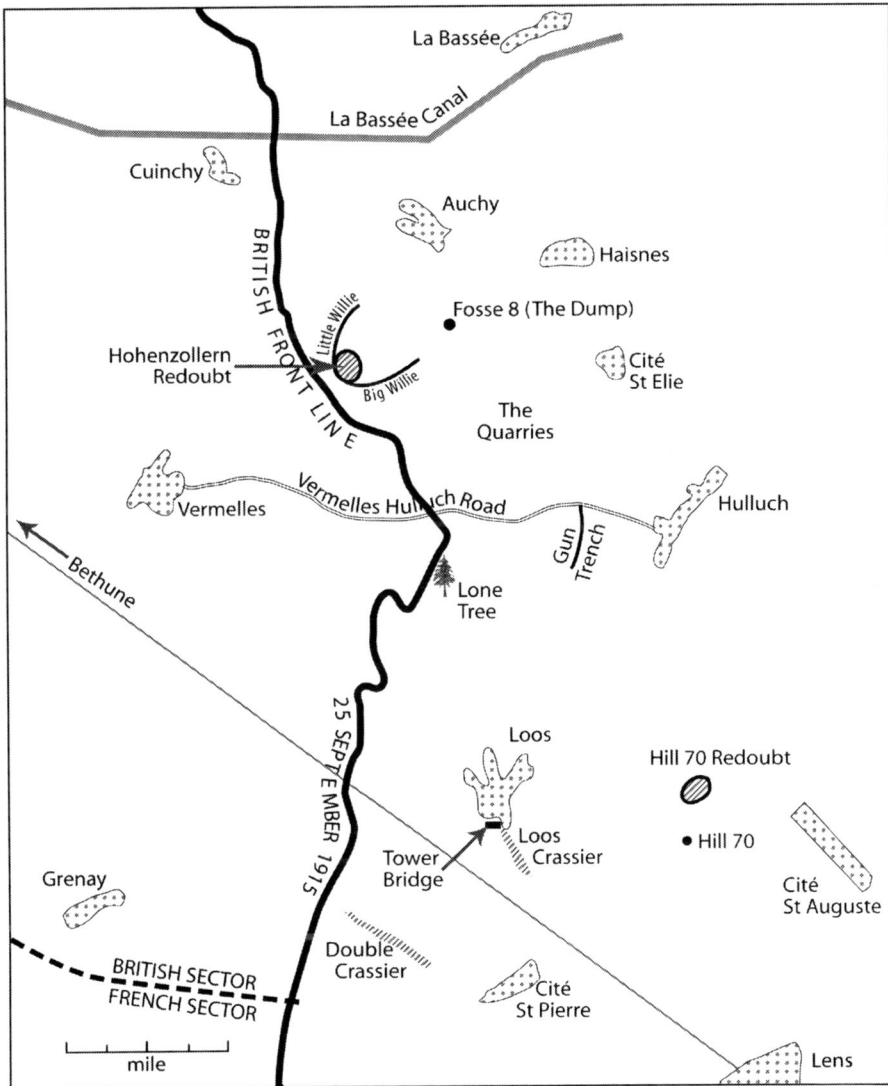

Map 4: Loos Battlefield: 25 September 1915

reserve two thirds of which was comprised of unblooded troops is puzzling. He could easily have brought in experienced troops from quiet parts of the front. Whatever reasoning went into the choice of 21st and 24th Divisions and their ultimate deployment, the consequences for them were to be catastrophic and would spark great controversy.

FM French decided to retain the reserve under his control and not hand it over to Haig. His reasons for so doing are still not entirely clear but may have reflected a concern to avoid Haig throwing it away in pursuit of a lost cause. Or he may have wanted to see how the battle went on the first day before deciding whether to release it to Haig. Ill-advisedly French positioned the reserve well behind the battlefield. As a consequence, when 21st and 24th Divisions were called forward, they had long distances to march over unfamiliar country. They arrived at their jumping off points tired, hungry, thirsty and 24 hours too late to exploit the opportunities that had arisen on the first day of the battle. Haig was understandably furious with French.

To compensate for the lack of sufficient artillery to support a 6 division assault, Haig decided to use 'asphyxiating' gas during the initial assault. This weapon had been introduced by the Germans at Second Ypres in April and it had only been a matter of time before the Allies responded in kind. As both sides still lacked the technology to deliver the gas by shell, the British plans called for the undetected deployment of over 5,500 cylinders along the length of their forward trenches. A favourable wind would then be required to carry the released gas away from their trenches towards and into the enemy's. If there were no favourable wind, the initial assault would use only 2 divisions. In the event, it was a knife-edge decision that Haig made to release the gas in the face of conflicting wind estimates. That IV Corps achieved deeper penetrations than I Corps on the first day can be largely explained by the fact that the wind in the south made their gas more effective than in the north where the wind was fitful at best, and sometimes downright perverse.[32]

The gas was released at 05h50 on 25 September and the infantry began their assault at 06h30. On the right of the British advance the 47th (London) Division's gas was reasonably effective. Aided by the use of smoke to cover their advance the Division captured all its objectives, notably the enormous Loos 'Crassier' (slag heap) and the Double Crassier.

Next to the 47th, the 15th (Scottish) Division were assigned the tasks of capturing the village of Loos, crossing Hill 70 beyond and occupying the Cité St Auguste. The Germans regarded Hill 70 as vital to them and had prepared formidable defences, including well-sited and dug-in machine guns. Initially the 15th had problems with their own gas but managed to occupy Loos by 08h00. Their advance continued but many units began to lose direction. Some 1,500 troops, largely leaderless because of officer losses, reached the slopes of Hill 70 but progressed southwards instead of eastwards. The few that did maintain direction, and traversed the summit, found themselves pinned down with all hope of help disappearing southwards. The failure to secure Hill 70 was to prove disastrous for the outcome of the battle as a whole and any hope of a major breakthrough. The chance had been there to effect a major disruption of the German defences and it had been lost at a heavy cost in 15th Division lives.

On 15th Division's left, 1st Division had been ordered to attack the Lone Tree Ridge area. Initial progress was very slow because the attackers soon caught up with their sluggishly moving gas. The artillery too had failed to cut the German wire, effectively stopping the advance in the centre of the division's front. Instead of seeking to outflank the obstacle the division persisted with frontal attacks – a classic case of commanders, whose communications had largely failed, reinforcing failure. On the left of the division's front, there was more success albeit at terrible cost. An advance party of the remnants of 3 battalions found a gap in the German wire and entered Hulluch village to find it abandoned. But the news was deemed to be too good to be true and eventually the advance party was driven out by the arrival of German reinforcements.

On the division's right, the attackers found themselves up against some of the strongest German defences, uncut German wire and defenders quite unaffected by the British gas. By the end of the day three quarters of the British attackers were casualties. Little progress had been made.

The area attacked by I Corps contained 3 major German strongpoints: on the right, the Quarries, a deep and wide chalk pit which had been extensively tunnelled; in the centre Fosse ('Pit' in the coal mine sense) 8 with its crassier known as 'the Dump', protected by the heavily fortified Hohenzollern Redoubt; and on the left Auchy village.

On 1st Division's left, 7th Division were charged with the capture of the Quarries. They gained no advantage from the guns and the gas did them more harm than good. But, despite heavy losses, the Quarries was captured by 18h00, only to be lost later in a German counterattack.

The 9th (Scottish) Division were allotted the task of capturing the Hohenzollern Redoubt, the strongest point in the German line, and Fosse 8. They secured a precarious hold in the redoubt but failed at Fosse 8 and took heavy casualties in their attempts. The 28th Brigade were virtually destroyed as a fighting force.[33]

Despite the failure of their gas and smokescreen the Indian Corps' feint attacks north of the main battlefield were initially quite successful. But their advances left them open to enfilade fire which eventually drove them back to their own trenches.[34]

The 2nd Division's preparations for their participation in the battle had begun with the arrival of nearly 900 cylinders of gas for distribution amongst the 3 brigades. On 20 September, I Corps had issued orders which, for 2nd Division, envisaged a subsidiary attack by 5th Brigade on the German trenches and beyond opposite Givenchy, north of the La Bassée Canal. The 6th and 19th Brigades were to assault the enemy trenches from the La Bassée Canal to the left of 9th Division, and take the village of Auchy.

The gas cylinders were opened at 05h50. The 5th Brigade were due to assault from Givenchy after 8 minutes of gas discharge and 2 minutes smoke bombardment. The gas moved very slowly, giving the enemy plenty of time to take countermeasures. In front of the left assaulting battalion the gas 'hung' very badly and interfered with their forward movement. On the other hand, the smoke barrage did its job well even though one part of it had to be stopped when the assault commenced, as the wind took it into the assaulting battalion.

The 2nd Highland Light Infantry and 1st Queen's rapidly overran the German front trench and moved on to their second line. The 2nd Oxford & Bucks Light Infantry also reached the front trench and began bombing down a diagonal trench. But all 3 battalions were driven out of the German positions by enfilade machine gun fire and German bombers, whose bombs, unlike those of the British, were working properly. Back in their own trenches, the attackers suffered accurate German artillery fire. The 2nd HLI were at the same time being affected by the British gas which had blown back into their section of trench. This delayed their attempt to make a further advance until 06h40. When it took place it was quickly halted by enemy machine gun fire. The 5th Brigade's attempts to carry out their orders had been defeated by the almost total ineffectiveness of the gas, the lack of impact of 2 mines which had been detonated 10 minutes prior to Zero Hour, and the difficulties experienced by the troops in igniting their bombs in the very damp conditions.

South of 5th Brigade and of the La Bassée Canal, 6th Brigade released the gas at 05h50 with the intention of attacking at 06h30. The Brigade Commander telephoned Horne within 2 minutes of the gas being released to report that the wind (south-south-west at 2 mph) was unfavourable. He was told to turn off the gas if it did not move forward. This was done, but too late to prevent some troops being badly affected by it. The 2nd South Staffs had 130 men totally incapacitated. At 07h30, Brigade HQ reported that their 2 attacking battalions, one of which was 2nd South Staffs, had made no progress. ' ... Gas had taken effect on our own men, but not on the enemy, and the attack was held up in front of the German trenches by heavy machine gun fire and bombs', which caused heavy losses. The 2nd South Staffs had made a gallant attack on the Embankment Redoubt, a German strongpoint, but had been obliged to return to their own trenches.[35]

Further south, 19th Brigade also released its gas at 05h50 and attacked 40 minutes later. At 06h48 the brigade informed divisional HQ that some of the gas was coming back into their own trenches. A few minutes later they reported that the leading platoons were stopped at the enemy's wire. The Germans appeared to be holding their front trenches without difficulty, even though many of them were without the protection of gas helmets. At 07h10 Brigade reported that their right hand battalion, 1st Middlesex, were meeting heavy opposition. By 08h00 the remnants of this battalion were lying in front of the German trenches; by contrast 2nd Argyll and Sutherland Highlanders had regained their own trenches after being driven back. Both battalions had suffered heavily.

At 08h30 Horne, recognising the failure of the initial attacks by 6th and 19th Brigades, ordered them to make a second attack at 09h30, following a 30 minute bombardment. The 19th Brigade pointed out they would have to replace 1st Middlesex and 2nd Argylls by 1st Cameronians and 2nd Royal Welsh Fusiliers and would need more time for this. They were told to report when ready. Both Brigadiers however represented that further attacks would be a useless waste of lives and, following consultation by Horne with I Corps HQ, the attack was suspended pending further orders. By midmorning, all of 2nd Division's attacking battalions were back in their own trenches except for 1st Middlesex, still lying out in front of the German lines.

The division's attacks had been thwarted by a combination of the damage wrought on the attackers by their own gas, with the lack of damage it had inflicted on the enemy; by the inadequacy in some cases of the smokescreen; and by the many craters in No Man's Land which had channelled the advancing troops into the German machine gun fire.[36]

Unsurprisingly, Horne's decision to release the gas on this 'day of tragedy, unmitigated by any gleam of success'[37] for 2nd Division, has been called into question. Given the lack, or at best fitfulness, of wind in the divisional area, the consequences were indeed tragic. But once the results became apparent, Horne was

quick to authorise the gas being turned off. Horne was fully aware of how funda-
mental the use of gas was to the attackers' chances of success, given their vulnerability over such unfavourable terrain. This may have swayed him into giving the
new technology a chance despite the unfavourable circumstances. One distinguished commentator was outspoken in his later criticism of Horne over his use of
gas at Loos. Captain Sir Basil Liddell Hart[38] wrote scathingly:

> In Horne's 2nd Division, the officer in charge of the gas on the 6th Brigade
> front declined to assume the responsibility of turning on the cylinders. But
> when this was reported to Divisional HQ, Horne replied with an order that
> "the programme must be carried out whatever the conditions". As a result of
> this stupidity many of the infantry were poisoned by their own gas. Those
> who were able to advance were soon stopped and slaughtered, by the ungassed
> German machine gunners.
>
> Nevertheless Horne ordered a fresh assault, which was only abandoned
> after his Brigade Commanders had protested against "the useless sacrifice of
> life".[39]

The first day of the Battle of Loos ended with one sixth of the attacking force
casualties but at least 2 claimed possibilities for exploitation by the reserves,
reserves which were too far back to intervene in the battle. They would only be in a
position to do so the following day.

To the generals, the results of the first day seemed gratifyingly positive. Severe
inroads had been made into the German defences which seemed ripe for exploitation by the original divisions and the reserves. This assessment however took little
account of the exhaustion and decimation of the troops involved on the first day.
Nor of the fact that the Germans were rushing up nearly 7 divisions to reinforce
their shaky defences. These divisions were immediately put to work shoring up and
wiring their second position and siting their machine guns.

In addition to their traumatic marches to reach their assembly points for their
attack on the second day of the battle, the 21st and 24th Divisions were to suffer
from a lack of maps of the area over which they were to attack Their artillery
support would also prove to be patchy, with some of it harming them more than
the enemy. They were deployed on the IV Corps front to advance over the ground
previously fought over by 15th and 1st Divisions. Attacking at 11h00 they were
scythed down in great numbers. Elements reached the summit of Hill 70 but were
cut down by machine gun and artillery fire as they tried to advance further. Further
north a German counterattack was only repulsed by 21st Division at the cost of
heavy casualties. At 12h00 1st Division tried to take Hulluch village, advancing
over 600 yards of open ground. The attacking battalions lost half their number
before they had got 100 yards.[40]

For the bulk of 2nd Division the orders for the second day of the battle were to
stand fast. Heavy artillery and machine gun fire was nevertheless kept up on the
German positions throughout the day, to leave them doubtful as to Horne's intentions. Late the previous evening Horne had received orders to organise a detachment to support 7th Division in front of Cité St Elie. He withdrew 2nd Worcesters
from 5th Brigade and 1st Royal Berks and 1st KRRC from 6th Brigade and placed
them under the command of Lieutenant Colonel B C M Carter with the designation 'Carter's Force'. They marched off at 04h30 to be in 7th Division's area by

07h00. The assumption had been that they would attack Cité St Elie after an early morning attack had once more secured the Quarries. But this attack had failed and German occupation of the Quarries precluded an assault on the Cité. Instead, therefore, Carter's Force was ordered to renew the attack on the Quarries. After a frustrating period trying to reach their jumping-off point, 2nd Worcesters and 1st KRRC, against strong resistance from enemy bombers, reached a trench still about 200 yards short of the Quarries. There they were ordered to consolidate. They had sustained heavy casualties on a day when the GOC of 7th Division, Major General Capper was mortally wounded. He was one of 3 divisional commanders to be killed at Loos.

The other battalion of Carter's Force, 1st Royal Berks, had been ordered to retake Fosse 8. This involved advancing for half a mile over badly cut up terrain unknown to them. Personally led by Colonel Carter, the attack was undertaken in moonlight which led to its detection by the enemy. The attackers nevertheless got to within 70 yards of the Fosse, where they were stopped by heavy fire. As daylight approached Colonel Carter ordered a retirement. The battalion had sustained over 300 casualties. Carter's Force was broken up the following day, although its 3 battalions were to remain with 7th Division.[41]

On the third day of the battle, the last of the reserves, the Guards Division, were given the task of pushing over and beyond Hill 70. They were driven back with heavy casualties.

By the night of 27/28 September the front line was beginning to stabilise. But the Germans were maintaining a heavy artillery bombardment. FM French told General Joffre that his reserves were exhausted. If he were to continue the offensive the French would have to make diversionary attacks. The French thereupon took over the Loos sector of the front. On the 28th the Guards, by now at only half strength, attacked once more just north of Loos. The Coldstreams were almost exterminated in this attack.

On 1 October, 5th Brigade made unavailing attempts to dislodge the Germans from 250 yards of Gun Trench, north of the Vermelles-Hulluch road, which they had taken from 7th Division.

For their part the Germans made persistent attempts to recapture the Hohenzollern Redoubt. They eventually succeeded on 3 October. On 8 October they launched a general offensive all along the line but were forced to abandon it after heavy losses.

On 13 October the British made a final effort to push their line a little further ahead before the onset of winter. It involved elements of 3 divisions, including 1st Queens and the bombers of 5th Brigade of 2nd Division. The attackers employed gas and smoke, but the gas merely served to warn the enemy of the attack. The bombers and 1st Queens attacked towards the Little Willie trench but with no result. A lack of bombs precluded a further attempt.

Thus ended the Battle of Loos.

Total British casualties amounted to over 60,000 for a maximum penetration of the German front of one and a half miles on an 8,000 yard length of front. German casualties were about half the British. The 2nd Division's casualties totalled 3,365 of whom over 1,400 were killed or missing.[42]

The main fallout of the battle was that patience with FM French's tenure as GOC-in-C of the BEF was virtually exhausted. He did himself no good by producing a mendacious dispatch on the battle, which, when added to the embarrassment he had caused the Government by his hostile leaking to the press over the shell shortage (which was by now the 'Shell Scandal'), and his perceived unfair dismissal of General Sir Horace Smith-Dorrien, led to his own recall in December 1915. His successor was General Sir Douglas Haig, a choice that could hardly have been bettered as far as Horne's future prospects were concerned.

These momentous changes would find Henry Horne a long way from the Western Front. On 4 November he received a telegram ordering him to hand over temporary command of his division to one of his Brigadier Generals and to join FM Lord Kitchener in Paris. He was warned that he would probably be absent for a month and to take one ADC with him. The telegram gave no indication of the reason for his orders.[43]

Chapter VII

November 1915–April 1916: Near Eastern Interludes

The day after Henry Horne's hastily arranged trip to Paris, Lord Kitchener told him that he was to be his Chief Military Adviser for the duration of an unforeseen and very secret visit to Gallipoli. The Field Marshal had formed a high opinion of Horne's abilities as long ago as South Africa, and this may have been the reason for his selection. It had nothing to do with Haig, who had been as mystified as Horne by the latter's sudden summons to Paris.

By November of 1915 a decision on whether to pursue the Gallipoli campaign, or close it down and evacuate, was well overdue. The campaign had been originally conceived by the then First Lord of the Admiralty, Winston Churchill, as a purely naval expedition to force the Dardenelles, open up the Bosphorus, bombard Constantinople and knock Turkey out of the war. When the Navy's attempt failed, Churchill persuaded Kitchener and subsequently their Cabinet colleagues to approve the use of troops to overpower the Turkish defences on either side of the Dardenelles and clear the way for the Navy to renew its efforts.

Cabinet support was never better than lukewarm and both Churchill and Kitchener had plenty of opposition from their professional advisers. Indeed, Kitchener committed the Army to the venture without formally seeking the advice of his. The vast bulk of the army high command were, and would remain, committed 'Westerners', firm in the belief that the only way to win the war was to defeat the German army on the Western Front, and avoid being distracted by sideshows. Kitchener himself was of this view in principle and therefore sought to mount the Gallipoli expedition without weakening the army's commitment to the Western Front. Predictably this had resulted in men and matériel urgently required for the Western Front being siphoned off to Gallipoli, but never in sufficient quantities to assure the success of that operation.

One of the most difficult operations in war is an amphibious landing on a hostile shore. This was what was attempted at Gallipoli with inadequate resources, sometimes poor leadership, changes of plan and indecision; all in the face of determined Turkish opposition under German military supervision. Despite sometimes superhuman courage (the 1st Bn Lancashire Fusiliers won 6 Victoria Crosses 'before breakfast') the British, ANZAC and French landings on 25 April 1915 failed to occupy sufficient ground to make the beachheads secure and capable of use to mount major future strikes inland. Subsequent attempts to retrieve the situation by attacks, and a further landing in August, were bedevilled by too few resources being provided too late.

The Commander of the expedition was General Sir Ian Hamilton. When asked in October by the War Office to estimate the number of casualties his force would suffer in the event of a withdrawal being ordered, he replied with a figure of 50%. He was recalled and the Commander of the BEF's Third Army, Horne's predecessor at 2nd Division, General Charles Monro, was appointed in his stead.[1]

Map 5: The Near East

As a convinced 'Westerner' Monro was unlikely to call for a continuation of the campaign. But it nevertheless came as a severe shock to Kitchener when, having visited all the beaches and consulted as many as possible of his corps and divisional commanders, Monro cabled London on 31 October recommending evacuation.[2] 'He came, he saw, he capitulated' was to be Winston Churchill's sardonic comment on Monro's recommendation.[3]

Kitchener's feelings were understandable. He had, at best, ignored his professional advisers in committing the army to the campaign. The conservation of his already rather tarnished prestige rested on its successful prosecution. Evacuation, especially if it resulted in heavy casualties, might deal it a terminal blow. Kitchener immediately replied requesting the independent views of Monro's corps commanders. When he received these, Lieutenant Generals Sir F Davies and Sir Julian Byng favoured evacuation and Sir William Birdwood opposed it, citing the physical dangers of withdrawal and the damage it would do to British prestige in the Moslem world.[4]

Hence Kitchener's precipitate decision to visit Gallipoli to see for himself.

For a short period prior to his departure from London, Kitchener had been espousing a plan to retrieve the situation and avoid the military and political dangers of evacuation. Proposed by Commodore Roger Keyes RN, this plan was to rush and force the Straits by naval action. Keyes was Chief of Staff to Vice Admiral de Robeck, the commander of the Gallipoli Expedition's naval forces, who was not in favour of his subordinate's plan. Kitchener tried to cobble together a plan combining Keyes' scheme with a fresh landing by troops.[5] But when, after initial lukewarm endorsement, the Admiralty cooled towards Keyes' plan, Kitchener withdrew his scheme. By the time of his visit to the area, the options had narrowed to a choice between staying put and evacuation. Although he had learned during his stopover in Paris that the French opposed withdrawal, Kitchener was moving towards favouring evacuation.

Kitchener and Horne sailed from Marseilles on 7 November on the cruiser HMS *Dartmouth*. They arrived in Mudros harbour early in the morning of the 10th and immediately transferred to Admiral de Robeck's flagship, HMS *Lord Nelson*. Horne spent the rest of the day obtaining and collating detailed information for the Field Marshal in preparation for their visits to the Gallipoli beachheads.[6]

The first of these took place the following day when they travelled to Cape Helles by RN destroyer. They were accompanied by General Sir John Maxwell,the C-in-C Egypt, Sir Henry McMahon, the British High Commissioner in Egypt, and Lieutenant General Birdwood, deputising for General Monro, who was absent in Egypt trying to get a feel for likely Moslem reaction to a British evacuation. Horne noted that they had no time to visit the front line, but they had a general view of the country and visited the beaches. 'Marvellous to think how the landing was ever made good', Horne commented.[7]

Kitchener and Horne learned that Maxwell and McMahon were agreeable to evacuation, with the proviso that a fresh landing should first be made at Ayas Bay near Alexandretta. Its aim would be to disrupt Turkish communications and minimise the political damage which a Gallipoli evacuation would do to Britain. Since he had learned that there was no prospect of reinforcing the troops already ashore,

Birdwood had come round to favouring withdrawal without a prior landing at Ayas Bay, which he opposed. According to Kitchener, Monro and Horne quite liked the Ayas Bay scheme.[8]

On 13 November, Kitchener and Horne visited the ANZAC position, where Horne was shown around by Major General Alexander Godley. He recorded his impressions.

> Precipitous cliffs, intersected by ravines rising direct from the beach. The attack and capture of these was a fine performance. Nowhere is the skyline of the ridge in our possession. Had a good view of general line and also of Suvla line stretching northwards. ANZAC and Suvla front extends to nine miles and I do not see how it can be shortened. The New Zealanders and the Australians gave Kitchener a good reception. Fine day, calm voyage.[9]

The following day it was the turn of Suvla to be visited.

> Landed at Suvla at about 14h45. Visit beach. Met General Byng. Walked to an observation station. This landing place is very exposed. A small harbour has been formed by sinking old ships and a great deal of work has been done. This is not a safe position. A supporting or second line are difficult. The Suvla Point and Lalla Bala are prepared for defence as final points. A re-embarkation would be very difficult at any time, but still more so in winter when the sea is liable to be rough for some days at a time. Left at 03h45 and reached Mudros at 07h30. Very wet voyage.[10]

The next 2 days were to be spent in meetings and conferences. The visitors had learned that the War Office was opposed to the Ayas Bay scheme on the grounds that it would require 10 to 12 divisions, which would effectively be tied down for the rest of the war. Little more was to be heard of the scheme.[11] Kitchener now favoured the evacuation of Suvla and ANZAC and the retention of Helles. But before formal proposals could be made to London there remained the need for a decision on the future of the Salonika operation. Kitchener and Horne headed for the Greek city, arriving at 08h00 on 17 November.

They were about to experience at first hand the 'extraordinary situation', to use Horne's words, that was Salonika. 'A neutral port, with many German, Bulgarian and Turkish officers, and others, present, who know exactly how many men we land.' The military and political situation of the Allies was 'absurd and unsustainable'. The visitors met the Commander of the British Forces, Lieutenant General Sir B Mahon, and the Allied Commander-in-Chief, the French General Maurice Sarrail, the latter of whom made a poor impression on his interlocutors. Kitchener was in favour of withdrawal from the Serbian front and the occupation of Salonika.[12]

No sooner had Kitchener and Horne returned to Mudros than they received a telegram directing Kitchener to proceed to Athens to interview King Constantine I of Greece. They sailed for Athens at 22h00 on 19 November and reached Piraeus the following morning. The interview took place later that same morning and lasted 75 minutes with only the King, Kitchener and Horne present. The King, who was of German descent, was known to be pro-German in his sympathies, despite his protestations to the contrary. He said he was in a difficult position and was determined not to allow Greece to be drawn into war with the Central Powers, though he would be prepared to fight Bulgaria when this could be done without leading to hostilities with Germany. He assured his guests that Greek troops would neither attack nor attempt to intern British or French troops if they crossed the frontier. But if they were driven back and crossed fighting with the Bulgarians, the Greek troops would be bound to protect the frontier from the Bulgarians, which would be considered an act of war by the Germans.

Kitchener pointed out the consequences of an attack by the Greeks on Allied troops, emphasising that the Allies were only just beginning to develop their resources. The King took the opportunity to complain of many acts of ill-treatment by the British, including the stoppage of supplies. He also showed his anger with his recently ousted Prime Minister, Eleutherios Venizelos, although he claimed that the latter had not invited allied troops to come in. Kitchener assured him that the contrary was the truth.

Horne subsequently met the Lord Chamberlain and the Chief of the Greek General Staff and sat between the wife of the French Ambassador and the Russian Minister at a luncheon at the British Embassy. In the afternoon Kitchener and Horne called on the new Prime Minister Alexander Zaimis, who later returned their call. He declared himself very friendly and said that if the Allies would formulate their demands over Salonika, he would ensure they were met as far as possible.[13]

As the visitors left for Mudros later the same day they could reflect with some satisfaction on the outcome of the visit. They had obtained the King's assurance that no Allied troops forced to withdraw from Serbia would be interned, thus enabling them to put to one side considerations of Salonika when deciding on the fate of the Gallipoli Expedition.

The day after their return to Mudros, Kitchener chaired a conference to discuss the question of evacuation from Gallipoli and the future defence of Egypt. Kitchener had formally recommended to London that Suvla and ANZAC should be evacuated and Helles retained.[14] London had however come down in favour of total evacuation. As his final acts before departure for London on 24 November, Kitchener appointed General Monro to be Commander-in-Chief Mediterranean and Lieutenant General Birdwood to command the evacuation of the Gallipoli Peninsula. He also notified Horne that he would be sent to Egypt 'to assist in connection with a line of defence east of the Suez Canal.'[15]

Kitchener's main aim in sending Horne to Egypt was to bring his Western Front experience to bear on what was required in terms of troop deployments and physical barriers to ensure the security of the Suez canal from Turkish attack. Such an attack was perceived as being more likely once the Allies had evacuated Gallipoli.[16] The C-in-C Egypt, Sir John Maxwell, and the War Office had slightly differing views on troop requirements. Sir John had recommended that defence of the canal would require 12 infantry and one cavalry divisions and 20 batteries of heavy and siege artillery. A further 2 divisions would be required to defend Egypt, protect communications and maintain order. Finally, an additional 3 infantry brigades, with supporting cavalry and artillery, would be needed to police Egypt's western frontier, where the Senussi were a constant menace.

The War Office's estimates were based on a fixed system of defence 12,000 yards east of the canal. They were proposing 5 mounted and 8 infantry divisions,

19 batteries of siege and heavy artillery, plus armoured cars and additional aircraft for defence of the canal. For the defence of Egypt one mounted brigade and 15 garrison battalions would be required. That country's western frontier would require a further 2 mounted and 2 infantry brigades with supporting artillery.[17]

Accompanying Sir Henry MacMahon and General Sir John Maxwell, Horne arrived in Alexandria from Mudros on HMS *Chatham* on 25 November. A special train took them to Cairo the same day and Horne at once set to work. Until 7 December, Horne was to be out in the field, conducting a detailed reconnaissance of the canal and surrounding areas and talking to senior officers. Back in Cairo he composed his report on a defensive line east of the Suez canal. Dated 8 December 1915, the report recommended the establishment of a first line of defence an average of 11,000 yards east of the waterway, which would include all important points from which observed fire could be directed onto the canal. This would suffice to prevent interference with canal traffic by shellfire.

A second line should be established 4,500 yards back. Although this would surrender many points from which the enemy could observe the canal, it would be sufficiently advanced to prevent any serious shelling of ships.

The third line would be the canal itself.

The report also recommended the garrisoning of advance points, the main purpose of which would be to deny their water to the Turks.[18] But there was no mention in this context of the Qatiya district, where several oases were to be found. Sir John Maxwell had suggested a light railway should be laid to Qatiya, on the coast road to Palestine, in order to establish a strong position there and deny the enemy the only approach to the canal relatively well supplied with water. The War Office, perhaps influenced by the use of this route by many great military leaders in history, had based their estimates of Egypt's troop requirements on its occupation. They reckoned that, if it were in Turkish hands, a force of 200,000 could be deployed by them against the Nile Delta by the end of January 1916, and 300,000 a month later; if it were in British hands, no more than 50,000 Turks would be able to operate in the Qatiya district. Two infantry divisions and 2 cavalry brigades would suffice to cope with this latter size of threat. (It was to be rapidly realised that the size of the Turkish threat in the former case had been greatly exaggerated, and it was downgraded to 130,000 by the end of March 1916.)[19]

Finally, Horne's report recommended that the Canal Defence Force should be divided into 3 corps with their headquarters at Suez, Ismailia and Port Said. The corps based at Suez and Ismailia should consist of 3 infantry and one cavalry divisions, and that at Port Said of 3 infantry and one mounted infantry divisions. The other troops in Egypt should be one division each in Cairo and Alexandria and 2 divisions at Camp El Warden.

His immediate work completed with submission of his report, Horne embarked for England on the SS *Mongolia* on 16 December. During his voyage the debate continued elsewhere on the question of Qatiya. The War Office now learned that Sir John Maxwell was moving away from the idea of garrisoning the district, as denying the enemy this well-watered approach would necessitate an advance of 45 miles beyond the Canal's easternmost defence line. The maintenance of troops this far out would consume all the available railway material and thus weaken the defence of the central route to the Canal, which the enemy's rail laying activities appeared to be favouring. Maxwell now believed the overriding priority to be construction of the main line of defence, especially as the most propitious season for an enemy assault was at hand. Horne, still at sea, agreed with Maxwell's new evaluation, and told London that he was not in favour of the occupation of Qatiya in the present circumstances. The decision was made to postpone all thoughts of advancing to Qatiya until the main defensive line was well on the way to completion.[20]

During his brief stay in England Horne learned that the fate of Qatiya was to be of more than academic interest. He was to be posted back to Egypt to command one of the 3 corps entrusted with the defence of the canal, on temporary promotion to Lieutenant General. It is not difficult to infer that, despite the very welcome promotion, Horne was not altogether pleased to find himself once more heading away from the Western Front which he, like most of his peers, saw as the place where the decisive struggle would take place. There was nothing to be done in the short term however and Horne duly met General Sir Archibald Murray, the newly appointed Commander-in-Chief of the Egyptian Expeditionary Force, at Victoria station on 1 January 1916, at the beginning of the journey back to Egypt.[21]

After a delayed sailing from Marseilles, Horne and Murray arrived at Port Said on 9 January. Horne was immediately appointed to the command of XV Corps, which comprised 11th Division (Major General E A Fanshawe), 13th Division and 31st Division (Major General Wanless O'Gowan). As recommended in Horne's report, responsibility for defence of the canal was to be entrusted to 3 corps. From south to north these would be IX Corps (Lieutenant General Sir Julian Byng), ANZAC Corps (Lieutenant General Sir William Birdwood) and XV Corps (Horne). Horne moved to his new headquarters at Port Said on 13 January. An advanced HQ was quickly set up at Qantara.[22]

During the voyage out Horne had once more become preoccupied with the matter of preferment. He had received a Mention in Dispatches in the New Year Honours but was clearly disappointed that there had been nothing more for him. In a letter to his wife he criticised the award of a KCB to a General Wilson 'who made such an awful mess of the Canal Defence when the Turks attacked last year. Everyone thought he would be sent home!'. He consoled his wife, implicitly more disappointed than he, pointing out that he had done rather well to reach the rank of temporary Lieutenant General without the benefit of attending Staff College.[23]

In a later letter he commented on how difficult it was to continue to do well in the changed circumstances of an army which was no longer close-knit and fully professional.

> It is a different matter dealing with the new Armies and with Territorials and Yeomanry to what it was with the old 2nd Division. There are so few trained or experienced officers and the men, although the very best fellows in the world, are not trained like the soldiers of the original expeditionary forces. Then the regimental traditions do not exist. In the old army, as soon as new officers or men joined a regiment, they became part of the regiment and were at once influenced by the regimental traditions and customs and soon became soldiers. It makes it much more difficult and throws much more detail on the shoulders of the few who know what is what … It is the ignorance of the officers that is the worst feature. However they all try and do their best.

Horne was even less equivocal about the Yeomanry. The officers are very good individually, but full of cliques and squabbles amongst themselves. A rum lot.[24]

Horne was speaking from experience, if very brief, as all three of his corps' divisions were New Army. He was soon to lose the 13th, who were moving to Mesopotamia, and would acquire in their stead the 52nd (Lowland) Division, a Scottish Territorial unit. In addition he had been given a brigade of Yeomanry originating from Warwickshire, Worcestershire and Gloucestershire, and the Ayrshire and Lanarkshire Yeomanry (Scottish Horse), which would fight dismounted.[25]

It was however looking increasingly unlikely that his corps would be engaged in any serious fighting in the immediate future. In another letter to his wife he wrote:

I do not think the Turks are going to come in any great strength and therefore we might be called back to France in a month or two. The signs are that the Turks are making preparations but their preparations are very backwards, and it does not seem possible that they can concentrate a large force before the hot weather sets in towards the end of April. Also they are being pressed in the Caucasus and are sending troops to Mesopotamia against us. I do not think they will have the troops to send here in any numbers. Certainly a few will come and they will probably endeavour to keep up the appearance of attacking us as long as ever they can in order to tie up our troops here, but I hope that we shall be able to see through that and form an accurate estimate of what is going on. At the present time, the railway is only a short distance beyond Beersheba, but the embankment is built as far as EL Auja (130 miles from the Canal). From there they have made or improved roads which bring them to within about 60 miles of the central position of the Canal (Ismailia). This road may be extended another 20 miles and then their troubles begin, because the sand gets very heavy and is blown up into high dunes. That was the way that they brought their main force last year. There is another road further south which is more mountainous and along which a small force might come, and then there is the main coast road which runs along the north of the Sinai Desert and which is opposite to me. There are far more wells and a better water supply along this road but the Turks do not like it because it is so near the sea and they are afraid of our warships firing on them or of our landing a force behind them. They are working on this route now, digging out wells and preparing stores for supplies and they are certain to send some force along this line, but whether it will be the main attack or not we do not know. I am sending out a small mounted force to have a look at what is going on but they cannot go far, as although there is water for horses it does not suit the white man's stomach and we have to carry the drinking water on camels ... I am establishing an advanced camp at one of the Canal Company's stations on the Canal Bank.[26]

Until mid-February the troops had been fully engaged in reorganisation, training and work upon the fixed defences. Air reconnaissance had established that there were no signs of the Turks massing for an attack. In the second half of February Horne sent mounted patrols out 20 miles where they found no sign of Turk or Bedouin. In mid-March work on a standard-gauge railway line between Qantara and Qatiya was put in hand. Within a month 16 miles of track had been laid. This necessitated the establishment of permanent posts up to and including Qatiya to protect the line and the labour force from armed Bedouin. In what was virtually his last act in command of XV Corps Horne gave the job to 5th Mounted Brigade and put its commander, Brigadier General E A Wiggin, in charge of Qatiya district.[27]

By early March Horne had become convinced that the threat of a Turkish attack on the canal had virtually disappeared. The Turks had suffered a serious setback in the Caucasus with the capture on 16 February by the Russians of the fortress town of Erzerum in Turkish Armenia. This was part of a more general Russian offensive in the region which had cost the Turks heavy losses in men and matériel. Horne wrote:

> I think that on the whole the Turks have withdrawn troops from Sinai, probably for the Caucasus. In another month all the water pools will have dried up, and no force of any consequence can cross the desert. Turkey is in a bad way, and would make peace tomorrow if only Enver[28] was out of the way. There was a report that he had been assassinated but it is not true apparently.[29]

Horne was clearly hoping that the way was opening up for him to be recalled to France. What might help him achieve his aim, in addition to the diminution of the Turkish threat, was a rationalisation of the army command structure in Egypt. On his arrival, Sir Archibald Murray had taken over responsibility for the canal and Eastern Egypt from Sir John Maxwell, who retained responsibility for the rest of the country. Horne was not alone in thinking that this sharing out of the Egyptian command was not necessary and looked to the day when the 2 commands would be reunified in one person. He wrote:

> If Sir A Murray goes to Cairo (when the Commands are unified) it will mean that one of the Corps Commanders must command the Canal defences. For the summer there will be no necessity to keep more than sufficient troops to guard the Canal and there will be no occasion to have more than one Corps Commander. Joey Davies is senior to me so he will probably command the Canal defences and that ought to release me to go to France.[30]

On 15 March Sir A Murray was appointed Commander-in-Chief Egypt in place of Sir John Maxwell, who returned to England to be handed the soon-to-be poisoned chalice of Commander-in-Chief Ireland. On 26 March Murray told Horne that he had placed his services at the disposal of the BEF in France. Horne immediately wrote to Sir Douglas Haig saying that he hoped Sir Douglas would get him back if he could manage it.[31] This was not his first direct intercession with Haig. He had written to him a month earlier asking him to get him back if he could. He had pointed out that he still had some energy and a great deal of experience at his disposal to fight Germans. He told his wife, 'I dare say he will get me if he can, but it may be difficult to get me out of this for a little while yet, until the whole threat of attack has passed by'.[32] Horne had also urged his wife to tell Ladies Haig and Robertson, with whom she was on friendly terms, that he was keen to get away to France again for the summer fighting. 'I do not look forward to kicking my heels in Egypt all the summer.'[33]

On 11 April, the anxiously awaited telegram arrived. 'Send Lt Gen Horne and his personal staff to France as soon as possible.' Horne was delighted. 'Well done Douglas Haig', he wrote to his wife, 'I am sure that it is he who has asked for me back.' Even the prospect of travelling to France in a transport vessel full of Australians could not dampen his relief and pleasure. He was also not sorry to be leaving Sir A Murray's command. 'I am glad to get away from him', he wrote, 'for he and I do not as a rule see eye to eye and he is not a popular man. However he has always had regard for me, I think, and I have done him well.'[34]

Horne left Alexandria on RMS *Scotian* on 15 April and disembarked at Marseilles 6 days later.

Part Three

WORLD WAR: APRIL–OCTOBER 1916

Chapter VIII

Corps Commander: The Somme: The Opening Days

Horne disembarked at Marseilles on 21 April and was ordered to report immediately to Fourth Army headquarters at Querrieu, near Amiens. On arrival there he was reappointed to the command of XV Corps, which was being revived.[1] Horne must have been very pleased that he was, after all, going to play a significant part in what was now being talked of as 'The Big Push' better known to history as the Battle of the Somme.

Allied military strategy for the Western Front in 1916 had been agreed at an inter-Allied meeting held towards the end of the previous year. Its centrepiece was to be a joint Anglo-French offensive in the Somme area of Picardy, to be mounted as early as possible in the summer. The choice had fallen on the Somme area less for its strategic potential than for the fact that it would be where the British and French sectors of the line conjoined. The French would be the main protagonists, but the BEF's input would be significant, commensurate with its growing size and strength.[2]

All this was changed by the wholly unforeseen German assault on the French at Verdun in February 1916. With France suddenly fighting for her very life, the Somme offensive became transformed into a mainly British operation, with the French contribution to the initial assault reduced to 5 divisions. It had also become vital to launch the offensive at the earliest possible moment to help relieve the German pressure on the French at Verdun. These changed circumstances put Haig under some very unwelcome pressure. He had been relying on a massive French presence to take some of the heat off his inexperienced divisions, many of which would not have completed their training by the sort of date for launching the battle now being called for.[3]

In March the newly formed Fourth Army took over the future battlefield area of the Somme Département from the French. General Sir Henry Rawlinson was placed in command.[4] He was initially given 4 infantry corps headquarters and staffs for the campaign, but in a letter to the CIGS, General Sir William Robertson, dated 8 April, he wrote:

> The four Corps commanders I have are Hunter-Weston, Morland, Putty [Pulteney], and Congreve. They are now well-staffed and I ask for no changes though the last is I think the weakest. After talking the matter over with DH [Haig], he has decided to give me another Corps Staff as Congreve was to have 5 divisions, too much for one man to handle in a general action. He tells me I am to have Horne, which delights me, so send him out as soon as you can for there is much for him to study in the problems that he will have to solve.[5]

When Horne arrived at Fourth Army headquarters on 22 April he learned that newly-promoted Brigadier General Louis Vaughan was again to be his Chief of Staff. Vaughan was an Indian Army officer who was to prove to be one of the outstanding British staff officers of the war. To Horne's regret, their renewed asso-

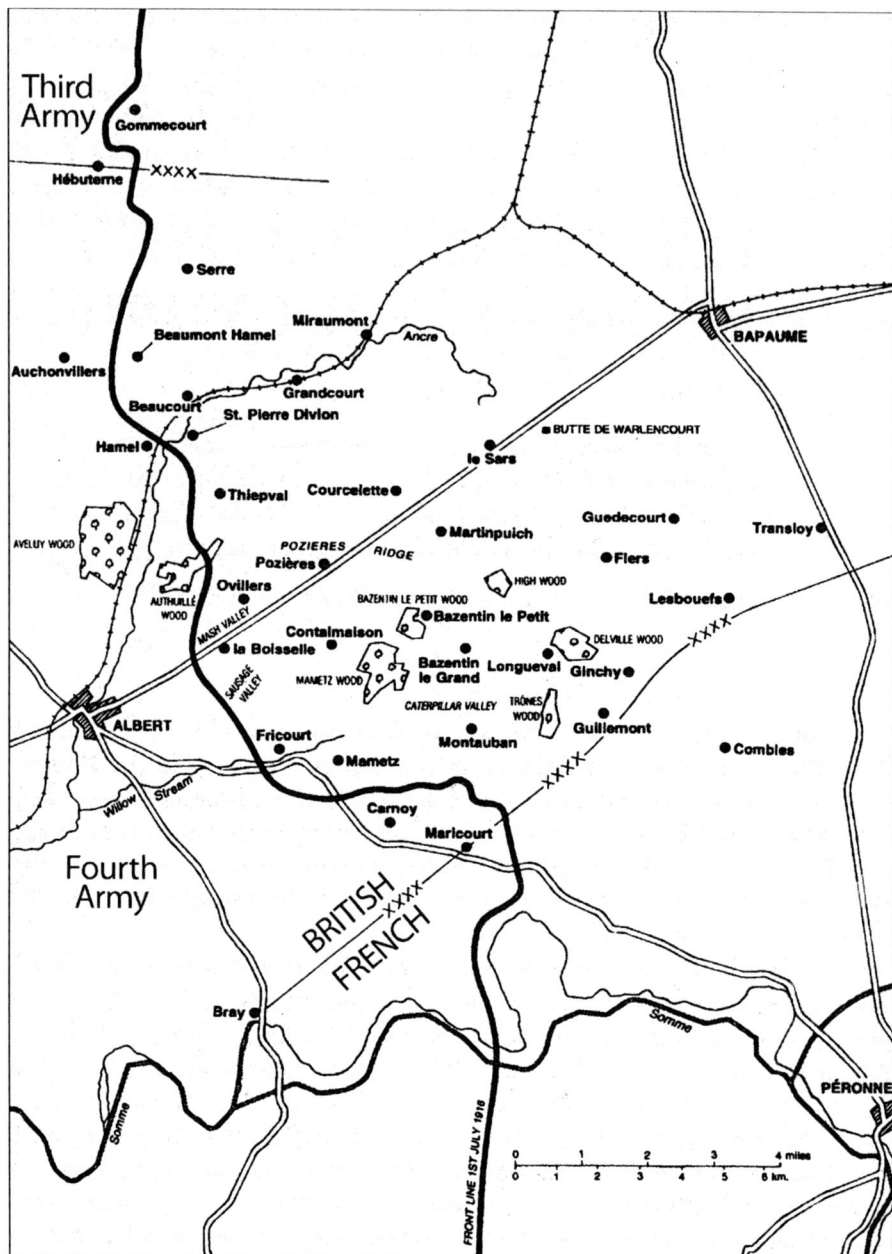

Map 6: The Somme Battlefields: 1916

ciation was to be brief. Horne was also lucky in being assigned an outstanding gunner, E W Alexander, as his Brigadier General Royal Artillery. Alexander had won the Victoria Cross at Elouges in the opening days of the war.[6]

The XV Corps initially consisted of the regular 7th Division, commanded by Major General H E Watts, and the New Army 21st Division, commanded by Major General David Campbell, who replaced Major General C W Jacob on 23 May. Another New Army Division, 17th (Northern) (Major General T D Pilcher), joined the corps a few days later.

New Army divisions would make up 60% of the overall attacking force on the first day of the battle. Most of them, including the 17th, were new to offensive operations. The 21st was less fortunate, having been disastrously blooded on the second day of the Battle of Loos, when badly led, exhausted and hungry, they had suffered terrible casualties.

Horne's plans for his corps would need to conform with the overall strategy for the conduct of the battle, which was largely in the hands of Rawlinson. One of the reasons Haig had given him command of Fourth Army was that he was an infantryman, and this was to be an infantry battle once the artillery preparation had paved the way. Tragically, Rawlinson's plans were not to serve his infantry well. His faith in the ability of the artillery to do their work efficiently and effectively was to prove sadly misplaced. In the absence of the protection the artillery were supposed to have provided, the infantry's planned initial role of walking across No Man's Land, to occupy the German positions unopposed, was to prove seriously at odds with what was required. Rawlinson's reason for imposing this role on his infantry was his apparent belief that it was about all his infantry was capable of, undertrained, inexperienced and unprofessional as he perceived his New Army divisions to be. Hence normal infantry assault tactics were to be abandoned in favour of the troops walking steadily across No Man's Land in open order, rifles at the high port, in broad daylight.[7]

In these circumstances, if disaster were to be avoided, the artillery would have had to have done its work thoroughly. The tasks set it were to destroy the enemy's wire, annihilate their front line positions and neutralise their artillery. Rawlinson put his faith in the largest concentration of guns yet seen on the Western Front, and a preliminary bombardment of long duration. Sadly the gunners were to fall well short of completing their tasks. They were still deficient in the really heavy guns required to destroy the German fortifications and deep dugouts; they still had too much shrapnel ammunition and insufficient high explosive; and an unacceptable number of the shells they fired, about one third by some estimates, proved to be 'duds'.[8]

Haig was not happy with aspects of Rawlinson's plans, especially the abandonment of normal infantry tactics and the reliance on an, in his view, overlong preliminary bombardment. But he did not feel able to insist on changes, given that Rawlinson was equal in rank to himself, if junior. As an infantryman he might too be expected to know better what was right for the infantry.[9] As Haig was surely correct over the infantry tactics, it was a tragedy that he did not prevail over his subordinate.

Just as worrying for the conduct of the forthcoming battle was the divergence of the two men's perceptions of its aims. Ever the cavalryman, Haig envisaged an infantry breakthrough which the cavalry could exploit. For this latter purpose he had created a Reserve Army of 3 cavalry divisions under Lt General Hubert Gough. This was conceived as an independent command, but Rawlinson persuaded Haig to subordinate it to Fourth Army. Rawlinson did not believe there was any serious role for cavalry in the conditions of the Western Front and his readiness to use it to exploit a breakthrough, should one occur, was only token. Not that he thought a breakthrough likely. He saw the battle more in terms of 'bite and hold'. This difference of perception was not the last to affect conduct of the battle. A later one, over the attack on Bazentin Ridge, would directly affect Horne's corps.

Rawlinson's plan for the opening of the battle had the virtue of simplicity. Four of his 5 corps would attack and occupy the German front line. North of the Albert-Bapaume road, where the German front and second lines were close together, the attacking troops were to seize both lines. The fifth, northernmost, Corps, north of the River Ancre, were to advance and wheel leftwards and form a defensive flank. As a diversion, Third Army (General Sir Edmund Allenby) were ordered to attack Gommecourt village, conforming to the timings of Fourth Army.[10]

If any attempt was made to grade the tasks of Fourth Army's various corps in terms of difficulty, this was not apparent in the planning; the corps facing the greater challenges were not assigned additional resources. The Fourth Army front ran roughly north to south from its junction with Third Army, south of Gommecourt, to Fricourt, and thence east to beyond Montauban, where the French Army took over. Fricourt and Montauban were 2 of the 9 fortified villages on the Fourth Army front forming part of the German front-line defences.[11]

Horne's XV Corps were given the sector of the line opposite Fricourt and, to the east, Mametz, another of the fortified villages. Horne busied himself in conferring with his neighbouring corps commanders to finalise their respective boundaries, in drawing up his corps' plan of attack and the complementary artillery plan, and in visiting the headquarters of his divisional commanders. He also visited the trenches and artillery emplacements and made at least one balloon ascent to survey the future battleground.[12] His divisions were adding to the already heightened nervousness of the enemy with trench raids. A notable participant in this activity, whether officially authorised or not, was the war poet, 2nd Lieut Siegfried Sassoon of 1st Bn Royal Welsh Fusiliers, 7th Division. Not to be outdone, the Germans made the occasional raid, but enjoyed little success.

Despite his preoccupations, Horne found time for a week's visit to England in the first half of May, during which he saw Lord Kitchener for the last time. Although, like most of his peers, Horne was no devotee of Kitchener's somewhat idiosyncratic methods of running the War Office and the army, he had come to like and admire him during their travels together in the eastern Mediterranean. When, a month after they last met, Kitchener's death from drowning on his way to Russia in HMS *Hampshire* was announced, Horne wrote, 'The grand work he has done has never been appreciated at its full value. Personally I felt quite an affection for him … I feel like I have lost a friend.'[13]

Horne's plans for the assault on the first day of the battle had to take full account of the fact that the front line curved round Fricourt in its change of direction from north-south to west-east. The village thus formed a salient in the German line, which would oblige Horne's divisions to attack in both an easterly and north-easterly direction to accomplish their tasks. Horne was confronted with German defences of considerable strength. Not only had the 2 villages been

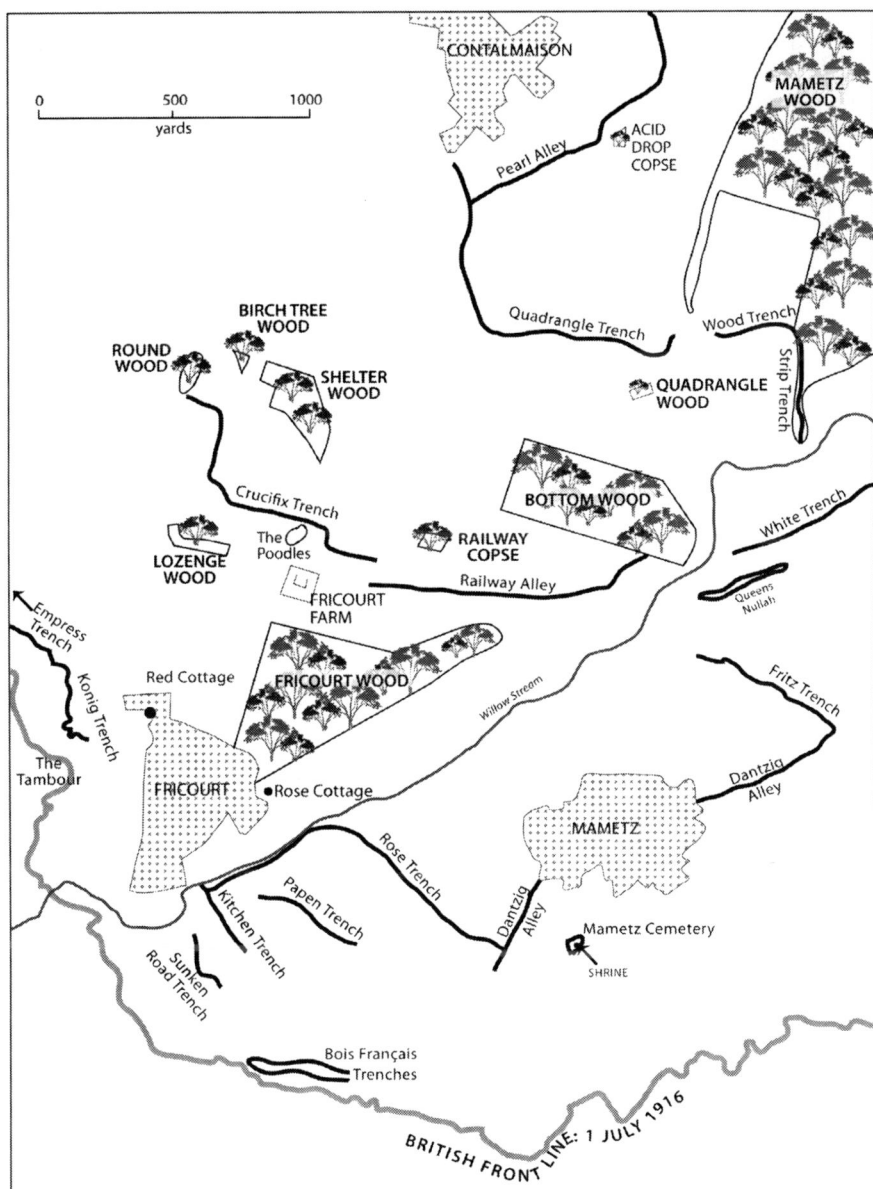

Map 7: The Somme: Fricourt and Mametz: July 1916

strongly fortified, but the front line was supported by 2 defensive positions respectively 1,000 and 2,000 yards behind the villages. The former consisted of Fritz Trench, Railway Alley and Crucifix Trench; the latter included White Trench, Wood Trench and Quadrangle Trench and protected the approaches to Mametz Wood. The sophistication of the German dugouts was to come as an unpleasant surprise to the British when they captured some on the first day of the battle. They were deep and usually immune to the calibres of artillery available to the British.

Horne was realistic in appreciating that, whatever assumptions were being made by Fourth Army headquarters on the efficacy of the planned artillery bombardment in eliminating the German defences, an immediate frontal assault on a village as strongly fortified as Fricourt would be a recipe for disaster. Being in a salient, it offered the potential for being enveloped from both sides, and this formed the basis for Horne's plans. He decided on a 2 phase attack. At Zero Hour (07h30) Mametz would be assaulted by 7th Division. Once the village was secured, the advance would continue north towards Bottom Wood. Simultaneously, 21st Division would assault the higher ground north of Fricourt village and then continue eastwards towards Bottom Wood. Both divisions would establish defensive flanks facing Fricourt, thus isolating and surrounding the village. Only these 2 divisions, with 50th Brigade of 17th Division, temporarily attached to 21st Division, were to be involved on the first day. The remainder of 17th Division would form corps reserve.

The second phase of Horne's plans, the attack on Fricourt itself, would be launched at a time to be determined by Horne, in the light of progress on the first phase.[14]

The XV Corps' artillery plans for the preliminary bombardment and the first day were to be reproduced in the Official History as models of their kind.[15] The preliminary bombardment was to prove to have been much more effective on this part of the front than on most others. Severe damage and loss of life had been inflicted on the enemy's defences and troops, and on the ability of their artillery to interfere with British troop movements on the first day. The first day plan also laid down the genesis of a creeping barrage, calling for lifts of 50 yards every minute with the infantry exhorted to keep close up – but not too close! Unfortunately the protection thus offered was not made available for the period when the troops would actually be crossing No Man's Land.[16]

Finally Horne's plans called for the detonating of a number of pre-placed mines 2 minutes before Zero Hour, notably 3 mines sited under the German lines opposite a small salient in the British line known as the Tambour, just outside the western edge of Fricourt. The resultant explosions were designed to throw up parapets which would prevent German machine guns enfilading the advancing British troops.

The 1 July dawned fine and clear. At 06h25 the artillery bombardment homed in on the enemy's front line systems and grew in intensity. For 10 minutes beginning at 07h15, gas was released from the centre of XV Corps' front to deceive the enemy into believing that an assault would come from this direction – the one area of the corps front where no initial assault was planned. At 07h22 a hurricane bombardment by Stokes mortars on the German positions opposite the whole corps front began.

At 4 minutes before Zero Hour the gas discharges were replaced by smoke. Two minutes later, the 3 mines under the German lines opposite the Tambour, containing respectively 25,000, 15,000 and 9,000 lbs of ammonal, were detonated simultaneously with smaller mines elsewhere on the corps front.[17]

The task of capturing Mametz village and then pushing on a kilometre north-wards towards Bottom Wood had been assigned to 7th Division. Their frontage ran from due south of Fricourt to a position southeast of Mametz. The division's plans called for the left-hand 22nd Brigade to make no move, the initial assault being entrusted to 20th and 91st Brigades. Between them they would assault on a 5 battalion front. The 2nd Bn Border Regt and 9th Bn Devonshire Regt would move off in a north-westerly direction, leaving Mametz on their right, as they made for the gap between that village and Fricourt. The 2nd Bn Gordon Highlanders and 1st Bn South Staffordshire Regt would also advance to the northwest and assault Mametz. The easternmost and last battalion, 22nd Bn Manchester Regt (7th Pals), would move due north towards the German-held Dantzig Alley, east of the village. To assist and protect the attackers 4 saps had been driven close to the German front lines.

The 4 small mines which were detonated 2 minutes prior to Zero Hour to the left of the area over which the division would assault, were unfortunately too small to have any serious effect on the German defences. When 2nd Borders went over the top they immediately found themselves the target of machine gun fire from both Fricourt and Mametz. But they pressed on and successfully formed the southern part of the defensive flank facing Fricourt.

On 2nd Borders' right, 9th Devons, on emerging from the shelter of Mansel Copse, suffered serious casualties from enfilade fire from an enemy machine gun sited in the shrine in Mametz village cemetery. The potential danger from this source had been spotted by Captain D L Martin of 9th Devons who, when on leave in England prior to the battle, had produced a plasticine model illustrating the danger. This was used in briefings to impress upon the artillery the need to eliminate this threat. Tragically, their attempts ended in failure and 9th Devons, including Captain Martin, paid the price. So cut to pieces were they, that they made scant progress and were unable to form the northern part of the defensive flank covering Fricourt. They also left 2nd Gordons on their right seriously exposed to heavy fire. Despite the resultant severe casualties, the Highlanders stuck to their task and got round the south of Mametz village. There, supported by 2 companies of 2nd Bn Royal Warwickshire Regt and 8th Bn Devons, who had passed through the remnants of their sister battalion, they eliminated the troublesome machine gun in the shrine. By 16h00 they were in occupation of a German trench west of the village.

Assisted by two mines detonated under the German lines opposite them, 1st South Staffs fought their way into the outskirts of Mametz village, where they and 22nd Manchesters on their right were held up by intense enemy rifle and machine gun fire. Despite bringing up reinforcements from 21st Manchesters and 2nd Bn The Queens, and ordering an additional artillery barrage, the German defences proved obdurate. But a further bombardment, coupled with the success of XIII Corps to their right, eventually enabled the attackers to take possession of Dantzig Alley, leading into the village from the east. By early afternoon, the southern part of the village was in British hands and the northern part was increasingly threatened with encirclement from the northeast. After a further bombardment of the whole area beginning at 15h30, the British were able to complete occupation of the village and the German trenchworks on its northern and north-eastern sides by

18h30. The 7th Division spent the rest of the day consolidating their hold on the territory they had gained.[18]

As has already been noted, the capture of Fricourt, albeit by indirect means, had been entrusted to 21st Division. Their plan called for the use of 3 brigades in the early phases. From right to left these were 50th Brigade (attached from 17th Division), 63rd and 64th. The 62nd Brigade would be in reserve. Only one battalion of 50th Brigade, occupying the stretch of line due west of Fricourt village, would assault at Zero Hour. The ill-fated 10th West Yorks would attack from the north of the brigade's sector in close cooperation with 63rd Brigade's assault.

The Yorkshire battalion were assigned the task of forming the defensive flank to the north of Fricourt village. As they were to have no close support to their right, their vulnerability to enfilade fire from that direction was to be neutralised by the explosion of the Tambour mines. Their detonation did in fact help the first waves of the West Yorks by slowing the initial German reaction. But by the time the 2 support companies advanced, the German machine guns, whose fields of fire had not been obstructed as a result of the detonations, were in action. Unprotected by the artillery bombardment, which by then had moved on from the German front line positions, the companies were virtually wiped out.

The fate of the support companies left the Battalion's 2 advance companies largely isolated. They had crossed the German front lines, known as König Trench, relatively unscathed and reached Red Cottage at the north end of Fricourt village. There, highly vulnerable, they were soon largely overcome. On a day justly notorious for its casualty figures, the unfortunate 10th West Yorks were to record the highest individual battalion losses of all. No fewer than 22 officers and 688 other ranks became casualties. Only one officer and 40 other ranks emerged unscathed, a loss rate of over 90%.

Mention must also be made here of the fate of A Company of 7th Bn Green Howards. This battalion, part of 50th Brigade and in the line south of the 10th West Yorks, were not due to participate in the initial assault. But for reasons still unexplained, A Company went over the top at 07h45, and were annihilated near their own trenches by the fire of a single machine gun. [19]

The tribulations of 4th Bn Middlesex Regiment, 63rd Brigade, to the left of 10th West Yorks, began even before Zero Hour. They left their trenches and crawled forward into No Man's Land at 07h25 and immediately came under murderous machine gun fire, which forced the survivors to retire. They were hastily reorganised and sent forward again. Once more they were cut down by enemy machine guns. Only 40 survivors of the 2 attacking companies reached the Sunken Lane within the German position. About 100 men of the battalion's support companies subsequently succeeded in securing the German front line.

The battalion on the Middlesex's left suffered almost as severely. The objective of the 8th Bn Somerset Light Infantry was the German front line known as Empress Trench. They suffered from heavy machine gun fire as they left their trenches shortly before Zero Hour. But, despite heavy casualties, their attack was successful, isolated groups of men even reaching, and advancing beyond, the German support trench.

It was quickly recognised in brigade headquarters that the assaulting battalions no longer had the numbers to be sure of clinging on to their modest gains. The decision was taken to send forward 2 fresh battalions, the 10th York and Lancs and the 8th Lincolns. Like their predecessors, they took heavy casualties in crossing No Man's Land before eventually reaching the Sunken Road, north of Fricourt. Here they became involved in bombing duels with the enemy in trying to push north from the village.

By comparison with the rest of 21st Division, 64th Brigade's day was one of relative success. It might have been greater but for the problems created for the brigade by the failure of 34th Division (III Corps) to their north and the patchy success of 63rd Brigade south of them. The brigade assaulted on a 2 battalion front due east from north of Fricourt towards Crucifix Trench, deep in the German defences. Both battalions were King's Own Yorkshire Light Infantry, the 9th and 10th. They too moved into No Man's Land prior to Zero Hour where they faced carefully sited enemy machine guns. However the preliminary bombardment appears to have been at its most effective here; the German wire was thoroughly cut and the initial German response was sufficiently muted to enable the assaulting troops to overrun the German front line quite quickly.

The Brigade's supporting battalions, 15th Durham Light Infantry and 1st East Yorks, were promptly sent forward. The now formidable force pressed forward and had taken possession of the Sunken Road north of Fricourt 30 minutes after Zero Hour. A further advance was made to the northern section of Crucifix Trench where the assault was halted by enfilade German machine gun fire from both north and south. The battalions were ordered to consolidate, and further reinforcements were sent up. To strengthen their rather tenuous hold on the northern section of Crucifix Trench, 21st Division ordered 2 battalions of their reserve forward, the 10th Green Howards and 1st Lincolns. Even though these battalions were moving through areas by now ostensibly under British control, they took significant casualties before they were in a position to reinforce the parties of troops holding the trench.[20]

While these events were unfolding, General Horne, as Corps Commander, could only be a bystander. He was soon however to make an important decision; if and when to launch the next phase of his plans, the attack up the Willow Stream valley on the village of Fricourt and Fricourt Wood. Horne's original intention had been only to implement this phase when the earlier phases had been successfully completed. These were, on the right, the capture of Mametz, the formation of a defensive flank facing Fricourt and the successful completion of an advance beyond Mametz and Fricourt Farm towards the German second intermediate line covering Mametz Wood; on the left, the eastward envelopment of Fricourt and the formation of a defensive flank facing the village.

When, at 12h50, Horne issued the order for the direct attack on Fricourt to begin at 14h30, virtually the only precondition that had been met was the partial formation of the southern defensive flank. He appears to have been swayed from his earlier caution by the encouraging reports he had received on their progress from XIII Corps on his right (in their case accurate) and III Corps on his left (in their case anything but). In the view of the Official History, he may also have been swayed by the apparent success of the preliminary bombardment of the Fricourt sector.[21]

The 2 battalions handed the poisoned chalice were 7th Green Howards, reduced to 3 companies by the tragedy which had befallen A Company that morning, and 20th Manchesters. They would be assisted by 2 companies and the bombers of 2nd Bn Royal Welsh Fusiliers. The Green Howards would attack from due west of Fricourt, passing the Tambour to their north. The Manchesters, holding the longest frontage of any battalion in action that day, would attack from the south of the village.

On receiving the order, 50th Brigade, to which 7th Green Howards belonged, signalled back urging that the attack should not take place until the objectives of 10th Bn West Yorks had been made good. They were overruled. After a short artillery bombardment, which did little to weaken the strongest part of the Fricourt defences, the Green Howards attacked. They immediately came under heavy machine gun and rifle fire from Germans standing on their own parapet. Only a small group got into the village where they were promptly killed or captured. Within a matter of minutes the attack was over. The battalion had suffered casualties of more than 350 officers and men. Two companies of 7th East Yorks who, on the initiative of their Commanding Officer, had attacked 3 minutes after, and in support of, the Green Howards, also lost heavily and unavailingly.

The 20th Manchesters initially made rather better progress although their left flank suffered heavily. Some detachments succeeded in getting into the German trenches. Bombing duels were fought but progress had been minimal as night fell. Only the Sunken Road trench and the Bois Français support trench, both well to the south of the village, had been taken and held.[22]

Plans for the capture of Fricourt Farm by 63rd Brigade were largely dependent on a successful outcome to the attack by 7th Green Howards and 20th Manchesters. In turn plans by 64th Brigade to take Shelter Wood, to the east of Crucifix Trench, would have been materially assisted by the success of 63rd's. Attempts by both brigades to push on nonetheless were thwarted. The 63rd Brigade were stopped by heavy enemy machine gun fire, and the 64th were forced on to the defensive by a series of German counterattacks, even though they were unsuccessful.

As the light began to fade on 1 July it was becoming apparent that the German defence of Fricourt was weakening. The 50th Brigade wished to exploit this by mounting an immediate attack, but their proposal was overruled by the divisional commander who preferred to carry out the relief of 50th Brigade by 51st, an operation which was to take most of the night.

With Mametz and Montauban already securely in British hands, and Fricourt apparently there for the taking, the German defences on the south-eastern area of the battlefield appeared to be close to collapse. If fresh troops could have been got up in time, the opportunity for the sought for breakthrough might have been there. But it was not to be. How far this hesitancy could be ascribed to Horne is a matter of conjecture. Had he had a clear picture of the situation, he might have been at fault. But almost certainly, his appreciation of the day's events would have been patchy and sketchy. He may not even have been aware of 50th Brigade's assessment of the state of Fricourt's defences. Be that as it may, the Official History described it as a lost opportunity.[23]

At 22h00 on 1 July, General Rawlinson ordered XV Corps to capture Fricourt village and Wood, push on to its original objective and link up with III Corps south of Contalmaison. XIII and XV Corps were also to prepare plans to attack Mametz Wood in conjunction. To implement the first part of these instructions, Horne ordered 17th Division to capture Fricourt by an attack to be launched at 12h15 the next day after a 75 minute artillery bombardment. The Division was then to link up with 7th Division north of Mametz.[24]

These orders were however rendered nugatory when it was reported that a patrol of 7th Division's 2nd Bn Royal Irish Regt had entered Fricourt unopposed at midnight on 1 July. Soon after dawn, patrols of 17th Division's 8th Bn South Staffs also entered the village and took unresisting prisoners. General Pilcher, the GOC of 17th Division, thereupon ordered 51st Brigade to occupy the village without waiting for the bombardment. But, according to the Official History, 'the changing of orders caused considerable delay, and Fricourt was not entered until noon. There was no fighting and only eleven German stragglers were rounded up.'

Once the village was secured the advance continued and Fricourt Wood was quickly occupied. The aim of 51st Brigade was now to reach Bottom Wood, but 7th Lincolns could not make any progress beyond Fricourt Wood. To their left units of 62nd Brigade were pushing towards Fricourt Farm. By the early afternoon 10th Green Howards were close to The Poodles, a small group of trees just north of the Farm. Late in the evening a further section of Crucifix Trench and 200 yards of Railway Alley were captured by 51st Brigade's 10th Sherwood Foresters.

By the early morning of the 2nd it was apparent that the area north of the village of Mametz was empty of enemy. This enabled units of 91st Brigade to push up and occupy Queen's Nullah and the western section of White Trench, 1 km northeast of the village, facing the southern edge of Mametz Wood. Likewise, units of 22nd Brigade were able to advance eastwards from south of Fricourt across Kitchen, Pearl and Papen Trenches towards Rose Trench.

At the end of the second day of the battle, XV Corps had achieved nearly all of the first line of objectives set for the first day. Similarly the objectives of the ill-fated attack by 7th Green Howards and 20th Manchesters had been reached. In the case of 7th Division, their second, and sometimes their third, objectives had been attained. But worryingly for future stages of the battle, Bottom Wood and the main German Second Position, barring the way to Mametz Wood, remained firmly in enemy hands.[25]

During the course of the day, Horne found the time to write to his wife. He was clearly upbeat at the way things were going.

All goes well. My Corps has taken over 1,600 prisoners and is still getting on.

We are getting on well, I am thankful to say, on my front. Yesterday we took Mametz and some 1,300 prisoners. Today we have got Fricourt and up to some 300 more prisoners. On my right the next Corps got on very well yesterday and are holding their line and improving it today. To the North of us things were not quite so successful but we have given the Germans a hard knock and ought to give him more still before we have finished. The French to our right are doing well.

> Altogether things go very well. Hard fighting of course. But my losses are not very great I am thankful to say. I hope we may inflict a severe defeat on the Germans. In fact we have already but want to make it heavier.[26]

Horne went on to tell his wife that he had received a visit from the Chief of the Imperial General Staff, Sir W. Robertson, who had congratulated XV Corps on its success. Sir Douglas Haig had also been to see him. Haig recorded this visit in his diary:

> I visited XV Corps HQ at Heilly and complimented General Horne on the success of his operations. He had had a most difficult problem. His troops had now taken Fricourt and were pressing on to Fricourt Farm. A prisoner (Sergeant Major) reported that the Commander of Fricourt had asked for reinforcements. The reply was that there were none to send except only 2 companies of divisional Pioneers. These were sent and were duly taken prisoner by us.[27]

Horne later returned to the events of the first 2 days in another letter.

> The artillery have done splendid work, the way we knocked about Mametz and Fricourt and the trenches round has been grand. All agree that the places were utterly demolished. My infantry fought splendidly, the old 7th Division in particular distinguished themselves. They took Mametz the first day. The 21st also did well north of Fricourt, about Shelter Wood, and the 17th took Fricourt on the 2nd day and Fricourt Wood and Railway Alley. All did splendid work and I did not have casualties as heavy as I expected to. The artillery covered the infantry advance so well. We are all very pleased with ourselves.[28]

One can only assume that Horne's claims to his wife that his casualties had been 'not very great' and 'not ... as heavy as I expected' were based on the incomplete information available to him at the time of writing or an understandable wish to spare her feelings. Although by no means the worst returns by the 5 corps engaged on the first day of the battle (only XIII Corps, consisting of only 2 divisions, suffered fewer), XV Corps' losses were very serious at 8,781, nearly all, it is believed, victims of machine gun fire. The 21st Division suffered the worst with 4, 256 killed, wounded and missing, followed by 7th Division with 3,380 and 17th Division, which only had one brigade involved, with 1,155.

Over the next few days, Horne's attentions were to be concentrated on the need to capture Mametz Wood. The relative success of Fourth Army to the east of Fricourt compared with the almost total disaster which had befallen it to the north of the village had persuaded both Haig and Rawlinson that the army's main effort for the immediate future should seek to build on this success. Haig appreciated that a northward advance from the line Fricourt-Montauban would, if successful, take in rear the westward facing German defences north of Fricourt, which were proving so obdurate. In Haig's view, if not in Rawlinson's, no attack on the Bazentin-Longueval Ridge, the next logical step northwards, could succeed unless Mametz Wood, on the left, and Trônes Wood, on the right of the line of advance, were firmly in British hands.[29]

While this view would lend more urgency to Mametz Wood's capture, it was in any case also the next significant obstacle to be overcome on XV Corps' line of advance. A preliminary to its capture, short of a *coup de main* by an aggressive commander, would have to be the seizure of the German trench systems and woods guarding the approaches to the wood itself. It was to this that Horne addressed himself from 3 July.

The first stage would be to complete the work outstanding from the first 2 days of the battle, namely the capture by 17th Division of Railway Alley and Bottom Wood; and, further north, the capture of Shelter and Birch Tree Woods by 21st Division. The 2 divisions went into action at 09h00 on the 3rd. By 11h30 Railway Alley, despite strong resistance, had been captured by 7th Borders with the assistance of other units of 51st Brigade. The Borders also entered Bottom Wood to find it already in the hands of 21st Bn Manchesters of 7th Division, who had entered it from the east without opposition.

Success had also crowned the efforts of 21st Division. Birch Tree Wood fell first, but before Shelter Wood could also be secured, 1st Lincolns and 12th and 13th Bns Northumberland Fusiliers had to repulse German counterattacks launched from it. When it in turn fell to the British in the early afternoon the Germans launched yet another unsuccessful counterattack in their efforts to retrieve the situation. By late afternoon the wood was completely cleared of Germans, with 800 of them made prisoner.[30]

At this stage an opportunity occurred, the failure to seize which was to lead to strong criticism of General Horne in the Official History. At 15h00, patrols pushed out towards and into Mametz Wood and Quadrangle Trench reported back that both were empty. Seemingly disregarding this information, XV Corps headquarters merely issued at 17h00 orders for the occupation after dark of Strip Trench, Wood Trench and the eastern end of Quadrangle Trench. According to the Official History, Horne was averse to patrol action which might bring on an engagement before he was prepared to accept it. Perhaps a more humdrum explanation of his apparent dilatoriness was the fact that at the time when urgent orders were called for, Horne was absent from his headquarters attending a meeting at Fourth Army HQ to discuss plans for the attack on Bazentin Ridge.

The task of implementing XV Corps' orders was assigned to 2nd Royal Irish and 1st Royal Welsh Fusiliers of 22nd Brigade, 7th Division. Under the impression that the trenches they were to occupy were already in British hands, the 2 battalions cluttered themselves up with all the equipment required to consolidate possession. Thus encumbered and slowed down, they were further delayed when the guide assigned to them contrived to get them lost. It was not until daylight that the troops were in a position to carry out their orders, too late as the circumstances were by now even more different from what they had expected. British patrols during the night had found and dispersed a German detachment in Mametz Wood and established that Wood Trench and Quadrangle Trench were by then held by the enemy, if only lightly. But by the time 2nd Royal Irish and 1st RWF were ready to advance it was clear that the Germans held Mametz Wood in some strength. The British battalions retired, but not before 2nd Royal Irish had sustained casualties. In the view of the Official History:

> It would appear that if the XV Corps had encouraged more vigorous action
> on the afternoon of the 3rd a hold on Mametz Wood could have been secured
> and Wood Trench and Quadrangle Trench occupied. The last-named objec-

tive was taken on the morning of the 5th, but the others were to cost many lives and much precious time.[31]

There is no suggestion in either Horne's diary or in his letter of the day to his wife that he sensed an opportunity missed. Nevertheless the criticism of Horne does appear to have validity, but he in turn appears to have been having some difficulty in getting one of his divisions, the 17th, to show much drive and determination. Haig, who visited Horne at his HQ, on 4 July recorded in his diary:

> General Horne was dissatisfied with 17th Division under General Pilcher. He could not get it to advance quickly. Ford, a young Brigadier General of 7th Division observed from a hill to the east that Bottom Wood was unoccupied by the enemy. He sent to tell the Brigadier of 17th Division (General Fell) of the fact. The latter apparently declined to move on. Then Ford occupied the Wood with his own men, and sent back to tell Fell that he had done so, and asked that his men might be relieved. It was not till then that a unit of the 17th Division was sent forward. General Horne is enquiring into the facts of the case.[32]

There is no suggestion in the Official History of any reluctance on the part of 51st Brigade to advance towards and into Bottom Wood. According to Brigadier General Fell, he had been ordered to take Railway Alley, Railway Copse, Crucifix Trench and Bottom Wood and then consolidate in front of Quadrangle Trench. Fell said these objectives had been achieved with the loss of about 600 men. He had then told General Pilcher that Quadrangle Trench was there for the taking but General Pilcher had disagreed and declined to approve an advance.[33] Whether this disagreement was known about by Horne or not, his unfavourable impression of General Pilcher was to come to a head as his frustrations over Mametz Wood grew.[34]

Chapter IX

Corps Commander: The Somme: Mametz Wood

The ridge of relatively high ground running between the villages of Longueval to the east and the 2 Bazentins (le-Petit and le-Grand) to the west constituted the German Second Line of defences. Its rapid capture was vital if full benefit were to be gained from the relative success achieved in this area of the Somme battlefield in the first days of the battle. There were however disagreements at the highest levels of the British command over how the Bazentin Ridge might best be seized.

As early as 4 July General Haig recorded in his diary that he had impressed on General Rawlinson the importance of getting Trônes Wood, to cover the right flank, and Mametz Wood and Contalmaison village, to cover the left flank of the attack against Bazentin Ridge.[1] That General Rawlinson did not attach the same significance as his Commander-in-Chief to Mametz Wood was rapidly to become clear.[2] This divergence of views and the failure of XV Corps to capture the wood promptly, which would have made the divergence irrelevant, were to complicate planning for the seizure of the ridge.

Unless Rawlinson could persuade Haig to see things his way, Mametz Wood would remain Henry Horne's top priority. On 4 July he issued orders for a surprise attack to be made at midnight on 4/5 July on Quadrangle and Wood Trenches. Horne described it to his wife as, 'A small attack, just to gain ground which will help me along. Mametz Wood is now in front of me and a serious obstacle.'[3] The attack was to be mounted on a 4 battalion front with 17th and 7th Divisions each supplying 2 battalions. Brigadier General Fell, who had been champing at the bit all day to attack Quadrangle Trench, was bitterly disappointed to be told that his brigade would be relieved by 52nd Brigade for the attack.[4] The latter brigade's 10th Bn Lancashire Fusiliers and 9th Bn Northumberland Fusiliers would be joined on their right by the 2 battalions which had had such a frustrating baptism the night before, 1st Royal Welsh Fusiliers and 2nd Royal Irish.

Horne's plans looked in some doubt when heavy rain began to fall in the afternoon. Major General Watts, the GOC of 7th Division, called to say that a surprise attack was impossible in such muddy conditions. Horne thereupon arranged a 30 minute bombardment immediately prior to the attack, which was postponed to 00h45 on 5 July.[5] An earlier, daylight, bombardment was also laid on to cut the enemy wire in front of the 2 objectives. It was reported that this had been quite successful in front of Quadrangle Trench, much less so in front of Wood Trench.

On a very dark night in appalling conditions, with rain still falling, the assaulting troops crept out of their trenches under cover of the second bombardment and advanced to within 100 yards of the enemy lines. As the bombardment lifted, to be replaced by concentrated machine gun fire to keep enemy heads down, the troops charged. In the centre and on the left success was almost total. Not only was Quadrangle Trench occupied, but Shelter Alley on the left, leading from

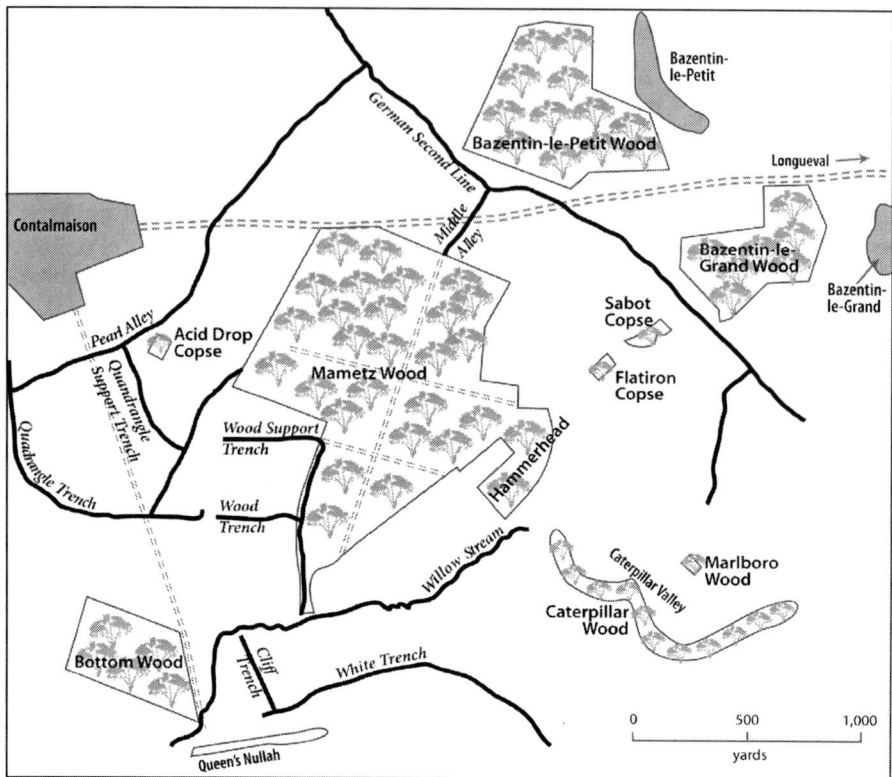

Map 8: The Somme: Mametz Wood: 5–12 July 1916

Shelter Wood to the northern end of Quadrangle Trench, was taken enabling the attackers to form a defensive left flank. Some troops even managed to push up Pearl Alley almost as far as Contalmaison. But they were unable to cling on to this gain.

The 2 right hand battalions came up against much tougher resistance and 1st RWF were only able to clear the eastern part of Quadrangle Trench after prolonged fighting. The 2nd Royal Irish, whose objective was Wood Trench, found the German wire almost impenetrable and the trench strongly held by the enemy. The battalion launched a total of 4 attacks. Having suffered 125 casualties, they finally retired to their own lines. A gap swept with machine gun fire, between the end of Quadrangle Trench and the start of Wood Trench, was sufficient to prevent 1st RWF coming to the aid of the Irish. Horne told his wife:

> My attack last night succeeded except in one place. We gained most of what I wanted and took some more prisoners. I am racking my brains to see the best way to do my next job. I have to take Mametz Wood – a large, very thick wood. A very difficult problem.[6]

As he wrestled with it, 7th Division were being relieved by 38th (Welsh) Division, the relief being completed by 01h00 on the 6th. This division's role in the attempts to capture Mametz Wood was to generate considerable controversy.

Even by the standards of the confusion and improvisation which accompanied the rapid expansion of the army following the outbreak of war, the creation of 38th (Welsh) Division followed an unusual path. It owed everything to that well-known Welshman, David Lloyd George, then Chancellor of the Exchequer, who conceived the notion of setting up a Welsh army of 2 divisions. When recruitment began, it was already too late to benefit from the flood of Welsh volunteers who enlisted at the outbreak of war; they had already joined other units. With recruitment sluggish, it was decided to restrict the scheme to one division. As battalions were filled up they were badged into one of the 3 Welsh infantry regiments; the Welch Regiment, the Royal Welsh Fusiliers or the South Wales Borderers. It was almost a year before the exercise was complete.

Officering the Division also presented problems, as it did for many Kitchener New Army units. To help offset this, retired officers were recalled to the colours and frequently promoted beyond their experience. The situation also offered opportunities for patronage which Lloyd George was not slow to exploit with his Welsh division. The command was entrusted to Ivor Philipps, a fellow MP and political ally of Lloyd George's. His career as a regular officer in the Indian Army had ended ten years earlier in the rank of Major. He returned to the colours as a Brigadier General and, only 2 months later, was promoted to Major General and appointed GOC of the 38th.[7]

By the end of 1915 the division were in France. To round off their training they were initiated into trench warfare in the First Army area under the supervision of Lieutenant General Sir Richard Haking of XI Corps. In early 1916 Haking told Haig that the division were good but that he had no confidence in Major General Philipps as a commander.[8]

The outbreak of the Battle of the Somme found the division in GHQ reserve. During the course of the first day they were released to Fourth Army and a couple of days later came into XV Corps reserve. When they moved up to take over the front line from Bottom Wood to Caterpillar Wood from 7th Division on the night of 5/6 July, they gave 2nd Lieutenant Siegfried Sassoon, whose battalion was one of those being relieved, a rather less favourable impression than they had made on General Haking.

> Our little trench under the trees was inundated by a jostling company of exclamatory Welshmen. Kinjack would have called them a panicky rabble. They were mostly undersized men, and as I watched them arriving at the first stage of their battle experience I had a sense of their victimisation. A little platoon officer was settling his men down with a valiant show of self assurance. For the sake of appearances, orders of some kind had to be given, though in reality there was nothing to do except sit down and hope it wouldn't rain. He spoke sharply to some of them, and I felt they were like a lot of children. It was going to be a bad lookout for two such bewildered companies, huddled up in the Quadrangle, which had been over-garrisoned by our own comparatively small contingent. Visualising that forlorn crowd of khaki figures under the twilight of the trees I can believe that I saw then, for the first

time, how blindly war destroys its victims. The sun had gone down on my own reckless brandishings, and I understood the doomed condition of these half trained civilians who had been sent up to attack the Wood.[9]

A Captain Glynn Jones of 38th Division saw the relief rather differently, recalling after the war how the guides from 1st RWF had lost their way, and the unseemly haste with which 1st RWF had departed the scene with no proper hand-over or any instructions or information being passed over. According to Captain Jones, his men soon settled down in the unpromising conditions of an only recently taken Quadrangle Trench, and even began to enjoy themselves putting pressure on the enemy.[10]

At about 10h00 on 6 July, Horne issued orders for attacks the following day by 17th and 38th Divisions. In a letter to his wife he wrote:

> ... tonight we push on to get a preparatory position for an attack on Mametz Wood tomorrow morning. It is a very difficult problem the attack on a big wood like that and our information is that it is very thick. However I have made my plan and I hope by a combination of artillery and gallant infantry to make our way through it ... A day full of preparation today. We have an attack at 02h00 when I hope to get a little bit to give me a better starting place against Mametz Wood tomorrow morning. I hope it will come off.[11]

The attack scheduled for 02h00 was to be launched by 17th Division. Its objectives were the capture of Pearl Alley and Quadrangle Support Trench. With these 2 trenches in British hands 17th Division could then attack Mametz Wood from the west at 08h00 on the 7th, the same time that 38th Division would attack the south-eastern part of the wood, known, because of its shape, as the Hammer-head. If 17th Division's preliminary attacks were unsuccessful, the main attack would nevertheless go in as scheduled, with the unfinished business of the early hours becoming 17th Division's first objectives in the main attack.

Major General Pilcher was not at all happy with the task handed to his division. Using up some more of his diminishing residue of goodwill he pointed out forcefully that even if his troops succeeded in capturing the 2 German trenches, they would be unable to hold them while subject to enfilade fire from Contalmaison to the west and Mametz Wood to the east. Horne responded that the capture of the trenches would make the subsequent capture of the village and the wood easier, and brushed aside Pilcher's protest.[12] The 52nd Brigade were thereupon assigned the task. The 10th Bn Lancashire Fusiliers and 9th Bn Northumberland Fusiliers were once again called upon, with 9th Bn Duke of Wellington's Regt in support.

After a 25 minute bombardment the attack went in on schedule at 02h00. The attackers found it very hard going against a fully alerted enemy not unduly disorganised by the bombardment. The 10th Lancs got into Pearl Alley and some small number even got as far as Contalmaison before becoming casualties or being driven back. The 9th Northumberlands were even less successful in the face of unbroken German wire in front of Quadrangle Support Trench. A German counterattack was successfully beaten off, but not before it had thoroughly disrupted the British brigade's preparations for the main attack scheduled for 08h00.[13]

Horne's plans for the main attack had foreseen the possible failure of the preliminary attack. It was now postponed for half-an-hour to enable a 70 minute preliminary bombardment to be laid down instead of only 40. However, in an early example of the sort of confusion that was to characterise this part of the Somme battle, Horne determined that 17th Division should make up for lost time by sticking to the original Zero Hour of 08h00 for their renewed assault on Pearl Alley and Quadrangle Support Trench. Orders to this effect were only issued by Corps at 05h25 and did not reach the 4 battalions concerned (10th Lancs and 9th Northumberlands were being relieved for the attack by 9th Duke of Wellington's and 12th Manchesters) until 07h00 or even later. The attackers' problems were compounded by an accurate German bombardment of their assembly trenches.

As a consequence the attack went in behind schedule with incomplete units, which lost the protection of the artillery bombardment which had stuck to the original timetable. Advancing in broad daylight the Manchesters were cut down by enemy machine guns in numbers reminiscent of the first day of the Somme. The 9th Duke of Wellington's, attempting to retake Pearl Alley, suffered a heavy enemy bombardment and a counterattack which forced them back with severe losses. In incessant rain a second attack was mounted on Quadrangle Support Trench in the early afternoon. It merely added to the casualty toll. A third attack was cancelled, and at 16h15 all units of 52nd Brigade were ordered to withdraw. Two battalions, 7th East Yorks and 6th Bn Dorsetshire Regt of 50th Brigade, which had been told off to mount an attack on the southwest corner of Mametz Wood, received the order cancelling it in the nick of time.[14]

The 38th Division's attack on the Hammerhead was entrusted to Brigadier General H. J. Evans's 115th Brigade. The attack would have to be made westwards along a narrow valley flanked on the south side by Caterpillar Wood and on the north by a ridge beyond which were Flatiron Copse and Sabot Copse, both in German hands. The attackers would be faced by fire from Mametz Wood itself in front of them, and by enfilade fire from Flatiron Copse if they were to get too high up on the ridge. Evans therefore decided on a 2 battalion attack, with one battalion immediately behind the other, to avoid his front becoming so broad as to expose its right flank on the ridge. A further battalion would be in support in Caterpillar Wood, and the fourth in reserve. As protection, an artillery bombardment would be laid on and smoke put down to blind the enemy to the north.

When these proposed dispositions were seen at Horne's headquarters, a message was immediately sent to the brigade, via the division, that the proposed concentration of 3 battalions so close to Caterpillar Wood put them at unacceptable risk from enemy artillery; only 2 battalions should be used in the attack. The other 2 battalions should be withdrawn from the immediate area. For reasons which are still not clear, Evans took this to mean that he should attack on a 2-battalion front and, in the limited time available, amended his orders accordingly. The battalion which would now find itself advancing on the right, along the ridge, was 16th Bn Welch Regiment. To their left, close to Caterpillar Wood, would be 11th Bn South Wales Borderers. The 10th South Wales Borderers would be in reserve.

Following the artillery bombardment the infantry attack began punctually. It was very soon in trouble. The smokescreen intended to protect the northernmost battalion from enfilade machine gun fire from Flatiron Copse and Sabot Copse did not materialise, according to the Official History, 'owing to the high wind'.[15] As soon as they came into view of the enemy, 16th Welch Regiment were pinned down unable to advance, despite being 'well supported by trench mortar and machine gun fire.' The 11th SWB on the left were scarcely any better off, being pinned down by heavy machine gun fire from the Hammerhead to their front. As soon as Brigadier General Evans realised that the attack had bogged down, he sought further artillery support from corps artillery. This was initially refused by Horne's HQ with the rider that no further battalions should be involved in the attack, as the 2 already committed were sufficient for the task in hand. However, Horne had a change of heart and a further half-hour bombardment was laid on, ending at 11h15. But the attack that followed this, and a subsequent one launched at 15h15, failed to improve the situation; this despite the fact that Evans had disregarded Corps and brought up his reserve battalion.

Despite the increasingly intolerable conditions brought about by the incessant rain, General Horne ordered a further attack by both 38th and 17th Divisions which, after two postponements, was to start at 20h00. However Brigadier General Evans was able to persuade his superiors that his disorganised battalions would not be ready in time to take advantage of the preliminary bombardment. Their participation was cancelled and the disorganised battalions were withdrawn, having sustained about 400 casualties during the course of the day. That night 2 companies of 17th Bn RWF moved up to hold the line opposite the Hammerhead.[16]

Despite cancellation of the Welsh prong of the attack, 3 battalions of 17th Division (10th Sherwood Foresters, 7th East Yorks and 6th Dorsets) renewed their assault on Quadrangle Support and Wood Trenches after a 30 minute bombardment. (They were supposed to be supported by 15th RWF of 113th Brigade, 38th Division, on the Dorsets' right but, apparently unaware that they were part of a larger operation, this battalion confined itself to sending forward a patrol.) Once again the bombardment failed to suppress the enemy machine guns and the attacks failed to make any progress, with heavy casualties. Thus ended a day of almost total failure for XV Corps.[17]

General Horne nevertheless contrived to strike a positive note in letters to his wife, despite his frustration at the lack of progress.

> We are stuck in the Wood. It is very difficult to find out what is going on, but I expect we shall make some progress by evening. The Germans are fighting hard, but reports and examination of prisoners show that they are hard put to it to hold on. The situation altogether looks well for us, thank God, who has been very good to us … I hope we may make some substantial progress by evening.[18]

> I am creeping slowly along around Mametz Wood but I have not got it yet. A wood is a very difficult thing to manage, it offers full scope for the German machine guns. The attacks of ourselves and the French to the east and south have gone well today, I hear, so that progress is being maintained. I really think that we are giving the Hun a good hustling.[19]

General Haig's diary entries for the period reflect the growing frustrations and anxieties being felt at high levels. On 7 July he wrote, 'I visited HQ Fourth Army and saw General Rawlinson. I directed him to get Mametz Wood and push on towards Pozières.'[20] And the following day:

> I sent General Birch, CRA, to see Fourth Army and arrange for the capture of Mametz Wood as early as possible – and about 15h30 I visited HQ Fourth Army myself.
>
> Sir H Rawlinson stated that his plan was now to pierce the enemy's second line near Bazentin-le-Grand. I pointed out the necessity for having possession of Mametz Wood before making any attempt of the kind. The moment for taking the enemy by surprise here had passed, and the fighting in the Mametz Wood showed that the enemy's 'moral' was still good. I therefore gave Rawlinson an order to consolidate his right flank *strongly* in the south end of Trônes Wood, and to capture Mametz Wood and Contalmaison before making any attempt to pierce the enemy's second line. This was later confirmed in writing.
>
> Rawlinson reported … the 38th Welsh Division which had been ordered to attack Mametz Wood had not advanced with determination to the attack. General Horne, Comdg XV Corps, is enquiring into General Philipps' conduct as Divl GOC. The artillery preparation was in both cases reported as highly satisfactory.[21]

The next stage in the mutual incomprehension which seemed to exist between Horne's and 38th Division's headquarters arose when the former ordered that the attack by 15th RWF on Strip Trench on the night of 7 July be 'supported and developed'. Unsurprisingly, given that the Commander of 113th Brigade was only aware of patrol activity by this battalion at the time in question, clarification of the order was sought. The division were told that the details of timing and place of action should be left to the Brigadier. Accordingly Division sent a message to Corps pointing out that 15th RWF had made a bombing raid up Strip Trench the previous night but had been driven back. The 113th Brigade were now preparing a battalion-strength attack, by 14th RWF, on the trench at a time yet to be fixed.

When Horne read this he personally telephoned Major General Philipps and told him that a battalion-strength attack would be inappropriate. Horne followed this up with an immediate visit to Philipps' HQ out of which emerged an order for a scaled-down attack to take place at 02h00 on the morning of 9 July. This change in the original plan only reached 14th RWF's CO late on the night of 8 July, too late in the crowded conditions of the approach trenches to carry out the necessary reorganisation. The CO declined to risk his men in the rapidly approaching daylight and cancelled the attack.

When news of this reached Horne from divisional HQ, Major General Philipps' fate was sealed.[22] Horne was already enquiring into his conduct as divisional GOC as a result of the division's disappointing first attack on Mametz Wood. Philipps had arrived on the Somme with a somewhat tarnished reputation, thanks to General Haking. He was going to find little support from Rawlinson or Haig, neither of whom would have been well disposed towards him, either from what they had heard or on the basis of his division's recent performance. His political background would not have helped either with soldiers who almost instinctively distrusted 'political' officers. By the middle of the morning of the 9th, Horne had summoned Philipps, dismissed him and ordered him back to England. Horne had planned to replace him with Major General C G Blackader, but was pre-empted by Haig, who wished to see the command given temporarily to Major General H E Watts, GOC of 7th Division. Watts was duly appointed.

Haig's diary for 9 July records:

> In the afternoon I saw Rawlinson at Querrieu, the CGS was with me. I urged the immediate capture of Mametz Wood.
>
> We then visited HQ XV Corps and saw General Horne. He was very disappointed with the work of the 17th Div (Pilcher) and 38th Welsh Div (Philipps). Both these officers have been relieved. In the case of the latter Division, although the Wood had been most adequately bombarded the Divn never entered the Wood and in the whole Divn the total casualties for the 24 hours was under 150 ... A few bold men entered the Wood and found little opposition. Deserters also stated enemy was greatly demoralised and had very few troops on the ground.
>
> I congratulated B Gen Alexander (CRA XV Corps) on the excellent work of the gunners.[23]

Although it was almost certainly Horne's intention by this time to relieve General Pilcher, he was not in fact do so until 11 July. Haig's figure for 38th Division's casualties is also at odds with the generally accepted figure of 400. If, in this passage, Haig is quoting what Horne told him, there is a degree of self-serving in what Horne said. It does less than justice to the difficulties confronting the troops on the ground. The artillery bombardment manifestly failed to suppress the German machine gunners and the planned smokescreen was not laid. No acknowledgement is made of XV Corps' contribution to the orders for the attack, which sought to impose too much control on details which were properly the responsibility of the Brigade Commander. On the other hand there is evidence that both Philipps and the Brigade Commander balked at sending waves of their men unprotected against machine guns.

Horne's patience had been wearing thin with Major General Pilcher since early in the battle. The failure of a further attempt by the division to capture Quadrangle Support Trench on 8 July was probably a further nail in his coffin. The battalions which had received such a mauling in the attack the night before had been relieved by 7th Borders and 7th Green Howards. They were ordered to bomb up the trenches on either side of Quadrangle Support and take it this way. The attacks went in at 07h00 but failed after 5 hours of effort in the face of mud and the enemy's machine gun and artillery fire. The attack was renewed at 17h50 after an artillery bombardment, even though a promised simultaneous attack on Contalmaison by 23rd Division of III Corps did not take place. This time some progress was made. At one point 6th Dorsets, who had returned to the front line, got to within 50 yards of Mametz Wood itself by taking and holding Wood Trench.[24] But Quadrangle Support remained firmly in German hands, to the intense disappointment of Horne.

General Pilcher was urged to renew his attacks on the trench, using fresh troops. Horne agreed however that it might be best to wait until 23rd Division made their attack on Contalmaison and co-ordinate with that. The attack, the seventh on Quadrangle Support Trench, was accordingly timed for 12h15. Despite the introduction of 7th Lincolns and 8th South Staffs and the retention of

7th Green Howards, the result was again failure. The attack cannot have been helped by 23rd Division's non-appearance; their plans had apparently been misconstrued by XV Corps. Horne was more inclined to ascribe the failure to poor troop deployment and lack of determination on 17th Division's part.[25]

With pressure still being maintained by Haig, in a further visit to Horne's HQ, that seizure of Mametz Wood was a vital prerequisite to any attack on Bazentin Ridge,[26] Horne in turn pressed Pilcher and 38th Division's new Commander, Watts, to make plans to renew their assaults as soon as possible.

The 17th Division's attentions remained focussed on Quadrangle Support Trench. Even if lightly manned by the Germans, it was a formidable challenge to capture as long as the junctions at either end with Pearl Alley and Quadrangle Alley were in German hands. Retention of these junctions enabled the Germans to feed in reinforcements at will. Further protection of Quadrangle Support was provided by the machine guns operating from Contalmaison and Mametz Wood which could enfilade any frontal attack. The attack launched by 17th Division at 23h20 on 9 July was intended to capture the 2 junctions and also seize the trench by frontal assault. The 7th Lincolns were to take the western and 7th Green Howards the eastern junctions. The 8th South Staffs were to carry out the frontal assault, with their bombers assisting 7th Lincolns.

Deep, clinging mud led to failure on the left; the much depleted numbers of 7th Green Howards and intense enemy fire to a similar outcome on the right. In the centre, the South Staffs, despite casualties from blind-firing enemy machine guns, got into the trench and cleared a section of it. (Their bombers even got as far as Acid Drop Copse where they set up a machine gun.) But lack of support from left and right made their position untenable and they withdrew, having suffered 220 casualties. Quadrangle Support Trench remained in German hands, but the repeated British attacks were taking their toll.[27]

Little attempt was made to co-ordinate the attacks of the 2 divisions, beyond ensuring that 38th Welsh's troops were aware of the presence of 6th Dorsets in Wood Trench, just to the left of the planned line of advance of the division's 113th Brigade. Major General Watts' plan called for a 4 battalion assault north from just north of White Trench to the southern tip of Mametz Wood between Strip Trench on the left and the Hammerhead on the right. The assault would be led, on the left by 16th RWF, followed by 14th RWF, of 113th Brigade and, in the centre and on the right, by 14th Welch and 13th Welch of 114th Brigade. All the assaulting battalions would be supported by additional machine guns. The remaining battalions of these brigades would be in support. Zero Hour would be 04h15 on the 10th.

A feature of the attack would be an attempt at a much more sophisticated artillery programme. The first part of this called for the 45 minute-long pre-assault bombardment of the enemy front line to be lifted as if the assault were coming in, and then return to the front line in the hope of catching the enemy manning it. The second part was the use of a creeping barrage, which would begin at Zero Hour by putting down a protective curtain just in front of the advancing infantry and lift forward 50 yards every minute to just beyond the first objective. At 06h15 it would lift to the second objective and, an hour later, to the third.

When the assault began it soon became apparent that despite the artillery preparation, which also included a smokescreen along the whole front, German resistance was going to be strong and tenacious. In the initial stages, there was considerable confusion amongst the Welsh. One battalion fell behind its creeping barrage and suffered as a consequence; another, in the centre of the assault, followed it so closely that they were into the edges of the Wood and onto the Germans before the latter were ready for them. Gradually, with determined leadership from regimental officers of all ranks, the Welsh made progress, except on the right where enfilade fire from the Hammerhead pinned down 13th Welch Regt, inflicting heavy casualties. But, with support battalions by now engaged, Strip Trench was finally secured and parts of no fewer than 7 battalions had gained footholds in the wood.

The main problems were now from congestion, the danger of outrunning the British barrage, the thick undergrowth which the attackers had found awaiting them and German infiltration through gaps between the Welsh units. The most successful German infiltration was between 13th and 15th Welch Regt. The latter had got into the Hammerhead with the former in the main Wood to their left. Before they could link up, the Germans got round behind 15th Welch and annihilated one of their companies. The Welsh hold on the edges of the Hammerhead was very tenuous and subjected to strong German counterattacks.

By 10h30 orders had been issued for the advance to the second objective, an east-west line about half way through the wood. The attacking battalions had been reorganised and thinned out because of the congestion. The 10th Welch got through at the second attempt but on the left 113th Brigade could make no progress against intense enemy fire from Wood Support Trench. They were told to bypass it in some way and 17th RWF, sent from 115th Brigade to reinforce them, succeeded in fighting their way through to the second objective. A further attack was arranged for 16h30 to complete the advance through the wood. It would be preceded by a further attempt to take Wood Support Trench.

Despite the capture of a number of prisoners, this further attempt on the trench did not succeed. But the main advance from the second objective met initially with little resistance and all the battalions made progress. By about 18h30 they were about 40 yards from the northern edge where they came under heavy fire from Middle Alley, a trench leading north from the centre of the northern edge of the Wood. After attempts to bomb the Germans out of the trench failed, the Welsh battalions were withdrawn some 2 to 300 yards back into the wood, where they dug in. A proposed further attack at 20h00 to complete the wood's capture was abandoned because of the exhausted state of the troops.[28]

Meanwhile 17th Division were ordered to make further attacks on Quadrangle Alley and Quadrangle Support Trench, and to push patrols forward to occupy the western edge of Mametz Wood. The first attempt to implement these orders, an attack on Quadrangle Alley and the eastern end of the Support Trench, was launched at 09h00 by 7th East Yorks. It failed.

By now the German defenders of Quadrangle Support Trench were in danger of being outflanked by 6th Dorsets moving north from Wood Trench. Spotting this, the acting CO of 7th East Yorks launched 2 attacks of platoon strength. But these, and 6th Dorsets, were stopped not only by the defenders in the trench, but also by German machine guns firing from Acid Drop Copse. The Germans had been able to reoccupy the copse after the 8th South Staffs machine gun crew, which had captured it, had been wiped out by a direct hit from a British shell.

The same evening, 17th Division made a further effort. This time, despite taking heavy casualties from enfilade fire from Quadrangle Support Trench, 6th Dorsets successfully occupied and cleared Wood Support Trench. The main attack was launched at 21h45 after an artillery bombardment. Despite an enemy counter bombardment, Quadrangle Support Trench was finally occupied and secured. Nearly all the German defenders, realising they had been outflanked on both sides, had already made good their escape.[29] Contalmaison also finally fell to 23rd Division.

General Haig recorded in his diary for 10th July:

> … I saw General Horne, Comg XV Corps at Heilly. He reported that General Watts (7th Div) had temporarily taken command of 38th Welsh Divn, and had nearly got the whole of Mametz Wood. What an effect on a Division has a good Commander! I urged on Horne the necessity for organising the north end of Mametz Wood with field guns for offensive purposes and to enfilade the enemy's line of trenches.[30]

Haig was clearly pleased that his intervention to secure the temporary appointment of Major General Watts appeared to have worked. There was still work to be done however before Horne could start organising field artillery dispositions at the north end of the wood. In his letter to his wife that day he wrote:

> We are in the middle of Mametz Wood (13h00). We attacked at 04h15 and have got about half the Wood. I hope that we may clear it by nightfall. It is anxious work, wondering whether things are going right or not, it is very difficult to know how matters stand in a wood. Troops get much mixed up. Prisoners are coming in from the Wood, there are 88 in now and probably more to follow. All reports show that the Germans are using up all their reserve troops, and the reinforcements which they are bringing up are being withdrawn from the garrisons of other parts of the line.
>
> (16h30) Not much news but the little there is points to our making progress in Mametz Wood. 136 prisoners have been brought in up to now. I hope to catch more in the Wood, as I am surrounding the Germans with a ring of artillery fire.[31]

The 11 July was to prove to be the Welsh division's last full day in Mametz Wood. By 05h30, following a series of unsuccessful attacks during the night, 10th South Wales Borderers finally gained full possession of the Hammerhead. Half an hour earlier Brigadier General Evans had arrived in the wood with the remnants of 115th Brigade, to take over command of all the troops in the wood. He had expected to find it fully in British hands, but quickly realised the true situation and reported to divisional HQ that the position was unstable; he needed time to probe the enemy's positions and strength. He was told in no uncertain terms that he must attack as the Germans were weak and could not be reinforced with British artillery interdicting their movements.

Evans decided on a surprise 3-battalion attack to begin at 15h00 and sent back messages designed to prevent a British barrage giving away his intentions. Either these messages were not received, or not acted upon, because a British bombardment began at 14h45. It not only wrecked any hope of surprise, but also inflicted serious casualties on the battalions preparing to attack, especially as it provoked a German counter barrage. There could be no question of the attack going in until the British bombardment had lifted, which it did at 15h30. But by then some of the attacking battalions were only able to push forward patrols or the odd company. Some of these piecemeal attacks did make progress; others failed, were repeated and failed again. German resistance was stubborn; they had been heavily reinforced, whatever divisional HQ believed, and were determined to hold on in the wood, recognising the threat its fall would pose to their Second Line. By late that night even those Welsh units which had made progress had been forced back to their start lines by the failure of attacks on their flanks or severe enemy artillery bombardments.[32]

During the night of 11/12 July, 38th Division were relieved by 21st Division. The Germans had, during the same night, finally accepted that they could no longer hold on in the wood and had begun a rapid withdrawal to their Second Line. The 21st Division thus had little difficulty in mopping up and taking full possession of the wood by a little after midday on the 12th.[33] Horne wrote:

> We have got Mametz Wood at last and I hope we shall hold on to it. It was a difficult problem. It is in a terrible state now. Full of German dead and some of ours too, the trees torn and many of them thrown down by the shellfire. It is difficult to get about in it I am told and no doubt it is. It took a long time to get hold of, but I had new hands doing it, not my old friends, and a wood is a difficult job at any time. We soon finished it up when I got my old hands back to it.
>
> Watts is a splendid fellow. The best general I have, and the most successful. It was he who fought on the Mametz side, and they did excellent work.
>
> We took four Howitzers, one of them very big, in Mametz Wood. XV Corps has taken 61 officers, 3710 men and 15 guns up-to-date and of course many machine guns. Not so bad.[34]

The 38th Welsh Division were not to participate further in the Battle of the Somme. During their 6 days in action they had suffered 3,993 casualties, of whom over 600 were killed and nearly 600 missing.[35] Despite these dispiriting figures, the division emerged from the battle with a sullied reputation, largely acquired as the result of the failure of their first attempt to capture Mametz Wood, in which, it was perceived, too few casualties had been taken to constitute their attack as a determined effort. Their subsequent bloodletting in the wood failed to restore their reputation. In a letter sent to the Chief of the Imperial General Staff on 14th July, General Rawlinson wrote:

> I only write a line to say how splendidly the troops have done. Only one Division, the 38th (Welshmen) turned out badly and if it had not been for their failure at Mametz Wood we would have brought off the action of today [Bazentin Ridge] at least 48 hours sooner.
>
> … Our Corps Commanders Horne and Congreve have done and are doing splendid work – so is old Putty [Lieutenant General Sir William Pulteney, III Corps] though he is of course not up to the standard of the other

two. Of the Divs in this last attack, all did well especially the 21st, 9th and 7th which had the bulk of the fighting. The 3rd and 18th did well also but had easier tasks … [36]

In this letter from the Fourth Army Commander can be seen the beginnings of a tendency to blame the unfortunate Welsh division for the failure of the British effort on the Somme to live up to its prior billing. This gathered momentum in a book published in 1922 entitled *Sir Douglas Haig's Command*, jointly written by George A B Dewar and Lt Col J H Boraston. Its authors posited that the delay created by the failure of the Welsh division to capture Mametz Wood quickly led directly to the failure to achieve rapid breakthrough in this sector of the front and hence the failure of the whole campaign except in attritional terms.[37] Such a claim hardly bears close examination when it is recalled that General Rawlinson did not regard possession of Mametz Wood as vital to the success of his planned attack on Bazentin Ridge. He could have made his attack on 11 July as he wanted, regardless of the situation in Mametz Wood, if he had been able to persuade General Haig and GHQ in time to his way of thinking.

While by no means exonerating the Welsh entirely from blame – some of the Division's actions are described as 'failures' – the Official History does not suggest that the ultimate lack of a clear-cut victory in the Somme campaign was caused by the delay in taking Mametz Wood. In stressing that time was of the essence at this early stage of the campaign the Official History blames the loss of momentum, not on the alleged shortcomings of one division, but on the failure to seize Mametz Wood when it was empty of enemy and there for the taking on 3 July.[38] Although little is made of it in the Official History, no small part in the Welsh division's perhaps disappointing performance might be ascribed to the repeated interference from XV Corps HQ in matters which should have been left to divisional or brigade staffs. In other words, the division's reputation may have paid the price for General Horne's inexperience of battlefield command at this level.

The 38th Welsh Division were to retrieve their reputation, even in the eyes of their earlier detractors, on future battlefields of the war. The sacked Commander, Major General Philipps, was to have no opportunity to retrieve his. He was unfortunate to have to carry the opprobrium for the failure of the first attack, especially as he seems to have acted merely as a conduit for the transmission of orders between XV Corps and the attacking brigade. But he does not seem to have demonstrated any great grip of the situation, nor any great desire to impose himself and show some necessary leadership. While, given the chance, he might have grown into the job, the most probable conclusion is that his shortcomings would have found him out at some stage.

Chapter X

Corps Commander: The Somme: Bazentin Ridge

Haig and Rawlinson's difference of opinion over whether British possession of Mametz Wood was an essential prerequisite to the attack on the German Second Line, was to effect its timing quite significantly. Rawlinson's first plan called for the attack to be launched at dawn on 10 July. The XIII Corps would attack the line Longueval-Bazentin-le-Grand village with 2 divisions. The XV Corps, also with 2 divisions, would attack Bazentin-le-Grand Wood-Bazentin-le-Petit village and cemetery from a line following, but to the east of, the northern edge of Mametz Wood. An auxiliary attack would be mounted on XV Corps' left by one division of III Corps. An essential element of Rawlinson's plan was surprise. To achieve this the 2 divisions of XIII Corps would advance into the 500 yards-wide No Man's Land in the dark and undetected, there to form up for the attack. Rawlinson contended that the attack could be mounted whatever the situation in Mametz Wood.

Haig was not at all happy with Rawlinson's plan. As has already been noted he forcefully rejected it and reiterated the need to take Mametz Wood as a first step. He thought it was asking too much of the skills of XIII Corps' troops to expect 2 divisions of them to form up unobserved in the dark. Haig proposed instead that XV Corps should initiate the attack about 2 hours before dark on 12 July. No Man's Land in their sector was narrower than in front of XIII Corps. Once they had advanced north and secured their initial objectives, they could wheel right to begin clearing the ridge towards Longueval. At this point XIII Corps could join by advancing from the south. III Corps would protect XV Corps' left flank by advancing towards Contalmaison (at this stage still in German hands). Apart from any other shortcomings it might have, Haig's plan sacrificed the advantage of surprise by calling for the attack to be launched in daylight after a lengthy preliminary bombardment.

Haig soon discovered that the commanders of the 3 corps involved all preferred Rawlinson's plan to his. Of the 3 (Horne, Congreve and Pulteney), probably the one that made the most impression on Haig was Horne, whose corps, under the Commander-in-Chief's plan, would bear the brunt of the fighting, with little support in the early stages. Horne made clear his strong aversion to attacking in the evening daylight without the support of XIII Corps on his right. Haig was not used to dissent from such a source; he and Horne usually saw eye-to-eye.[1] Indeed the authoritative military writer, Captain Basil Liddell Hart, was to suggest unkindly that Horne's rise through the senior ranks matched his capacity for agreeing with his C-in-C.[2]

The array of dissent against him made little initial impression on Haig, such was his unhappiness with Rawlinson's concept. He did however modify his plan to try to meet Horne's concerns, proposing that the latter's initial attack should have all the support necessary on the right to secure the right flank. This would include

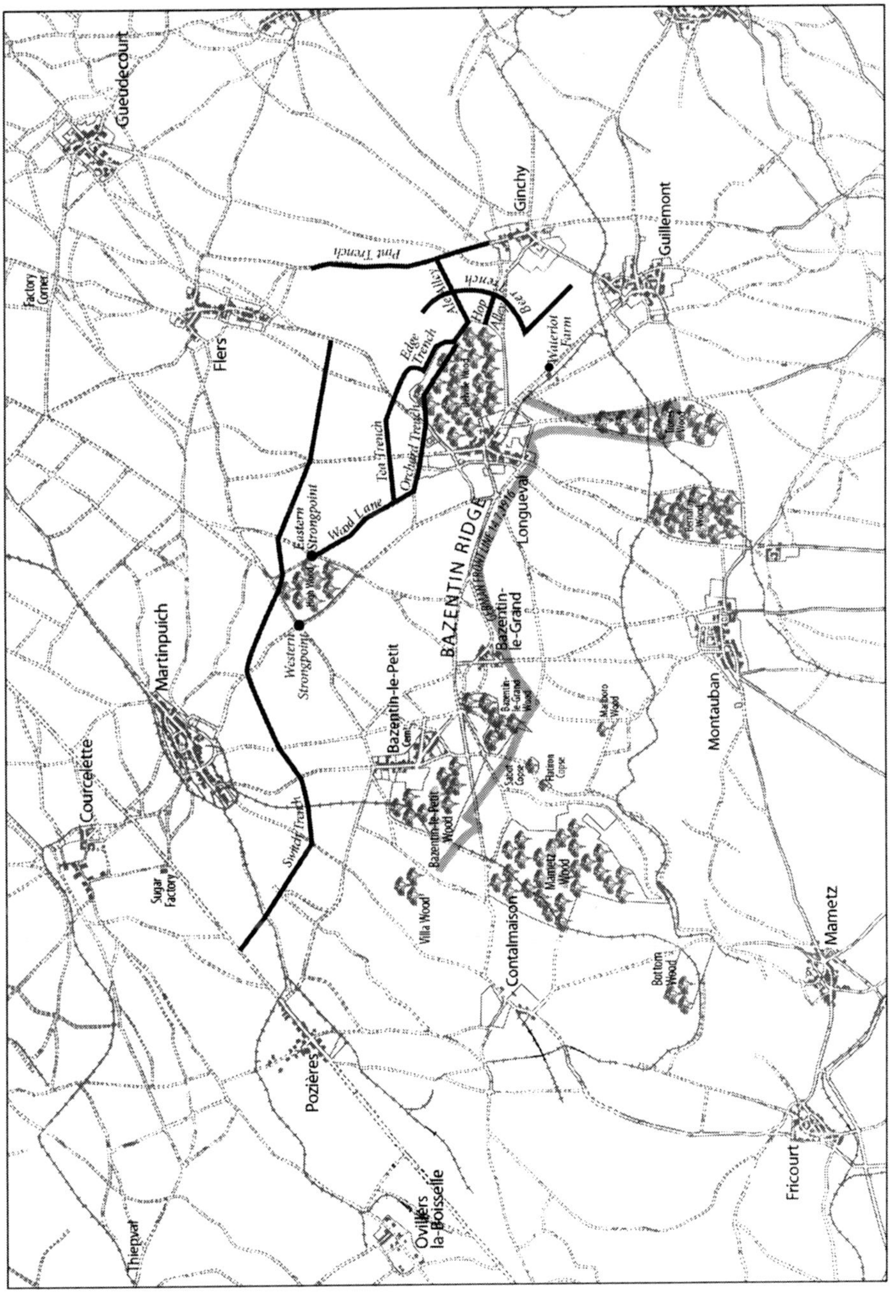

Map 9: The Somme: Bazentin Ridge: July 1916

strong patrolling by XIII Corps.[3] Haig's diary entries for 10 and 11 July reflect his worry and concerns.

> After lunch I visited Querrieu and saw Rawlinson and his Chief of Staff Montgomery. I questioned him about the plan of attack against Longueval Ridge. He proposes to form up two divisions in the dark and attack at dawn over an open maidan against the front Bazentin-le-Grand Wood to Longueval. Further to the West the attack will be made by XV Corps.
>
> As regards the first day of the bombardment, I said Mametz Wood and Contalmaison must be in our hands to secure our left flank, while Trônes Wood must be held on our right. At present the enemy is in Trônes Wood, but we'll get it again tonight. Progress in Mametz Wood is satisfactory and we should capture Contalmaison this afternoon.[4]
>
> I am not quite satisfied with Rawlinson's plan of attack against Bazentin-le-Grand – Longueval. He is proposing to attack at dawn over an open plateau, for 1,000 yards distance, after forming up in the dark, and this with a force of two divisions, appears to me a manoeuvre which one cannot do successfully against flags in time of peace! Rawlinson explained his plan, and I gave him my opinion that it was unsound. He at once, in the most broadminded way, said he would change it, making, as I suggested, the main attack against the line Contalmaison Villa – Bazentin-le-Grand Wood Farm – Mametz Wood, while threatening from the rest of our front, from Ovillers to Trônes Wood. General Montgomery was most anxious to adhere to the original plan but I declined to discuss the matter further.
>
> Rawlinson was accordingly ordered to attack the line Contalmaison Village – Bazentin-le-Grand Wood with XV Corps reinforced by a Brigade or Division as Horne might desire to be prepared to reinforce him. To establish a good flank on West of Bazentin-le-Petit and then work eastwards and capture Longueval, Ginchy, Guillemont etc. The XIII Corps to organise supporting points just under the slopes opposite Longueval, Bazentin etc and be ready to push in when the XV Corps begin to work towards Longueval.
>
> The whole question of the attack of the German Second Line is a difficult problem.[5]

At this point, despite the arguments of Rawlinson and the tenacious Montgomery, Haig was insisting on his plan being implemented. In accordance with this the bombardment began, with the intention still being that the infantry attack would go in late on the 12th. This timetable quickly slipped when Horne reported to Rawlinson that his artillery's wire-cutting programme could not be completed before the 14th. The attack was thereupon postponed to that day.[6]

At some stage during this enforced delay, Haig was finally brought round to accept that the attack would follow Rawlinson's plan rather than his. Neither Haig's diary nor Horne's letters indicate how this conversion was achieved – indeed neither source indicates that any transformation took place. The Official History puts it down to further appeals finally persuading Haig. Revised orders called for the infantry of XV and XIII Corps to begin their assault simultaneously at 03h25 on 14 July.

The bombardment had inevitably warned the Germans that something was up. To try to ensure tactical surprise therefore the pre-assault intensification of the bombardment, which had so often in the past alerted the enemy to the imminence of an attack, would last only 5 minutes. The concept of the creeping barrage also edged forward with a decision that this latest version would only use high explosive shells with delay fuzes. No shrapnel would be used. This experiment was to be rated so successful that shrapnel would only rarely be used in future creeping barrages.[7]

As the build-up to the attack reached its climax, Horne wrote to his wife:

> All goes very well. Hard at it again tomorrow. Bazentin is now in front of us and is part of the German second line.
>
> We have Bazentin-le-Petit and Bazentin-le-Grand – two woods and two villages – to tackle. We are giving them a good bombarding but they are strong as they are part of the Boche second line! However I think that the guns followed by determined men will get through all right. The Boche is having a terrible time of it, but I think that they have got a fresh division coming in, either last night or tonight – but we keep the whole place under a good artillery fire all night, including the roads and villages for miles back and the Boche suffers many casualties coming up. Our artillery has quite got the supremacy, and with the splendid assistance given us by the aeroplanes we are able to keep down a great deal of the Boche artillery fire. The longest ranging guns I have shoot up to 10 miles, but we have some in other places, which carry much further, probably up to 15 miles at least.
>
> The weather is dull and cold today, I want clear bright weather to get full value out of the aeroplanes. The Flying people have done splendid work; no-one could praise them too highly.[8]

In detail General Rawlinson's plan saw as its first objective the seizure of the Germans' first and second lines of trenches from the southwest corner of Delville Wood, through Longueval, the southern end of Bazentin-le-Grand village and Wood to the south face of Bazentin-le-Petit Wood. The second objectives were Delville Wood, the rest of Longueval, and Bazentin-le-Petit Wood and village. The III Corps would secure Contalmaison Villa, nearly a mile northeast of the village of the same name, as soon as possible.

In addition to these objectives Rawlinson attached great importance to the seizure of High Wood (Bois des Fourcaux), which lay on the crest of the ridge some 2,000 yards northwest of Longueval. The plan called for 2nd Indian Cavalry Division, under the temporary command of XIII Corps, to achieve this. They were to be ready to move at 04h00 on the first day of the attack.[9] It is curious that Rawlinson was prepared to entrust such a vital operation to a cavalry unit, given his infantryman's scepticism of the value and efficacy of cavalry in the prevailing conditions of the Western Front. He may well have determined that his Commander-in-Chief Haig had lingering suspicions about his failure to commit the cavalry on the opening day of the Somme battle, when an opportunity for breakout had seemed to offer itself on XIII Corps' front. Hence a greater willingness to contemplate the use of cavalry against High Wood. It was to prove a fateful decision.

The battle that was about to take place was to have a seminal effect on the military thinking of Captain Basil Liddell Hart. The revival of the use of surprise, which the battle exemplified, was to influence strongly his approach to battlefield tactics in later life. He was to advocate the outwitting of an enemy, preferably by a paralysing combination of surprise and mobility, as a way to avoid future repetitions of the opening day of the Somme battle.[10] Liddell Hart did however take some time to reach this evaluation of the conduct of the Somme campaign. He was a junior officer in 9th Bn King's Own Yorkshire Light Infantry, part of 64th Brigade, 21st Division, which in turn was part of Horne's XV Corps. In the notebook he kept at the time of the battle, Liddell Hart wrote that Lt General Horne seemed to be a very capable man and quite young.[11] His immediate experience of the battle did nothing to dent his estimation of Horne, for in an article he wrote for the *Daily Express*, which was published on 21 December 1916, he described Sir Henry Horne as a man of genius, the captor of Fricourt, Mametz Wood and Bazentin, who had just been promoted to the command of an army for his great work.[12]

In the same month he recorded, apparently uncritically, an interview he had conducted with John Buchan, the celebrated novelist who by this time was on Haig's personal staff for the purpose of drafting his dispatches and communiqués. In the interview Buchan described General Sir Hubert Gough and the Russian Chief of Staff, General Mikhail Vasilevich Alekseev as the 2 military geniuses thrown up so far by the war. He ranked Henry Horne with Gough. 'Horne ... was a wonderfully scientific soldier and one who had done wonders on the Somme. It was his Corps which had introduced the 'creeping barrage' on July 1st and the excellence of the artillery and road organisation on 1st July was unique on the whole Somme front.'[13] Buchan may have been in a better position than most to make these sort of judgments, but they appear to owe more to his talents for fiction than for military analysis. Doubts about Gough were already being voiced, notably by the Australians and Canadians, and Alekseev, while undoubtedly a highly competent staff officer who succeeded in overcoming many of the deficiencies in Russian military organisation, hardly matches up to the general conception of a military genius.

Liddell Hart's view of Horne, along with many other British generals, was to change drastically in the post-war years. His criticism of Horne's use of gas at the Battle of Loos in 1915 has already been recorded as has his suggestion that Horne's rise through the senior ranks of the army owed much to sycophancy. He also recorded approvingly the view of James Edmonds, the Official Historian of the Great War, who, speaking on 31 October 1929, said, 'Haig's trouble was that he would not sack Corps commanders – Horne, Congreve, Hunter-Weston, inefficient or miscalculating. But he sacked underlings ...'[14]

Liddell-Hart's view of Henry Horne may have undergone drastic change, but he remained constant in his admiration for the conception and execution of the Battle of Bazentin Ridge. He wrote:

> Rawlinson framed a plan to attack and break the German defences on a four-mile front between Delville Wood on the right and Bazentin-le-Petit Wood on the left. His right was fully three quarters of a mile distant from his second line, with the vital tactical feature of Trônes Wood between still in German hands. Thence towards his left No Man's Land gradually narrowed until in front of Mametz Wood it was only about 300 yards wide; but Trônes Wood enfiladed a large part of the line of advance. If the obvious course was adopted and an attack delivered only on the left, the prospects were barren. For the

experiences of 1915 had shown that an attack on a narrow frontage against an enemy with ample guns might gain an initial success, only to be blown out of the captured fragment by the concentration of hostile gunfire thus facilitated.

Instead of the obvious, Rawlinson took a course which for all its risks – calculated risks – was more truly secure and economical of force. The troops were to cross the exposed area by an advance under cover of darkness, followed by a dawn attack, preceded by a hurricane bombardment of only a few minutes' duration. This plan revived the use of surprise, which lay rusting throughout the greater part of the war, until in fact the last year from Cambrai onwards.

In 1916 the ideas of a night advance and of such a brief bombardment were alike so fresh in revival as to be a shock and appear a gamble to orthodox opinion. That he should attempt the manoeuvre with New Army troops, men who had been civilians less than two years before, made his plan yet more rash. The C-in-C was strongly opposed to it, preferring a more limited alternative, but Rawlinson persevered, his own confidence reinforced by the confidence of the actual troop-leaders in their ability to carry out the night operation. For once, Horne, whose capacity for agreeing with the C-in-C was as consistent as his own rise, agreed instead with his immediate superior, and this fact may have helped to tilt the scales. Rawlinson gained his way, but instead of the already delayed attack being launched on 13th July, as he intended, the reluctance of the Higher Command caused it to be postponed until 14th July – a day's delay that was to have grave consequences. Another drawback was the lack of French co-operation, owing to lack of faith in the prospects of the attack.[15]

It was not just French lack of faith in the ability of Fourth Army to mount a night attack that determined their uncooperative attitude, but also the failure of XIII Corps to complete the capture of Trônes Wood. The wood was too close to the French left flank for them to regard its possession by the Germans with equanimity.[16] Haig had been insistent all along that its capture was essential to the success of the Bazentin Ridge attack. Unlike the case of Mametz Wood, Rawlinson did not dissent from this view. The wood had been partially captured on 11 July, but Lieutenant General Congreve was left in no doubt that it had to be entirely in British hands by the morning of the 14th, at any cost. Following the failure of 30th Division's efforts, the task was assigned to 18th Division. They launched their attack at 19h00 on 13 July. After bitter all-night fighting, which lasted well into the following day, the wood was finally secured. Fortunately for the main attack on Bazentin Ridge, the Germans in the wood had been far too busy defending themselves to interfere in it to any extent.[17]

Horne entrusted his sector of the main attack to his 2 most reliable divisions, the 7th and 21st. The XIII Corps used 3rd and 9th Divisions. From their jumping off points north of Marlborough and Mametz Woods, Horne's troops had to advance between 350 and 600 yards, mainly uphill, to reach the German lines. Five minutes before Zero Hour the bombardment which had been going on for 3 days erupted into a hurricane barrage. The infantry assaulted at 03h25, achieving complete surprise. In Horne's sector there were no setbacks. Within a short period his troops were in possession of the 2 Bazentin villages and their eponymous woods. Casualties were light. On his left III Corps had moved up to protect his flank and Horne was planning his next moves which foresaw 21st Division moving north and then west to get behind the enemy facing III Corps, and a fresh brigade of 7th Division preparing to relieve the cavalry once they had seized High Wood.

The enemy managed to mount a couple of counterattacks on Horne's troops. The first established a machine gun position at the northwest corner of Bazentin-le-Petit Wood; the second temporarily regained Bazentin-le-Petit village. The village was quickly retaken and secured, but the machine gun position remained in German hands.[18]

In XIII Corps' sector all had initially gone very well. By midmorning, taking into account XV Corps' success, Fourth Army had breached the German Second Line from Bazentin-le-Petit to Longueval, a distance of 6,000 yards. But XIII Corps had not taken their second objectives, the northern part of Longueval and Delville Wood. Their attempts to secure these places were met by well-organised and determined German counterattacks well supported by artillery. These German successes were to induce a sense of caution in the minds of the British commanders just when a bold approach might have paid dividends. They were, in addition, to provide the Germans with a covered approach for future counterattacks.[19]

By midmorning both 7th Division of XV Corps and 3rd Division of XIII Corps had High Wood in their sights. Patrols sent forward confirmed that everything was quiet in the wood. The GOC of 3rd Division proposed that he should send his reserve brigade to seize the wood. General Watts, back in command of 7th Division after his brief sojourn with 38th Welsh, confirmed his reputation for dash (so appealing to Haig in the context of Mametz Wood), by urging that his 91st Brigade should also get on and take the wood. Both Lieutenant General Congreve and Horne respectively declined these suggestions, with the approval of Fourth Army. The cavalry would take the wood. Horne reiterated his order that 7th Division would relieve the cavalry in the wood once they had seized it.

The cavalry had been ready to move since 04h00. Urged on by Rawlinson, Congreve called them forward at 07h40. Unfortunately they had 12 miles to cover, largely over ground torn up by shellfire, and for the most part could go no faster than walking pace. By noon there was no news of the leading cavalry brigade and anxiety was growing at Fourth Army headquarters. At 12h15 they suggested to Horne that he take advantage of 7th Division's anxiety to get forward by ordering them to occupy High Wood. At this point Horne chose to take a broad view of the battlefield. He decided that the continuing enemy occupation of Longueval would offer too much of a threat to an advancing 7th Division. Congreve recognised some validity in this; when the Secunderabad Cavalry Brigade at last arrived at Montauban at 12h40 they were ordered to stand fast until Longueval was captured. This was the first example of how the momentum of the early morning was to be dissipated. More were to follow.

The enemy machine gun post at the northwest corner of Bazentin-le-Petit Wood also contributed to the loss of momentum. Reducing it was to take some time, helped as it was by a 2 battalion counterattack on Bazentin-le-Petit Wood and village, which threatened the new British salient for two and a half hours up to 17h30. While this was going on Horne was erroneously informed that Longueval had been fully secured by XIII Corps. He thereupon told Congreve at about 15h40 that 7th Division's 91st Brigade would move on High Wood at 17h15. Could the cavalry cover their right flank? Congreve affirmed they could but somehow failed to tell the cavalry Brigadier until 17h40. It was not only XIII Corps' communications that were suspect; the Commander of 91st Brigade did not get his orders to advance until about 17h20. This was the first he had heard of what was in store for his brigade; there had been no opportunity for detailed planning or reconnaissance. Meanwhile, despite these delays enforced on the original plan, the pre-assault artillery bombardment of High Wood went ahead as scheduled, thus ending at 17h15, much too soon to be of any use.

The 91st Brigade finally crossed their start line at about 19h00, approximately 9 hours after 7th Division had sought permission to make this advance. The brigade were screened on the right by a squadron each from 7th Dragoon Guards and 20th Deccan Horse. A brigade of 33rd Division (now part of XV Corps), who were supposed to cover the left flank, failed to put in an appearance.

This British dilatoriness had allowed the Germans to move some troops forward to prepare an ambush just to the southwest of the wood. Fortunately the weather had cleared sufficiently to allow air observation. An RFC aircraft spotted the Germans and drew their fire, causing them to give away their position. The aircraft dropped a sketch map to the cavalry to be doubly sure they were aware of the danger. As a result its crew were rewarded with that rarest of sights on the Western Front, a cavalry charge with lances, which successfully dispersed the German threat.

As the infantry and cavalry entered the wood and pressed north they came increasingly under German sniper fire. This later intensified into concentrated machine gun and rifle fire from the Switch Trench near the northern edge of the wood. With the light gone the British troops took up defensive positions for the night with the wood only half-occupied. The Germans were to take full advantage of this further respite to reinforce and strengthen their positions. It was to be 2 months before the wood came fully into British possession, 2 months of bitter and costly fighting. The first day's fighting had already cost the British 9,194 casualties, of which 5,713 were from XV Corps.[20]

When Horne wrote to his wife the following day he was under the impression that High Wood had been taken.

> The troops fought brilliantly yesterday. In the evening we got forward a bit further and occupied High Wood. Today I am working forward towards Martinpuich and the Corps on my left are attacking Pozières. Up to now the fighting is going first one way and then another, and it is difficult to say how we are getting on, but I hope we shall gain a bit. The Germans appeared much mixed up and demoralised yesterday but some fresh ones must have come up today I think, judging by the resistance we are meeting.
>
> The C-in-C has just been in, very pleased with the success of our attack yesterday. He says that everything is going very well indeed. We are gradually widening out our bulge in the German defences, and we have accounted for many Germans since this day fortnight.[21]

During Haig's visit Horne told him about the cavalry action. Haig recorded, 'He told me that the 7th Dragoon Guards charged last night and killed with lances 16 enemy and took over 30 prisoners. All Cavalry much heartened by this episode and think their time is soon coming.'[22] Horne was fully aware of Haig's devotion to the cavalry and must have been delighted at this opportunity to show Haig that there might still be a role for them on the Western Front.

Fourth Army's orders for 15 July called for a resumption of operations with the purpose of completing the capture of all the previous day's objectives and exploiting those gains already made. It was to prove a very frustrating day for both XIII and XV Corps. The Germans had brought in reinforcements overnight that enabled them to contest every inch of ground. The British were not helped by deteriorating weather conditions which hampered air spotting.[23] The one positive success was the almost complete capture of Delville Wood by the South African Brigade (9th Division, XIII Corps). It was to prove both a Pyrrhic and ephemeral victory as furious German counterattacks for the rest of the month were to lead to the virtual annihilation of the South Africans as they just clung on in the wood.[24]

Horne's efforts to complete the clearance of High Wood resulted in failure. The 91st Brigade made the first attempt of the day but were stopped by machine gun fire from the Switch Line. They were then pushed back by an enemy counterattack. They tried again in the late afternoon, equally fruitlessly. The 33rd Division's 100th Brigade attacked the Switch Line to the west of High Wood. Had they been successful, they might well have been able to clear the wood from the west. But they were not, and suffered badly from enfilade machine gun and artillery fire. Late that night Horne ordered a complete withdrawal from the wood, which was completed by 08h00 the following morning. He had decided that it should be shelled into submission.[25] He wrote the following day:

> Yesterday I failed to make any progress as the German has been reinforced and I could not get in without a regular artillery preparation. I shall get at them again shortly. I drew my men back from High Wood where they were being too much exposed in order that I may be able to shell it. I thought we had got the whole of it, but we only had half of it and it is so placed in a slope that the Hun's artillery can see into it and ours cannot. The clouds are low and the sky overcast which makes it difficult for aeroplanes to see well enough to direct our artillery onto the Hun trenches. He has succeeded in digging a line in front of us but of course it is very light and thin but we cannot see it and if we can only get the guns put on by aeroplane we will soon have them out again.[26]

Haig recorded in his diary, without comment, 'About noon I heard our troops withdrew from High Wood at dawn in accordance with orders. That point makes our position too extended until our flanks are safe, in General Horne's opinion.'[27]

The orders issued by Fourth Army headquarters for 16 and 17 July emphasised the importance attached to High Wood's early capture. The XV Corps were directed to seize it all as a preliminary to a joint attack by all 3 corps on the 17th. In this, XIII Corps would attack the villages of Guillemont and Ginchy, XV Corps the stretch of the Switch Line between the village of Martinpuich and High Wood, and III Corps the German defences further to the west, including Pozières. The French Army and the Reserve Army (Lieutenant General Sir Hubert Gough) were to cooperate on either flank.[28] Horne was however concerned that the indifferent weather was hampering the artillery from registering their targets; he was reluctant to resume the offensive until this had been properly carried out.

As a consequence Fourth Army initially agreed that the renewed attack on High Wood should form part of the main attack, which was later postponed to 20 July. The XIII Corps' assault on Guillemont and Ginchy would precede it by a day. On 19 July Rawlinson reiterated his order to Horne to attack High Wood the following day.[29] This not only reflected his own concerns but also Haig's displeasure at the situation at Longueval and Delville Wood which was recorded in his diary.

> I saw General Rawlinson at about 15h00 (17th July). He is as much dissatisfied as I am with the action of the 9th Division in failing to occupy the whole of Longueval. I also think there has been a lack of close cooperation between XIII and XV Corps. The latter occupied High Wood with Cavalry on the right, on the night of 14th inst. and the latter dug a trench from that Wood towards Longueval while infantry (7th Div) dug a line from High Wood to Bazentin-le-Petit. I think the XIII Corps should have at once connected up with XV Corps in the direction of High Wood.[30]

Horne recognised that an attack by his corps on High Wood would relieve some of the pressure on XIII Corps as they made a further attempt to expel the Germans from Longueval and Delville Wood. It had little else to recommend it. It was made under distinctly unfavourable conditions. The infantry were tired, having been under constant artillery bombardment; the weather was indifferent and visibility poor.

Despite heavy casualties, largely from German artillery, neither of the Corps' objectives, the wood itself and Switch Trench, were finally secured, although at one stage virtually the whole wood was in British hands. A heavy German artillery bombardment forced a retirement.[31] Horne's letters of that day and the day after reflected the ups and downs of the fighting:

> We are fighting very hard. I attacked High Wood again this morning and we got in all right, but there is a great deal of confusion there now and I do not feel too sure that we are going to hold on to it. The Hun is counterattacking pretty hard and the situation in Longueval is also not too good.
>
> 16h30. Fighting goes on still in High Wood and in Longueval and it is difficult to learn exactly how things are. One has to be patient. Once we get to close quarters in a wood it becomes a difficult matter to assist with the guns, as the gunners cannot tell where our own men are.[32]
>
> We got the whole of High Wood yesterday by evening time. But about 23h30 I was woken up to tell me that the Hun had shelled it very heavily and counterattacked and that we had lost the Wood. I could not of course know whether we had lost the whole or only part, so I could not turn the guns on and had to wait till morning when I found that we were still holding a portion of it. So it has remained today and I am busy arranging to attack it again. We have arrived at the most intricate part of our operations. The Huns have fallen back and selected very cleverly sited positions where it is not possible or at any rate not easy to get observed artillery fire and the approaches are very open so it is difficult to get to close quarters. However we must press on and see what we can do. The weather is nice and fine again. The French did well yesterday, taking 2,900 prisoners south of the Somme.[33]

It was at this time that Fourth Army redrew its corps' boundaries resulting in Longueval becoming Horne's responsibility. In exchange he lost Bazentin-le-Petit village to III Corps. By now Horne's corps consisted of 5th, 7th, 33rd and 51st (Highland) Divisions, the last-named having replaced 21st Division. They were soon in action, relieving 33rd Division in and near High Wood on the night of 21/22 July.[34]

It was planned to resume attacks to loosen the German hold on High Wood and Longueval at 00h30 on the 23rd, following a bombardment which would begin at 19h00 the previous evening. The specific aims would be to secure the orchards at the northern end of Longueval, the whole of High Wood and the Switch Line on either side of it. As a preliminary, 5th Division were ordered to secure Wood Lane, which led up to the Switch Line east of High Wood, at 22h00. The start time of the main attack was postponed for an hour, to 01h30, to avoid any problems with III Corps' barrage, not due to lift until that time.

Both the preliminary and main attacks were total failures. The 5th Division were taken in enfilade by machine guns firing from the eastern end of High Wood and fell back with heavy losses. Two battalions of 154th Brigade of 51st Division, seeking to secure High Wood and the sector of the Switch Line to the northwest, were shelled and machine-gunned back to their start lines. The general failure was shared by XIII Corps' and Reserve Army's attacks on either side of XV Corps.[35] About this latest abortive effort Horne wrote:

> ... we are going for High Wood again tonight. We are in possession of half of it, but we want the rest badly. The German has brought up much more artillery during the last few days.[36]
>
> The weather here is dry but overcast all day. Most annoying as I cannot get full use out of the aeroplanes – it leaves me in the dark as to what the Hun is doing ... We have got a portion of High Wood but not all of it, and as things are now it is very difficult to get on any further. I puzzle my brains how to do it. We attacked again last night but it was not successful – the Hun has been reinforced to a considerable degree and has a strong position.[37]

The Fourth Army were already planning the next general assault. As a preliminary they instructed Horne to seize the German strongpoints at the eastern and western corners of High Wood, and connect them with a trench line. He was also told to capture the enemy strongpoints in the orchards north of Longueval. This piecemeal approach to the unfinished business of the Battle of Bazentin Ridge may have seemed a sensible way forward given the failure of an all-out approach. Both Haig and Rawlinson were worried about the threat of German counterattacks so long as Longueval and Delville Wood were not fully secured. The preliminary assault would therefore be enlarged into a joint XV and XIII Corps operation. The 2nd Division (XIII Corps) would assault the greater part of Delville Wood, while 5th Division would attack Longueval and the western part of the wood, now part of XV Corps' sector as a result of the realignment of corps' boundaries. The attack was timed to start at 07h10 on 27 July following an hour-long bombardment.[38]

The bombardment was strikingly effective, killing many Germans and persuading many others to surrender. The 2nd Division, when it advanced behind a creeping barrage, made good progress through the wood to within 50 yards of the northern edge, even though they suffered from enemy enfilade artillery fire. The

5th Division also made good progress through the western side of the wood, where they linked up with 2nd Division. Longueval proved more difficult and the northern part of the village remained in German hands, well protected by German machine guns which had survived the bombardment.

The following day was spent coping with heavy German artillery bombardments and counterattacks, which were only repulsed with difficulty. On the 29th, 5th Division made a further attempt to complete the capture of Longueval. Some progress was made but the job was not completed. To the west 51st Division set about implementing Fourth Army's order to reduce the German strongpoint at the eastern corner of High Wood. Horne had told Haig that he thought Major General Harper, the GOC of the 51st had been a little slow in getting on, but that he (Harper) knew his work.[39] The Highlanders stormed the strongpoint at 21h20, but were repulsed by heavy machine gun fire.[40]

On 29 July General Rawlinson had agreed to mount a joint attack with the French the next day between the Somme river and Guillemont. The Fourth Army part of this would fall to XIII Corps but Horne was ordered to assist his neighbouring corps with all available guns. He was also told once again to complete the clearance of the orchards north of Longueval and secure as much as possible of Wood Lane. A heavy British barrage which began at 16h45 on the 29th failed to subdue the German artillery which saturated Longueval and Delville Wood and disrupted British communications.

When 5th Division's infantry assault went in at 06h10 on the 30th it was broken up by concentrated machine gun and rifle fire. Following this failure, Horne told the Division's GOC that he must secure his objectives without delay. Major General Stephens responded that his brigades were too exhausted for a further effort, and another division should be given the task. Horne accordingly arranged for 17th Division to relieve the 5th.

At the same time 153rd Brigade renewed 51st Division's assault on the eastern strongpoint of High Wood as well as attacking Wood Lane. They were beaten back with heavy casualties. Horne tried to have the assault renewed at 21h45 but was told by Major General Harper that it was impractical. He told Horne that in his view only a massive bombardment with heavy guns would subdue the Germans holding High Wood.[41]

Apart from an attack by 17th Division on Orchard Trench (between Wood Lane and Delville Wood) which was repulsed with heavy losses, there was no major infantry effort from the British during the first week of August. The relative calm would be broken on 8–9 August by an attack by XIII Corps on Guillemont and Waterlot Farm. (This was to be the swan song of Lt General Congreve and his corps HQ as he was forced out by ill-health. Lt General the Earl of Cavan and XIV Corps took over on 10 August.) The XV Corps had not been involved in the XIII Corps operation; their time had been spent in preparation for future operations. The corps artillery concentrated on locating and eliminating German guns, and trenches and saps were pushed out towards future objectives.

The corps were once more in action on 18 August. The 14th (Light) Division, which had just joined Horne's command, attacked, after a 36 hour bombardment, on either side of Delville Wood, now wholly in Horne's sector as a result of further corps boundary adjustments. The 6th Bn Somerset Light Infantry captured and held Hop Alley and Beer Trench with relatively little loss. But 6th Bn Duke of Cornwall's Light Infantry, which initially captured Edge Trench, were bombed out of it with heavy losses by a German counterattack. To the north of Delville Wood, 7th Bn KRRC captured and pushed beyond Orchard Trench. On their left 7th Bn Rifle Brigade managed to secure only a small section of Wood Lane. The 33rd Division, who were attacking the northern sector of Wood Lane and the eastern edge of High Wood, failed to make any permanent progress. They did succeed initially in reaching Wood Lane Trench but were ousted by machine gun fire from High Wood. An innovative attempt to use burning oil drums and flame throwers in the attack on the wood did not work as planned; the flame throwers were buried by shellfire and the oil drums simply failed.[42]

Haig noted in his diary the failure of 33rd Division but expressed pleasure at the success of 14th Division south of Delville Wood. This had brought Fourth Army to within 200 yards of Ginchy. When coupled with the already secured station and quarry at Guillemont, this would be of considerable military value for the next advance. Haig also noted a drop in German morale; some of the prisoners had given sad accounts of their great losses.[43]

Over the next week Horne made a couple of attempts to improve his position in Delville Wood. The second of these made progress but was not entirely successful in clearing the wood. This would have to wait until an attack launched by 14th Division on 27th August which drove the Germans out of Edge Trench and allowed a barricade to be placed in Ale Alley, leaving Delville Wood completely in British hands.[44] Horne wrote:

> All went very well and we are now established on the far side of (Delville Wood) and I am glad as it was a source of anxiety and difficulty to me. The job was excellently done by the troops concerned and I am pleased.[45]
>
> The German infantry does not fight as they used to. It is only their artillery and machine guns which keep them going as well as they do.[46]

If Horne thought that his problems with Delville Wood were over he was in for an unpleasant surprise when on 31 August the Germans launched a counterattack in strength on XV Corps' positions in and to the north of the wood. Horne wrote the following day:

> The German counterattack yesterday was the heaviest they have delivered. It came all along my front and they pushed us back a little at two points. In both cases it is a nuisance as they are tenacious people and difficult to dislodge, but I hope to have them out again shortly. They put up a very heavy artillery fire against us yesterday, that was what caused the trouble.[47]

At the expense of heavy losses the Germans had succeeded in retaking Orchard Trench, part of Hop Alley, and all of Edge Trench, together with a small part of the north-eastern and eastern edge of the Wood. Horne's confidence that the setback would be only temporary did not prove entirely misplaced. By the following evening, some of the German gains had been retaken after hard fighting, largely by the newly arrived 24th Division. But the Germans remained in possession of the eastern part of the wood and Tea Trench north of Orchard Trench. It would not be until 6 September that the German gains were more or less eliminated.[48]

At the same time as trying to rectify the damage done by the German counter-attack, Horne was mounting an operation to capture the village of Ginchy as part of the wider Battle of Guillemont. A first attack was launched at 11h55 on 3 September after an hour's bombardment. Subsequent attacks secured parts of the German trench system. 'A' Company of 1st Bn Royal Welsh Fusiliers got into the northern part of the village, never to be heard from again. Two other battalions got toeholds on the eastern and south-eastern edges of the village but were forced out by counterattacks. The end of the day found the Germans still in complete posses-sion of the village.[49] Horne's claim in the following extract was therefore not correct.

> Yesterday was a successful day but at the same time disappointing as it was nearly a *very* successful day. There was an attack on quite a wide front. I had a very difficult job, the attack on Ginchy with my left flank exposed. However it was necessary to undertake an attack on Ginchy in order to take Guillemont which has been giving a strong resistance and was very important. All went well to begin with and my neighbours on the right (XIV Corps) took Guillemont all right. We got right into Ginchy but the battalion on the left which had the difficult task of forming the left flank was held up and the result was that we were counterattacked and driven out of a good part of Ginchy. We held on however to the southern end and today we are still in the village and a further attack is now being made. But once you are close quarters with the Germans in a village or a wood it becomes very difficult to turn them out as you cannot use the guns for fear of hitting your own men.[50]

The next few days were to prove very frustrating for Horne. A series of attacks were mounted; some succeeded in getting into the village, but none secured a permanent lodging in the face of invariably successful German counterattacks. By the night of 7/8 September a thoroughly exhausted 7th Division, which had also been trying to restore Delville Wood fully to British possession, was relieved by 55th Division, and 16th Irish Division of XIV Corps. The Irish were ordered to take Ginchy on the 9th and succeeded in doing so despite heavy casualties in the 6 battalions involved. On the same day Horne's troops secured the eastern end of Delville Wood but made little impression on the German-held Beer Trench and Ale Alley.[51]

While these efforts to clear up the loose ends of the Battle of Bazentin Ridge were continuing, planning was well-advanced for the next major set piece battle of the Somme campaign, to be launched on 15 September. It was to be remembered best for the sensational first appearance of the tank on a battlefield.

Chapter XI

Corps Commander: The Somme: Flers-Courcelette

Planning for the attack later known as the Battle of Flers-Courcelette had begun in August. Its timing was set for mid-September when the highly secret new weapon, the Tank, was expected to be available in sufficient numbers to make an impact. The Fourth Army would play the main part but General Gough's Reserve Army would also have an important role.

Just as at Bazentin Ridge, there was a significant divergence between Haig's and Rawlinson's perceptions of the aims of the battle and how it should be fought. This time, however, Haig's views would prevail. Rawlinson conceived the battle as 3 successive night operations which would capture the German defence lines from Morval in the east through Gueudecourt in the centre to the outskirts of Martinpuich in the west. Rawlinson thought that a series of night attacks would prolong the surprise impact of the tank; they would go in each night and be withdrawn before dawn. With luck the enemy would not work out for a time what they were up against.

Rawlinson's perception was essentially of a bite and hold operation; Haig's was much more ambitious. He wanted a powerful daylight assault aimed at setting up a defensive flank from Morval to Bapaume, with the main thrust to the north to cut off the German troops facing the Reserve Army between Pozières and Serre. Once again the cavalry featured strongly in Haig's concept, which foresaw a resumption of the war of movement. Once the enemy's main defences had been breached, 5 cavalry divisions would pass through and seize the high ground between Bapaume and Roquigny, northeast of Morval, and hold it until relieved by the infantry. They would then prey on the German lines of communication seeking to cause maximum disruption. GHQ's directive laid great emphasis on boldness.[1]

> All arrangements are to be made with a view to overwhelming the enemy at the outset by a powerful assault and following up every advantage gained with rapidity and vigour. The exploitation of success to the full during the first few hours is essential to a decision and it must be impressed on all Corps and Divisional Commanders that the situation calls for great boldness and determination on their part. It lies with them to feel the pulse of the battle and to turn favourable opportunities at once to the fullest account. In particular it is of great importance to reach the enemy's artillery positions quickly and capture his guns. Risks must be minimised not by declining to accept them but by skilful handling of reserves. The necessity for great vigour and determination in this attack, and the great results that may be achieved by it, must be impressed on all ranks as soon as considerations of secrecy will permit of their being informed of what is required of them. It will also be necessary then to impress on all leaders that the slow methods of trench warfare are unsuited to

the style of operations they will be called on to undertake after the enemy has been driven from his prepared lines of defence.[2]

The calls for boldness at senior levels of command clearly reflected a sense of what might have been had such enterprise been evident at earlier crucial stages of the Somme battle, like Mametz Wood and High Wood. The directive was also implicitly setting great store on the impact of the first appearance of the tank to overcome the problems of achieving the elusive breakthrough.

In line with Haig's wishes, and fully reflecting his call for vigour and boldness, Rawlinson submitted revised proposals which set the villages of Sapignies, Achiet-le-Grand and Miraumont as the ultimate targets for the main northwards thrust. Four successive objectives, well short of these villages but nevertheless still ambitious, were specified for the first morning.[3] Detailed planning was however complicated by 2 concerns. First, that III, XV and XIV Corps, on which the brunt of the forthcoming battle would fall, were still engaged in fighting on their fronts as they sought to expel the enemy from areas which should already have been secured. Second, the question of how to integrate tanks into the overall operation.

There is still an ongoing debate over whether tanks should have been committed to battle at all until they were more mechanically reliable and available in sufficient numbers to exploit to the full the shock effect their sudden and totally unforeseen eruption was bound to have. Leaving this issue aside there were more mundane questions which had to be addressed by Rawlinson and his senior subordinates. These officers had been made fully aware of the new weapon and had, at least briefly, seen it demonstrated. But there had been little time or opportunity to examine the options for their use and to determine how to maximise their effectiveness.

Prior to their introduction, an advance in single line abreast had been posited. This was rejected in favour of a diamond formation, which in turn was discarded for the forthcoming battle in favour of a single file advance in lines of 3 tanks. On the assumption that they would move ahead of the infantry, lanes would be left for them in the otherwise blanket artillery creeping barrage (which would have the inevitable effect of leaving some enemy positions untouched if there was a no-show by the tanks). The new weapon was seen essentially as infantry support. The latter were left in no doubt that they were to get on with their tasks willy-nilly should the tanks break down or fall behind.[4]

Formal orders for the battle were issued on 11 September. The following day, General Horne told a XV Corps conference that when the general attack was launched he proposed to clear up the situation east of Delville Wood. The awkward re-entrant in his line there, caused by the continued German possession of Hop Alley and Ale Alley, was liable to hamper both his own right and XIV Corps' left. He would use 2 tanks for this purpose. 'Liable to hamper' was perhaps an understatement; from these positions German machine guns would be able to enfilade very effectively British advances on either side.[5]

Aside from the clearance operation, XV Corps' 4 objectives for the first stage of the battle were, successively, the German forward defences and Switch line (codenamed Green Line); the German 3rd position in front of Flers (Brown Line); the village of Flers (Blue Line). Once the fourth objective, the village of Gueudecourt and its defences, was taken Horne's troops were to form a northwest

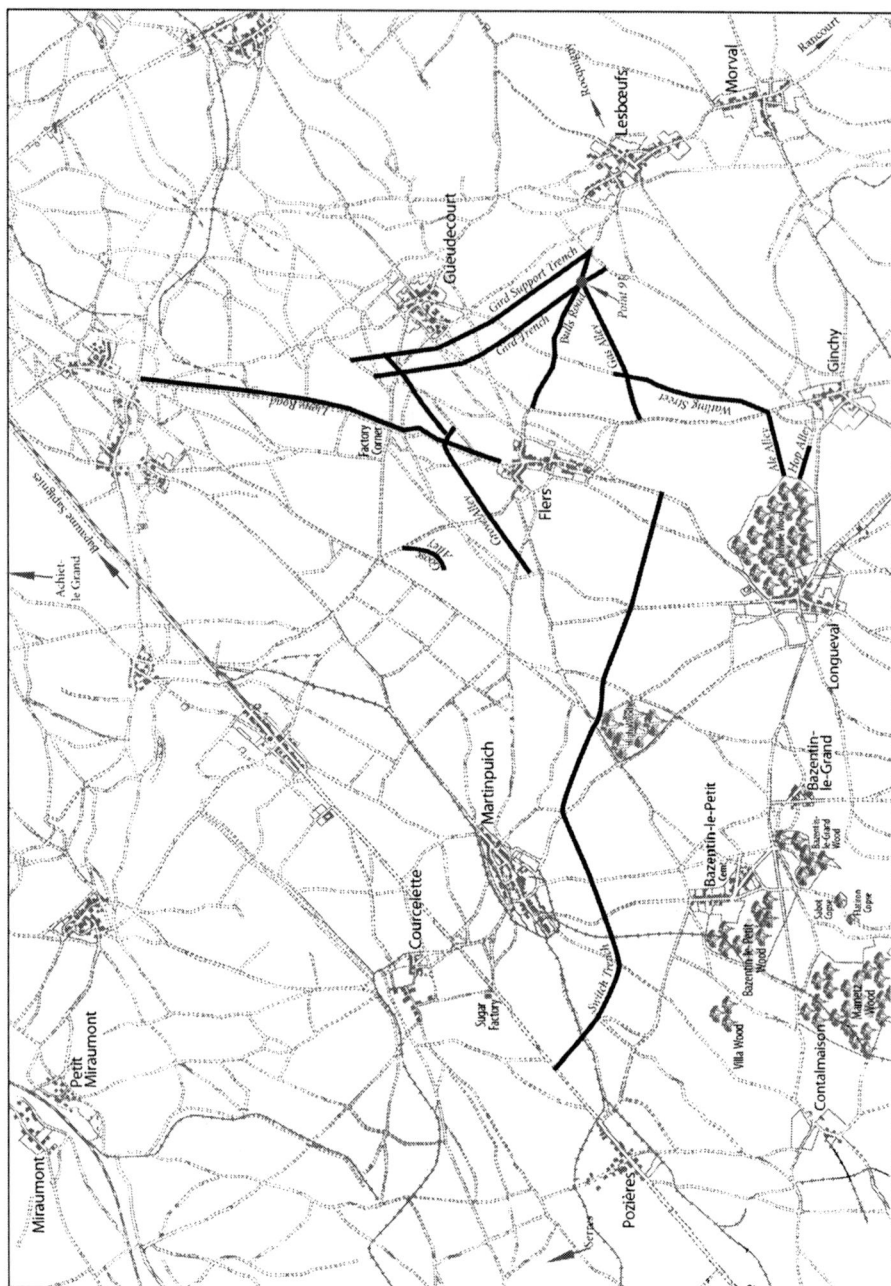

Map 10: The Somme: Flers-Courcelette: September 1916

facing flank between Gueudecourt and the German 3rd position beyond Flers (Red Line). From their starting positions just north of Delville Wood, the north-easterly advance to their fourth objective would represent for XV Corps (and XIV Corps to their east) a breakthrough of the enemy defences on a frontage of nearly three and a half miles. If the attackers could reach and consolidate their fourth objective by midday, there would be 8 hours of daylight left to exploit the success. Two cavalry divisions would be on standby to advance with the least possible delay.

Horne would commit 3 divisions to the battle. Two of them were new to his command. From right to left as they lined up they were the 14th (Light), the 41st and the New Zealanders. The 14th Division, which had already served Horne well at Delville Wood, had been on the Western Front since May 1915 and had previously seen bitter action in the Ypres Salient. The 41st were a New Army division. Most of the battalions carried the names of London and south-eastern county regiments. The New Zealand Division had arrived in France covered in glory from the forlorn Gallipoli campaign of the previous year. They would be the first Empire troops to serve under Horne thus beginning his association with Empire formations which was to bring great credit to his commands.

The XV Corps, which were to provide the main thrust of the overall attack, were allocated 18 tanks, 10 of which were given to 41st Division in the centre of the corps' sector. They were to be largely deployed to deal with Flers village and nearby German strongpoints and sunken roads. The remaining 8 were allocated equally to the other 2 divisions. In all, 14 of these tanks made it to the start line.

Zero Hour for the main assault would be 06h20 on 15 September.[6] But as all previous attempts to dislodge the Germans from their little salient to the east of Delville Wood had failed, Horne ordered a preliminary operation to be launched 50 minutes prior to the main attack. This fell to 2 companies of 6th Bn KOYLI (43rd Brigade), who were supposed to be supported by 2 of the tanks allocated to 14th Division, plus 1 tank borrowed from XIV Corps. Only one of these tanks, D1, made it to the start line, thus making history as the first tank ever to go into action. It was fairly quickly put out of action but it did help the KOYLI, despite the loss of all their officers, to eliminate the German salient.[7] Tragically the shell which did for D1 was almost certainly British.

The preliminary bombardment for the main attack had begun at 06h00 on 12 September. At Zero Hour a creeping barrage was laid down just in front of the British trenches while an intensive stationary barrage hit the first objective. On the right 14th Division were due to advance northeast for a total of 4,400 yards, bypassing Flers to the east and going on to take Gueudecourt. The New Zealanders were due to bypass Flers on the other side before helping to form the flank to the west of Gueudecourt. The 41st Division were due to take Flers before also forming a flank north and west of Gueudecourt.

The performance of the tanks might best be described as good in parts. Some of those that got past the start line were quickly disabled, either by enemy guns, by mechanical failure or by becoming ditched in the cratered landscape. Where this happened the attacking infantry almost invariably suffered at the hands of German strongpoints left undealt with. Not sufficiently in the early stages to pin them down, but nevertheless leading to severe losses. Those tanks that did engage the enemy proved of invaluable assistance to the infantry in doing precisely what had been intended of them – flattening barbed wire and engaging and silencing field artillery batteries and machine guns.

One of the tanks assigned to 14th Division, D5 Dolphin, was to travel 4,800 yards before being destroyed by a German shell. This was the longest distance recorded that day by a tank. It reached a point between the third and fourth objectives just south of Gueudecourt, outrunning all but a handful of infantry, before turning back. It had provided material help to the advancing infantry and its retirement effectively brought to an end the infantry's capacity to get forward. Having overwhelmed the German battery responsible for the demise of D5, the infantry dug in just south of Bulls Road, their third objective.

The 4 tanks assigned to the New Zealand Division were late arriving and the 2 attacking battalions set off without them. The tanks soon caught up and helped mop up resistance in the enemy trenches. When tank D10 was put out of action by shellfire, tank D11 took over its role and flattened German wire which was holding up the infantry's advance on the New Zealand left. With this dealt with, the infantry were quickly able to reach their third objective. On the right of the New Zealand advance things were going less smoothly as elements were being sucked into the outskirts of the village of Flers. A second tank, D12, fell victim to enemy shell fire, but D11 was able to help the infantry overcome a German strongpoint and resume their advance north towards the fourth objective. However they found themselves increasingly exposed and subject to counterattack and were forced back. D11 earned the great appreciation of the New Zealanders by apparently ignoring an order to withdraw to stay with them to help fight off any counterattack that might be launched against their flank.

Five of 41st Division's 10 tanks failed to make it much beyond the starting line. The initial infantry assault was to be undertaken by 2 battalions each from 124th Brigade on the right and 122nd Brigade on the left. As soon as they left the shelter of their trenches the attacking battalions came under withering fire from German guns sited behind their front line, which had been destroyed by the British bombardment. A sixth tank, D15, soon became a casualty, but the remaining 4 pushed on. One of these, D17, caught up with the infantry pinned down in front of the German wire protecting Flers. Crushing the wire, the commander placed his tank astride the Flers Line where it crossed the road in front of the village and enfiladed the occupants. German resistance melted away and the infantry were able to follow D17 into the village. This event was famously recorded in a message delivered by an RFC aircraft observing the scene; 'A tank is walking up the High Street of Flers with the British army cheering behind.'

D17 soon outran the infantry and turned back. The Germans subjected the village to a heavy bombardment which led to a great deal of confusion and forced some, but not all, of the infantry to retreat south of the village. Order was later restored and troops pushed forward through the village to occupy the third objective on its northern edge.

The other 3 tanks still in action had an adventurous time. Two of them, to the west of Flers, helped the infantry to subdue a German defensive pocket northeast of the village and to resist enemy counterattacks. D6 took on 2 enemy batteries to the east and north of Flers as it headed towards Gueudecourt. It was destroyed by the latter battery.[8]

To the right of Horne's corps, XIV Corps attacked with 3 divisions supported by 16 tanks. The results were to prove disappointing largely as a consequence of the failure of 6th Division in the centre of the attack. The division were supposed to capture Morval, but were held up by a German strongpoint known as the Quadrilateral about 400 yards from their starting line. The tanks, which might have made light work of reducing the Quadrilateral, had failed to materialise. No progress could be made without them despite the brave efforts of the infantry.

The failure to subdue the German strongpoint left the divisions on either side vulnerable to enfilade fire and infiltration, and they suffered accordingly. The 56th Division on the right did however make fair progress in masking off Combles by occupying some of the enemy's trenches west of the village. They were helped in this by 2 of the 3 tanks allotted to them. The help came to an end when the tanks were put out of action, one through ditching and the other by shellfire. The infantry then came under fire from the Quadrilateral.

The Guards Division on the left were to advance 3,600 yards northeast from Ginchy through and beyond the village of Lesboeufs. This would take them past enemy positions on both their left (Pint Trench) and their right (Straight Trench, behind the Quadrilateral and unsubdued by 6th Division). Although 7 of the allotted 10 tanks crossed the start line, they seemed to lose all sense of direction and were of no help to the Guards, who were soon taking heavy casualties, especially among the officers. The Guards themselves became disorientated and at one stage were under the impression that they had already passed through Lesboeufs. Realising this was not the case, they continued to move ahead, but in ever diminishing numbers until they were too weak to make further progress.[9]

To the left of Horne's troops, III Corps also attacked on a 3 divisional front. On the right 47th (London) Division was tasked with the capture of High Wood, still in German hands 2 months after XV and XIII Corps' advanced patrols had found it empty. While the wood remained in German hands progress to the west would be prevented by enfilade fire from it, as 50th (Northumbrian) Division were to find out. Of the 4 tanks assigned to the Londoners, only 1 proved to be briefly effective before it was hit by shellfire. One of the others lost its bearings and fired on its own side. Their misfortune could largely be put down to their being ordered to advance through the wood, hardly ideal tank country. The failure of the tanks compounded the infantry's problems, already significant through the decision not to lay on an artillery bombardment because of the close proximity of the German and British front lines in the wood.

The infantry suffered heavy casualties initially as they attempted to get forward unsupported. They made no progress until, in an attempt to break the deadlock, a mortar bombardment was ordered for 11h40. This finally broke the resistance of the German defenders, the survivors surrendering en masse. High Wood was at last in British hands. To the left of the Londoners, the Northumbrian Division had made no progress against the enfilade fire from High Wood and by 10h30 they had been ordered to curtail their operations.

The left hand division of III Corps' attack were the 15th (Scottish). They were supported by only one tank, the survivor of a pair, which nevertheless did excellent work mopping up the German trenches. Such was the infantry's enthusiasm that they ran into their own creeping barrage as they rapidly advanced into and through the village of Martinpuich. Possession of this village had been deemed indispensable to the operations of the Reserve Army to the west of the Scots.[10]

The Reserve Army's task was the capture of the village of Courcelette. Newly arrived on the Somme, the Canadian Corps were given the job. Their British GOC, Lieutenant General Sir Julian Byng, assigned it to his 2nd and 3rd Divisions. All 7 tanks allotted to the Reserve Army were put at 2nd Division's disposal. It was planned that they would precede the infantry, but preparations were slightly disrupted by German bombardments in support of bombing raids designed to secure prisoners. The raids were beaten off, the last one at dawn, and the 6 battalion Canadian assault was able to go in on schedule behind a creeping barrage. Good progress was made; an intermediate objective, the Sugar Factory, was taken by 07h00 and preparations begun for the advance on Courcelette. The tanks had played little part as they had been outpaced by the infantry. They had however been instrumental in persuading Germans in overrun and bypassed positions to surrender. The attack on Courcelette went in at 18h15 and the village was completely in Canadian hands 45 minutes later. Meanwhile 3rd Canadian Division attacked westwards and seized a number of German trenches.[11]

On XV Corps' front, Horne had learned that by just after 10h00 his infantry were advancing towards their third objectives along the whole corps front. It was however becoming apparent that the fourth objective was likely to prove an objective too far. At 14h40 Horne told the GOCs of 14th and 41st Divisions that the corps artillery would begin a fresh bombardment of Gueudecourt village and the Gird trenches protecting it. He would give them 2 to 3 hours' notice if a fresh advance were to be ordered. Immediately afterwards he issued orders that all units should consolidate on their third objectives.

Horne then contacted Fourth Army HQ and told them that he proposed to renew the attack at 17h00. He asked if the reserve brigades of his divisions should be used as he only had one division in reserve. General Rawlinson's response was to cancel any planned further attacks that day by Fourth Army units; at 15h45 all the attacking divisions were instructed to link up securely and consolidate on their third objectives. All tanks still operational were ordered to return to base to prepare for action the next day when the advance might resume. Predictably the Germans took advantage of the respite to trickle forward reinforcements into the Gird Trenches, from where they mounted several unsuccessful counterattacks.

From Fourth Army's perspective the results of the first day of the battle were clearly disappointing. Instead of being on their fourth objectives by noon, the troops had only attained their third objectives on a front of 4,500 yards when the fighting died down for the day. Both XV and XIV Corps still had work to do to complete the capture of those parts of the German defences covering Morval, Lesboeufs and Gueudecourt. No breakthrough was conceivable while these localities remained in enemy hands. General Rawlinson realised that the initial impetus of the attack was spent and the shock effect of the tanks dissipated. Reserves would need to be committed if the attack were to be continued, given the heavy losses sustained on the first day. Nevertheless orders were issued for the resumption of operations at 09h25 on 16 September.[12]

Horne's letter of 16 September to his wife reviewed the previous day's events:

Yesterday the villages of Flers, Martinpuich and Courcelette were all taken, the first one by my men. We are pushing ahead again this morning and I hope for further success as the Germans must be very much rattled. My troops did splendidly. The New Zealanders did well for me, 41st Division did very good work – they took Flers. Also my other lot, who are old and well-tried friends. The Gunners did splendid work. Had there not been some obstruction in the south towards Combles we should have got on further still. The French are also pushing ahead.[13]

The attempts to retrieve the shortcomings of the first day of the battle were to prove almost entirely unproductive, beyond adding substantially to Horne's corps' casualty figures. Only a handful of tanks were available to support the attacks and, unusually for troops under Horne's command, the infantry were to suffer from inadequate to non-existent artillery support. With the exception of the New Zealand Division, the infantry attacks gave the impression of being ill-conceived, ill-reconnoitred and ill-supported. As usual it would be the infantry which would pay the price.

The New Zealanders decided on a one battalion attack. It was to be supported by Tank D11, which had stayed with the New Zealanders overnight in contravention of the order to return to base. While waiting in their trenches for Zero Hour, the New Zealand battalion were attacked by a force of 500 Germans who, unfortunately for them, had to cross open ground as they advanced. They were cut down by the New Zealanders' and D11's machine guns. Very soon after the New Zealand attack began, D11, moving forward in support, was hit by an enemy shell and immobilised, although it continued for a time to fire its guns. The New Zealand battalion rapidly secured their assigned sector of Grove Alley, to the west of Ligny Road. Plans for further advances were cancelled in the light of developments to their right.

These developments involved 41st Division and, in particular, 64th Brigade from 21st Division, which had been attached to the 41st, to carry out the required advance over the Gird Trenches to Gueudecourt. The Brigade Commander, Brigadier General Headlam, had only learned of his unit's assignment at a late night meeting at 41st Division's headquarters in Albert. Although he was able to warn his battalion commanders orally by 01h30, written orders were not issued until after 05h00. These had to be hastily revised when it was thought, erroneously as it turned out, that the units engaged the previous day had withdrawn to points south of the planned starting line. With the usual confusion endemic in any attempt to set things up in a hurry in battlefield conditions, the attacking battalions found themselves moving up to their assembly positions in daylight and without the protection of an artillery bombardment. Moving across open ground east of Flers, they were subjected to enemy machine gun and artillery fire.

The attack nevertheless went in, supported by 2 tanks which had ditched the previous day and been recovered. Unfortunately, they were quickly put out of action by German shells. The infantry attack faltered through a combination of exhaustion and heavy casualties. Orders were issued postponing any further attack to 16h30, later further postponed to 18h30. As orders for this only reached Brigadier General Headlam at 17h25 there could be no question of organising it in the time available; the attack was abandoned. Much of the blame for the tragic fiasco of the day's events must be attached to 41st Division which initially led Horne to believe that they could carry out the planned attack from their own resources. Only belatedly did they change their mind and ask for the operation to be assigned elsewhere. Hence the lateness in handing the task to 64th Brigade.

To the east of the unfortunate 64th Brigade were 43rd Brigade of 14th Division. They were tasked with assaulting the Gird Line and capturing Gueudecourt. They would assault on either side of Watling Street from starting points on both sides of Bulls Road. The root cause of the brigade's failure to achieve any of their objectives appears to have been the lack of adequate support from the artillery. The pre-attack bombardment, which began at 06h00, was described as 'desultory and too scanty to be effective'. Between 09h00 and the launching of the attack 25 minutes later, when it should have been at its most intense, it was said to 'have slackened off very considerably and until about 09h15 few shots were fired. To the left of our line the bombardment had been even weaker.[14] The effect was to leave the enemy wire and trenches largely undamaged. Just as disastrously, the creeping barrage failed; although fired it did not creep, The enemy machine guns were not neutralised. There were no tanks available to support the attack.

The infantry assault nevertheless began on schedule. It was very soon in trouble from machine gun and rifle fire, both enfilade and from in front. Despite heavy casualties some of the troops managed to occupy a trench just short of Gird Trench itself. Here they clung on as attempts were made to get the artillery to eliminate the German strongpoints which were preventing any serious advance by the attackers. These attempts appear to have been largely unavailing, mainly through communications breakdowns. Even where bombardments were organised, they appear to have been ineffective. With the survivors of the attacking battalions pinned down, the Brigade Commander received orders to renew the attack at 18h55 after a bombardment beginning at 18h30. Although this bombardment was a little more effective, it still failed to eliminate vital German strongpoints. The renewed attack was a predictable failure despite the courage displayed by exhausted troops. The brigade had suffered over 1,400 casualties.[15]

The following day 14th and 41st Divisions were relieved by 21st and 55th Divisions respectively. The next major attack was first planned for 18 September but was successively postponed to the 21st and then the 25th. The delays were partially caused by the increasingly wet weather. But they also gave the time for artillery ammunition to be replenished and for the operation to be synchronised with French plans. This hiatus did not prevent bitterly fought minor operations taking place as Horne's front line troops sought to eliminate German strongpoints and trenches which had given serious trouble on the first 2 days of the battle. The New Zealanders spent 3 days capturing Goose Alley, a German trench northwest of Flers, and holding it against determined counterattacks. Less successful were 21st Division's attempts to clear Gas Alley and Point 91 at its junction with Bulls Road, despite the heavy casualties suffered by 1st Lincolns and 13th Northumberland Fusiliers. Here again deficiencies in the artillery barrage compounded the infantry's problems, inaccuracy rather than inadequacy being the failing this time.[16]

The tasks facing Horne's Corps on 25 September were essentially those remaining unfinished from the 15th and 16th, the capture of Gird and Gird

Support Trenches and Gueudecourt village. These tasks would fall to 21st Division on the right and 55th Division in the centre. On 55th Division's left, the New Zealanders were ordered to attack north-westward from Grove Alley to form a defensive flank between Factory Corner and Goose Alley, which fed into Gird Trench further north. Unlike their comrades on their right they were to achieve their objectives quickly and relatively painlessly in a 3 battalion attack conducted with great Élan.

On XV Corps' other flank 2 brigades of 21st Division would participate in the attack. The 64th Brigade would attack north-eastwards towards Gird Trench from positions astride Bulls Road. From positions north of Bulls Road and west of Watling Street, 110th Brigade would attack north and north-eastwards on lines that would take them over the Gird Trenches and into Gueudecourt. When 64th Brigade's 2 battalions attacked at Zero Hour, 12h35, they immediately came under heavy machine gun fire and found themselves pinned down in front of uncut enemy wire. The survivors were forced to remain there until nightfall.

The 110th Brigade's 2 battalions likewise found the enemy ready for them; a well-targeted artillery barrage caught them as they crossed No Man's Land. The survivors of the right-hand battalion (9th Leicesters) nevertheless managed to seize part of Gird Trench but then found themselves being enfiladed by machine guns to their right. The intensity of the enemy's fire pinned down attempts by support troops to get forward. The left-hand battalion (8th Leicesters), by dint of veering left of their planned line, fared a little better and managed to get a good number of troops into Gird Trench. From there some may have got into Gueudecourt itself. Realising that a gap had opened up between them and their sister battalion they attempted to close up in Gird Trench. But a German counterattack eliminated 9th Leicester's toehold in the trench, and put their own under threat, before they managed to block any further enemy progress.

The 21st Division had been allocated 2 tanks for their attack. One of these had ditched. Horne decided that the other should be used to help clear Point 91, at the junction of Gas Alley and Bulls Road, which had caused grief on the first days of the battle and was continuing to do so. He was keen for the attempt to be made that day, but the GOC of 21st Division was able to persuade him that his men were in no fit state to mount a further attack so soon. The attempt was postponed until the next day.

The failure to complete the capture of the Gird Trenches caused difficulties on XIV Corps' left flank. Despite these, they were able finally to seize and secure their principal objectives, the villages of Morval and Lesboeufs.[17] Further to the east the French took Rancourt. Horne wrote:

> A big battle again today and up to now (14h50) it has gone well. I hope that I shall have got Gueudecourt or at any rate the system of German trenches which defend it. I hope also that [XIV Corps] may get Les Boeufs and Morval, and the French report that they have taken Rancourt so all goes well. Please God we may be able to stand the counterattacks and hold on all right. I trust however to the artillery to cover the front and keep the enemy off.
>
> (18h00) The fight has gone well on the whole and we will finish off the odd bit tonight, I hope. We have not got into Gueudecourt, but we have the trenches round it.[18]

The 26 September would finally see the capture of Gueudecourt. This was in no small part due to the intervention of a new tank, D4, which got astride Gird Trench after setting out from Flers. It forced those Germans who were not killed by its guns, or by those of a strafing RFC aircraft, or by bombing parties of 7th Leicesters, to surrender. The loss of the Gird Trenches apparently persuaded the Germans that the village was no longer tenable. As they withdrew, infantry patrols and later cavalry, fighting dismounted, moved in. The village was fully secured by 19h00. The seizure of the village of Combles by XIV Corps and the French capped a relatively successful day for Fourth Army.[19] General Haig recorded the day's events in his diary.

> The Battle was continued on the Fourth Army front and at 12h30 the Reserve Army began an attack on Thiepval Ridge by parts of 4 divisions. Their troops were everywhere successful.
>
> By 09h00 it was reported that our patrols were in Combles village. The French sent in patrols from the southeast. The enemy had withdrawn most of his garrison so the village was soon in our possession.
>
> A strong redoubt which was holding out between Lesboeufs and Gueudecourt was captured easily this morning. A tank was sent against it and an aeroplane flew over at about 500 ft elevation. The enemy at once held up his hands.
>
> Thiepval Village was taken by the 18th Division (Maxse) and the 11th Division on the right got the high ground east of it, including Zollern Redoubt. The Canadians, further on the right, attacked and gained the ridge Southwest of Courcelette village, which they also hold.
>
> I saw General Horne at Heilly. He confirmed Cavan's (GOC-in-C, XIV Corps) statement that losses were small. The 21st Division had one Brigade which suffered because [of] its attack on the Redoubt Southeast of Gueudecourt.
>
> Southeast of Gueudecourt today, enemy counterattacked in force. Over 100 guns were turned on him and he literally ran away, throwing down his arms. We now have the observation which makes so much difference to the success of our operations.[20]

The aims of the battle had by now been largely, if belatedly, achieved. But there remained some work to be done and this was undertaken by 55th and New Zealand Divisions which launched an attack at 14h15 the following day against the Gird Trench between Gueudecourt and the Trench's junction with Goose Alley, well to the northwest of the village. The 55th Division were fully successful but one of the New Zealand battalions sustained severe losses. The Germans remained in possession of the Trench-Alley junction. An attempt to renew the assault the following day was cancelled when a tank, which was supposed to offer support, failed to arrive and the New Zealanders were heavily shelled as they moved up. The battle was effectively over.[21]

The battle ended just as Horne's tenure of command of XV Corps also came to an end. On 28 September, Horne handed over command to Lieutenant General J Du Cain and took his leave. The following day he arrived at First Army headquarters at Lillers where, on 30 September, he formally assumed command.

The vacancy at the head of First Army had arisen when, at the beginning of August, Haig had received instructions to inform its Commander, General Sir Charles Monro, that he was being appointed temporary Commander-in-Chief of the Indian Army. When informed, Monro was predictably reluctant to go. He was fully aware that reputations in this war would be made on the Western Front and seldom elsewhere, and he feared, with reason, that his temporary appointment would prove to be permanent. But there was nothing to be done; his move had been decreed by the new Secretary of State for War, David Lloyd George.

Haig asked Monro for his recommendation on who should act as Commander of First Army until his return. Monro suggested Lieutenant General Sir Richard Haking, GOC-in-C XI Corps, the choice of whom Haig thoroughly approved.[22] Haking was, Haig thought, his sort of general, aggressive and thrusting. Haking deplored the live-and-let-live attitude which had inevitably begun to permeate the officers and men manning the Western Front as the realisation grew that trench warfare was becoming the norm. He believed that this could, and should, be overcome by ensuring that the troops were regularly ordered to attack, thus inculcating an offensive and aggressive spirit into them. In what passed for normal conditions at the front, this meant frequent trench raids and not just leaving it to the artillery to carry the war to the enemy.

Opportunities for even greater bursts of aggression were provided by the BEF's set piece attacks. At Aubers Ridge in May 1915 Haking had to be ordered by his corps commander not to renew an attack by his !st Division after their initial assault had ended in failure and chaos. By the Battle of Loos in September 1915 Haking, now a Lieutenant General, was in command of XI Corps which was given the role of GHQ reserve. Field Marshal French was to take most of the blame for the mishandling of the commitment to the battle of the corps' inexperienced New Army 21st and 24th Divisions. But the Army Commander, General Haig, and Haking were also not without fault. There is no suggestion that Haking tried to protect his vulnerable divisions from the manifest shortcomings surrounding their participation. Both suffered very heavy casualties and achieved nothing.

Although not directly involved in the Battle of the Somme, Haking proposed that his corps should undertake an attack designed to pin down German reserves and prevent their transfer to the Somme battlefield. His Army Commander, by now General Monro, did not like the plan and wanted to cancel it, but was overridden by Haig. Haking's idea was to capture the German positions between Aubers Ridge and the village of Fromelles. Following a 3-day bombardment, the attack, involving the 61st and Australian 5th Divisions, went in on 19 July 1916. After 2 days of severe fighting the attack was called off. It had achieved nothing beyond heavy casualties in the attacking divisions. It also began the process of Australian disillusionment with British generalship on the Western Front. No admirers of this and British staff work after their experiences in Gallipoli, the Australians were only too ready to fear something similar for them in this new theatre of war. They had been given ample justification for their fears.

It is perhaps surprising that only a few days after the Fromelles fiasco, General Monro was prepared to recommend Haking as his temporary successor. As Haking's immediate superior, some of the mud attaching to Fromelles had stuck to him and may have been partly responsible for London choosing him to go to India.

Possibly he realised that Haking was the sort of general, regardless of results, that Haig admired. Fortunately for Henry Horne's future prospects, this admiration was not shared by the authorities in London.

Haig first realised that something was wrong when he received letters from the Military Secretary at the War Office and the CIGS, General Sir William Robertson, telling him that the War Committee did not sanction General Haking's appointment to command First Army 'in succession' to General Monro. On one of the rare occasions when the CIGS was not fully supportive of Haig, Robertson wrote that he could not support Haking's appointment and nor would the Secretary of State and the Prime Minister. In his diary Haig recorded:

> I did not appoint him "in succession" but to "act temporarily" in Monro's absence. No other Corps Commander, who is fit for it, is available, e.g. Byng, Horne, Cavan. I reply pointing out misunderstanding. I am afraid the WO willing(ly) misread my letter or telegram, and an effort to limit my powers of appointment are (sic) noticeable.[23]

Robertson's letter alluded to above had continued:

> You may reckon on Monro not returning. We are sending you four names to choose from. I think the best selection would be Cavan or Horne, in this order, unless you feel you can rely upon Wilson. He undoubtedly has the necessary ability but of course other qualifications are necessary. I doubt if Birdwood is up to an Army, and he is wanted for the Australians. It is awkward having to move Horne now, but you have other good men to put in his place. I have the highest opinion of Cavan, and should myself select him. But any of the four you like.[24]

Haig received a telegram from the War Office confirming that Monro's appointment to India would be permanent. He wasted no time in informing Haking that the Home Authorities would not confirm him in his appointment, but that he should remain in temporary command until the Battle of the Somme had ended and it might be possible to spare someone to take over.[25] Haig quickly decided to recommend Horne to London and was able to tell him on 20 August that the Cabinet had approved his appointment to command the First Army. He also told Horne that in his opinion it was in the interest of the Somme operation that he should continue to command XV Corps until a decision in the battle had been reached. Horne readily agreed and told Haig that he would prefer to finish this fight as a corps commander, but was ready to do whatever Haig judged best.[26]

During their earlier correspondence over the Monro succession Robertson had recommended to Haig that General J Du Cain should be given a corps. He was soon nominated as Horne's successor. In mid-September he was attached to XV Corps headquarters. On 26 September Horne told Haig that Du Cain was quite fit to take over command of XV Corps forthwith and that this might be a favourable time for him to hand over.[27] Two days later Horne was on his way.

Horne's elevation to army command had been remarkably rapid. He had commanded a corps in action for only 12 weeks, a period in which it could hardly be claimed that he had demonstrated the outstanding gifts for high command that would have set him head and shoulders above his peers. But nor had any of his rivals particularly distinguished themselves, or were that much more greatly experienced. He was fortunate that Haking was *persona non grata* in the War Office because, almost certainly, despite Haig's bluster about 'succession' and 'temporary command', he would have been the Commander-in-Chief's first choice for the vacancy. At the same time, Haig would not have been too sorry to have been forced into choosing Horne. His faith in his abilities was unshaken, despite the disappointments at Mametz Wood, High Wood and Gueudecourt. Horne now had the opportunity to prove that his Commander-in-Chief's faith was not misplaced.

Chapter XII

The 'Creeping Barrage'

From the day of his entry into the Royal Military Academy at Woolwich until he took over command of 2nd Division at the start of 1915, Henry Horne's career had been exclusively focused on gunnery in all its aspects. Until the advent of trench warfare, at about the same time as Horne ceased to be a gunnery specialist, the concept of the role of artillery on the battlefield had undergone little change from that ruling at the time Horne received his commission. The artillery's role was seen as supporting the infantry by firing shrapnel over open sights at mass, and obligingly visible, formations of the enemy, using mobile field guns. Even the experience of facing the tactically more sophisticated Boers in the South African War, hardly dented the concept. The Boers might conceal themselves but, once located, the same artillery tactics applied.[1] When it became increasingly likely, in the early years of the twentieth century, that Britain could be faced with a war with Germany in the foreseeable future, there was little thought that such an event would call for a revolution in artillery strategy and tactics; not surprisingly given that the events of 1914–18 were to surpass even the wildest imaginings of the most doom-laden prophet.

Thus Britain went to war in August 1914 with its infantry and cavalry divisions of the Expeditionary Force supported by batteries of field guns armed largely with shrapnel, and very little else in the way of artillery firepower and ammunition. As long as the war remained mobile the guns were to prove their worth. But once trench warfare came about, the shortages of heavy calibre guns and howitzers, trench mortars and, above all, high explosive ammunition were to place severe constraints on the effectiveness of the BEF. These shortages were, in some cases, to persist until the war was over 2 years old. It was as a direct consequence of the shortage of shells that the 'Shell Scandal' erupted in mid-1915, contributing to the political crisis that led to the replacement of Asquith's Liberal government by a Coalition.[2]

Bearing in mind that the Entente's strategic imperative was to attack the enemy and expel them from Northern France and Belgium by defeating them in the field, the problems which the advent of trench warfare were to pose for the Royal Artillery may be summarised as: how to destroy the enemy's barbed-wire entanglements: how to pulverise the enemy's trench systems and neutralise their garrisons: how to neutralise enemy artillery in a position to engage friendly infantry and artillery (counter battery work): and how to protect friendly infantry as they moved across open ground to engage the enemy. The developments which led to the solution of these problems cumulatively amounted to a revolution in artillery tactics and the emergence of the artillery as a main contributor to the winning of the war on the Western Front.

The plentiful availability of high explosive shells and the development of the 106 instantaneous fuze dealt with the problem of wire entanglements; the advent of the tank also played its part. The development of heavy howitzers and trench mortars took care of trench systems and deep bunkers. (The enemy rapidly learned to thin out their front line defences and adopt defence in depth to counteract the increasing vulnerability of the former.) Counter battery work was perfected by developments in air observation, flash spotting, sound ranging and formulae allowing for gun barrel wear and meteorological conditions to be taken into account. These ultimately enabled counter battery firing to wait until an assault was imminent, thus restoring the potential for surprise to the attackers. Finally, protection of attacking infantry was greatly improved, if not totally perfected, by the development of the creeping barrage. It is with this that Henry Horne's name was popularly associated in the years immediately following the end of the war and beyond.

Despite being in his early fifties at the outbreak of the war, Horne rapidly showed in the few months available to him in an artillery role before he took over 2nd Division that he was an enthusiastic disciple of new technology. This should not come as any surprise; it has already been noted that the 'gun-arc' was first developed and used under his watch in India in 1895.[3] Once the frenzy of activity of the opening weeks of the war died down, Horne energetically threw himself into the problems of making the best use of the new weapon of war, the aeroplane, to enable the artillery to see beyond the horizon. On virtually a daily basis he supervised a series of experiments designed to enable the aircrew to understand what they were looking at and to communicate it to the ground.[4] The experiments established the practicality and methodology of the idea. Horne was frequently to allude in later entries in his diary and in his letters to his wife to how frustrated he felt when the observations of the Royal Flying Corps were denied to him by adverse weather conditions.

Horne's receptiveness to new ideas and technology must certainly have played a part, and probably a significant one, in the development of the technique known as the creeping barrage. Whether it could be claimed, as it frequently was by the popular press of the time and, sometimes, by more august sources, that he was its inventor, is highly questionable. One of those more august sources was John Buchan. In his interview with Liddell Hart in December 1916 he described the creeping barrage as the leading tactical novelty of the Somme battle and that its inception was chiefly due to Horne, 'the outstanding artillery officer. It was first put into partial use on July 1st, but by Horne's Corps alone.'[5] Horne himself would have no part of such claims and tried to discourage them. But they were persistent. Even today, on the very rare occasions when Horne's name finds itself in print, it is likely to be associated with the creeping barrage.

The first true creeping barrage, identical in detail to what is now understood by the term, was almost certainly fired during the Battle of the Somme and very probably by Horne's XV Corps at the opening of the Battle of Flers-Courcelette on 15 September 1916.[6] Its genesis as a concept and its evolution into the finely tuned instrument it was from then onwards to be, must be open to a certain amount of speculation. Although what follows will largely focus on the British development of the concept, the French and Germans were certainly developing similar techniques in the same time scale. No less a personage than the future Field Marshal Lord Alanbrooke, the Chief of the Imperial General Staff for most of the Second World War, but in 1916 merely Major Alan F Brooke, a gunnery officer with 18th Division of XIII Corps, described conversations he had in March 1916 with a

French officer, Colonel Herring. The Frenchman told him about the *'barrage roulant'* which the French were already employing on their section of the front. Herring told Brooke that this rolling barrage was fired by one 75mm gun for every 10 to 15 metres of front being attacked at a rate of 4 rounds per minute per gun. The range of the guns was increased by increments of 50 metres at periods corresponding with the predicted rate of advance of the infantry.[7] We shall revert to what Brooke made of these revelations. But they left him in no doubt that they entitled the French to claim invention of the concept; he dismissed any pretensions to the honour on the part of either Horne or himself.

Brooke's recollections perhaps lend further credence to the view that the creeping barrage was an evolution rather than an invention. Developments which would result in the creeping barrage had been taking place on the British front since the onset of trench warfare. It might have been developed even earlier if John Headlam, the CRA of 5th Division in September 1914 had had his way. He had suggested that the divisional infantry, charged with capturing an enemy held hill, should advance in the open in full view of their own artillery, which would then fire just in front of them throughout their advance. Perhaps understandably this was rejected in favour of an attack through woods which the artillery was helpless to support closely. Had Headlam's proposal been tried and been successful, it might well have resulted in a quicker adoption of the creeping barrage.[8]

One of the developments on the way to the creeping barrage was the introduction of the lifting barrage. This generally entailed the artillery barrage lifting from the enemy's front line trenches to their second, then third lines, and so on as required. It was probably first employed by the BEF at the Battle of Neuve Chapelle in March 1915. After lifting from the first to the second enemy lines at Zero Hour, a further lift was made beyond the infantry's final objective to discourage the enemy from bringing up reinforcements. The barrage was fired to an artillery timetable, in itself a new development which would become a permanent fixture subjected to greater and greater refinement.

The lifting barrage technique was also employed at the Battles of Aubers Ridge and Festubert. Under cover of its first stage at Festubert however there was a new development, when the infantry left their trenches prior to Zero Hour and formed up for the assault in No Man's Land. Even though this manoeuvre brought the infantry that much closer to their own barrage before it lifted further back, it was achieved without any reports of friendly fire casualties.[9]

The next stage in the development of the lifting barrage was the recognition that it would become a much more effective aid to the infantry if some way could be found to ensure that it did not lift to its next objective until the infantry were close up behind it and ready to move on. By the time the Battle of Loos opened on 25 September 1915 the firing of a lifting barrage was general throughout the attacking divisions, thus indicating that it had received official approbation as a means of offering some protection to the infantry. But it still had to lift according to a pre-fixed timetable or after a predetermined number of rounds had been fired. The control and communication systems which would be needed to adapt it to the actual speed of the infantry's progress simply did not exist. Loos also pointed to a need for the infantry to be trained to implement the new methods required of them to benefit from a lifting barrage. Understandably, untrained troops with a strong sense of self-preservation might hang back when they needed to get up close to the barrage; conversely overeager ones might walk into their own gunfire.[10]

The next big challenge to the artillery and its developing techniques would be the Battle of the Somme. Planning for it was based on the belief that, for the first time, the British would have sufficient guns and ammunition. These, when coupled with a prolonged preliminary bombardment, would accomplish the tasks of destroying the enemy wire, pulverising their front line trenches (eliminating those unfortunates manning them), and interdicting their artillery in a position to take on the assaulting infantry. These men, it was assumed, would be protected as they crossed No Man's Land by there being no enemy left capable of taking them on.

This assumption was to prove tragically unfounded. The number of guns, especially heavy calibres, was still insufficient. Too much of the ammunition was shrapnel when high explosive was needed. Too many of the shells proved to be duds, up to a third by some estimates. When the assault took place, the enemy machine guns, manned by men who emerged from virtually impregnable dugouts when the barrage lifted at Zero Hour, took a murderous toll as the attackers struggled to find a way through largely uncut German wire.

There had been no discernible attempt to impose a rigid artillery pattern throughout the Fourth Army except for it being made clear that a lifting barrage was now the desired norm. In an order issued during the run up to the battle, General Rawlinson wrote:

> The lifts of the artillery timetables must conform to the advance of the infantry. The infantry must be given plenty of time. The guns must "arrose" [spray] each objective just before the infantry assault it. Timing is a matter of most careful consideration.

Rawlinson went on to warn that lifts on earlier occasions had been made too quickly; not enough time had been allowed for the infantry to advance before the barrage moved on.[11] He clearly was looking for an ideal of short lifts with the artillery fire staying immediately in front of the infantry. But he seemed to regard this as a counsel of perfection difficult, if not impossible, to attain in practice.

Beyond this, corps were left to their own devices; they could impose a rigid pattern on their subordinate divisions or leave them to devise their own form of barrage. It is perhaps more than coincidence that the 2 Corps that did best on the first day of the battle were the XIII and XV, whose artillery programmes came nearest to an approximation of the creeping barrage. The Official History shares the view of John Buchan that XV Corps made the most sophisticated use of the 'creeping barrage' on 1 July.[12] But this honour must rightfully be shared with at least 18th Division of XIII Corps.

The insights which Major Brooke of that division had gleaned as a result of his encounter with Colonel Herring have already been mentioned. Brooke was able to persuade his superiors in the divisional artillery to propose a rolling or moving barrage, as Brooke termed it, to accompany the initial assault. Brooke realised that the Germans often sited machine gun posts in the areas between trench lines precisely because they would be safe from a barrage that lifted from trench line to trench line. A barrage which lifted by 50-yard increments just in front of the advancing infantry would go a long way towards countering their threat. When the

Gunners made their proposal at a divisional conference it was met with incomprehension from the divisional GOC and his brigadiers. They were adamant that the barrage should focus exclusively on the trenches. But Brooke and his colleagues partially got their way when it was agreed that the field artillery shrapnel barrage should lift from trench to trench until the last trench was covered; thereafter it would increase its range in lifts of 50 yards every 90 seconds.

When this plan was implemented on 1 July Brooke claimed that it was the first time a rolling barrage had been fired on the British front. The Division were to secure all their first day objectives with the infantry indicating full satisfaction with the support provided by the artillery.[13]

At XV Corps headquarters Horne was blessed by having E W Alexander, VC, one of the outstanding British gunners of the war, as his BGRA. He and Horne both realised that the fortified villages which the corps had been ordered to capture were highly unlikely to have been rendered toothless by the preliminary bombardment, however effectively this might have been implemented. So, in addition to an effective preliminary bombardment, their artillery plan also sought to offer as much protection as could be devised for the assaulting infantry. The corps' plan, reproduced in full in the Official History as an example of best practice, was described by the History as containing the most sophisticated use of the 'creeping barrage'. It represented an advance on that fired by 18th Division in that, while the howitzers and heavy guns were called upon to lift directly from objective to objective, the 18 pounders were to search back by increasing their range by 50 yards per minute from the first objective. A map, showing 6 proposed lifts from the German front line back to Caterpillar Valley and the west side of Mametz Wood, accompanied the plan. Divisional instructions filled in the details. They lend some credence to claims that the first creeping barrage was fired by Horne's XV Corps on 1 July 1916.[14]

Brigadier General J G Rotton was BGRA of the corps' 7th Division. His Operation Order No 11 of 18 June instructed that:

> a barrage of artillery fire will be formed in front of the infantry according to the timings shown on the tracing ... At the times shown heavy guns will lift their fire direct to the next barrage line. The divisional artillery will move their fire progressively at the rate of 50 yards a minute. Should the infantry arrive at any point before the time fixed for the barrage to lift, they will wait under the best cover available and be prepared to assault directly the lift takes place ...[15]

The division's 20th Infantry Brigade's Instruction No 2 dated 19 June contained the following under the heading 'Method of Assault'.

> The assault will be carried out steadily behind the artillery barrage. At the hour named for the barrage to lift the leading line will be as close to the hostile line as possible, and on the barrage lifting will at once move forward steadily, keeping touch and only halt and lie down when next compelled to do so by awaiting the lift of the artillery barrage.[16]

(As a result of the brigade's experiences on 1 July, its Commander became even more convinced that it was essential for the attacking infantry to reach and enter their objective immediately the barrage had lifted off it. This view was clearly shared by his divisional GOC, Major General H E Watts. The creeping barrage was to form part of the division's future assault plans as a matter of course. It was also used by 38th Welsh Division for the assaults they undertook under General Watts' temporary command.)

The 21st Division's Artillery Instructions indicated that the barrage would 'drift forward' and that the troops must move forward as it advanced so as to take all advantages of its protection. The division's 64th Brigade elaborated that, 'the line of the barrage must be constantly watched by the infantry whose front lines must keep close up to it.'[17]

Both these divisions and their subordinate formations clearly recognised the potential protection offered by keeping up close to a forward moving barrage. That the idea had not been universally recognised, even within a given corps, is exemplified by the bombardment fired for 50th Brigade, attached to 21st Division (from the 17th) for the start of the battle. Their 30-minute preliminary bombardment lifted back 500 yards at Zero Hour. Fifteen minutes later it lifted a further 250 yards where it stayed until Z+1 hour 45 minutes. None of its guns were called upon to 'creep'.[18] That one of his brigades was able to go its own way to this extent over the pattern of its artillery bombardment would indicate that Horne, if moving towards advocacy and adoption of the creeping barrage, did not yet feel able to insist on it throughout his command. It may have been that he believed it appropriate for such decisions to be taken at divisional or brigade level. If so, this contrasts with his readiness to interfere with his divisions' infantry assault plans, which was to leave him open to criticism.

In the event, in the cases where a forward moving barrage was fired, the infantry were not generally able to keep up with it and lost its protection. Moreover the concept still offered no protection at all to the infantry as they crossed No Man's Land.[19] Even though the casualties suffered by the infantry during the day were by no means light, it was generally accepted that the Artillery Plan's relative sophistication had made a significant contribution to the corps' performance

As has already been seen, XV Corps were to get very heavily involved in efforts to wrest Mametz Wood from the enemy's grip. Major General Watts, in temporary command of 38th Welsh Division, laid on a creeping barrage in support of their attack launched in the early hours of 10 July. The plan called for the barrage to begin at 04h15 and lift forward 50 yards every minute to just beyond the infantry's first objective. The troops were allowed 2 hours to take and consolidate their hold on their first objective before the barrage resumed lifting to the second objective, just beyond which it would hold until 07h15. At that point it would move on again to the northern edge of the wood. Given the relative inexperience of everyone concerned, this was an ambitious plan, the more so as Mametz Wood would prevent the artillery having a clear idea of where their shells were falling. But although the unfortunate Welsh were to suffer grievously from friendly fire during their assault on the wood, this was largely due to later bombardments falling in the wrong place at the wrong time and much less so to the initial creeping barrage. It did however make some contribution to their misfortunes when shells burst above the Welshmen on impact with the upper branches of trees.[20]

The next refinement or development of the creeping barrage was already in the last stages of planning as the Welsh struggled to secure Mametz Wood. It was introduced on 14 July when XV and XIII Corps assaulted Bazentin Ridge. It was decided that the barrage should make use of high explosive shells with delay fuzes exclusively instead of the usual shrapnel. The change was deemed so successful that only on very rare occasions in the future would shrapnel solely be used.[21]

Feedback from the experiences of the July battles had persuaded GHQ of the potential value of the creeping barrage in future operations. Haig's Chief of Staff, Lieutenant General Sir Launcelot Kiggell, bestowed the Commander-in-Chief's official blessing on the technique in circular memorandum OA 256, issued on 16 July, which read in part:

> One of the outstanding artillery lessons of the recent fighting has been the great assistance afforded by a well-directed field artillery barrage maintained close in front of the advancing infantry. It is beyond dispute that on several occasions where the field artillery has made a considerable 'lift', that is to say has outstripped the infantry advance, the enemy has been able to man his parapets ... It is therefore of first importance that in all cases infantry should be instructed to advance right under the field artillery barrage, which should not uncover the first objective until the infantry are close up to it (even within 50/60 yards) ... An infantry Brigadier, whose command has met with considerable success, ascribes it largely to the fact that his men have insisted in advancing close under the field artillery fire ... on more than one occasion his men were thus enabled to gain an enemy's trench almost without loss, and in time to meet the defenders hand-to-hand as they emerged from their dugouts and before they could mount their machine guns.[22]

It will be noted that the term 'creeping barrage' was not used in this memorandum. Although the word 'creep' was used in the artillery instructions for 1 July of both VIII and XIII Corps, it was not until XV Corps' Artillery Operations Order No 47, issued in preparation for the Battle of Flers-Courcelette, that a separate section was devoted to the technique under the heading 'Creeping Barrage.' Thereafter the term enjoyed general and official acceptance.[23]

It was on the first day of this battle, 15 September 1916, that a comprehensive creeping barrage was fired. Plans for it were complicated by the need somehow to accommodate the advent of the tank onto the battlefield. It was decided that they should advance slightly ahead of the infantry along lanes kept clear of the creeping barrage which otherwise was to be laid down initially just in front of the British lines and creep forward from there, thus offering its protection to the infantry as they crossed No Man's Land.

The modification of artillery plans to accommodate the new weapon may have seemed theoretically sound, but they took insufficient account of the unreliability and vulnerability of the tanks. If and, all too frequently, when they failed to put in an appearance, there were areas of the German defences, not covered by either the creeping barrage or tanks, in which the Germans could man their parapets and operate in relative impunity as soon as the main barrage had lifted. Furthermore if a tank which had made it to the start line strayed for any reason from its assigned lane it was in immediate danger from the creeping barrage. At least one of the tanks fell victim to this.[24]

Despite these problems the creeping barrage, where it was allowed to operate as intended, demonstrated its effectiveness conclusively at Flers-Courcelette. There was no looking back. By the end of September the terminology and methodology had been agreed, disseminated and accepted throughout the BEF. It was, for example, to become generally accepted that a creeping barrage required one 18 pounder gun for every 25 yards of front. Experimentation went on, aimed at achieving the best results, with mixtures of creeping, sweeping back and forth, and lifting being tried.

One problem for which there was no universally applicable answer was the pace of the barrage. If it crept too fast the infantry lost its protection; if too slow the Germans might be able to reinforce their defenders and organise counterattacks. There was a prolonged debate on whether the ideal creep was one of 50 yards or 100 yards. Eventually 100 yards was settled on, largely because this meant the gunners only had to adjust their guns half as often.[25]

Thus by the end of September 1916 the creeping barrage had become an established and essential part of all infantry offensive operations and would remain so in the future. Improvements and developments were introduced as circumstances required and permitted. One slight drawback was that the infantry were to grow so accustomed to advancing under the cover of an accurate and effective creeping barrage that they were to become possibly over-reliant on it. When, for one reason or another, the gunners were unable to provide a barrage up to the infantry's expectations, they found themselves having to suggest that the infantry should do more of their own work. A case in point might be when the infantry had made an advance which had outstripped their artillery cover. It was not always possible to bring up the guns to new positions in the time scale required, given the frequent problems with torn up ground and mud. The gunners could console themselves with the fact that the infantry's dissatisfaction in such circumstances was a reflection of the gunners' overall success in mastering the demands of fighting on the Western Front.

Were there any grounds for the at-one-time popularly held belief that Henry Horne was the inventor of the creeping barrage? It has already been noted that Horne himself never claimed ownership of the technique and deprecated attempts to ascribe it to him. In doing so he was not lending himself to false modesty. The fact is that the creeping barrage was less an invention than an evolution. It evolved out of the need to solve a clearly recognisable problem; how to offer artillery protection to infantry obliged by the circumstances of the Western Front to assault their enemy frontally and not by outflanking them. How this might be done was recognised as early as September 1914, by Brigadier General John Headlam. He was not given the chance to prove his point at the time. Had he had the opportunity it may have proved premature as the techniques and equipment required to fire an effective creeping barrage were only beginning to evolve. This process was to continue through 1915 and the first half of 1916, up to which point there had been little to indicate that Horne would be anything more than a peripheral figure in the adoption of the creeping barrage.

But this was to change at the Somme where Horne was in a position of power as a corps commander. There could be little doubt that he would be innovative in the handling of his artillery. As a Gunner of long standing himself Horne could be expected to understand and appreciate how developments in gunnery techniques and equipment could be applied in a practical manner for the benefit of the troops he commanded. He was strongly of the view that whatever the artillery could do to ease the tasks of the infantry and preserve their lives should be done. There was no place in his make-up for beliefs, such as those espoused by General Haking, that infantry should not be allowed to shelter behind the artillery but should have their sense of aggression nurtured by constant trench raids in the absence of anything more momentous like a full-scale battle. This is not to say that Horne did not want his troops to show aggression, but that when they did, it should be for a purpose and they should enjoy whatever protection the artillery could afford them.

There can be no question that Horne's XV Corps was at the leading edge of developments in the first two and a half months of the Battle of the Somme, at the end of which period the creeping barrage was an established shot in the BEF's locker. Of the other 4 Corps initially engaged on the Somme only XIII Corps seemed to be similarly leading the way in the same direction. In both corps a great deal of the impulsion clearly came from outstanding Gunners in corps or divisional headquarters. In Horne's corps' case it was Brigadier General E W Alexander VC. There can be little question that this officer played a major part in perfecting the creeping barrage. When disclaiming any credit for himself, Horne was disposed to give it to Alexander. He was delighted when Alexander, whom he had had to leave behind when he left XV Corps to take over First Army, rejoined him, becoming his MGRA at First Army in early April 1918 and remaining so until the end of the war.

It is impossible to tell at this stage how much interplay there was between Horne and Alexander as they put together the Artillery Plans at XV Corps Head-quarters which played such a part in the perfection of the creeping barrage. Although this would certainly have been greeted with astonishment by his divisional commanders at XV Corps, it was to be Horne's general practice to interfere as little as possible in the plans of his subordinates, provided that they conformed with the broad lines he had laid down. But in the summer of 1916, Horne was still feeling his way at senior command level, and was perhaps less inclined to adopt a hands-off approach than he would later be. It is therefore quite possible that his input into Alexander's plans was significant. In any case, as the Corps Commander, he was ultimately responsible for the actions of his subordinates. If they got it wrong, he should have been to blame. If they got it right, should he not receive the credit?

Although Henry Horne manifestly did not invent the creeping barrage, he does deserve to have his name associated with it in a way that recognises the significant contributions made to its development in the corps under his command.

Part Four

WORLD WAR: OCTOBER 1916– NOVEMBER 1918

Chapter XIII

Army Commander: Vimy Ridge

In taking over command of First Army, General Sir Henry Horne was returning to a stretch of the BEF's sector of the Western Front already familiar to him from his previous service there with 2nd Division. His 3 corps, totalling about 12 infantry divisions (the number of divisions might vary in the light of the overall pressures on the BEF at any given time) were responsible for the sector of the front between Third Army to their south and Second Army to their north. In geographic terms, it ran northwards from the southern end of Vimy Ridge to an area about 5 miles south of Armentières. It encompassed the area of all the attempts by the BEF to take the fight to the enemy in 1915. Except for Neuve Chapelle, these operations had been carried out against the better judgment of the senior BEF commanders at the time, who had regarded the area as not well suited for offensive operations. Now, with Field Marshal Haig's strategic ambitions for 1917 firmly fixed on an offensive north of the River Lys designed to clear the Belgian coast, Horne might have found his army marginalised if it had not been for the imperatives of the Anglo-French entente.

Horne arrived at his new headquarters at Château Philomel near Lillers, a village about 12 kilometres west of Béthune, on 29 September. The following day he formally took over First Army from the temporary incumbent, Lt General Sir Richard Haking, who returned to XI Corps, one of the 3 corps comprising Horne's new command.[1] The other 2 were I Corps and IV Corps, the latter of which would be replaced towards the end of October by the Canadian Corps as its divisions disengaged from the fighting on the Somme. It would not be until the battle there had ended in late November that the 4 Canadian divisions would be reunited as a corps. Over the next 2 years they were to be in the forefront of virtually every offensive launched by First Army.

Unsurprisingly, given what was going on on the Somme and at Verdun, Horne found his sector of the front to be quiet. He took the opportunity to spend a few days at home from 5 to 10 October. The highlight of his brief break was his investiture with the KCB by the King at Buckingham Palace. The ceremony took place on the 9th, surely to Horne's intense and immense satisfaction. His letters to his wife reveal a constant preoccupation that he was not receiving the recognition he deemed his due. This award put all that behind him. He was, in addition, to be gazetted temporary full General on 28 October, the promotion being backdated to the day he took command of First Army.[2]

Before this happy interlude in England he had been summoned to GHQ. Over lunch, Haig told him to make preparations (as far as the means at his disposal admitted) for an attack on Vimy Ridge.[3] The ridge was a tactically important part of the Western Front running north to south for about 12 kms to the northeast of, and overlooking, the key town of Arras. Sloping gently upwards from the west to its crest, the highest point of which was 145 metres above sea level, it then fell sharply away to the Douai Plain, which it completely dominated. Allied possession of it would provide matchless observation to the east and seriously limit German freedom to exploit the mines, railways and other industrial assets of the area. The Germans had occupied the ridge in September 1914. Since then, they had made it a pivotal point in their Western Front defences, linking their northern defensive line, running north from here to the sea, with the new Hindenburg Line system to the south. They had taken advantage of the chalky soil to dig artillery-proof tunnels and storage facilities under the ridge.

During the fighting of 1915 the French had made strenuous efforts to capture the ridge. On 9 May, General Philippe Pétain's XXXIII Corps had launched an assault. The famed Moroccan Division broke through the German lines and took the ridge, having advanced 4 kms in just a few hours. But their effort had exhausted them and they desperately needed reinforcements, which were too far back to reach them before the next day. The Germans retook the ridge that evening, materially assisted by 'friendly fire' from the French artillery.[4]

A further attempt on the ridge was made during the Second Battle of Artois, which began on 25 September. Despite great bravery in the face of heavy losses, the French troops did not advance as far as they had in May. When the French handed the area over to the BEF in March 1916, they had sustained over 200,000 casualties in their unsuccessful efforts to expel the Germans from the ridge.[5]

The capture of this dominant (and, in the view of the Germans, impregnable) feature was to be part of the Allied strategy for the Western Front in 1917, which was being hammered out by General Joseph Joffre and Haig in exchanges which were making it clear that it was still the French who were the senior partner of the alliance. The two Commanders-in-Chief had agreed that there would be no great differences in their approach in the New Year. But before the detailed plans could be finalised, two significant events took place in December 1916 that would have important consequences for Allied operations on the Western Front in the following year. The first was the fall of Joffre and his replacement as French Commander-in-Chief by General Robert Nivelle; the second, the replacement of Herbert Asquith as British Prime Minister by David Lloyd George.

General Nivelle, who was, like Horne, an artillery officer, had achieved prominence and fame during the Battle of Verdun. Almost as soon as General Pétain had restored order out of the chaos of the early days of the defence of the fortress city, he had been appointed to command the French Army Group Centre and been replaced at Verdun by Nivelle. He and his subordinate, the unquenchably aggressive Major General Charles Mangin, took the fight to the Germans, recaptured the Forts Vaux and Douaumont and, at the cost of huge casualties, pushed the Germans back to a defensive line close to where they had started the battle. Their achievements gave a great, and sorely needed, boost to French morale and national pride. The French success owed much to Nivelle's skills in handling his artillery. It has even been suggested that he copied the concept and use of the creeping barrage from Horne, although, as has been noted earlier, the French almost certainly evolved the technique separately.[6]

Apart from his military skills Nivelle was a very good communicator who had a natural charm. The French Government, long resigned to the taciturnity of General Joffre, and alarmed at the ever growing casualty lists with little prospect of improvement whilst he remained Commander-in-Chief, warmly embraced Nivelle and his confidence that he could win the war with one massive offensive.

Joffre's position had been seriously undermined by his failure, despite warnings, to anticipate the German assault at Verdun. He had had to go, consoled by his elevation to the rank of Marshal of France.

On the British side, David Lloyd George had been at the heart of the political conduct of the war from the outset, initially continuing in his senior Cabinet post as Chancellor of the Exchequer. Following the establishment by Prime Minister Asquith of a Coalition government on 25 May 1915, Lloyd George was appointed Minister of Munitions and charged with sorting out the alarming deficiencies in the production of shells. A year later, on 7 July 1916, he was appointed Secretary of State for War in place of Lord Kitchener, who had been lost at sea on his way to Russia. Within 5 months, on 9 December, he was Prime Minister. Appalled by the casualty rates on the Western Front and the apparent lack of anything positive to show for them, Lloyd George believed that his role was to conceive and pursue a strategy that would marginalise the Western Front and reduce the scope for Haig and his generals to amass huge casualty lists in further fruitless offensives. It is fair to say that, had he felt politically secure enough and there had been an obvious and acceptable successor, Haig would have been relieved of his command very early on in Lloyd George's premiership.

As it was, the Prime Minister decided that one way in which Haig's freedom of manoeuvre could be curtailed, would be by subordinating the BEF to the French. This must call into question Lloyd George's judgment, given the French Army's horrendous casualty rates on the Western Front and their unshakeable belief that this was bound to be the decisive area of operations. Almost certainly, like the French politicians, his judgment had been impaired by the charm and plausibility of General Nivelle, augmented in his case by the latter's panache and fluency in English (he had an English mother). After a period of intrigue, and at the expense of poisoning military-political relations, Lloyd George partially achieved his aim when Haig was subordinated to Nivelle, but for the duration of Nivelle's planned offensive only. Haig retained the right to appeal to his government if he felt the BEF was facing unreasonable demands. It was also agreed that if the Nivelle offensive were to fail, Haig would then be able to launch his own offensive from north of the River Lys, and would be supported by the French.[7]

Although by no means as susceptible to Nivelle's charms as the politicians, Haig struck up a good working relationship with the Frenchman. At their first meeting on 20 December 1916 Nivelle outlined his plan for a rapid victory, specifying that if the looked-for breakthrough had not occurred within 48 hours he would call off the battle.[8] Over the next few weeks at meetings, sometimes involving the politicians, and in correspondence, details of the Nivelle Plan emerged. It called for a massive attack by 28 French divisions north across the River Aisne, over the Chemin des Dames and beyond to St Quentin, the River Oise and Cambrai. Subsidiary French attacks would be mounted on either side of the main offensive. Starting roughly a week earlier, the Third Army of General Sir Edmund Allenby would attack eastward from Arras, in the general direction of Cambrai where, if both allies had been successful, they would link up. The Third Army would be supported to the north by Henry Horne's First Army and to the south by Hubert Gough's Fifth Army. Originally envisaged to begin in February, successive postponements were to delay the start until April. To enable the French to mass the necessary troops for the offensive, the BEF agreed to take over more line from their ally.

On 22 December 1916 Haig briefed Horne on the results of his first meeting with Nivelle and confirmed that First Army would need to capture Vimy Ridge.[9] Allenby considered possession of the Ridge essential to the security of his army's left flank as it advanced east from Arras. Horne had already warned Lieutenant General Sir Julian Byng, the Commander of the Canadian Corps, that his divisions would be assigned the task of taking the northern half of the ridge, with a British corps taking the remainder.[10] In mid-January 1917 Byng was told that his corps would now have to take the southern part of the ridge as well. Horne had suggested that Allenby's concerns about his flank might be eased by the capture of the southern part of the ridge, leaving its more northern portion and the village of Thélus out of the operation. But Allenby was adamant that the area thus captured would be so shallow and so overlooked from the higher ground to the north that it would be very difficult to hold if counterattacked by the Germans. Furthermore, the northern part of the ridge, if left in German hands, would give them a jumping-off point from which to launch an attack towards Arras, thus threatening the Third Army's flank and lines of communication. Called upon to adjudicate, Haig supported Allenby and confirmed his order that the whole of Vimy Ridge should be assaulted and captured by First Army.[11]

As 1916 gave way to 1917, Horne, Byng and their respective staffs were fully engaged in planning the attack on Vimy Ridge. On 1 January, Horne was officially promoted to the substantive rank of Lieutenant General (he was already a temporary full General). In the early weeks of the New Year there were several key changes to his senior staff. At the beginning of February, Hastings Anderson, whom he had known briefly at XV Corps, was appointed as his Major General General Staff on promotion to that rank, in place of General Barrow. Anderson recorded the 'characteristic' interview he had with Horne on arrival.

> He told me frankly that he had been anxious to get his old Brigadier-General, General Staff, on the Somme [Louis Vaughan] as his senior Army Staff Officer, but on being told that other officers senior to him could not be passed over, he had asked for me, having known me for a short time on the Somme.[12]

Two other changes followed soon afterwards. Major General Frederick Mercer became MGRA and Major General Gerald Heath was appointed MGRE. Both were old friends of Horne. The changes were completed when Major General Hobbs was replaced by Geoffrey Twining as the senior Administrative Staff Officer (DA & QMG) on 3 March. Hobbs resigned his position because he and Horne could not get on. The breakdown in this relationship was regretted by Haig whom Hobbs had previously served at Aldershot and in France until Haig became Commander-in-Chief.[13]

In the weeks leading up to the opening of the Battle of Arras (as the British part of the Nivelle offensive was to become known) Horne spent a great deal of his time away from his headquarters visiting the corps and divisional headquarters of the troops under his command, as well as reviewing the troops of various units. The emphasis of this activity was on the Canadian Corps, understandably given the vital role assigned to them in the forthcoming battle. Horne walked the corps'

Cité de
Caumont

Bois en
Hache

Givenchy-
en-Gohelle

The
Pimple

Souchez

0   1000   2000

yards

DOUAI

La Chaudière

PLAIN

Hill
145

Petit
Vimy

Bois de
la Folie

Vimy

Zwischen
Stellung

La Folie
Farm

FRONT LINE APRIL 9

Bois du
Goulot

Neuville-
St Vaast

Hill
135

Les
Tilleuls

Farbus

Thélus

Bois de
la Ville

Farbus
Wood

To Arras

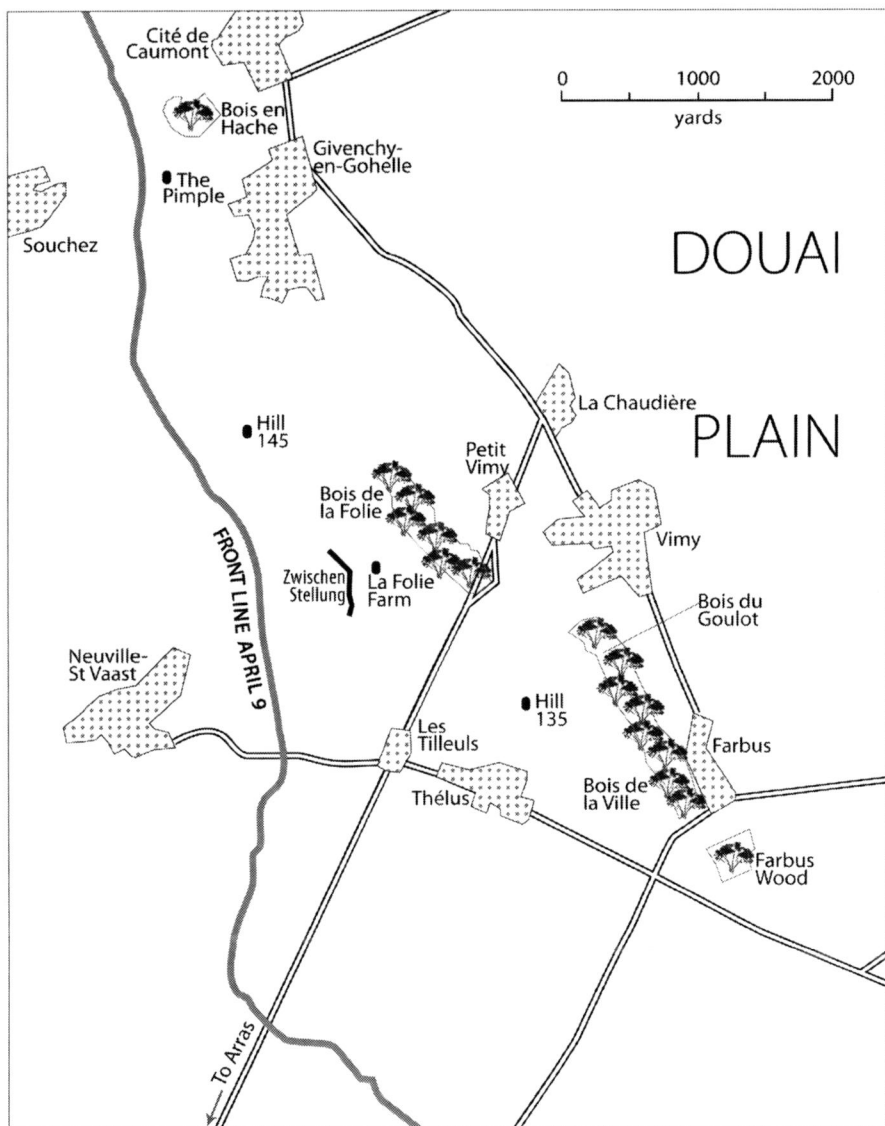

Map 11: Vimy Ridge: 9–12 April 1917

front areas with Lt General Byng to get a feel for the area over which the Canadians would attack.

The principal ingredient in the stunning success the Canadians were to achieve at Vimy Ridge was undoubtedly the painstaking and detailed preparation. While Horne would certainly have insisted on this, he was pushing on an open door given the nature of the Corps Commander. When he assumed command of the corps in May 1916, Lt General Sir Julian Byng had already had a very active war. A cavalryman, he commanded the 3rd Cavalry Division at Ypres in 1914. He then briefly commanded the BEF's Cavalry Corps in 1915 before being transferred to Gallipoli to take over IX Corps, although too late to make any difference to the outcome of that campaign. Having returned to the Western Front and assumed command of the Canadian Corps, his first challenge arose when the corps replaced the Australians on the Somme, as part of General Gough's Reserve Army, in time for the Battle of Flers-Courcelette.

As has already been recorded, the Canadian attack on Courcelette went well. It was in the subsequent fighting which began on 26 September, as the Canadians pressed north from Courcelette as part of Reserve Army's efforts to take the Thiepval Ridge, that they came under severe pressure from well-organised German defences and artillery bombardments. In truly attritional style they slogged forward until, on 1 October, they were in a position to attack the heavily fortified German line known as Regina Trench. In bitter fighting over the next week, with interruptions dictated by bad weather, the Canadians sometimes occupied, but never managed to hold, the trench. When 3 of the divisions were relieved at the end of the second week of October, the trench was still in German hands. It was finally largely taken by 4th Canadian Division, left behind on temporary attachment to II Corps, on 21 October. The division attempted to complete the job 4 days later but failed. They were to be involved intermittently on the Somme up to and including the final British attack of the campaign.[14]

Their involvement in the Somme battle had left the Canadians with a sour taste in the mouth. They had suffered over 17,000 casualties. Neither the senior officers nor the rank and file blamed Byng for the ordeal they had undergone. Their admiration of, and liking for, him, warmly reciprocated, remained undimmed. Rather, they laid their misfortunes at the doors of General Gough and his staff at Reserve Army. The Canadians were to refuse to serve ever again under Gough.[15]

Horne's introduction to the Canadians was a gentle one. They arrived in First Army still under General Byng's command. As fellow senior British officers, Horne and Byng knew each other well and Horne found no difficulty in entrusting Byng with the detailed planning of the Vimy Ridge assault.

If Byng had not already been convinced of the value of detailed and thorough planning for an attack, the experiences of his corps on the Somme would have persuaded him of the need for it. Confronted with what the Germans regarded with some assurance as an impregnable obstacle, Byng and Horne and their staffs quickly identified the areas where new thinking and solutions would be required to shatter German complacency. The attackers were faced with 3 main lines of defences consisting of trenches, machine gun strongpoints, barbed wire and dugouts capable of sheltering entire battalions at a time, all linked by connecting tunnels. They were manned by the 3 divisions of 'Gruppe Vimy'. The Germans would, by now, have preferred a rather more flexible defence system but had not yet been able to start work on it. Part of the reason for this was the pressure they had been put under by an intense programme of trench raiding instituted by the Canadians not long after they had come into the line. Apart from stretching the nerves of the defenders to near breaking point, these raids were of value in probing the enemy defences and acquiring more detailed information on their layout and strength. Some of these raids were mounted in considerable force and most were highly successful. But some failed and were costly. In the 2 weeks ending 5 April, the Canadians sustained 1,653 casualties, most suffered as a result of the raids.[16]

Much of the new thinking that went into the planning of the attack would focus on its 2 main ingredients, the infantry and artillery. But the favourable geology of the area for underground activity also offered opportunities which the planners were quick to seize on. The British had begun to mine assiduously as soon as they had taken over the area from the French, and during the rest of 1916 the British and German miners sought to blow up the others' positions and frustrate their countermining efforts. Gradually the British gained the upper hand and, by the time the Canadians arrived, were in a position to undertake the extensive construction of a network of subways designed to allow the assaulting troops to move to their front line trenches, and sometimes into No Man's Land, fully protected. Over 5 kms of subways were excavated, the work being done largely at night to maintain secrecy and enable the spoil to be removed undetected. The subways were constructed to a high standard with adjoining chambers included for brigade and battalion HQs, communications centres, dressing stations and ammunition stores. They were illuminated by electric light and fresh air was pumped through. Fully equipped soldiers could pass along the passages comfortably upright, and passing areas facilitated two-way traffic. In addition to the subways, a series of tunnels were driven under the German front lines and 21 mines laid and primed.

As far as infantry tactics were concerned, Byng was of the view that the army had lost its way in employing the rigid tactics seen on the first day of the Somme. In this he was reflecting the conclusions of GHQ itself, which had issued 2 pamphlets (SS143 and SS154) on the subject. Like GHQ, Byng favoured a reversion to the methods of mobile warfare in which the infantry would operate in highly mobile platoon-sized groups acting independently. They would be assigned natural features as their objectives rather than, for example, a trench which might be obliterated by the artillery. If an enemy strongpoint could not be quickly overrun the troops would be instructed to bypass it, throwing up a defensive flank towards it. Reserves coming up would be fed into the parts of the line where there was no hold-up thus reverting to the tried and true, but sometimes neglected, doctrine of reinforcing success and not failure. On the assumption that officers and NCOs could well become casualties, the troops were trained to become interchangeable with them and with each other. Byng had a full-scale replica of the battlefield laid out behind the lines and the troops were thoroughly trained on it in their roles. At Horne's HQ a detailed plasticine model of the ridge was built which all the officers and NCOs participating in the assault were given time to study and discuss.

Probably for the first time in the war the artillery and shell supply available was more than adequate for the task in hand. In addition to the Canadian Corps' own resources, Byng was able to count on the big guns of 11 heavy artillery groups and the artillery of I Corps to his left. The total density this gave him was one heavy gun for every 20 yards of front and a field gun for every 10 yards, proportionately 3 times as many heavy and twice as many field guns as on the Somme. 42,500 tons of shells were allocated to the operation with a daily quota of 2,465 tons. Although still not readily available, Byng managed to obtain an adequate supply of the new instantaneous '106' fuze, which was proving so effective in a wire-cutting role.

The tasks which this profusion of artillery would be called on to perform were the familiar ones of bombarding the enemy strongpoints and entrenchments, cutting their wire, and providing as much protection to the assaulting infantry as possible. This last task would be achieved firstly by eliminating their worst enemy, hostile artillery, by counter-battery work; and secondly, by firing a standard creeping barrage, supplemented by a concentrated line of machine guns firing over the heads of the assaulting troops to keep the enemy's heads down. What would be different from previous artillery programmes would be the precision with which these tasks would be carried out.

An essential part of the counter-battery programme was to be conducted by so-called silent batteries. The presence of these batteries would be concealed from the enemy by their not firing to register targets prior to the battle. In many cases their targets were identified for them by aerial reconnaissance; no less than 80% of the German artillery was thus spotted. Those that the aircraft missed could well have been pinpointed by the pioneering work of an outstanding Canadian scientific gunner, A G L McNaughton, whose counter-battery organisation attached to Byng's headquarters, was the leader in the fields of flash spotting and sound ranging.[17]

The grim weather and resultant mud of a northern French late winter and spring notwithstanding, the apparently intractable problems of getting men and matériel into the right place at the right time were well on the way to being solved, when Byng put before Horne his detailed plan for the capture of Vimy Ridge. He did this on 5 March. Byng's proposals were based on the Plan of Operations issued by Horne on 31 January which had called for a Southern Operation to capture the main crest of the ridge, the village of Thélus and Hill 135. If this operation were successful the Northern Operation would be launched to capture the Pimple and Bois en Hache. If the enemy lost these last 2 positions they would be totally deprived of Vimy Ridge. Since mid-January, Horne had envisaged the Southern Operation as an entirely Canadian affair, with the Northern Operation entrusted principally to the right flank of I British Corps assisted by the left flank of 4th Canadian Division. As late as 5 April, this was changed to give 4th Canadian Division the full responsibility for the capture of the Pimple. The Commander of the Division gave the task to his reserve Brigade, the 10th.[18]

As all the Canadian divisions would be committed to the battle from the outset, Horne added the British 5th Division to Byng's command as a reserve. One brigade of this, the 13th, would go into action with 2nd Canadian Division. The decision to assign the Northern Operation, except for the Bois en Hache, to the Canadians may well have been because the Southern Operation only called for an advance of 700 yards on the left compared with over 4,000 yards on the right.[19]

Byng's plan fully recognised that total surprise could not be achieved. The Germans were well aware that a major Allied offensive was in the offing and that Vimy Ridge would be an important objective.[20] Efforts were made to keep the Germans as much in the dark as possible (the Canadian fighter ace, Billy Bishop, was to win an MC for shooting down a heavily defended German observation balloon over the ridge) but all that could be realistically hoped for was to keep the precise time and date of the assault secret. What remains one of the unresolved mysteries of the war was why the Germans made no more than desultory attempts to interfere with Canadian preparations. This inertia led to some nervousness on the part of Horne that the Germans were planning to abandon Vimy Ridge as part of their withdrawal to the Hindenburg Line, which was taking place further south (and was to play a major part in the failure of the Nivelle offensive). In fact the Germans had no such plans; possession of the ridge was simply too vital for them.[21]

In mid-March the date of the attack was set for 8 April, although this was later postponed for 24 hours at the request of General Nivelle. The preliminary bombardment, using only about half of the available batteries, was to begin on 20 March. On 2 April the rest of the artillery were to join in, thus beginning what the Germans were to term 'the week of suffering'. The heavy guns concentrated on the villages and lines of communication behind the lines, the heavy mortars on the German front lines, and the smaller calibres on wire-cutting. To deceive the enemy on the precise time of the assault there would be no intensification of the bombardment in the run up to Zero Hour. As this moment arrived a barrage would be laid on the German front line where it would remain for 3 minutes before lifting 100 yards every 3 minutes. Gas and high explosive shells would rain down on known German strongpoints, artillery batteries and ammunition dumps.[22]

Byng's plan called for all 4 Canadian infantry divisions to go into action together for the first time in the war. They would assault in line abreast on a front of 4 and a half miles in numerical order from 1st Division on the right to 4th Division on the left. The 4 stages of the assault were delineated by coloured lines. The Black Line, about 750 yards from the Canadian front lines, incorporated all the German forward defensive line. The Red Line ran north along a German trench called Zwischen Stellung to the crest of the Ridge and included La Folie Farm and Hill 145. The Blue Line included Thélus, Hill 135 and the woods above the village of Vimy. The Brown Line marked the German Second Line including Farbus Wood, Bois de la Ville and the Bois du Goulot. The German Third Line of defences in the area was situated to the east of the ridge and was not an objective of the assault.

The plan called for the capture of the area up to and including the Black Line within 35 minutes of Zero Hour. There would then be a pause of 40 minutes to ensure the synchronisation of the artillery barrage and the infantry advance to the Red Line which would be reached in 20 minutes. At this point 3rd and 4th Divisions would have achieved all their objectives and could consolidate. For 1st and 2nd Divisions there would be a halt of 2 and a half hours before fresh troops would resume the advance to the Blue Line. There, after a further pause of 96 minutes, the advance would continue to the Brown Line, scheduled to be reached at 13h18. The 51st Highland Division of XVII Corps of Third Army, would advance in tandem with, and on the right of, 1st Canadian Division.[23]

Unsurprisingly, given the close liaison between their respective headquarters, Horne only felt the need to make minor modifications to the artillery section of the plan presented by Byng. The First Army issued its Operation Order on 26 March and Byng's headquarters sent out detailed orders based on the now finalised plan to all concerned.[24]

Zero Hour was 05h30 on Easter Monday, 9 April. By 04h00 30,000 men had assembled in the Canadian forward areas, the leading companies within 100 yards of the German outposts, all without raising the alarm. At Zero Hour the planned assault barrage erupted, 2 mines were detonated under the German positions and the infantry went over the top. A bitter northwest wind and a snow blizzard made conditions unpleasant for the attackers, but more so for the defenders who were partially blinded by the snow driving into their faces, as well as the very dim light of an early spring morning. The attackers' main problem, given the dazed, disoriented state of most of the front line defenders, was to negotiate the pulverised, and glutinously muddy ground in the poor visibility. Although resistance stiffened the further forward the attackers got, 1st, 2nd and 3rd Divisions had reached the Black Line less than an hour after Zero. Fresh units now took over the lead. Having taken La Folie Farm, 3rd Division reached Red Line at 07h30; the 2 divisions on their right 30 minutes later. The 1st Division had surprised and routed a battalion of Bavarians on their way. In heavy fighting, 2nd Division had cleared the hamlet of Les Tilleuls, captured 2 battalion headquarters and 500 enemy troops.

The 3rd Division could now consolidate and send out patrols. The 1st and 2nd Divisions had to continue their advance to the Blue Line which they secured shortly after 11h00. Ninety minutes later they began their advance to the Brown Line. Farbus Wood and the guns it contained were taken without difficulty. German artillery in the Bois de la Ville was silenced by a downhill bayonet charge which finally yielded 250 prisoners. The 2 divisions were now in full possession of their final objectives and could consolidate. Patrols were sent out and advanced observation posts set up.[25]

In contrast to the other 3 divisions, the attack by 4th Division, despite having the shortest distance to cover, had run into problems. These stemmed from their need to capture Hill 145, the highest point of the ridge (where the Canadian memorial now stands). Such an important vantage point was bound to be heavily defended, the physical obstacles augmented by old, deep, shell-proof mine workings manned by large garrisons easily reinforced from reserves sheltered in deep dugouts on the reverse slope. The fighting was to go on all day but, despite heavy casualties, the Canadians were unable to secure the crest. The brigade to the left of the one attacking Hill 145 did manage to secure its objectives despite the fire directed at them from the Hill and the Pimple to their north. They succeeded in blocking off these 2 German positions from each other.

The next day, 2 battalions of 10th Brigade, the divisional reserve, were added to the attacking troops. Following a fresh artillery barrage further attacks were mounted in the afternoon which finally secured the crest of Hill 145, the German reserve dugouts beyond and the whole of La Folie Wood. The Southern Operation of Horne's plan was now complete with the 4 Canadian divisions, and 51st Highland Division to the south, having achieved all their objectives. The way was now open for 4th Division's attack on the Pimple, rescheduled for 12 April.[26]

Following a preliminary bombardment 2 battalions of 10th Brigade launched their attack at 05h00. In darkness and with a blizzard blowing in their faces the German defenders were taken by surprise but put up a strong if uncoordinated defence. Nevertheless the Pimple was securely in Canadian hands by 06h00. To their north, 2nd Bn Leinster Regt and 9th Bn Royal Sussex Regt of 73rd Brigade captured the Bois en Hache.[27] The battle was over.

Field Marshal Haig recorded in his diary for 12 April what Horne had told him about this day's events.

> [Horne] told me that the going this morning (owing to the snow and the shell holes) when the Canadians attacked the Pimple was very bad indeed. Yesterday Horne had visited Thélus and found it difficult to discover where the German front line trenches had been. All had been so terribly destroyed by our shell fire. Horne thought he had used too many shells! It had broken up the soil so frightfully that all movement was made so difficult.
>
> Owing to the amount of Artillery and ammunition now available, the frontal attack on a position had become, Horne thought, the easiest task. The difficult matter was to advance later on when the enemy had organised a defence with machine guns. He also said that many officers in the First Army had said to him that their chief joy in gaining Monday's victory was the knowledge that it would put the stopper on all the disgraceful intrigues which had been going on at home in certain quarters against me. Especially was this feeling marked in the Canadian Corps, who had resented very much the attacks to which I had been subjected by certain politicians and others in England.
>
> … When I think over the fine work of the 4th Canadian Division in taking the Pimple notwithstanding the mud, shell holes and snow, I come to the conclusion that no other people are comparable to the British race as downright hard fighters. This operation of Hilliam's Brigade (ex Sgt Major 17th Lancers) this morning was a fine performance.[28]

In the space of 4 days the Canadians of First Army, with some assistance from British units, had completed a stunningly comprehensive victory, the most complete to this date by the BEF in the war. It proved to be a real shot in the arm for the Allies, both military and civilian, who were by this time more expectant of news of inconclusive battles and disproportionate casualty figures. The CIGS, General Sir 'Wullie' Robertson, had wired Haig after the first day's fighting.

> You had a splendid success yesterday, and I cannot help thinking that you really have now got a moral superiority over the Germans. I was afraid that the effects of the Somme might have worn off, but I do not think they have or it is unlikely you would have made such a big bag of prisoners as you had yesterday.[29]

Congratulations poured into Horne and Byng from the King, the Governor-General of Canada, the Commander-in-Chief and many others. The French press, effusive in its admiration and gratitude, described the victory as Canada's Easter gift to France.

The Canadian victory had not been bought lightly. Over 10% (10,602) of the 100,000 troops involved had become casualties, of whom 3,598 were dead.[30] These losses were however well below what had become the norm for the Western Front. The intensity of much of the fighting was reflected in the award of no fewer than 4 Victoria Crosses. Only 2 of the recipients survived the battle, one of whom was to be killed 2 months later.

The fact that the battle was the first in which all 4 Canadian divisions went into action together and achieved such a stunning success gave a huge boost to Canadian national identity. At the purely military level Haig, as Commander-in-Chief of the BEF, was to come under persistent and, in effect, almost irresistible, pressure to keep the corps together as a single unit and not allow its divisions to be fed into actions separately. Haig's exasperation at the constraints this placed on his freedom of action is well documented in his diary, which includes his comment that some Canadians regarded themselves rather as 'Allies' than fellow citizens of the Empire.[31] The Canadian Corps had, by this victory, earned their right to be considered amongst the elite shock troops of the BEF. They were rather relentlessly to be used in this role for the rest of the war. They were never to shirk a task they were called upon to perform, however unpromising and difficult it might be. The prime example of this was to be their attack on Passchendaele Ridge and village in the last days of Third Ypres. Their success here was bought at heavy cost, but when they returned to First Army it was with their offensive spirit intact. Horne was to be able to harness this in the subsequent months, to the great benefit of his Army.

On a national level, Canada was to date its coming of age as an independent sovereign country, no longer sheltering in the shadow of the Mother Country, from Vimy Ridge. The first recognition of this new international standing came when Canada was granted signatory status for the Treaty of Versailles in 1919.

As Commander of the Canadian Corps, Lt General Sir Julian Byng's already good reputation received a significant boost. He had demonstrated that, even in the conditions of the Western Front, it was possible with limited objectives, meticulous planning and training, and the ready embrace of technological advances, to achieve success. Within weeks of Vimy Ridge Byng was promoted to the command of the BEF's Third Army, a promotion he gave the impression he would much rather not have had, if he could have stayed with the Canadians.[32] But, apart from any other considerations, the assiduity with which Byng had ensured that Canadian officers should replace British secondees to the Corps as soon as their competence was proved, could have only one logical outcome; his replacement as Corps Commander by a Canadian officer. (Byng's connection with matters Canadian was not to be entirely severed. He was to become a popular Governor-General of the Dominion from 1921 to 1926.)

Horne always regarded Vimy Ridge as one of the most significant achievements of his tenure in command of First Army. It was, of course, his first offensive. He had determined the overall framework in which it was planned and fought. He had agreed with, and fully supported, the detailed operational plan, despite criticisms levelled at it by General Nivelle's staff. Above all, it had worked. Although it is most often Byng's name that is popularly associated with Vimy Ridge, there is little doubt that the chemistry between the Army Commander and the Corps Commander and their staffs was crucial to the success of the operation. Byng was fortunate in his Army Commander. Some others of this exalted rank might not have been as willing as Horne to back the Corps Commander's ideas and proposals. Horne may not have been a technically-minded man steeped in the mysteries of gunnery. But he was ready to support those, like Byng, who were prepared to innovate. His rapport with the Commander-in-Chief ensured that he could be a persuasive advocate on behalf of his subordinates. He was a General to whom Haig would always listen.

Horne might have relished the success of Vimy Ridge more had he not, the day after the close of the battle, while mounted and on the rearward slopes of Vimy Ridge, come off his horse on one of the muddy plank roads laid by the Canadians. The horse rolled on top of him and broke a bone in his leg.[33] For the next few weeks he was to suffer considerable pain and discomfort as he hobbled about on crutches. But this at least gave him time to put pen to paper and summarise the success of his troops at Vimy Ridge.

> The Vimy Ridge has been considered as a position of very great strength; the Germans have considered it to be impregnable. To have carried this position with so little loss testifies to the soundness of plan, thoroughness of preparation, dash and determination in execution, and devotion to duty on the part of all concerned.[34]

Chapter XIV

Army Commander: Arras: 'The Stationary Army'

The acclaim which attaches to the Canadian triumph at Vimy Ridge notwithstanding, the action itself was but a supportive part of the mainly Third Army Battle of Arras. This in turn was intended to be secondary to the major French offensive known as the Second Battle of the Aisne or, more popularly, the 'Chemin des Dames'.

General Robert Nivelle, whose brainchild the offensive was, was seen by an increasingly desperate French government as something akin to a knight in shining armour riding to his country's rescue. He planned to repeat, on a much grander scale, the tactics that had proved so successful for him at Verdun and achieve the breakthrough and defeat of the Germans that had eluded the Allies so far. He proposed a massive French offensive, the main thrust of which would start off between Soissons and Reims, sweep over the Chemin des Dames and head north, through St Quentin, over the River Oise towards Cambrai and the Belgian border. The main French attack would be supported by a British advance eastwards from Arras and a subsidiary French attack starting off between Roye and Soissons and heading northeast. These supporting thrusts were intended to draw the Germans away from the main French onslaught northwards. Within 48 hours, according to Nivelle, the attacks would link up leaving the Germans in disarray.

The British operation would mainly involve General Sir Edmund Allenby's Third Army supported, as has been seen, by Henry Horne's First Army on its left flank; and on its right by General Sir Hubert Gough's Fifth Army. The thrust of the Third Army attack would be eastwards towards the area of Cambrai where it would link up with the French. The initial assault would be mounted by 10 divisions of Third Army advancing from positions around Arras and supported by Horne's assault on Vimy Ridge. The Fifth Army would attack towards the village of Bullecourt and the Hindenburg Line at a slightly later date. The main British attack would precede that of the French by a week.[1]

Surprise had become almost impossible to achieve at a period of the war when every major attack was heralded by a prolonged and intensive bombardment of a week or more. General Allenby nevertheless proposed to achieve some tactical surprise by reducing his bombardment's length to 48 hours. But his Artillery Adviser, Major General Arthur Holland, was unable to persuade Haig's, Major General Noel Birch, that the surprise that might be achieved was a fair trade-off for a short bombardment that would have left necessary work undone. A compromise of a 4 day bombardment was agreed.[2]

Simultaneously with First Army, the Third Army attacked in the predawn hours of a bitterly cold Easter Monday, 9 April. Like the Canadians, they were initially assisted by a blizzard blowing in the Germans' faces and the attack achieved some degree of surprise. Allenby's centre units achieved an advance of 3 and a half miles, up to that point the BEF's greatest one-day advance on the

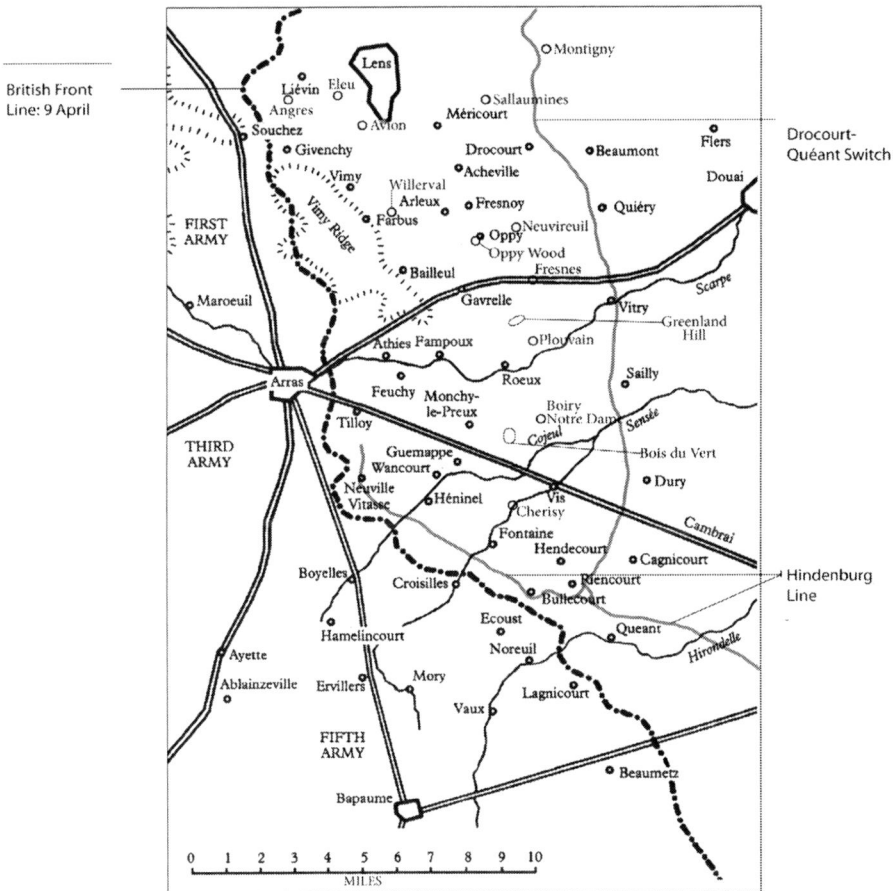

Map 12: The Arras Battlefield: April–May 1917

Western Front. They had been helped by the Germans holding their reserves too far back to be able to intervene until the following day. There had been just a slight window of opportunity for the elusive breakthrough but the weather, and the state of the ground churned up by the artillery, effectively prevented the cavalry exploiting the situation.

The offensive was resumed on the next 2 days but progress became more and more difficult in the face of the artillery's problems in moving up their guns over ground they had all too successfully churned up, and the Germans' hardening defence and counterattacks. In effect, most of what the Third Army were to achieve was accomplished on the first day. But it was by no means the end of the battle.[3]

The Fifth Army's planning for their share in the battle had been greatly complicated by the German decision to shorten their front by withdrawing several miles to their new defensive system, the Hindenburg Line (*Siegfried Stellung* to the Germans). The operation, codenamed *Alberich*, began in great secrecy on 9

February and was completed by 20 March. Tens of thousands of French civilians were uprooted from their homes as the Germans carried out a scorched earth operation intended to deny to the Allies any useful infrastructure for future exploitation. They were all too successful. The Fifth Army became aware that something was up when their patrols failed to find the enemy where they expected them. Gough ordered his troops forward to close the gap and, he hoped, disrupt construction of any new defence system.

For their part the Germans were acutely aware that neither the *Siegfried Stellung* nor the secondary *Wotan Line* (known to the Allies as the Drocourt-Quéant Switch) were likely to be complete before the anticipated Allied offensive was launched. They therefore fortified several key villages in front of the new system to hold up the British advance.[4] By the time the Battle of Arras was due to start the Fifth Army were 3 miles from the Hindenburg Line with no real idea of whether the Germans had ended their retirement or not. Gough decided to gamble that the Germans would not defend the village of Bullecourt in force and planned to pinch it out by attacks on either side. In fact Bullecourt was especially sensitive to the German defences, being close to where the Hindenburg Line and the Drocourt-Quéant Switch linked up. They had every intention of defending it fiercely. The stage was set for some of the most savage fighting of the war which would rank Bullecourt alongside Gallipoli and Pozières in the Australian national memory.

After an abortive start the previous day, Gough launched his full-scale attack on 11 April, 2 days after those of First and Third Armies. The V British Corps assaulted Bullecourt directly and from the west and I ANZAC Corps approached from the east. They were confronted by the experienced and battle-hardened 27th Württemberg Division which inflicted a bloody repulse on them. The Anzacs lost 3,500 men, including a record number of over 1,200 prisoners. Recriminations were quick to follow with the Australians blaming their supporting tanks. The main blame lay however with their own artillery. Three days later a German counterattack at Lagnicourt surprised the Australians who quickly lost 5 guns and 1,000 men. But by the end of the day they had rallied sufficiently to drive the Germans back and inflict heavy casualties.[5]

General Nivelle's offensive was launched at 06h00 on 16 April. 53 French infantry divisions faced 21 German divisions in the front line and 17 counterattack divisions poised behind. Not only were the Germans alert to the imminence of a French offensive but, through documents captured a week previously, they were fully aware of all the details of the French plan of attack. Their new strategy of defence in depth, and the confusion caused by their withdrawal from positions which the French were planning to bombard and assault, meant that they were not as badly affected as they might have been by the preliminary French bombardment. For their part the French infantry were ill-served by a creeping barrage which crept forward much too fast and tanks which proved to be ill-equipped for the tasks assigned to them. The result was a slaughter, one of the greatest disasters to befall the French in a war of disasters for them.

Despite Nivelle's undertaking to win the battle in 48 hours or give up, the battle was to drag on into the next month. The French were to achieve some successes, but the offensive had manifestly failed to live up to the high expectations which had been rashly fostered by Nivelle. This, perhaps more than the casualties, was to lead to signs of open disaffection in the French ranks rapidly turning to mutiny. Within a matter of weeks only 2 divisions could be considered totally reliable. It was fortunate that the French army proved a great deal more adept at keeping this information from the enemy (and incidentally, for a time, their British allies) than they had been in the case of their battle plans. It was inevitably to mean that Haig would come under great pressure from the French to continue the Battle of Arras, when there was little military point in doing so, in order to keep the Germans distracted from looking too closely at the misfortunes of the French.[6] At a time when Haig would have preferred to have been focussing all his attention and resources on his proposed offensive north of the Lys, he was prevented from doing so by the need to continue the battle further south.

The prolongation of the battle would involve Horne's army in some serious fighting although the leading role would continue to be taken by Allenby's troops. Immediately following completion of the occupation of Vimy Ridge, Horne pushed his divisions forward along a line from just south of Loos to his Army's junction with Third Army near the village of Fampoux. Against relatively light, or non-existent, resistance, as the Germans adjusted to the loss of Vimy Ridge, 21st Division occupied the town of Liévin just west of Lens. The villages of Angres, Givenchy, Vimy, Willerval and Bailleul-Sir-Berthoult were also occupied by Horne's troops. There were clear signs that the German withdrawal had been precipitate; large quantities of war matériel had been abandoned. But as 24th Division passed through the 21st in Liévin and pushed on towards Lens, German resistance stiffened as they made clear that Lens would not be lightly taken. The division did, however, secure the Cité St Pierre, a north-western suburb of the town. By 14 April Horne's troops had advanced about 3 miles east of Vimy Ridge and were confronted with the Germans' Oppy Line in front of the villages of Arleux, Oppy and Gavrelle.[7]

On Monday 16 April, Haig convened a meeting with Horne, Allenby and Gough and their chief staff officers at Allenby's headquarters, Château Bryas.

> I decided that all three Armies should attack next Friday simultaneously. First Army will break the Oppy Line, take Gavrelle, etc and push advanced guards on to the Drocourt-Quéant line. Third Army to advance towards Boiry, Vis-en-Artois and gain the rising ground on the right bank of the Sensée in co-operation with an attack by Gough (on the right flank) having as objective Riencourt, Hendecourt and the rising ground north and northwest of the latter. As a preliminary operation Allenby is to take the high ground on either side of Guémappe village, and then a detachment (covered by a creeping barrage) will move down to take the village itself. The object of this operation is to be able to use the valley of the Cojeul for gun positions above Guémappe and Héninel.[8]

The following day Horne told Haig that his preparations were being delayed by the wet weather. He asked for a postponement of 48 hours. Haig agreed and notified the 2 other Army Commanders.[9] The wet weather continued to hamper Horne's preparations. The advance of his guns and ammunition and the wire cutting programme had been so delayed, he told Haig, that he would not be able to attack the full length of the Oppy Line. Haig agreed that Horne's part in the operation should be confined to the taking of Gavrelle and an operation south of Loos. This would give the necessary cover to Allenby's left, whose troops would carry out their part of the operation as laid down. The First Army would complete the outstanding parts of their share of Haig's plan when the Third Army's advance had taken it across the Sensée river.[10]

While preparations for this operation went ahead, Horne's troops were continuing to exert pressure on the German positions in and around Lens. Horne described it as, 'biting off bits and putting the Germans back gradually'.[11] Every advance invited German counterattacks which were generally fought off satisfactorily. But not always. In fighting southeast of Loos on 22 April a dynamite factory was captured but was almost immediately lost to a German riposte.[12]

After a further delay of 24 hours the second phase of the Battle of Arras, known as the Second Battle of the Scarpe, was launched on 23 April. On the previous night it had been found that the wire in front of Gavrelle had been insufficiently cut, too late for a further postponement. It proved less of an obstacle than was feared and the 63rd (Royal Naval) Division of XIII Corps (now part of First Army) succeeded in taking the village, but were unable to get beyond to their final objective 300 yards to the east. The division consolidated in the village and beat off several strong counterattacks.[13]

Two other attacks were mounted by First Army, one on either side of the Souchez river. To the north, 139th Brigade of 46th Division, on the mistaken assumption that the Germans were preparing to evacuate Lens and that their positions would therefore be lightly held, attacked in insufficient strength. They sustained heavy losses with no progress to show for them.[14] It is curious that an imminent German withdrawal could have been expected. Horne himself appeared to have no such illusion. His letter to his wife of that day mentioned that the Germans were reinforcing round Lens and suggested that his strategy might be to work round the town rather than take on the Germans in house-to-house fighting.[15]

South of the Souchez 2 brigades of 5th Division assaulted even though one of the brigade commanders questioned whether the enemy wire had been adequately cut, as had been claimed by patrols and air reconnaissance. The Brigadier's fears proved well-founded and the battalions of the leading wave of the attack suffered severely from machine gun fire. The attack failed. Horne cancelled any further operations on either side of the Souchez.[16]

Meanwhile Third Army's renewed offensive had made little progress at the cost of over 8,000 casualties. An advance of nearly a mile had been achieved and the village of Guémappe secured but the attack by XVII Corps on the village of Roeux, with its chemical works, failed.[17] The Third Army tried again on 28 April, Allenby throwing 2 depleted divisions into an attack shrouded in mist. It achieved little.[18] It was left to First Army to derive something positive from this otherwise disappointing day with the capture of the village of Arleux by 1st Canadian Division.[19] Haig's diary for the day put a rather more positive gloss on events.

> The First and Third Armies attacked at 04h30 today with the object of taking Arleux-Oppy-Greenland Hill-and spur about 2,000 yards east of Monchy-le-Preux where our line now is.

Very severe fighting took place and most of the objectives were taken. We now hold Arleux, the wood west of Oppy and half the village, and we have advanced on the western slopes of Greenland Hill.

But between Greenland Hill and the Scarpe our troops did not progress as well. The 34th Division (Nicholson) attacked here. A weak battalion and a half attacked Roeux by advancing along the left bank of the Scarpe. The battalions which were to have attacked Roeux from northwest came under heavy machine gun fire as soon as they left their trenches, and were forced back to their original line. The enemy retained the wood west of Roeux, the cemetery and the Chemical Works. The troops which entered Roeux from the south were therefore cut off.

Otherwise the day was most successful. The Enemy was driven out of a wide stretch of front and 2 villages and suffered very heavily in making fruitless counterattacks. Our artillery did splendid work, both field and heavies had numerous excellent targets. 7 or 800 prisoners were taken today.[20]

Two days after this, *pace* Haig, disappointing day, the Commander-in-Chief convened a conference with his Army Commanders and their chief staff officers. He was accompanied by his Chiefs of Staff, Operations and Artillery. He opened the conference by describing developments in the French sector of the front and drawing the inferences for the BEF.

I explained the general situation and the results of the French attacks on the Aisne: that Nivelle (though still nominally C-in-C) must now carry out Pétain's orders. The latter would be based on 'avoiding losses'. Consequently all hope of piercing the enemy's lines, and of the French joining hands with the British after we had passed Cambrai, must be given up. My orders therefore were to work forward deliberately and methodically and *without hurry* to a good defensive line by the 15th May. I indicated the general line as follows:-
First Army: Hill 70 east of Loos-Lens-Acheville-Fresnoy-east of Gavrelle.
Third Army: Greenland Hill-Bois du Vert (east of Monchy)-Riencourt.
  This line must be consolidated. By the time our troops are established in it, I will be in a position to decide whether to proceed to the attack of the Drocourt-Quéant line, or to transfer troops elsewhere for active operations. The events on the Russian and Italian fronts must greatly affect my decision.[21]

The first stage of implementing these orders was to be a joint attack by all 3 armies on 3 May. Horne's army would try to take the villages of Fresnes-les-Montauban, Oppy, Neuvireuil, Fresnoy and Acheville; Allenby's Fontaine-les-Croisilles, Chérisy, Vis-en-Artois, Boiry-Notre Dame and Plouvain; and Gough's Bullecourt, Riencourt and Hendecourt. To have any hope of achieving surprise all 3 armies would have to assault at the same time. Some of Horne's troops needed daylight to get through a wood in front of Oppy; Gough's Australians, on the other hand, needed the protection of darkness as they advanced across some flat open ground in front of Bullecourt. Haig initially set Zero Hour at 04h45, which was just about acceptable to Horne and Allenby. Gough wanted 03h30 and, in the face of his protestations, Haig changed the timing to 03h45. Despite the general outrage expressed by their divisional and brigade commanders, Horne and Allenby had no choice but to comply. In the view of the Official History the decision was to prove 'unfortunate, even disastrous' for their troops. They were in general completely unprepared for night operations and facing an enemy well able to take full advantage of the moonlight against which the advancing troops would be silhouetted.[22]

The day proved to be a serious disappointment with little to show for the 3 armies' efforts except long casualty lists. They had encountered an enemy almost fanatically determined not to give ground and prepared to counterattack repeatedly if forced to. Many of Horne's troops were becoming tired and some units were seriously depleted by casualties suffered earlier in the campaign and not yet replaced. One of the 2 divisions used in the attack by XIII Corps, the 2nd, was reduced to 1,800 rifles in 4 battalions; the other, the 31st, was fresh. The terrain was also unhelpful, with the felled trees in the wood in front of Oppy acting as a defensive barrier against 31st Division. Their supporting field artillery was forced to fire from unusually long ranges. One of their brigades nevertheless managed to reach its objectives but was forced back by the failure of the brigade on its left and enemy counterattacks. The division suffered 1,900 casualties.

The 2nd Division, despite being shelled prior to going over the top, made some progress on their left and managed to link up with the Canadians southeast of Fresnoy. Elsewhere was failure. The Canadians, attacking on a 2 brigade front, achieved surprise and managed to get 250 yards beyond the village of Fresnoy where they successfully resisted 2 German counterattacks. The capture of this village was virtually the only noteworthy achievement of the day.[23] The following day, Horne wrote home describing the previous day's events.

> Yesterday's operations were successful on my front insofar that we gained about half of our objective and inflicted very heavy loss on the Germans. The fighting seems to have been very stiff all along the line. The Germans have made great efforts to prevent our further advance and have brought up many new divisions. I am quite pleased with the results of yesterday and the taking of Fresnoy was very good. Today there is the usual comparative calm after the storm except that my guns do not give the Germans any rest. I endeavour to maintain the horror which the Germans now have of the British artillery.[24]

Four days later Horne's letter home recorded some doleful news.

> The Germans put in a heavy attack on Fresnoy this morning and have gained possession of the village. It was a very misty morning and I fancy that their approach was not seen till too late to get the guns going. I am arranging for a counterattack shortly and hope to turn them out again. It is annoying but one must be prepared for a setback occasionally and I have been very fortunate up to now. It is of no great importance of course. Our line is very much stuck out in a salient at that corner and consequently liable to attack. I must have a good try to get it back again.[25]

The German attack had fallen on units of XIII Corps, which had relieved the Canadians. They were subjected to a heavy bombardment with HE and gas prior to a surprise night assault by the enemy who broke through at the second attempt, retook Fresnoy and advanced to the eastern outskirts of Arleux, inflicting heavy casualties. Horne's counterattack failed and left him no longer in a position to make further attempts to restore the situation.[26] By now his army, like those to his south, were feeling the effects of the build-up of Second and Fifth Armies in preparation for Haig's planned offensive north of the Lys. No fresh troops were coming his way to replace his losses. Some of his artillery units had been sent north. Between 8 May and the closure of the Battle of Arras near the end of the month, the fighting was to be intermittent with little progress made by either side.

With the drawing to a close of the battle, Horne and his army were about to enter into a period of relative inactivity which would last until the major German offensives of spring 1918. Horne himself was keen to press on, especially to complete the capture of Lens, but the demands of events further north were to place severe constraints on his room for manoeuvre. If the rather sardonic appellation 'Stationary Army' could ever have been applied to First Army, this was the period when it would have been less unfair than at other times. But, constraints or not, Horne's army contrived activity in this period which belies the adjective 'stationary'.

As an army commander, Henry Horne found himself having to play host to a burgeoning number of VIP visitors, from the King downwards. The bulk of his visitors were senior politicians, including Government ministers, and journalists. Like most of his senior colleagues on the Western Front, Horne was becoming increasingly exasperated at what he saw as the undermining of the BEF's leadership by the Prime Minister and other members of the government and their success in slowing down the despatch of reinforcements to France and Flanders. A visit by *The Times* military correspondent gave Horne the opportunity to 'rub the manpower question into Colonel Repington' in the hope that he would write about it.[27] A few days later he confessed to his wife, 'I loathe all politicians nowadays'.[28] When Winston Churchill, Minister of Munitions, asked to visit him on 3 June, he told her, 'I am sure I do not wish to see him but I must be civil I suppose'. (In fact the visit went quite well.)[29]

Two events which were to have a long term impact on the First Army occurred in mid-1917. The first was the arrival in the line in May of the first Portuguese troops of what was eventually to become a 2 division presence; the second, a change of command for the Canadian Corps in June.

Horne's Chief of Staff, Major General Hastings Anderson, recorded that the attachment of the Portuguese Corps to First Army was to give great anxiety to Horne, not without reason as it was to turn out. Anderson wrote:

> The methods and training of our Allies differed materially from those of the British Army, and their national pride made their assimilation in the British front a matter of anxious thought and difficulty. It was on crutches from his Vimy accident that General Horne inspected the Portuguese troops which first took over a portion of the line between Neuve Chapelle and Festubert in May 1917.[30]

Horne's anxieties were at least partially shared by his Commander-in-Chief who recorded in his diary a meeting he had had with the Portuguese Minister of War, Sr Norten de Maddas.

> He seemed quite an energetic and keen little man. The Portuguese Divn, though the first units began to arrive soon after the new year, have now only *one battalion* in the line! The delay is due in great measure to the Chief Staff Officer of the Force (Major Baptista) who has made difficulties and would

not take advantage of the knowledge of the British officers whom I sent to the Divn to be instructors. I told the Minister of this, and suggested that Baptista should go back to Portugal. He promised to go into the matter, and on his return from London is to spend a fortnight with the Division here. His Staff Officer, Major Aquas, and General Tomagnini also lunched. The latter, the old General I mean, seems generally appreciated.[31]

A change at the head of the Canadian Corps became necessary in June when, following General Allenby's departure for the Middle East, Lt General Sir Julian Byng was promoted to succeed him. Although loath to leave his Canadians, Byng was given no choice in the matter and departed on 9 June.[32] On his recommendation, Haig selected Major General Arthur Currie, GOC 1st Canadian Division, to take over the corps on promotion to Lieutenant General, thus becoming the first Canadian to achieve this position. Haig shared Byng's admiration for Currie's qualities and it was to prove a felicitous choice. It was not one which met with wholehearted approval in Canadian military and political circles. But Haig, fully supported by Horne, remained resolute. Currie wholly deserved his promotion. Although most unmilitary in pre-war background and appearance (he was the only senior BEF commander not to sport a moustache!) Currie had fully shown his competence as a brigade and divisional commander and was to prove to be one of the outstanding corps commanders of the war. Under his command the corps were to garner further laurels right through to the last day of the war. For much of the time this would be as part of First Army under Horne's command. The two men were to strike up a very good, if not entirely problem-free, working relationship.[33]

Even though he was being denuded of his artillery and his British infantry units were increasingly under strength, Horne was told by Haig that he must keep up the pressure on the enemy. This was not only to unbalance them should they attempt any voluntary retirement to free troops for use to contain the BEF's next major blow, but also to help keep them guessing where that blow would fall.[34] Horne was to rely heavily on the Canadian Corps, less affected by the drying up of drafts than his British units, to maintain this pressure. An earlier plan, to attack with all 3 of his corps on a 14 mile front from Gavrelle to Hill 70, just north of Lens, would of necessity have to be scaled back to something more in line with his depleted resources.

At midnight on the night of 2/3 June, 4th Canadian Division attacked German positions at la Coulotte, just to the southwest of Lens. The power station, brewery and brickworks were seized, but could not be held in the face of a furious enemy response with artillery and counterattacks. The Canadians were pushed back to their original line. Two days later they were able to reoccupy the power station, this time unopposed. This was the first, but not the last, time when the effectiveness of an operation was to be inhibited by First Army's shortage of artillery.[35]

Just 4 days later, on 7 June, implementation of Haig's cherished 1917 strategy began when the infantry of the Second Army assaulted Messines Ridge. Haig had long seen strategic possibilities for an offensive from the Ypres Salient. He foresaw it capturing the ridges on 3 sides of Ypres, then advancing northwest to Roulers and Torhout, then north to the Belgian coast. Simultaneously with this last step, British units on the Belgian coast would advance from Nieuwport to overcome the

German defences at Middelkerke. There would also be an amphibious landing on the Belgian coast behind the German lines. All 3 operations would converge between Ostend and Zeebrugge, liberating the 2 ports and driving the Germans northwards. They would thereby be deprived of 2 submarine bases and suffer a great strategic, and possibly terminal, defeat.

The first stage of this strategy was the seizure of Messines Ridge south of Ypres. In an operation which owed a great deal in conception and implementation to Horne's successful assault on Vimy Ridge, General Sir Herbert Plumer's Second Army were to achieve an equally stunning success on an even larger scale. A huge concentration of guns pounded the German defences for over 2 weeks prior to Zero Hour at which point 19 mines laid and primed under the German front lines were detonated simultaneously in the largest manmade explosion in history to that date. Confronted by only a few dazed German survivors, the infantry quickly overran and consolidated their objectives. Casualties were sustained over the ensuing days as the attackers sought to advance further, but when the battle ended after a week it had been a complete success and had opened the way for the full implementation of Haig's strategy.

But Haig had already planted the seeds of his strategy's failure by his decision, taken over a month earlier, to give the leading role to General Sir Hubert Gough and his Fifth Army, rather than Plumer and his Second. Instead of the relatively rapid follow-up which the latter might have been able to achieve there was to be a pause of over 6 weeks before Gough, distracted, as he had been, by his problems at Bullecourt, was ready.

Horne managed a quick trip to Messines immediately after the battle to have a look round. He was hugely impressed by the destruction wrought by the artillery, on a par with that achieved at Vimy Ridge, despite the fact that the Germans had prepared a great many more concrete dugouts at Messines.[36]

Horne's strategy was now to advance towards Lens from the southwest astride the Souchez river using the Canadians on one bank and I Corps on the other. After one or two minor operations which successfully seized stretches of German trench, Horne was ready to launch a more general assault involving all 3 of his corps.[37] In attempts to persuade the Germans that this was to be a large scale offensive against Lens, rather than the more limited operation it was, Horne hit upon the subterfuge of organising a First Army Horse Show – for him no doubt also a personal pleasure – on 25 June. It was held on high ground about 8 miles behind the front line. The resulting concourse of spectators and heavy motor traffic, as well as a gaggle of observation balloons floating above the event, were well designed to give the Germans the impression of a major concentration prior to an assault taking place.[38] The impression would have been reinforced by some preliminary operations on 24 and 25 June which saw 46th British and 3rd and 4th Canadian Divisions push forward astride the Souchez river.

On 28 June at 19h10, Horne's main assault began when XIII Corps attacked between Gavrelle and Oppy in a move intended to improve their positions on a front of 2,300 yards. At the same time the Canadian and I Corps attacked on a frontage of 4,800 yards to cut out a German salient between Avion, south of Lens, and the western suburbs of the town, and to capture Reservoir Hill (Hill 65) which overlooked the town. Despite a torrential thunderstorm, both attacks went well with only light losses and the objectives were largely secured. The exception was the main German defences in the north-eastern part of Avion, access to which had been prevented by the swollen Souchez river.

Horne was keen to resume the operation in early July with the aim of completing the encirclement of Lens. He was forced to postpone it through his shortage of artillery. For the time being follow-up was confined to a further push forward on 1 July by 46th Division, which had been responsible for the capture of Reservoir Hill 3 days previously. They gained all their objectives but were partially pushed back on one flank by a counterattack.[39] Horne was anxious about the growing weakness and tiredness of the 46th and concerned about their ability to hold on. This was no reflection on the division *per se* but on the general manpower situation. Horne had been very pleased at the way his army had performed as his letters testify.

> The last few days we have been closing in on west and southwest of Lens, and I hope this evening to find myself on the very outskirts of the town. There are so many suburbs and mine villages and one thing and another that Lens extends a great way, and once we get into the houses street fighting sets in and progress is difficult. I do not intend to let it be expensive if I can help it, and my plan is to drive the Germans out of their positions by the guns as far as possible. I am waiting now to hear results.[40]

> Our operations yesterday evening were a great success. We attacked in two places, north of Gavrelle and west and southwest of Lens. We gained all our objectives, inflicted very heavy losses on the Germans and have taken over 300 prisoners and 12 machine guns. In addition we made raids and feint attacks and drew the German fire over a front extending in all to about 15 miles. I think we fairly hustled him about. Up to now he has made no counterattacks and there has been but little hostile artillery fire. We are quite pleased with ourselves and our losses slight.[41]

Haig was equally pleased as his diary entry for 30 June records.

> The success of the First Army operations near Lens, a front of 4 miles to a depth of near 1 mile, has been highly satisfactory and most creditable. The enemy evidently thought he was to be attacked on a very wide front. He also withdrew his guns. General Horne and his Staff note a considerable change in the enemy's moral. Many prisoners now state that they cannot stand the British shelling: it is so terrific, all are ready to surrender on first opportunity.[42]

Three days later, Haig noted in his diary that the Germans appeared to have reinforced their front about Lens with 2 divisions withdrawn from the Ypres sector. He inferred from this that Horne's operations of the previous week had succeeded in one of their aims of misleading the Germans as to Haig's intentions.[43] When the 2 men met on 5 July Horne assured Haig that he would be able to continue the attacks around Lens by the Canadians, who were in fine fettle. His main worry was his 18 pounder guns which were in danger of wearing out if usage were to carry on at the desired rate. Should he go on as planned? Haig told him he would have to give the question of guns further consideration but he hoped it might be possible to reinforce Horne with a few more heavy guns taken from Third

Army.[44] Three days after their meeting Horne took advantage of favourable weather to maintain his pressure on the enemy by discharging 50 tons of gas at points along his line from Loos northwards to beyond the La Bassée Canal.[45]

In the forefront of Horne's mind was a desire to complete the capture of Lens which he hoped could be managed during the summer before his army's capacity for offensive operations was completely nullified by the need to sustain Fifth and Second Armies to the north. The obvious next move would be the capture of Hill 70 to the north of the town thus more or less completing three-quarters of its encirclement. Hill 70 was an objective with strong emotional overtones for the British. It had been a major objective on the first day of the Battle of Loos nearly 2 years previously and the failure to capture it – largely through bad luck and inexperience – had been a prime reason why Loos had turned out to be a costly failure.

On 10 July the Canadian Corps were ordered to relieve I Corps in front of Hill 70 and to formulate a plan for the capture of Lens from the northwest by the end of the month. The new GOC of the Corps, Currie, persuaded Horne that Hill 70 should be the 'Immediate Main Objective' of the operation. Not only was its possession essential to any successful attack on the town itself, offering as it would observation over the German defences, but its capture would be bound to lead to a furious enemy reaction. This would fit neatly into Haig's strategy of First Army holding the enemy on their front and keeping them guessing as to the Commander-in-Chief's broader intentions.[46]

On 11 July orders were issued to 1st and 2nd Canadian Divisions for the capture of Hill 70. Zero Day would be the 30th of the month. At a meeting on 24 July, Horne assured Haig that he had sufficient guns to give the Canadians all the artillery support they needed. The plan called for a major application of artillery power at all stages of the battle, from the initial wire cutting and reduction of the enemy defences, through the provision of protective barrages for the attacking infantry, to the main role in breaking up enemy concentrations as they prepared to launch the inevitable counterattacks. It was to be dissatisfaction with progress in destroying the enemy wire which led to the first of a series of postponements, most of them necessitated by bad weather, which finally saw the assault take place on 15 August.

Even though the Germans were fully alert to the imminence of an attack they were successfully deceived as to where precisely the blow would fall. The response of their artillery was thus spread over a much wider area than it should have been for full effectiveness. At 04h25 the First Army bombardment erupted and the assaulting Canadian battalions went over the top. In addition to the usual high explosive, the barrage also projected drums of burning oil which, combined with smoke bombs fired from Stokes mortars, covered Hill 70 with dense smoke, very effectively blinding the German defenders and their observers behind the lines. The surprise achieved by the simultaneous eruption of the bombardment and an infantry assault delivered swiftly and in strength ensured that the latter had gained their first objectives 600 yards away in 20 minutes. By 90 minutes after Zero Hour the Canadians had gained all their objectives except for a further advance of 500 yards down the eastern slopes of the hill. Attempts to complete this last challenge failed with heavy casualties among the 2 battalions involved, which had by then lost the protection of the smoke. The area concerned was taken with heavy loss 2 days later, but not before the Canadians had been forced to endure a whole series of German counterattacks on their gains of the first morning. No fewer than 18 of these were broken up by the artillery, and machine gun and rifle fire. When the battle came to an end after 4 days, the Canadians had successfully repulsed further German attempts to reverse their gains.[47]

General Horne was clearly delighted as he recorded in letters to his wife.

We have had a great day. At 04h25 we attacked a position known as Hill 70 north of Lens and we took the whole position and have held it throughout the day against a number of counterattacks. The Germans have endeavoured to counterattack across the open and we have inflicted very heavy losses on them with artillery and rifle fire. The heavy counterattacks show the importance which the Germans attach to the position. I hope we shall be able to hold what we have gained against the heavier attacks which I anticipate either at daylight tomorrow or perhaps tomorrow evening. I think we shall as our arrangements are complete and the troops, the Canadians, are staunch and good. The troops themselves are very delighted with their success, and full of fight, and I feel very thankful for our success.[48]

We have taken over 900 prisoners … I think they were determined to hold or recover Hill 70 and so far they have failed. I am very pleased as it is an unqualified success, and I am very thankful to God for his mercies.[49]

Our total of prisoners is now 23 officers and 1,161 men, … very heavy losses inflicted on the Germans and we shall be at them again before long.[50]

For his part General Currie described Hill 70 as, 'altogether the hardest battle in which the Corps has participated'. Canadian casualties amounted to about 5,600, mostly sustained on the first day, testifying to the effectiveness of the artillery in breaking up the German counterattacks.[51]

But there was to be no time for the licking of wounds or resting on laurels. With Hill 70 firmly in his hands, Horne turned his Canadians' attentions to the main prize, the town of Lens itself. On 21 August at 04h35 elements of 2 Canadian divisions attacked towards the town from the west and northwest on a frontage of 3,000 yards, from Eleu to the east of the Cité St Emile. Over the next 4 days the fighting was bitter as the Germans showed no signs of relinquishing their hold on the town. The strongpoints of the Green Crassier, Puits No 4 and the Fosse St Louis were taken by the Canadians but could not be held by them in the face of heavy enemy shelling. These points were to remain in German hands until their general retreat of the last few weeks of the war.

When added to the earlier battle for Hill 70, the Canadians were not exaggerating in regarding the 2 engagements as as bitter as any fighting they had experienced in the war to date, including Mount Sorrel and the Somme. Their casualties amounted to over 9,000. But they were able to draw consolation from the fact that 2 of their divisions had engaged and largely bested 7 German divisions, 4 of which were elite formations, which might have been employed elsewhere, to the detriment of Haig's overall strategy.[52]

Immediately after the fighting had died down and the 2 Canadian divisions involved had been relieved, Haig took the opportunity to inspect them. In the past, like most other senior British generals, he had been critical of their perceived slovenliness and lax discipline, although never of their fighting abilities. Now he commented:

> The experience and training of the past year have done wonders for the Canadians. Their moral is now very high, and though they have been opposed by the flower of the German Army (Guards etc) they feel that they can beat the Germans every time! They have now made up their minds to take more prisoners in future. It will be less trouble, because now they have to dig so many graves for the slain Germans! This is hard work!! ... I was greatly pleased with the smart turn out and earnest determined look of all ranks.[53]

The Canadians were notorious for their reluctance to take prisoners, a reputation which was well-known to the enemy and would have contributed to the last ditch resistance which the Canadians usually met. Horne would have welcomed this change of attitude on the part of the Canadians not so much for its humanitarian or labour-saving aspects – he held no sentimental attachment to human enemy life – but because the number of prisoners taken in a given operation was a useful measure of its success or otherwise, a measure to which he was much attached.

On 12 September Horne called on Haig and produced his plan for completing the capture of Lens and the cutting off of the enemy garrison's retreat. It called for an advance northeast from Eleu to the Sallaumines high ground and a simultaneous advance south east from Hill 70. Five infantry divisions and 70 tanks would be involved. When the 2 advances met, the encirclement of Lens would be complete. Horne was confident of success and thought that it would give a great boost not only to the Army's morale but also civilian, both French and British. He had all the infantry he needed, but was anxious about the number of guns that Haig could put at his disposal. Haig said he would send him direct from England a large number of a new type of 6 inch heavy mortar with a range of 1,500 yards, and some sections of 6 inch howitzers which would enable Horne to make his batteries up to 6 guns each. Haig, in approving the plan, told Horne to carry on with his arrangements as it was pretty certain that any other guns he required would be found.[54] Zero Day was set for 15 October.

Horne's planning had been taking place in the context of the momentous events taking place further north and it was in the same context that they were to founder. On 31 July, following a 2-week long bombardment, 9 divisions of Gough's Fifth Army went over the top on a 14,000 yard front east of Ypres. They were supported by 2 French divisions to the north and a Second Army diversionary attack to the south. Despite some initial success, the failure of Gough to give sufficient regard to repeated strictures by Haig on the prime importance of securing the Gheluvelt Plateau, led to the offensive becoming bogged down, literally as well as figuratively, as heavy rain turned the battlefield into a quagmire. Even the passing back of responsibility for the offensive to Plumer and the Second Army in mid-September could not stop the battle turning into an attritional slog with its overall strategic objectives well beyond the capacities of the attackers to achieve. By the end of the first week in October the ambition of Haig and his 2 Army Commanders was confined to the seizure of Passchendaele Ridge as an adequate outcome to the offensive. With the Anzacs having joined the rest of the 2 armies in exhaustion by mid-October, Haig was forced to call on the Canadians to complete the job.

This was not quite as simple as once it would have been. The Canadians were increasingly conscious of their apparent indispensability to the BEF and were no longer willing to accept unquestioningly orders from above. They had to be persuaded rather than ordered. General Currie had already told Horne that he was not prepared to place his corps under the command of Gough and Horne had passed this on to Haig's Chief of Staff, Lt General Kiggell. The latter in turn had warned Haig that if the Canadians were to be needed at Ypres they would have to be incorporated into Second Army. Haig accepted this, ascribing the blame for Gough's unpopularity with the Canadians to his Chief of Staff, Major General Neil Malcolm, who had driven them too hard on the Somme.[55] On the other hand Plumer of Second Army and Currie knew each other well and got on together.

Their mutual esteem did not however mean that Currie was prepared to commit his corps to the battle for Passchendaele Ridge. Having seen the ground and discussed it with Plumer he urged that the attack should be cancelled. Haig was forced to appeal to the corps' officers direct to seek their agreement to take on the task. In a rare outburst of articulateness, he managed this. Handed the poisoned chalice, Currie prepared his plans with his customary thoroughness, insisting on adequate artillery preparation at each stage. On 4 separate days over the period 26 October to 10 November the Canadians gradually advanced, capturing Passchendaele village on 6 November and, 4 days later, completing occupation of the Ridge. They had suffered over 15,000 casualties.[56]

Their involvement at Passchendaele had entailed the Canadians' departure from Horne's First Army on 13 October, thus effectively putting paid to Horne's plan to invest Lens. Although they were back under his command by 18 November, there could be no question of reviving his plan in the foreseeable future. Haig noted in his diary for 19 November:

> I explained to Horne my proposed operations [the Battle of Cambrai was to start the following day] and pointed out that by crossing the Sensée River east of Arleux I turned all the enemy's defences facing First Army and the Drocourt-Quéant Line. I could not expect the First Army, owing to weakness in guns and numbers, to do more than reconnoitre until our advance from Cambrai direction caused enemy to withdraw from his front. Then he must do his best to follow up and press the enemy.[57]

After its initial stunning success through the use of massed tanks for the first time in warfare, the Battle of Cambrai turned into a major disappointment when Third Army were caught unprepared by a major German counterattack. By the time the battle was over it was becoming increasingly apparent that the strategic initiative was passing over to the Germans. The conclusion of hostilities on the Eastern Front would soon enable them to transfer large numbers of relatively fresh but battle-hardened divisions to the Western Front at a time when the Allies were suffering manpower and morale crises. The bloodletting of Passchendaele had persuaded Lloyd George that repetitions could best be avoided by starving Haig and his generals of the human raw material they consumed so prolifically. The effects of this were becoming so painful that divisions were of necessity being reduced in size from 12 to 9 battalions with all the pain to cohesion and morale that this entailed. (The Canadians were not affected by this downsizing, another reason for their increasing importance in the BEF.)

At the same time the French were only in the early stages of recovery from the nadir of the mutinies and were a long way from resuming their willingness to assume the offensive. Finally, the build-up of the American Expeditionary Force in France was proceeding painfully slowly and it could not be counted on for a significant contribution until the second half of 1918 at the earliest. The realisation was sinking in that the BEF and its Allies would have to look to their defences over the next few months before there could be any question of resuming the offensive other than in strictly limited and local operations. Along with his fellow army commanders, Horne's defensive skills were to be sorely tested in the spring of 1918.

Chapter XV

Army Commander: The German Lys Offensive

It had been a long time since the BEF had been called on to fight a major defensive battle but, as 1917 gave way to 1918, this was the prospect that faced Haig and his army commanders. It called for a massive readjustment of mindset for commanders whose recent experience of defensive operations had been largely confined to beating off enemy counterattacks following successful offensive operations of their own. An unwelcome complication was provided by the need to reduce the size of the BEF's divisions from 12 to 9 battalions, an exercise forced on the unhappy generals by the increasing shortage of manpower. The heavy casualties suffered at the Third Battle of Ypres had effectively reduced the size of the BEF by the equivalent of 12 divisions. The drafts being sent out from England were proving wholly inadequate in numbers to restore the situation. There was little option but to reduce the size of divisions, thus enabling over 140 battalions to be disbanded and their troops redistributed among those battalions that remained. The reorganisation had been ordered by a War Office committee in the teeth of Haig's opposition and to the general distress of the army. Its effect on the fighting efficiency of an army, which would be engaged in one of the greatest battles of the war within days of the changes being implemented, can only be guessed at.[1]

Horne had completed the reorganisation of his army to the new format by 19 February.[2] His task was relatively easier than the other army commanders as his Canadian Corps was, for the time being at least, to continue to enjoy the 12 battalion format. Haig had confirmed this at a meeting in mid-January with Sir Edward Kemp (the Agent for the Canadian government in London) who agreed that the Canadian divisions should stay as they were until Haig's scheme to persuade the Americans to attach 3 of their battalions to each British division (thus restoring the *status quo ante*) was finally settled one way or the other.[3] Haig was thus able to reassure Lt General Currie, when the latter called on him on 5 February, that he would be continuing to command 4 full-strength divisions.[4]

In the event, Haig's scheme involving the Americans came to nothing. But the Canadians continued to field full-strength divisions until the end of the war. It was not that they did not have manpower problems. A fifth Canadian division, formed in early 1917, had had to be broken up a year later to provide replacements for the other 4.[5] Conscription, introduced into the Dominion in the winter of 1917/18 after much political soul-searching, was not proving to be a huge help in maintaining numbers.[6] But the Canadian Expeditionary Force were just able to maintain their full-strength presence on the Western Front partly because of their lack of direct participation in the great defensive battles which were to engage the British and French armies in the spring and early summer of 1918. The circumstances surrounding their non-involvement were to lead to a rare, and fortunately temporary, souring of relations between Currie on the one side and Horne and Haig on the other.

Preoccupied as he was with putting his army's defences in order, Horne was nevertheless able to keep in touch with political developments at home and the fallout from them affecting the fortunes of the BEF. The 5 months since Winston Churchill's visit to his headquarters had done nothing to allay Horne's suspicion of politicians; in mid-November 1917 he told his wife that he did not trust Lloyd George a bit![7] The immediate cause of this comment was Lloyd George's latest attempt to circumvent what he saw as the dead hand of Haig and his generals on the conduct of the war by setting up an Inter-Allied Supreme War Council at Versailles. Horne wrote:

> We are all much interested and not a little exercised over LG's latest production, the Allied War Council and its Military advisers. It is difficult to see how it is to work without clashing with the C-in-C and the General Staff at the War Office. It looks like an attempt on the part of LG to get the control of the strategy and of the army, and I fear he is very dangerous.[8]
>   ... No, this "Supreme Allied Council" does not impress me, and you know that I have no great opinion of the other man.[9] He is more of a politician than a soldier! I cannot see how it is all going to work without friction, and I cannot follow LG's arguments in its favour as given in his speech at Paris, which I have read through. However we will hope for the best and I am sure that we will muddle along as we always do.[10]

By early February Lloyd George's efforts to undermine Haig in France and General Robertson, the Chief of the Imperial General Staff, in London bore partial fruit when Robertson, unable to accept the dilution of his role implied by the existence of the Supreme War Council, resigned. He was replaced by Sir Henry Wilson despite an unequivocal warning from Haig direct to the Prime Minister and the Secretary of State for War that Wilson was distrusted by the Army, hardly an ideal qualification for its military head.[11] Although Horne very quickly struck up a good rapport with Wilson at meetings they had at Versailles and then at Horne's headquarters, he had been greatly saddened by Robertson's departure.

> We are awfully distressed to read that Wullie Robertson has been pushed out. I am so sorry. It appears to me madness at this most critical period of the war, and so very unjust. I am sure that there is no one who has done more for the British Empire during this war than Wullie Robertson! I have known for a long time that Lloyd George had got his knife into him, and he has managed to get him out at last! It is a great shame! I feel very angry as well as sorry about it. Such a splendid man. I do not know how we shall get on without him.[12]
>   ... I feel very cross to think that Robertson has been badly treated and, besides, the loss of his commonsense to steady the War Cabinet will be very great and very bad for the country at this critical time.[13]

These political manoeuvrings could not be permitted to distract Horne from putting his army on as sound as possible a defensive footing in anticipation of the German offensive. Labour was short but plans were drawn up, and the preparations made, for the destruction of bridges and important road centres which, if left intact, would prove useful to an advancing enemy. By 21 February Horne was sufficiently satisfied with the state of his preparations to deem it possible to request 2 weeks' home leave. Haig agreed but, before Horne's departure, spent a couple of days with him travelling round the First Army front examining the defensive dispositions that had been put in place. Haig was especially concerned about arrangements around the junction of First Army's sector with Third Army's, recalling that it was here that the two armies had made such spectacular advances on the first day of the Battle of Arras, nearly a year previously. What could be done by his armies, could equally be done by the enemy. He was well pleased with what he saw and thought a further 2 weeks' work would see the defences as sound as human endeavour could make them.[14]

The following week Haig spent a day with 2 of Horne's corps commanders, Lt General Holland of I Corps and Lt General Currie and his Canadians, and came away well impressed with what he had seen. It gave him a feeling of confidence, he noted, to have such reliable troops and such methodological defensive arrangements in such a very important area of the front.[15]

Horne's principal concern remained the Portuguese Corps. Since raising the matter with Haig on 15 January[16] his nervousness about them had mounted as the ground hardened in the Neuve Chapelle-Givenchy area where the Portuguese held the line. The hard ground, which would materially assist any German assault, had been brought about by a combination of measures designed to drain the trenches and keep them dry, and an unusually dry winter. When Haig visited the Portuguese Corps headquarters and the 2 divisions on 1 March he took some comfort from the fact that the men looked very much fitter than when they had arrived a year previously. He realised however that morale was unlikely to be good when the junior officers took prolonged leaves in Portugal and, even when at the front, neglected the welfare of their men.[17] The most satisfactory solution would have been to relieve the Portuguese with British divisions. But this was not, unfortunately, an option at a time when the BEF was severely stretched and still unsure of where and when the German blow might fall.

By 10 March, GHQ Intelligence was anticipating that the main German blow would fall in the Arras-Cambrai sector (Third Army). There might possibly be a 5 division diversionary operation against First Army between Armentières and Neuve Chapelle, and possibly on Hill 70, north of Lens.[18] When there was a sudden upsurge in enemy artillery activity aimed at Armentières, Houplines and Fleurbaix, Horne moved a reserve division up to the River Lys.[19] There were no further developments and by 17 March GHQ Intelligence thought a German attack was no longer imminent.[20]

Only 4 days afterwards, on the 21st, the Germans launched *Operation Michael.* As had been anticipated a major assault was made on Third Army on the Cambrai front. But an even heavier assault fell on the British Fifth Army further south in the Somme area. General Sir Hubert Gough's army had only recently taken over much of the sector from the French and were weak in numbers. The Germans, helped by a mist cloaking their movements, a sophisticated artillery programme, overwhelming force and refined infantry tactics, advanced rapidly. On Horne's front the anticipated diversionary operations did not eventuate; German activity on this first day in his sector was limited to heavy gas shelling of Armentières and Fleurbaix.[21]

On the outbreak of *Operation Michael,* Horne's army were defending a line 33 miles long stretching from Armentières in the north to Gavrelle in the south. He had 14 divisions at his disposal, including the 2 Portuguese, and 1,450 guns and howitzers. Behind Horne's lines were the Béthune coalfields and Vimy and Lorette Ridges, important economic and strategic targets for the Germans. But Haig's first priority was to reorganise the BEF in the light of developments in the Fifth and Third Army areas, where the immediate crisis was unfolding. On 26 March, during a meeting with his army commanders at Doullens, Haig instructed Horne to withdraw 3 of his Canadian divisions from the line and place them at some central point behind the Third Army from where they might quickly be deployed to meet any developing threat to the vital city of Amiens.[22] This wholesale move of a key part of Horne's army was forced upon Haig, not only by the overall military situation, but also by General Currie's insistence that the divisions of his corps must not be split up and fed piecemeal into the line.

On the same day that he met his army commanders Haig also participated in an inter-Allied conference at Doullens at which the momentous decision was taken to appoint General Ferdinand Foch to co-ordinate the actions of the Allied armies on the Western Front. A week later Foch's role was expanded to cover the 'strategic direction of military operations' making him in effect Supreme Allied Commander, or *Generalissimo*.[23]

Two days after the 26 March meeting of army commanders, Horne's army became involved in the battle for the first time when the German Seventeenth Army launched *Operation Mars*, an attack north-westwards and westwards on both sides of the River Scarpe towards Arras. Nine German divisions, with 2 in support, formed the southern prong of the assault (*Mars South*) and 7 divisions the northern prong (*Mars North*). Ready to receive them were XVII Corps of Third Army to the south and XIII Corps of First Army further north.

Horne's intelligence had predicted accurately both the extent and timing of the German assault. In line with the latest concepts of defence in depth, and his belief that the front line should be regarded as an outpost line, Horne ordered 56th and 3rd Canadian Divisions to evacuate their forward zone on the night preceding the German attack, leaving only outposts in the area. A further reason for Horne's order was that it would bring his troops under the protection of the artillery batteries firing from Vimy Ridge. It was quickly realised however that Horne's dispositions conflicted with Third Army's intention of fighting in their well-developed Forward Zone. If they were to conform with First Army they would have to give up some of their strongest defences. A compromise was agreed whereby both Armies would maintain a strong presence in the Forward Zone but the front line would be only nominally held. When the German barrage erupted at 03h00 it fell on largely empty trenches. Nevertheless the sheer weight of the German heavy artillery bombardment, which included phosgene gas, put great pressure on the British defences.[24]

Despite the great strength in numbers of the German assault in the south, it only succeeded in pushing back the Third Army defenders a short way before the attack petered out with heavy losses. In the north only 4th (Third Army) and 56th (First Army) Divisions faced the 7 division-strong German onslaught. After stubborn resistance, and the infliction of heavy casualties, the British divisions were forced out of the Forward Zone but stabilised their positions in the forward area of the Battle Zone. Here they successfully repelled all further attempts by the enemy to get forward. Like *Mars South, Mars North* had failed; Horne's army had passed its first defensive test.[25] There were accumulating signs that the next one would not be long in coming.

The main problem for Haig, Horne and Byng was to determine precisely where the next German blow might fall. As March gave way to April it was felt that the enemy would still try to envelop Arras from the southeast and northeast, but that they might possibly extend their assault northwards to the La Bassée Canal. This indication of a northward shift was not sufficient to persuade Haig that a reserve division, the 57th, should go to Horne rather than Byng. But Byng was ordered to concentrate his reserves behind the north end of his line where they would be better placed to come to Horne's assistance should the need arise.[26]

A shift north had obvious attractions to the Germans. It would mean them attacking where the British lines were only 50 miles from the Channel, with the area in between chockfull of vital infrastructure and logistics for the BEF. A northward wheel, once the British lines had been breached, would put the Germans in possession of the last remaining French coalfields in Allied hands.[27] The French were understandably nervous about this and the responsibility for their defence being in the hands of Horne, whose defensive capabilities had not, in their eyes, been proven.[28]

At daybreak on 2 April, First Army observed a German concentration between La Bassée and Vendin-le-Vieil which they sought to deal with by gunfire. Aircraft reported considerable railway activity around Douai, Valenciennes and Cambrai which tended to bear out the assessment that the attack would come south of the La Bassée Canal. As late as 6 April this was still Haig's belief, and would remain so, although by this time he was not discounting a possible surprise attack against the Portuguese. He commented that Horne was quite alive to these possibilities and was prepared to meet them.[29]

The previous day, the Germans had brought *Operation Michael* to an end in the Somme area. Not that Haig could be immediately sure of this. But this development did open up the possibility that British troops might soon be available to relieve the Portuguese. Horne's letters for these early days of April reflect a quiet confidence that his army would be no pushover for the Germans should they attack it, as he was fairly sure they would. He fretted that the wet, dull and hazy weather was preventing him from receiving the air reconnaissance reports he craved. At the same time, he recognised it would also be hindering the German preparations and be of little help to them when they eventually attacked.[30]

In these nervy days Horne was to lose the services of his friend and Major General Royal Artillery, Freddie Mercer. He could not, however, have wished for a better replacement than Major General Ernest Alexander, VC, who had served under him at XV Corps and been the brains and driving force behind the development and refinement of artillery tactics which had taken place there on Horne's watch. Alexander took over from Mercer in the first week of April and was to remain with Horne at First Army for the remainder of the war.[31]

Despite his confidence in his Army's ability to withstand anything the enemy could throw at him, Horne put in hand preparations to move his headquarters rearwards and told his wife:

I am working up back lines because it is prudent to do so. We have no intention of going back unless compelled to by finding our flank turned! These are anxious times as during this lull the Boche must be preparing a fresh attack and a heavy one and I think it may extend southwards from the La Bassée Canal this time, with perhaps a small attack north of the Canal.[32]

As this letter was written only a few hours before the German attack was launched, the enemy's attempts to deceive the British as to where the blow would fall had clearly proved successful. They had been helped by GHQ's conviction that the main intention of any German attack in the area would remain to pinch out Vimy Ridge and threaten Arras. This had led GHQ to downplay the clear evidence of enemy preparations opposite the Portuguese stretch of the line – much increased road and rail traffic and the stockpiling of ammunition – as a diversion intended to draw British reserves to the sector, when they should be kept further south.[33]

Concerns about the Portuguese, should any sort of attack fall on them, were not only preoccupying Horne but also his 2 corps commanders most directly affected. Most of 1st Portuguese Division had already been withdrawn from the line and the 2nd, which now had responsibility for both divisions' stretch of line, had been incorporated into Lt General Haking's XI Corps. Another division of the corps, the 55th West Lancs, held the line to the Portuguese right. To the left of XI Corps were Lt General Du Cane's XV Corps, whose 40th Division were deployed to the left of the Portuguese. To the 40th's left were 34th Division. All the British divisions, except the 55th, were tired and depleted from their recent involvement in the heavy fighting further south.

Like Horne, Haking entertained no illusions regarding the fighting qualities of his Portuguese Division. Even by the standards of most Allied units by this stage of the war, their numbers were well below establishment. Their morale was poor and their apprehension great as they realised that the protection from attack they had been afforded by the generally waterlogged nature of their area of line had been lost as the ground had dried out. Haking had strongly and urgently recommended that British troops should relieve their allies. In the meantime he and Du Cane had agreed that such reserve troops as they could muster should man the Battle Zone behind the Portuguese should the latter be attacked.[34] If he needed any reminding of the frailty of the Portuguese, Horne received it when on 8 April one of their battalions refused to go into the trenches. He thereupon arranged for them to be relieved on the night of 9/10 April, a decision made easier now that the end of *Operation Michael* had eased the manpower crisis slightly.[35]

Sadly this was to be 24 hours too late to help the Portuguese, or First Army, to withstand the initial enemy onslaught. It was also to give Basil Liddell Hart another stick with which to beat Horne, which he wielded with one-sided relish. He wrote:

The Portuguese Corps had been holding a six-mile front on both sides of Neuve Chapelle. It had been in the line for a long time, and increasing cases of insubordination had been a warning of declining morale. The remedy applied was an inverted example of military judgment. General Horne, reshuffling his dispositions, withdrew the 1st Portuguese Division, all but one brigade, from the line on April 5th. The 2nd was also to be relieved by British divisions on the night of the 9th, but meanwhile it was given the whole Corps sector to hold. We might aptly coin the phrase "First Army Aid" as a satirical definition for misguided first aid. Horne's solution is the more curious in that he had been warned by his "Q" staff that the convergence of German railways made the Lys sector the most probable point of attack; indeed the only point where an attack could be mounted.[36]

The German offensive was given the codename *Georgette* in recognition of the fact that it had been scaled down from the originally planned *George*. The scaling down had been necessitated by the unanticipatedly high demands on their resources generated during *Michael*. The German strategy was to break through

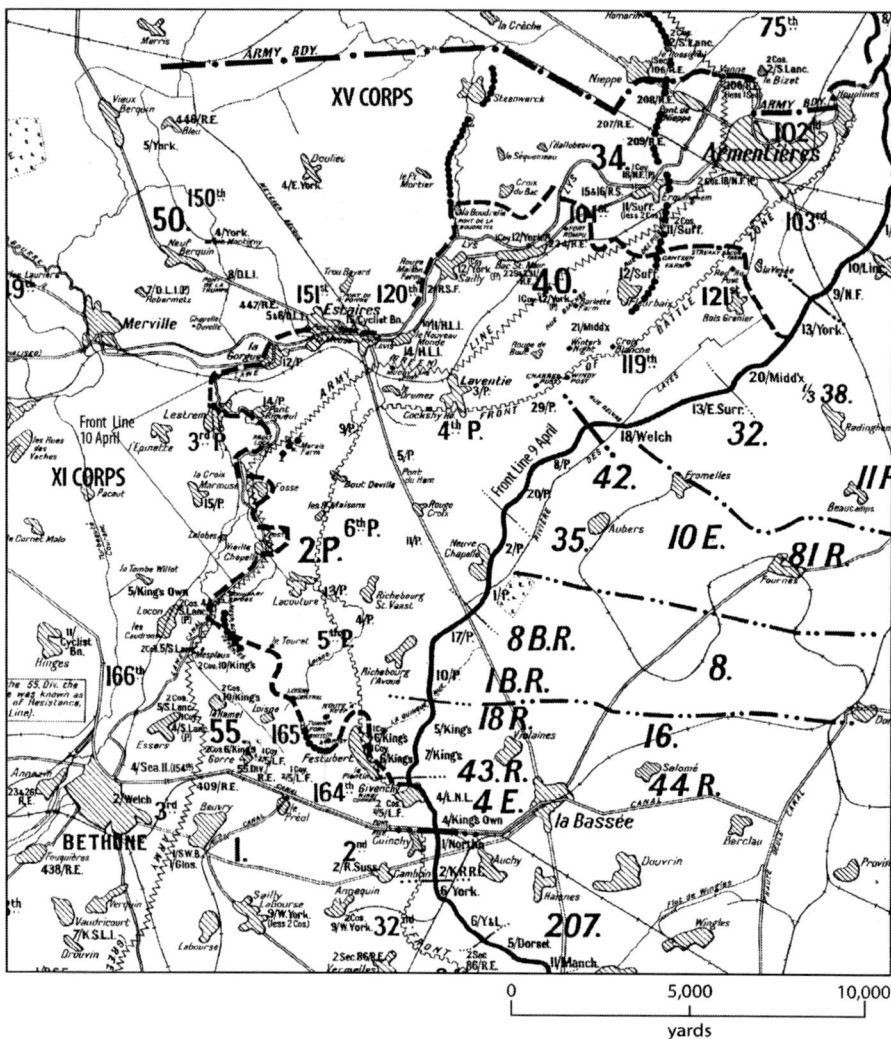

Map 13: The Lys: April 1918

the British lines and seize the vital railway junction of Hazebrouck. If circumstances were propitious the advance might even be continued to the coast. A
second prong would capture the important Flanders heights of Mount Kemmel,
Cassel and Mont des Cats and force a British withdrawal from the Ypres Salient.
The first stage of the German plan called for 4 divisions of their Sixth Army to
attack between La Bassée Canal in the south and Houplines, east of Armentières, in
the north, a frontage of 17 miles. Two other divisions would guard the left flank
along the La Bassée Canal and a further 2 would advance behind the German right
flank with the intention of exploiting the breakthrough by wheeling northwards
towards Hazebrouck.[37]

The German attack was prefaced by a heavy bombardment of the rear areas of
the Portuguese and 55th Divisions which began at 04h15 on 9 April. Singled out
for attention were Allied artillery batteries, road junctions and headquarters, from
Horne's at Ranchicourt, nearly 12 miles behind the lines, right down to those of
battalions. Although the distance to Ranchicourt was too great for the Germans to
achieve the desired accuracy, they were sufficiently effective with nearer HQs to
inflict severe disruption on command structures. The bombardment included the
intensive gas shelling of Armentières. For 2 hours, between 06h00 and 08h00, the
bombardment decreased in intensity. When it resumed in full fury it concentrated
on the Portuguese and British front positions, with trench mortars joining in 10
minutes before the infantry assault began at 08h45. It was one year to the day since
the triumphant assault of Horne's army on Vimy Ridge.[38]

The assaulting German infantry were helped by a heavy mist which lay over
the battlefield. It did not begin to dissipate until the early afternoon. The main
thrust of their attack fell squarely on the Portuguese, although both 55th and 40th
Divisions on either side, were rapidly and heavily engaged. Many of the Portuguese
of the 3 weak brigades manning the front lines had not waited for the infantry
assault; they had begun heading for the rear during the German bombardment,
some as early as 07h30. By 10h00 the vast majority of the Portuguese had passed
through the front line of the Battle Zone (being hastily manned by British reserves)
on their way to the rear and out of the battle. According to General Haking their
precipitate retreat greatly impeded the British reserves trying to get forward. Some
Portuguese even took their boots off to run the quicker. Others stole the bicycles of
XI Corps' cyclists, who had been sent forward to bolster the British line.

This sad account is not entirely fair to the unfortunate Portuguese. To their
credit, they did take their guns with them. Some isolated pockets of Portuguese did
stand and fight bravely, but were quickly disposed of by the enemy. By 11h00 the
battlefield was virtually empty of Portuguese troops and guns.

Although the likelihood of a Portuguese collapse had been anticipated, the
speed and extent of the disintegration had not. Nor had the Portuguese failure to
demolish bridges and other vital points in their rapid retreat.[39] The British were
consequently left with insufficient time to implement fully their emergency
contingency plan. Essentially this called for the 51st (Highland) Division to come
up on the left flank of 55th Division. It would link up there with 50th
(Northumbrian) Division coming up on the right flank of 40th Division. The 2
new divisions, tired and depleted from their recent exertions further south, were to

occupy the forward Battle Zone and try to contain the German advance there, about 3 miles behind the original front line.

The 40th Division had been ordered to place one of its brigades behind the Portuguese and to link up with 50th Division. The brigade had great difficulty in distinguishing attacking Germans from retreating Portuguese, as a result of which the Germans were allowed past the brigade's south facing defensive flank virtually unhindered. The Germans, turning north, began to envelop the brigade. It was only with the utmost difficulty that they were able to close the gap and link up with 50th Division.[40]

The 55th (West Lancashire) Division were to receive great acclaim for their successful defence of Givenchy and Festubert during this and the ensuing days. A Territorial Force division established in 1908, many of its constituent units had been sent to France in the early months of the war to join other formations. It was not until January 1916 that it was reconstituted in France as an operational division. As their full name would suggest, the division recruited largely from the area of Lancashire between Liverpool and Lancaster. The command was entrusted to Major General Hugh Jeudwine, who would remain in command for the rest of the war. Like Horne a Gunner, Jeudwine had a reputation for ruthlessness in his dealings with the enemy and his colleagues. But he knew how to handle the rather independent-minded Territorials, ensuring that he was aware of, and took account of, the views of the officers and men in the trenches on how tactics might be modified and improved.[41]

As his division awaited the German assault, Jeudwine almost certainly felt that he had a point to prove. The division's last period of intensive action had been during the Battle of Cambrai over 4 months previously. By the time the initially spectacular British advance in that battle had ground to a halt on 29 November, 55th Division, then part of the Third Army's VII Corps, had found themselves manning the front line by the Banteux Ravine. Jeudwine and his neighbouring Divisional Commander, Major General Scott, were convinced that a German counterattack was imminent but were unable to persuade their superiors of the danger. According to the Official History, 'Third Army issued no warning, ordered no movement of reserves, took no steps to ensure that troops in the rear area should be readily available'.[42]

In the face of this indifference the 2 divisional commanders did what they could to prepare their divisions for a possible onslaught. When it came after a heavy hour-long bombardment, they found themselves under attack from 3 enemy divisions employing storm troops and flamethrowers, and supported by strafing aircraft. Jeudwine's machine guns took a heavy toll of the attackers but their momentum was irresistible and 55th Division were forced to withdraw, suffering heavy casualties and losing some guns.[43] The German counterattack would soon wipe out, and more, the British gains of the first 9 days of the battle. Inevitably, the recriminations began. Jeudwine and his division came in for some largely unjustified criticism, but the axe, when it fell, descended on 3 corps commanders, including Lt General Sir Thomas Snow of VII Corps, who were all sent home. For their part 55th Division were transferred to Horne's army and were sent into reserve to begin a period of 2 months out of the line. This gave them the time to absorb replacements, re-equip and retrain before they found themselves once more back in the line on 15 February 1918.

Jeudwine's retraining of his division in the 2 month period available to him had concentrated on defence and involved a pragmatic and modified application of the new concept of defence in depth. He could not embrace the concept fully; he saw it as offering too many excuses to surrender or retreat. He assigned to his units either a garrison or counterattack role and their officers and men were intensively trained accordingly. The garrison units, which would man keeps or strongpoints, were ordered to fight on even if surrounded and cut off; the counterattack units would react immediately to join up with stongpoints holding out and thus cut off in turn the attacking enemy. Jeudwine's defensive philosophy, and its successful absorption by the troops under his command, was to prove of vital importance in the ultimate containment of the German offensive.[44] Retreat would have been disastrous both for his division and for First Army. As long as 55th Division held their ground, the enemy's scope to exploit its breakthrough of the Portuguese positions to the north would be inhibited.

As the battle opened, 55th Division were holding the line from La Bassée Canal northwards, passing to the east of Givenchy to La Quinque Rue, about a mile and a half east of Festubert. Two brigades were in the line, with one, on its way to relieve part of the Portuguese Division, fortuitously placed to act as a reserve. The division came under attack from elements of 3 German divisions. Under cover of a creeping barrage and the heavy mist the Germans were able to get within 20 yards of the British positions before they were spotted. In the initial exchanges the enemy succeeded in penetrating the division's line at several points. The brigade defending the Givenchy sector soon found that several of their strongpoints had been fully or partially surrounded and the ruins of Givenchy Church had been occupied. But no strongpoint was overrun and, as had been foreseen, counterattacks quickly re-established the division's line virtually in its entirety by nightfall.

The story was similar for the brigade defending the Festubert sector except that here 3 important keeps were overrun in the initial German assault. Only 2 were recaptured by immediate counterattack. In the case of the third, the Route A Keep, the initial counterattack failed and a set piece operation with artillery support had to be mounted. This took place, successfully, on the night of 12/13 April. (But this was not the end of the story; Route A Keep was to change hands no fewer than 8 times during the battle.) The British division, realising that the Portuguese had collapsed, formed a defensive flank facing north. The 51st Division, coming up from reserve, were able to plug the gap left by the Portuguese and ensure that there was a continuous, if tenuous and slowly retreating, British defensive line in front of the Germans.[45]

Held up on their left by 55th Division, and by 40th Division around Fleurbaix on their right, the German attackers nevertheless made considerable progress through the centre where the 2 tired and depleted British divisions, brought up to plug the gap left by the Portuguese, fell back slowly. But by the end of the day, the German timetable had already fallen behind. Their plan had called for them to be across the River Lys along the whole length of their assault by this time. Instead they had only secured a small bridgehead of the far side of the river at Bac St Maur.[46] Horne could take little consolation from this; the British position remained serious and losses had been heavy. With all available reserves committed, Horne's troops were holding a thin line around the edge of a German crescent-shaped penetration 10 miles wide and 5 and a half miles deep at its furthest extremity.

The enemy penetration had had the effect of extending the length of First Army's frontage north of the Scarpe from 16 to 29 miles, creating further pressures on Horne's resources.[47] The rejection by Foch of Haig's appeals to order the French to take over British line further south, which would have released British divisions for use further north, threw the BEF back onto its own resources. General Plumer of Second Army readily agreed to send 2 relatively fresh divisions, the 29th and 49th, to assist Horne; 3 brigades of these units would be available on the 10th.[48]

Despite his understandable anxieties Horne was able to sound upbeat in letters to his wife.

> The Germans attacked the front held by the Portuguese this morning and included in their attack my old spot Givenchy. We have had a very trying and anxious day. The Portuguese of course went back. Givenchy has been gallantly held all day by General Jeudwine's Division. The Germans have penetrated deeply in the centre of what was the Portuguese front and the situation is of course not entirely clear. I hope it may straighten out by morning time. There was a terribly thick fog this morning and noone could see what was going on. That was very much in favour of the attackers. The German certainly has luck in his weather. I am hoping to be able to hold them all right – a good deal depends on whether the Boche can renew his attack tomorrow in any great force. I am inclined to think that he will not be able to. The ground is very wet with deep mud and his roads will soon be bad. It is an anxious time but I am all right and my staff working splendidly.[49]
>
> The attack yesterday was very heavy between La Bassée Canal and Armentières but we got it stopped, except in one place where the Boche managed to get through and across the River Lys. I hope to put that right this evening and I hope that he may be in so congested a state behind that he cannot continue to attack in force. I am full of fight and shall do my best, so do not feel anxious. Fighting against superior numbers is always anxious work but one must not let it upset one but just go at it, hard. General Jeudwine and his Division did well and held Givenchy. The C-in-C came to see me this afternoon and was pleased with our defence.
>
> The Boche is making a big effort, there is no doubt of that. Our troops have a very hard time but they do fight well.[50]

The 10 April brought no respite for Horne's hard-pressed troops as the enemy's Sixth Army maintained the pressure on First Army's attenuated defences. At the same time, the German Fourth Army launched an assault on General Plumer's Second Army by advancing westwards north of Armentières towards the Messines-Wytschaete Ridge, which had been so triumphantly captured by Plumer in June 1917. For both British armies it was a day of desperate defence. As gaps appeared in the line the process of 'puttying up', reminiscent of the days of First Ypres, reappeared. Even though it did not prove possible to stop the enemy from advancing, their progress was much slower than they wanted or had planned.

Nevertheless, they did enlarge the Bac St Maur bridgehead, secured other passages across the Rivers Lys and Lawe, and obtained a foothold on the Messines Ridge. This last development, coupled with the town's saturation with gas, necessitated the evacuation of Armentières. But the Germans had failed to pierce the British front or drive a wedge between First and Second Armies.

Much of what little success the Germans enjoyed at the southern end of the battle was at the expense of 51st Division. Despite being driven back and losing a couple of river crossings the Highlanders did nevertheless manage to cling on to the village of Vieille Chapelle. To their right Jeudwine's 55th Division stood firm throughout the day. Further north, 50th Division, with much of their frontage facing south as a result of the Portuguese collapse, were unable to prevent the Germans crossing the Lys and establishing a small bridgehead at Estaires. The division withdrew to a previously prepared line about 1,200 yards to the west of the river. There they successfully resisted all further German attempts at penetration. The Germans fanned out to the north and south but were contained about 1,000 yards from the river by the 50th and elements of the newly arriving 29th Division. Along with the 49th, this division had been in the process of moving from Second to First Army when Plumer's army became directly embroiled in the battle.

At the northern end of First Army's sector, enemy attacks initially pushed 40th Division back about 1,500 yards, but a third of this was regained in determined counterattacks. The German advance to the Messines Ridge in the Second Army sector took them through the villages of Messines, Ploegsteert and Wytschaete before they were held. Wytschaete was later retaken by the British.

Even though an optimist may have detected signs that the usual norm of the Western Front – initial striking success followed by the onset of the law of diminishing returns – was beginning to reassert itself, Haig, Horne and Plumer could draw little comfort from the situation confronting them as the second day of the battle drew to a close. The new circumstances brought about by the widening of the German offensive to encompass Second Army's front led to Horne and Plumer meeting. They agreed that, as far as possible, Horne would release whatever reserves he could conjure up to Plumer in the expectation that these would be replaced by troops sent north to Horne by Third Army. In implementation of this arrangement Haig ordered the immediate despatch of 33rd Division to Plumer to be followed by 5th Division to Horne. In addition, 61st Division of I Corps were placed at the disposal of Horne's XI Corps.[51]

Overall, Haig now had only one Australian and the 4 divisions of the Canadian Corps available for deployment, with the latter still reluctant to being committed other than as a corps. Foch however was finally persuaded of the seriousness of the threat to the British. At a meeting with Haig late on the 10th, he agreed to order a French force of 4 infantry and 3 cavalry divisions northwards, initially to provide cover for the BEF's Third and Fourth Armies. This would enable them to free units for use in the First and Second Armies' sectors. If necessary, the French could subsequently be committed to the battle itself. Haig now felt able to order the immediate entrainment of 1st Australian Division to positions in Plumer's sector where they could block an enemy advance on Hazebrouck.[52]

Whatever relief Haig may have felt at Foch's belated support was insufficient to stop him issuing his uncharacteristic and famous 'Backs to the Wall' Order of the Day on 11 April. The reaction of its recipients, at least as recalled in retrospect, appears to have ranged from inspired to outraged. But the fact that the normally reserved Haig could be driven to such a pitch of eloquence reflected his belief that a, if not the, major crisis of the war for the Allied cause was being fought out by Horne's and Plumer's exhausted armies.[53]

Whatever disappointment the Germans may have felt in their achievements of the first 2 days of the battle was not reflected in their plans for the third. They were to exploit their successes in the direction of Hazebrouck and Calais. Their attacks began at 04h30 under cover of a mist which was not to clear until the middle of the day. Once again the Germans were able to make very little impression on 55th Division. Against the 51st however they were more successful, pushing them back. Vieille Chapelle, defended to the last man, fell. The Highlanders were saved from complete disaster by the arrival of the leading troops of 39th and 61st Divisions. Fed into the line as they arrived, they, with the remnants of the 51st, were able to stabilise the line 2,500 yards back from where it had been overnight. The XV Corps' divisions, the 50th, 40th and 34th, were also pushed back with heavy losses. The line, which was beginning to lose cohesion, was restored by a timely counterattack. Nevertheless Merville, 4 miles west of Estaires was lost. Overall, the serious casualties being suffered by First Army, facing odds of 5 or 6 to 1, were making its line ever thinner in numbers.

The day's fighting had made it clear that a serious threat to the vital town of Hazebrouck was developing. As Plumer would have responsibility for its defence and XV Corps' role in it would be vital, the decision was made to transfer the corps (except for 50th Division which went to XI Corps) from Horne's to Plumer's command with effect from midday the following day. The effect of this, and the transfer of 55th and 3rd Divisions to I Corps, was to shift XI Corps' and I Corps' responsibilities respectively further northwards.[54] Unsurprisingly, with all his problems, Horne sounded less upbeat than usual in his letter of 11 April.

> This is the third day of hard fighting and the Boche is in great strength and keeps gradually pushing us back about Merville. He is getting out on a very pronounced salient and I hope we may be able to stop him before long. He cannot go on for ever. Our troops are very tired and we are of course very short of reserves. However we keep in good heart and fight hard and must do our best.[55]

At 07h30 on 12 April Horne issued an order for the recapture of Merville. It was cancelled when orders were received from GHQ for Horne's and Plumer's armies to organise a line Kemmel-Neuve Eglise-Bailleul-Nieppe Forest-Hinges which was to be held at all costs.[56] On this, the fourth day of the battle, Horne discerned a slight easing in the relentless German pressure.

> Things have been a little easier today and I feel I have got the Boche a little more in hand, and have managed to stop him for the moment. I was woken up this morning early with rather alarming information of his having got through at a weak spot in the night but it turned out better than it first appeared, thanks to the splendid fighting of our men. He attacked this evening but selected a place where I had some pretty fresh troops and he took it "in the neck" and was repulsed with heavy loss. I expect the attack will commence again Arras way before very long.[57]

The Germans had in fact made no serious attacks, contenting themselves with probing which paid off at several points because of the exhaustion and weakness of the British defenders. The British centre near the hamlet of Vierhouck, just north of Merville, resisted the Germans' attempts to overrun it. But the Germans made significant advances on either side of it, which they sought to exploit the following day, when they threw 3 fresh divisions into the battle in an attempt to reach Hazebrouck. The brunt of their attack this day fell on Second Army which, while managing to hold their line in most places, were forced back in 2 areas, one of which was at their junction with First Army. The 95th Brigade of 5th Division, the left-hand unit of Horne's army were forced back a small distance in conformity with 4th Guards' Brigade which had been driven back about 1,000 yards with heavy losses, to the line now manned by 1st Australian Division. This division's timely arrival effectively blocked any prospect the Germans might have had of reaching Hazebrouck.[58]

Further south the stubborn defence of Givenchy by 55th Division was turned into offence when, during the night of 12/13 April, the Division recaptured Route A Keep. The Germans counterattacked furiously during the day but to no avail. Generally, Horne's I Corps were now confident that they had the measure of the enemy and would be able to cope with whatever was thrown at them.[59] Horne's daily letter noted the switch of emphasis in the German offensive.

> During the night the Germans made one or two small attacks against me but were repulsed with loss and now the battle has passed more towards General Plumer's front and he has been having a hard time yesterday evening and today. But I think he is holding out well and the German must be slacking off as his troops are very tired and his roads and communications generally in a very congested state. It looks like rain this evening and hard rain for 48 hours would completely stop him. He has had the most extraordinary good fortune in the weather. However we have beaten off all his last attacks with great loss to him, and I have just heard that 2nd Army has been doing well this afternoon also. I *think* that this attack will now gradually slacken down and that it will reopen before long south of Arras. The Germans are sure to push for all they are worth as soon as ever they can in order to take advantage of the effects of this attack and I expect before long to have my hands full at the other end of my line.
>
> General Foch came to see me this afternoon. Very pleasant and pleased with our arrangements.[60]

The previous day Horne had also had a visit from the French Prime Minister, Georges Clemenceau, and had somehow given him the impression that he was not seized of the vital importance of protecting the Bruay coalfields. Clemenceau had lost no time in taking up the issue with Haig, who recorded in his diary of 12 April:

> Clemenceau was anxious about our covering the Bruay coal mines effectively. He saw Horne this morning and had formed the opinion that the British were going back at once to the La Bassée Canal! There are only five days' reserves now at the French munitions factories, and as 70% of their coal comes from the Bruay district, it is of very great importance to cover the mines as long as possible. I assured him on this point.[61]

It was on the day of Foch's visit to him that Horne issued an Order of the Day to his Army affirming his complete confidence that, 'at this critical moment, when the existence of the Empire is at stake, all ranks will do their best'.[62]

The next 3 days were to be comparatively quiet on the First Army front, but less so for Plumer's army which lost Bailleul on 15 April and Meteren, Wytschaete and Spanbroekmoelen the following day. Counterattacks succeeded in stabilising the situation without recovering any of these places. The comparative quietness did not mean complete inactivity on the part of the enemy opposite Horne's troops. There was fighting on all 3 days, most notably on XI Corps' front on the 14th, but the enemy made no progress. Indeed, they had to give ground when I and XI Corps pinched out a salient between them.[63]

The next 2 days were to see the resumption of furious German assaults which were to prove both expensive and largely unsuccessful. So severe were the German losses on 17 April, when their assaulting infantry were cut down by concentrated machine gun fire, that serious thought was given by their High Command to breaking off the Flanders offensive. But the decision was made to continue. The following day, attacks were launched aimed at capturing Givenchy, Festubert and Béthune in Horne's sector, and Mount Kemmel in Plumer's. Following bombardments lasting between 4 and 7 hours, 6 German divisions assaulted at 08h10 under the protection of mist and a creeping barrage. The attack had been anticipated by First Army intelligence and, in furious fighting, was largely repulsed. Small gains made by the enemy at Givenchy, where 55th Division had been relieved on the night of 15/16 April by 1st Division, were rapidly reversed by counterattacks. The Second Army and French troops also turned back the German assault on Mount Kemmel.[64]

Horne had taken full advantage of the few days' relative lull to reorganise his troop dispositions and strengthen his defences in anticipation of the renewal of the German assault. On its eve he complained once again at the want of men and the short-sightedness of the country's failure to organise its manpower. But for that, the country would not be fighting for its existence now. Even at this point of crisis, in Horne's view, there was too much talk but not enough action.[65] The next letter to his wife described the events of the 18th.

> … a hard day's fighting. The Boche attacked my line from Givenchy-Festubert to east of Robecq. He commenced with a bombardment early this morning and towards Robecq he endeavoured to cross the canal near Pacault Wood by bringing up bridging material but he was knocked out by our rifle fire – 2nd Seaforths – and fled leaving about 200 prisoners. Further southeast he attacked Givenchy and Festubert in great strength. Bombarded very heavily and advanced in masses. He has been repulsed after very heavy fighting and his losses must have been very severe. The old 1st Division held Givenchy and Festubert on this occasion and they have fought splendidly. I *think* our line is held intact but of course reports are not very clear yet. It has been a day of great loss to the Boche. I *think* he must have employed five divisions at least. It has been an anxious day of course but all has gone well as far as I know at present – 20h00. The weather remains unfavourable for us. Northeast winds, mist and dry on the whole though we have had a little drizzle. 22h00 Still a lot of artillery fire going on but no report of any further attacks.

> The C-in-C came this afternoon. Very pleased with our successful defence. The *talk* that is going on in the House of Commons makes one sick. Home Rule! We want *prompt* action to get men. If we can get men and America will hurry up we shall beat the Boche yet.[66]

When the fighting on 18 April died down it was not to be renewed at anything like the same level of intensity for several days. Both sides' artillery remained active and there was aggressive infantry patrolling, but day succeeded day without a major renewal of the German offensive. Horne ascribed this to the hot reception that the Germans had suffered on the 18th, but was still expecting a further attack at any moment. He was especially nervous that the enemy would have another go for Givenchy and Hinges on the 22nd, as a result of 1st Division's success in eliminating their toehold in the Givenchy defences 2 days previously. But nothing transpired. Horne was confident that his army would be able to cope with anything the enemy could throw at them.[67]

In point of fact there was to be no further serious German attack against First Army before the Battle of the Lys was officially suspended by General Ludendorff on 29 April. Second Army were less fortunate; on 25 April, the Germans once again assaulted Plumer's army and this time were successful in taking Mount Kemmel from the French 28th Division which, according to Haig, 'did not fight well'.[68] The previous day, the Germans had also renewed their ultimately unsuccessful attempt to break through the allied defences at Villers Bretonneux which were blocking the enemy's road to Amiens.

Perhaps appropriately the last First Army involvement in the battle was at the Route A Keep where 54 prisoners were taken as the strongpoint was fully and finally secured.[69] It had been the German failure to overrun the British defences around Givenchy that had acted as a drag on their ability to exploit to the full their initial breakthrough in the area.

General Horne went to see Haig at GHQ on 28 April. He floated with him and Lt General Herbert Lawrence (who had replaced Lt General Kiggell as the C-in-C's Chief of Staff) proposals for a major counterattack designed to push the Germans out of all their gains on the First Army front since 9 April. As the detailed preparations would take some time, Haig authorised Horne to set these in motion. He agreed to relieve the 3 Canadian divisions holding the line in the Vimy sector so that they could begin training for their part in the operation. As a result of their non-participation in the defensive battles, the Canadian divisions were at full strength and had adequate reserves in their depot behind the line on whom they could call.[70] Agreeable though it was for Haig and Horne to have the full-strength Canadian Corps to call on at this time of general manpower shortage, the Canadian insistence throughout the defensive battles, in continuation of a policy adopted much earlier, that their corps should remain in being and not be committed to action piecemeal, still rankled with the 2 British Generals. When Haig had called at Horne's headquarters on 18 April the latter had told him that Lt General Currie, the Canadian Corps Commander, was, in his view, suffering from a swelled head![71]

> He [Currie] lodged a complaint when I [Haig] ordered the Canadian Divisions to be brought out of the line in order to support and take part in the battle elsewhere. He wished to fight only as a "Canadian Corps" and got his

Canadian representative in London to write and urge me to arrange it! As a result the Canadians are together holding a wide front near Arras, but *they have not yet been in the battle*! The Australians on the other hand have been used by divisions and are now spread out from Albert to Amiens, and one is in front of Hazebrouck.[72]

It was probably fortunate for Anglo-Canadian harmony that the defensive battles in the British sector were coming to an end. As a force of elite shock troops there would never be any question of splitting up the Canadian Corps, once the Allies resumed the offensive.

In the event, Horne's proposals for a major counterattack were not implemented. He was not to know it for a further 3 months or so, but he had successfully weathered the worst that the Germans could throw at him and had prevailed, even if at times it had been a close-run thing. His largely tired and depleted divisions had contained an offensive of overwhelming force. They had prevented the enemy from achieving a breakthrough which would have done immense, possibly irreversible, damage to the viability of both the BEF and the French economy. The cost had been high. The First and Second Armies had suffered a total of 82,000 casualties, about the same as they had inflicted on their attackers.[73] But, despite the BEF's manpower crisis, this particular numbers game was moving inexorably in favour of the Allies as Germany's manpower resources moved rapidly towards exhaustion, and more and more American soldiers arrived in France.

Horne was always subsequently to take great pride in the fact that he was the only BEF army commander who was not obliged to move his headquarters to the rear as a result of the German offensives of spring 1918. He appreciated that such a move might have an adverse effect on the morale of his troops and determined only to do so *in extremis*, a situation that was not quite reached.[74]

The main criticism of Horne's conduct of the battle has centred on his leaving the Portuguese in the line when their morale and fighting efficiency were so low. Quite apart from the scarcity of British troops to relieve them, this discounts the fact that neither GHQ nor Horne were expecting more than a diversionary attack to be launched in the Portuguese sector, a failure of intelligence or interpretation of intelligence, for which Horne must take his share of the blame. When Liddell Hart spoke to General Jeudwine, who had done more than anyone else to limit the initial damage caused by the German offensive, he was perhaps disappointed to learn that the latter entertained a high opinion of his Army Commander. He described Horne as a good man in a tight corner and strongly rebutted any suggestion that he was of low mental capacity, even if he was no genius.[75] There is no gainsaying the fact that, as evidenced by his letters home and the testimony of General Jeudwine and his Chief of Staff, Major General Anderson, Horne never lost his nerve and retained his optimism even at the darkest moments of the battle.[76]

Chapter XVI

Army Commander: The Scarpe and Drocourt-Quéant

The late spring and early summer of 1918 would see Henry Horne's army making the occasional small-scale attack to improve its position. For much of the period there was a recurrent expectation that the Germans would mount a further offensive on the First Army's section of the line. But by late July it was becoming possible to believe that the greatly overstretched Germans were losing the capacity to mount large-scale offensive operations. The initiative was once more passing back to the Allies whose thoughts could increasingly concentrate on going over to the offensive.

The beginning of May saw the onset of a series of small operations on Horne's front. They were designed not only to improve his army's position but also to keep the Germans from shifting troops around as they pleased without fear of punishment for their temerity. Typical examples involved 3rd and 5th Divisions. On the night of 3/4 May 3rd Division attacked and pushed their line forward slightly north of the La Bassée Canal. On 21 May 5th Division successfully closed a re-entrant in their line northwest of Merville. Rather more dramatically, on 13 May I Corps discharged 5,000 cylinders of gas in one vast cloud between Hulluch and the Hohenzollern Redoubt. At the same time 1,000 drums were projected into the German positions near Cité St Elie, south of La Bassée, and Le Cornet-Malo, north of Béthune.[1]

For 6 tense weeks the gas cylinders had been in I Corps' front line positions waiting for a persistent east wind to drop and be replaced by one which would take the cloud into the German lines. Horne had needed no reminding that a similar number of gas cylinders had been released in the same area on the first day of the Battle of Loos, for his part controversially, and harmfully for the division under his command. After this latest operation Horne told Haig, with some feeling, that he never intended to install this kind of gas in his front trenches again![2]

On the day after I Corps' gas attack, Haig was made aware by Horne of his dissatisfaction with the Commander of XVIII Corps, Lt General Sir Ivor Maxse. Haig's diary recorded their conversation.

> He spoke to me about Maxse who commands XVIII Corps. When he arrived he made difficulties; and after his troops had been in the line a few days, he said that unless he got two more divisions he would not be responsible for the front. Horne told him that his Corps was considerably stronger than the Canadians whom he relieved, and that there were no more troops to give him. If his dispositions were not satisfactory, it was his (Maxse's) fault and if he still felt that he could not hold his front line let him say so and another corps commander would be put in to relieve him at once! Maxse's tone at once changed! I asked Horne not to judge Maxse too quickly but if he found he could not work in sympathy with Maxse I would arrange to change him.[3]

In taking on Maxse, Horne had chosen an adversary with a formidable reputation. He had commanded the Guards Brigade in the early days of the war before being sent home on promotion to command and train one of the Kitchener New Army divisions, the 18th (Eastern). The division fought with distinction on the Somme and in January 1917 Maxse was promoted to the command of XVIII Corps. As part of Fifth Army during the German 1918 spring offensive *Operation Michael*, the corps was severely mauled and indeed broken up before being reconstituted and transferred to First Army at the beginning of May.[4] In addition to his reputation as a fighting soldier, Maxse was without peer as a trainer of troops. This may have offered Haig a solution to Maxse and Horne's apparent incompatibility. Haig had for some time been considering appointing an Inspector General of Training for the BEF, an appointment for which Maxse was the obvious choice. Coincidentally or not, the post was established and Maxse appointed to it within 5 weeks of Haig becoming aware of Horne's problem with his subordinate. Appropriate or not, the timing of his new appointment rankled with Maxse who saw it as reflecting on his conduct as a corps commander.[5]

The question of whether the Canadians would continue to fight only as a corps was again raised during a visit Haig received in early May from Sir Edward Kemp, the Canadian government's London agent. The latter told Haig his government was anxious to have a Canadian army and to this end hoped that the 4 Canadian divisions would be employed together. Haig reassured him that only extreme urgency would make him depart from the principle of a united Canadian Corps. In the privacy of his diary however he could not prevent a hint of exasperation.

> Kemp was very friendly, but from some of the remarks which fell from him inadvertently I could not help feeling that some people in Canada regard themselves rather as "Allies" than fellow citizens of the Empire![6]

This was not to be the end of Haig's badgering by Canadians over the disposition of the corps. In July Haig was to receive a visit from the Canadian Ministers of Defence and Marine, respectively Major General Newbarn and Colonel Ballantyne. The former told Haig of the great deal of upset among Canadians that the Canadian divisions were not all together under Lt General Currie. This alluded to the fact that while 2 of the divisions were in the line and one in reserve in the First Army sector, 3rd Canadian Division were currently in the line as the leftmost division of Third Army. Even though this meant they were alongside the right hand Canadian division in the First Army sector, they were not being administered by Canadian Corps HQ. Haig responded robustly to a rather taken-aback Minister.

> I at once told the Canadian Minister that the British Army alone and unaided withstood the first terrific blow made by 80 German divisions on the 21st March until the 27th May when the Aisne attack was launched: that since March units of the British Army had been constantly engaged until the present moment, when four British divisions are fighting in the Battle of the Marne. *During all this severe fighting the Canadian Corps has not once been engaged.* Why? Because the Canadian Government only wished it to be engaged as a Corps!! I was on the point of employing Canadian Divisions in the battle. They would have had to go into the fight separately to start with but a wire arrived from the War Office emphasising the Canadian Govern-

ment's desire to fight together. So I at once put the Canadian Divisions back into the line and employed British Divisions!! .... These remarks of mine at once made the Canadian Minister shut up and he became quite bearable. .... Later when leaving the Minister said, "My only object is to do all Canada can to support Great Britain at this time of trial."[7]

Not long into May strong evidence had accumulated that a German attack on the First Army front, and possibly Third Army's, might be imminent. The intelligence came largely from prisoners. It was the same source that disclosed that an attack on the Givenchy sector had been planned for 10 May but had been cancelled for unknown reasons. The British speculated that the German preparations had been disrupted by harassing artillery fire and by their awareness that their plans could have been disclosed by prisoners. But Horne regarded this setback to German plans as only fleeting. He told Haig on 14 May that he believed the Germans were ready to attack from Calonne to Hill 70, north of Lens, and from Oppy southwards to beyond the Scarpe. Although his divisions were each holding fronts of 5,000 yards or more he was very confident of being able to hold his ground.[8] Four days later, GHQ Intelligence concluded an enemy attack astride the Scarpe was probable but that the main blow would fall against Third Army between Arras and Albert.[9]

In the event, when the German blow was launched on 27 May it fell on the French in what was to become known as the Third Battle of the Aisne. Over the next 11 days, until the offensive petered out, the Germans were to make striking gains and inflict severe losses on the Allies (4 tired British divisions sent to the French area for rest and recuperation were severely mauled in the initial German assault and suffered 29,000 casualties). But once again the offensive was ultimately a German failure as no decisive breakthrough was achieved and a salient vulnerable to counterattack had been created.[10]

The switch of German attentions to the French sector did nothing to diminish Horne's and Haig's belief that the British sector was still clearly in the German sights, if not in the immediate future. A week into this latest German offensive Horne told his wife that the enemy still had enough troops in reserve to put in another heavy attack somewhere. He rather thought this would seek to exploit their current success against the French, as Paris must be a tempting target, but he admitted he did not know. The following day he observed that prisoners were insisting that an attack against his army was coming, although there was little discernible sign of enemy preparation.

A couple of days later the signs were more apparent. Considerable enemy movement was noted opposite Hulluch and north of Merville. Gas, trench mortars and bridging material were being brought up and ammunition stockpiled near guns. But contradictorily, the enemy had reinstituted home leave for their troops. Horne acknowledged it would make sense for the Germans to attack in the British sector to stop any notion of BEF troops being sent south to help the French. But he wondered whether it was not all a bluff.[11] GHQ thought this was all leading to attacks on the Hulluch front and towards Ypres and Poperinghe. Haig believed, once again, that the Germans were about to launch attacks north and south of Vimy Ridge intending to pinch it out.

The Germans seemed determined to provide the evidence to confirm Haig's and Horne's worst fears. Artillery bombardments and troop movements were being stepped up opposite the First Army front.[12] At a meeting of army commanders on 11 June Horne was in a bullish mood reassuring Haig and his fellow commanders that his men were in wonderful spirits and only anxious that the enemy should attack them.[13] His confidence was not just for the benefit of his colleagues; he was equally positive in his letters home. He thought the attack would come before long but cautioned that:

> ... the Boche take great pains nowadays to keep the troops who are holding the line in ignorance of his real intentions. They one and all say an attack is coming, but that may mean that it is *not*, but that the Boche wishes us to think it is coming here while he prepares to put in a surprise attack elsewhere. We are beginning to understand pretty well his little dodges.[14]

The understandable concern about a possible German attack did not prevent Horne from ordering 3rd Division to carry out a surprise attack on the night of 14/15 June on a 2 mile front between the Lawe river and La Pannerie, 2 miles north of Béthune. Under a creeping barrage and against wire known to be weak, the attack penetrated to a depth of 450 yards and took all objectives and nearly 200 prisoners. Counter battery work effectively silenced the German artillery and resistance was very slight. Some of the prisoners taken indicated that there were no reserves behind them and, had the attack been pressed further, Estaires might have been reached. Nevertheless a German counterattack was mounted but was broken up by the British artillery. The gains were successfully consolidated.[15]

By mid June 2 new factors were beginning to have an impact on the Western Front. The first was the steady arrival of British reinforcements which had been denied to Haig until the authorities in Britain had been galvanised into response by the German spring offensive. Artillery ammunition was also by now available in almost unlimited quantities. On the debit side, but affecting both friend and enemy alike, was the arrival in the front line trenches of the first cases of Spanish 'flu which was to end by killing millions more world-wide than the war itself. Sickness had already led to the cancellation of a joint First and Second Army operation and there was a growing belief that the German failure to launch their expected attack against First Army was at least partially due to their growing sick list.[16] It was to be rare for the pandemic to be allowed to interfere with the British Army's operations in the remaining months of the war.

Although there was a continuing expectation that it was only a matter of time before the Germans launched an attack, Haig was increasingly thinking in terms of taking the battle to the enemy. It would fall to Horne's army to begin implementation of his Commander-in-Chief's new approach. The 5th Division of Lt General Haking's XI Corps, reinforced by 31st Division (XV Corps) temporarily placed under Haking, were given the task of advancing the British line east of the Nieppe Forest a distance of 1 mile on a frontage of 3 and a half miles. The purpose was to provide room for an outpost zone clear of the forest, which had constantly been subjected to gas shelling by the enemy.

The attack was launched at 06h00 on 28 June without a preliminary bombardment. It took the enemy by surprise and achieved all its objectives without severe casualties. Surprise had been achieved not only by foregoing a specific preliminary bombardment but also by misleading the enemy by firing a barrage in the early morning on several days prior to the attack. The 1st Australian Division's artillery on the left fired a barrage and smoke to confuse the enemy over the extent of the front of the attack. Each division employed 2 brigades in the assault. The infantry advanced under a creeping artillery and machine gun barrage which lifted at the rate of 100 yards every 4 minutes. It worked so well that the attackers were into the enemy's positions before they could raise their heads. There was no counterattack.[17] Horne was delighted with the outcome.

> The attack yesterday was a great success and the Boche has not, as yet, coun-
> terattacked and no signs of his doing so. The total of prisoners came to 9 offi-
> cers and 424 men, 2 field guns and a lot of machine guns. In addition the
> Boche suffered very heavy casualties. The troops are very pleased indeed and
> they did well.[18]

On 21 July another chapter of the history of Horne's army drew closer to its end when General Tomagnini, the Commander of the Portuguese Corps, took his leave of the British Commander-in-Chief on being recalled to Portugal. With some sympathy Haig recalled what a difficult time the General had been given by his staff, many of whom had intrigued against him. His Chief of Staff had had a private cypher with which, unknown to General Tomagnini, he communicated with the Minister of War in Lisbon. Despite the debacle of 9 April there were still around 20,000 Portuguese troops in France, 4,000 of whom remained under Horne's command. The rest, deemed to be of little military value, were waiting for shipping to repatriate them to Portugal. Soon to be transferred to the newly formed Fifth Army, the nucleus would take no further significant part in the war.[19]

On 5 July, the day after a successful Australian operation at Hamel, Haig saw Generals Horne and Byng and told them to consider a plan for taking Orange Hill, west of Monchy-le-Preux, and the village itself. The plan would have to include capture of the Boiry-Wancourt Spur to the south between the Sensée and Cojeul rivers to protect the advance on Orange Hill from being taken in flank. Haig wanted the operation to involve the Canadian Corps and 3 or 4 other divisions with the assistance of tanks. It would need to be conducted by one army commander, probably Horne, but a decision on this and any necessary modifica- tion of army boundaries would have to await receipt of the 2 army commanders' report.[20] This was presented orally at a further meeting between the 3 officers on 15 July.

Both army commanders were opposed to making the attack. In their view unless Henin Hill further to the south were taken and retained at the same time, the retention of the Boiry-Wancourt spur would be very costly and not worth its capture. The extension of the operation implicit in Horne and Byng's report would require more troops than could be found at this stage. Haig bowed to the advice of his generals and dropped the idea. Instead he told Byng to mount some small-scale operations and Horne to instruct the Canadians to reconnoitre and advance their line step by step as opportunity offered.[21] An attempt by the Canadians to do this a few days later came up against a well-entrenched and determined enemy near Oppy and achieved nothing.[22]

Immediately after his meeting with Horne and Byng, Haig saw General Rawlinson, the Fourth Army Commander, and set in motion the planning of the

Battle of Amiens. He confided to Rawlinson that the instructions he had given Horne and Byng had been intended to ensure that the Germans were distracted from the preparations for his, the main, operation. In good time and the greatest secrecy, the Canadian Corps would be transferred to Fourth Army for the duration of the battle.[23]

On 15 July the Germans struck once again against the French in Champagne. Horne wrote:

> Great excitement. German attack broke out on the French front this morning. The reports we have received up to now (22h00) are most satisfactory. The French seem to have held the Germans well east of Reims and to be recovering some of the ground lost this morning west of Reims. It is *most important* that this attack should end in failure for the Germans. It is not yet clear whether it is a really strong attack or not but it is on a wide front and I expect it is a big try. If so, and it fails, it will mean that the Germans will not be able to put in another very strong attack for some time if at all again this year. I feel very excited about it, success or failure will mean so much. It is very quiet on my front and we are waiting eagerly to see to what extent the German has moved his troops from in front of us. If he takes much away it will show that he is not going to attack here.[24]

Three days later the French Tenth Army under General Mangin counterattacked the German right flank and transformed the situation.[25] General Ludendorff was forced to postpone the attack he had been planning against the British in Flanders which Haig had been expecting to fall largely on Second Army between Hazebrouck and Ypres. The German postponement was to prove permanent even though it would be some days before Haig could be certain that the initiative had passed firmly to the Allies. On 26 July a captured German aviator confirmed that the operation had been abandoned 'because the British had evidently received warning and were prepared'.[26]

When Haig submitted his proposals for the Battle of Amiens to the *Generalissimo*, Foch, when approving them, urged that Horne should be told to continue preparations for an attack between Festubert and Robecq, as it would free a particularly valuable area. Neither Horne nor Haig was in favour of pushing forward over the flat and wet country that this operation would entail; Foch's urgings were conveniently sidelined. Nothing further was to be heard of the proposal for an advance into 'the waterlogged basin of the Upper Scheldt.'[27]

On 29 July the Canadian Corps were still part of the First Army's order of battle. Shortly thereafter, in great secrecy, their transfer south to Fourth Army began. By now the Germans would assume that a sudden move like this by Canadian Corps would presage an attack on whatever part of the front they turned up. Elaborate deception measures were therefore carried out. Horne was ordered to send 2 Canadian battalions, 2 Canadian casualty clearing stations and the Canadian and Tank Corps' wireless sections to the vicinity of Mount Kemmel in the Second Army sector with orders to prepare an assault there. Fourth Army put out the cover story that the Canadians were relieving XXII Corps, sent south to help the French, in accordance with Foch's wish for a British corps to be held in reserve west of Amiens.[28] The ruses were completely successful. When the Canadian, Australian and III Corps, with French support on their right, attacked on 8 August they achieved complete surprise and brought about 'the Black Day of the German Army', in Ludendorff's famous phrase.[29]

The second and third days of the battle, while still yielding gains, were showing the usual symptoms of diminishing returns as German resistance stiffened. By the fourth day Rawlinson was calling for a halt which Haig tacitly accepted.[30] He ordered a renewal for 15 August but cancelled it when the Canadian Corps Commander, through Rawlinson, pointed out the strength of the German defences and defenders it was proposed to assault.[31] Haig had however already set in motion measures which would bring Byng's and Horne's armies into play. On 10 August he had instructed Horne to finalise his plans for the capture of La Bassée and Aubers Ridge in conjunction with advances by the Third Army to capture Bapaume and the Second Army to take Mount Kemmel.[32] By the 15th Haig had modified his orders in reaction to a voluntary retirement the Germans had initiated on Byng's front. Without waiting for promised reinforcements and tanks, Byng was to press on with Bapaume as his objective. Horne should take advantage of Byng's advance to assault and capture Orange Hill and Monchy-le-Preux.[33]

With the German voluntary retirement at an end, Byng launched his attack on 21 August. To help deceive the enemy over the frontage of the attack, Horne laid on a heavy bombardment that morning. In a further refinement of Haig's strategy he had been ordered to continue his preparations for attacks on Orange Hill and Monchy-le-Preux while at the same time holding 3 divisions and tanks available either to reinforce Byng or to exploit any success he might have.[34] Despite spirited German opposition, Third Army, and Fourth Army on their right, made good progress especially during night attacks mounted in the small hours of 25 August. On 29 August the New Zealand Division occupied Bapaume after the Germans had been forced to evacuate the town.[35]

In the light of the progress by Byng's and Rawlinson's armies Haig, on 24 August, issued very ambitious orders to Horne. Horne had told his wife how much he was looking forward to joining in as the battle moved northwards.[36] In the meantime his troops had mounted 2 minor operations on the night of 23/24 August at Fampoux, now securely in British hands, and Givenchy, where 55th Division retook the old British front line area north of the village.[37] Haig detailed his new orders to Horne at a meeting also attended by Lt General Currie (whose Canadian Corps was in the process of rejoining First Army) and senior staff officers of both GHQ and First Army. Haig recorded:

> I explained that I wished the First Army to advance by surprise and attack as rapidly as possible astride the Cambrai road with their left secured on the River Scarpe. First the Monchy-le-Preux position has to be taken, then the position of the Drocourt-Quéant Line which is south of the Scarpe, and next the Marquion-Canal du Nord Line. For these operations the Corps should be formed in depth. The 4th Division and the Cavalry Corps would be added to the First Army. If all went well and the advance was accomplished rapidly the enemy might still be holding his positions in front of the Third Army. It would then be the role of the First Army to operate against the right flank of this part of the enemy's forces.[38]

On the same day GHQ issued formal orders to First, Third and Fourth Armies. In First Army's case these confirmed what Haig had already said during his meeting with Horne. The Third Army were ordered to continue their advance, which was currently taking them through the old Somme battlefield. They were to strengthen their left in order to be in a position to afford all necessary support to First Army when the latter's attack went in. Fourth Army were instructed to protect Byng's right. Horne's attack was set for 26 August.[39] In preparation for it 2nd Canadian Division, cooperating with 52nd Division of Third Army, captured most of the village of Neuville Vitasse, at the junction of the two armies, and a sugar factory south of it.[40]

In expectation of making an attack south of the River Scarpe Horne had set in train an elaborate deception plan. It was aimed at persuading the Germans that his main assault would be north of the river, not easy to achieve if the presence of the Canadians south of the river were detected. Horne employed a mixture of artillery bombardments, combined tank and infantry training which it was made sure the enemy would observe, the establishment of dummy ammunition dumps and casualty clearing stations and an intensification of wireless traffic. The enemy were so far persuaded that the attack would take place north of the river, that they kept their reserves in position to intervene there. When the attack was launched, complete surprise was achieved.[41]

Horne still had some concerns however which he shared with Haig at a meeting the day before the attack. Horne had been to see Byng and had learned that the Third Army's 32nd and 56th Divisions had been checked on the line Henin-Croisilles in front of the Hindenburg Line, when they should have been further north-eastwards on the Heninel Spur. Horne was clearly nervous that this might expose his right flank. Haig told him that the object of his army's operations was to take the Hindenburg Line from the rear and press on as fast as possible against Marquion where the enemy's depots supplying the whole of the German Seventeenth Army were located. Reassured, Horne indicated that it was Lt General Currie who was understandably being a little 'sticky' as the Canadians would form First Army's right flank. Haig said he had seen the GOC of 2nd Canadian Division, who understood what Haig was about and was more relaxed than his Corps Commander. The 2nd would be on the extreme right of the First Army advance.[42]

The First Army's plan for the Battle of the Scarpe, as the attack later became known, called for 2nd and 3rd Canadian Divisions, the only 2 divisions to have returned in full at this stage from Fourth Army, to attack in line. The 2nd would do so between the Arras-Cambrai road and the junction with Third Army, and the 3rd between the road and the Scarpe river. They would be supported by 14 brigades of field and 9 brigades of heavy artillery. Each division would in addition be allocated 9 tanks. Air support would be lavish. They were set the first day objective of reaching a line just east of Monchy-le-Preux having captured Orange Hill, Chapel Hill and the village itself on the way. North of the Scarpe, 51st Highland Division would advance in step with 3rd Canadian Division. The Highlanders were given no specific objective and were merely to keep pace with the Canadians on their right.[43]

The surprise secured by the deception plan was not dissipated by the firing of a preliminary bombardment before the assault began at 03h00 on 26 August. The attackers were helped by dry conditions, but only just; heavy rain began to fall later in the morning. Less helpful was the late arrival of the tanks, despite which the

Map 14: The Scarpe, Drocourt-Quéant: August–September 1918 (I)

Canadians, supported by accurate artillery and machine gun barrages, initially carried all before them. Chapel Hill was taken by 06h00. Orange Hill followed and by 07h40 Monchy-le-Preux, attacked from both the north and west, was in Canadian hands. A heavy German counterattack was successfully broken up by artillery. The villages of Wancourt and Guémappe were also taken.

There were however some problems for the attackers. Their first attempt to carry the ridge between the Scarpe and the Cojeul rivers was stopped by machine gun fire and uncut wire. The attack was renewed that night without artillery support and was successful. Less so were attacks against the village of Pelves, which remained in German hands. The 51st Highland Division, north of the Scarpe, reached the outskirts of Roeux and the western slopes of Greenland Hill, and captured the chemical works north of Roeux, scene of much bitter fighting during the Battle of Arras, 16 months previously.[44]

Overall, the day was a huge success for First Army. The Canadians had advanced about 3 miles and called into question the viability of the German Lys salient to the north. That very night the Germans decided to retire from it voluntarily, beginning 3 nights later. Despite the evidence already accruing of the success of the day, when Haig saw Horne at 14h30 he found him anxious about the security of his right flank. Haig was sufficiently impressed to drive immediately to the headquarters of XVII Corps, on the left of Third Army, to point out to the Commander that he could now avoid frontal attacks against the Hindenburg Line. Instead he could bypass and envelop it by using the gap created by the Canadians. Lt General Sir Charles Fergusson took the point.

On the day as a whole Haig noted in his diary:

> Today has been a most successful one. The capture of Monchy-le-Preux at the cost of 1,500 casualties was quite extraordinary. The enemy knew the value of the position and devoted much labour to strengthening it.[45]

At 19h10 on the 26th Horne issued his orders for the following day. The Canadian Corps were to continue their advance in the direction of Cagnicourt, Dury and Etaing, villages well beyond the Drocourt-Quéant Line. North of the Scarpe a defensive flank was to be formed. If, on reaching it, the Canadians found the Drocourt-Quéant Line to be held in force, they were to prepare to attack it on the 28th (later postponed to the 30th). For this purpose 4th (British) Division were moved from Army reserve to the Corps.[46]

The weather on the 27th was to prove a great handicap for the attackers. The rain and low cloud badly affected the RAF's operations and artillery counter battery work. Nevertheless Vis-en-Artois, Chérisy, Bois du Sart and Bois du Vert were captured although Pelves and Greenland Hill remained unattainable in the face of stiffening German resistance. Lt General Currie had hoped that the day would end with the German Fresnes-Rouvroy Line, about a mile in front of the Drocourt-Quéant Line, in First Army hands. But it was not even to be reached despite savage fighting.[47] All the same, Horne could look back on 2 very successful days when he wrote to his wife.

> The battle is going well for us. We have taken Monchy, Vis-en-Artois, Chérisy and are getting on well. We have now the Boche's back defences before us, a line that joins the old Hindenburg Line. It is known as the

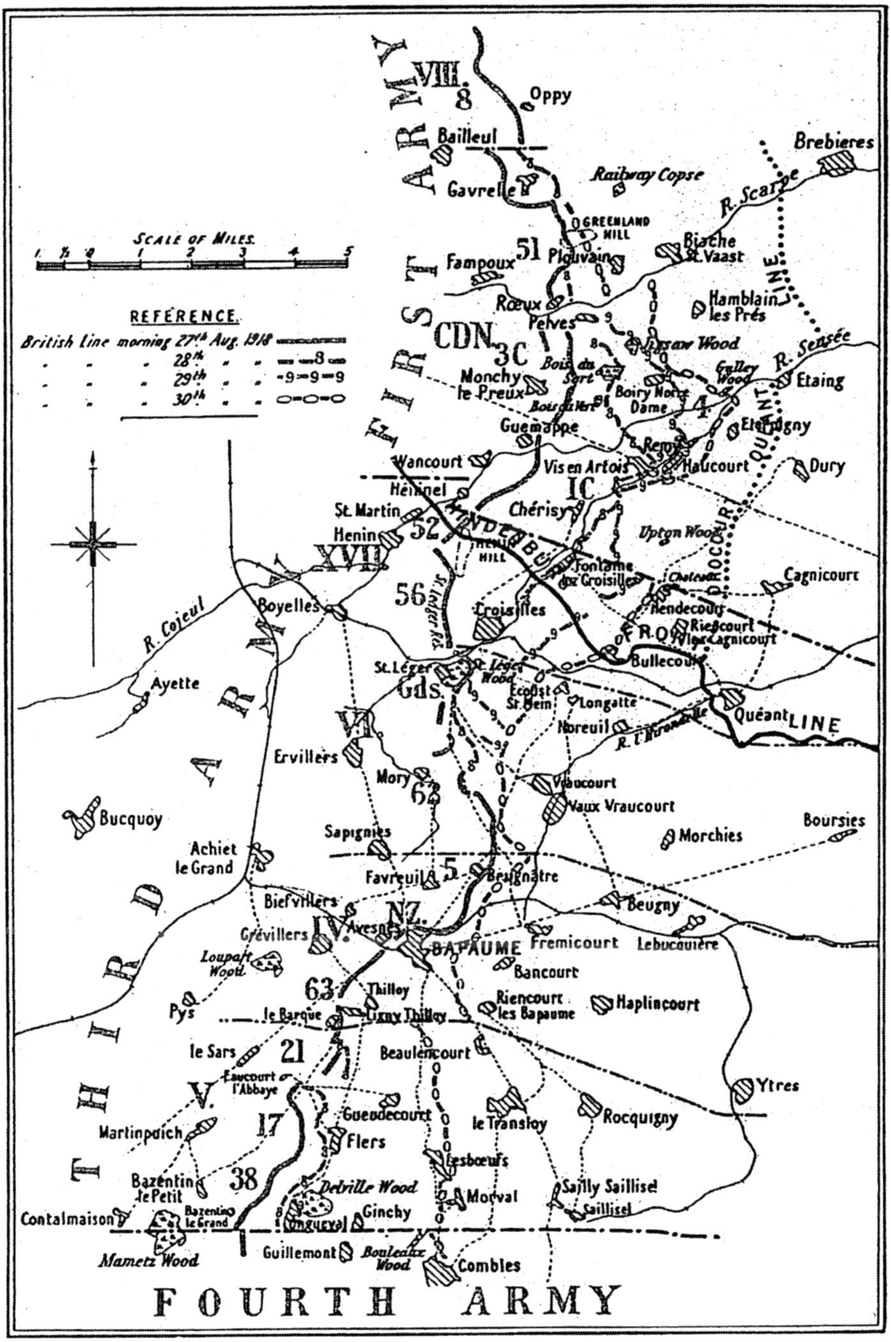

Map 15: The Scarpe, Drocourt-Quéant: August–September 1918 (II)

'Quéant-Drocourt Line'(sic) That will be the next nut to crack. Then after that he has the line of the "Canal du Nord" and then no further defences at present. We have taken over 3,000 prisoners. I am satisfied with the rate of progress and very pleased. The French have made a big advance today, taking Nesle and Noyon. The Boche is being hit hard along a very lengthy front and must be having a bad time.[48]

Horne's orders for the 28th repeated the rather curious formulation of the previous day. They instructed the Canadians to continue to advance towards Cagnicourt, Dury and Etaing. These villages were well beyond the Drocourt-Quéant Line which, in accordance with Haig's orders to Horne, was not to be attacked until he had all the means available to follow up and reach the Canal du Nord. Horne instructed the Canadians to be ready to attack the Line on 30 August. Currie ordered his attacking divisions to advance to within 2 miles of the Drocourt-Quéant Line on the 28th and capture the enemy trenches at the limit of this advance. It was to prove a day of mixed fortunes. The Canadian 2nd Division managed to advance about 1,000 yards but still failed to reach the German positions. The 3rd Division took Pelves, Boiry-Notre Dame and Jigsaw Wood.

After 3 days of often ferocious fighting, Currie felt obliged to relieve his 2nd and 3rd Divisions. Between them they had suffered nearly 6,000 casualties. With 4th Canadian Division still not fully returned from the Fourth Army area, the relief was effected by 1st Canadian and 4th (British) Divisions. Along with 51st Highland Division, their initial task was to prepare for the assault on the Drocourt-Quéant Line by mounting local attacks to improve their positions and close up to the Line.[49] The Highlanders completed the capture of Greenland Hill and moved within a quarter mile of Plouvain. The 4th Division crossed the Sensée river and took the villages of Rémy and Haucourt.[50]

The following day, the 30th, 1st Canadian Division successfully attacked the Vis-en-Artois Switch, the German defence line linking the Fresnes-Rouvroy Line with the Drocourt-Quéant Line. They advanced an average of 2 miles and came up level with 57th Division of Third Army on their right. The 4th Division also made progress and took the village of Eterpigny in front of the Drocourt-Quéant Line. In the meantime the artillery were carrying out a programme of wire-cutting.

The next day the Canadians advanced further, capturing some German trenches. The 4th Division took, lost and retook St Servin's Farm. On what was to prove to be the last day before the actual assault on the German Line proper, the Canadians on 1 September captured Hendecourt Château and the Crows Nest, a strongpoint on a prominent knoll north of the Château. The 57th Division took Hendecourt village.[51]

By the evening of 1 September the stage was set for the breaking of the Drocourt-Quéant Line, the most formidable defensive system to have confronted the BEF thus far. The assault would take place simultaneously with major attacks by Third and Fourth Armies. Orders for the First Army attack had been issued by Horne at 19h45 on 31 August.

1. Canadian Corps, with III Brigade Tank Corps, 1 regiment of cavalry and 17th Armoured Car Battn attached, will attack the Drocourt-Quéant Line on 2 September. Success will be exploited by pushing forward rapidly to seize the crossings over the Canal du Nord between Sains-lès-Marquion and Palluel

Map 16: The Scarpe, Drocourt-Quéant: August–September 1918 (III)

inclusive and the high ground (just beyond the Canal) Deligny Mill – Oisy-le-Verger. Zero Hour will be notified later.

2. XVII Corps, Third Army, is cooperating in the attack, and after the line has been forced, is intended to operate southeast of Quéant.

3. XXII Corps will secure the left flank of the attack by holding the crossings over the Trinquis Brook, and will exercise pressure on the enemy with advanced troops. The Commanders of the XXII and Canadian Corps will direct special attention to the necessity for close touch between their troops at the boundary of their respective Corps. RA XXII Corps will be employed to assist the operations of the Canadian Corps by engaging hostile batteries which can fire on the left flank of the attack, and by blocking the crossings over the Scarpe River between Biache-St Vaast and Brebières with its fire.

4. VIII Corps will continue to exercise pressure on the enemy with advanced troops, and will employ all available artillery to engage hostile batteries which can fire on the left flank of the Canadian attack.

5. Cavalry Corps will be held at 4 hours' notice to move, from Zero Hour on day of attack.

6. 1 Brigade RAF will assist the attack according to arrangements made direct with the Canadian Corps.[52]

> After issuing his orders Horne reviewed matters for his wife.

> Today we have been making a certain amount of ground and getting ready for another strong attack. All is going well, though somewhat slowly. There is a good deal of opposition as the Germans do not want us to get on along the Scarpe. You were pleased to see that the papers were making more mention of First Army. It was not realised at first that it was my Army that was at work! We have well over 4,000 prisoners and 26 guns and a large number of machine guns, etc since the 26th.[53]

Field Marshal Haig was showing uncharacteristic concern about the forth-coming attack. Having ordered it, his worries about the manpower situation had resurfaced. He told Byng on 1 September that he was opposed to doing more attacking than was absolutely necessary; the BEF's objective should be to keep the battle going as long as possible until the Americans could attack in force. On the same day he sent his Chief of Staff to tell Horne that he was only to attack the following day if he and his troops were satisfied that they could carry the enemy's position. A probably rather surprised Horne reassured General Lawrence that everyone concerned was quite confident and the attack would go in as planned.[54]

General Currie's orders to his divisions envisaged a 2 stage assault. The first stage would be a breakthrough of the Drocourt-Quéant Line where it was crossed by the Arras-Cambrai road. Thereafter the assault would fan out, rolling up the German line to both north and south. The end of the stage would see the Cana-dians on the line Cagnicourt-Dury-high ground south of Etaing, beyond the Drocourt-Quéant Support System. At Zero plus 3 hours the second stage would start with the resumption of the advance until it reached a line from Sains-lès-

Marquion to Récourt via Baralle and an area east of Ecourt-St Quentin. From Récourt the line would swing westwards back to the high ground south of Etaing. This stage would involve the occupation of the high ground west of, and over-looking, the Canal du Nord and the Sensée river.[55]

Zero Hour was at 05h00. It heralded a day of almost unbroken success for the Canadians. The Drocourt-Quéant Line was ruptured on a frontage of 7,000 yards and the Buissy Switch, the villages of Cagnicourt and Villers-les-Cagnicourt, as well as 8,000 prisoners, were taken before it was fully daylight. By the end of the day the Canadians had established a line well beyond the German line, except at the northern end of their attack. German opposition had been patchy but, where it was resolute, it had been very resolute indeed. The Cana-dians had suffered heavy casualties, opposed as they were by much of 7 German divisions. It was fortunate that the elaborate defences of the Drocourt-Quéant Line, with their excellent fields of fire, did not at any point give anything like the trouble that had been expected.[56]

The Canadian success, together with events further south, notably the Australian capture of Péronne, had made the German Winter Defence Line largely untenable. Horne subsequently noted with some satisfaction that Ludendorff, in his *My War Memories* (Vol. II, p 696), admitted that the success of the First Army on 2 September necessitated the retirement of the whole German front from the Scarpe to the Verle to the 'Siegfried Position' (i.e. the Hindenburg Line).[57] At midday on the 2nd the German High Command set in motion a general withdrawal which would begin that night with the Seventeenth Army, facing the Canadians and V Corps of Third Army, retiring behind the Canal du Nord and the Sensée.[58]

The enemy departure became apparent at dawn on 3 September. It rendered nugatory the detailed orders that had been issued by Horne at 20h15 the previous night for a resumption of the attack, again synchronised with attacks by Third and Fourth Armies. Horne's orders had foreseen a fighting advance to the Canal du Nord between Sains-lès-Marquion and Palluel. Even with the German retirement, these orders were daunting, as Currie's divisional commanders had indicated to him that their severe casualties would compromise the prospects of a successful further advance without adequate preparation. Currie thereupon secured Horne's assent to the cancellation of his orders. They were replaced by instructions to maintain close touch with the enemy and to follow up any with-drawal. With the enemy obliging by withdrawing, the 3 divisions were able to press forward beyond their objectives of the previous day. The only major excep-tion to this quieter day was the capture by 4th British Division of Etaing and Lock Wood, where almost the only Germans still on the west side of the Canal du Nord were found and dealt with.[59]

By 4 September the Canadians had taken Ecourt St Quentin and were in possession of the west bank of the Canal du Nord from south of Sains-lès-Marquion to Sauchy-Cauchy. The eastern bank was found to be strongly held by the enemy and all bridges blown except those at Palluel where the enemy retained a bridgehead on the western bank. A major attack in force would be required to secure a way across. Until this could be mounted, major operations on the army's right flank would cease.[60]

Horne was predictably pleased at the events of early September.

The battle of yesterday went awfully well and has had important results. The breaking of the Drocourt-Quéant Line has shaken him badly and he is hurrying back to the line of the 'Canal du Nord' ... It was a very great victory yesterday. We are all very pleased. Winning battles is more exhilarating than rearguard actions.[61]

Am very pleased with the success and the splendid way in which the troops must have fought. An advance of about 12 miles in 8 days through a succession of strong positions is really a very fine performance and all may be proud of it.[62]

Chapter XVII

Army Commander: Canal du Nord, Cambrai and Douai

The next serious challenge confronting Henry Horne's army would be the crossing of the Canal du Nord. He had already noted that this was the Germans' last major prepared defensive position on the First Army's line of advance and unlikely for that reason, if for no other, to be given up without a significant struggle.[1] However there were no longer any certainties, given the German readiness of recent days to withdraw rather than fight to maintain difficult positions, and this was reflected in Horne's orders issued at 21h10 on 3 September. The Canadian Corps were told to continue their advance in cooperation with XVII Corps. The importance of securing crossings over the Canal du Nord was emphasised. If these were found to be held only by rearguards, they were to be driven back and the advance continued towards Cambrai and the Escaut Canal.[2]

The First Army was now operating within a strategic framework which saw its main task as securing the Third Army's left flank in operations involving First, Third and Fourth Armies in breaking the Hindenburg System between St Quentin and Cambrai, and destroying the enemy's communications system by capturing Maubeuge. Its successful implementation required Horne's army to secure as far as possible its own flank of attack. In this it was helped by the favourable topography of the area with its 3 river valleys running parallel to the direction of advance. One of them, the Escaut Canal, would be a formidable obstacle to any enemy counter offensive from the north. The danger of such an enemy move had been much diminished by First Army's capture of the Drocourt-Quéant line, but could still not be entirely discounted. Moreover the threat posed by the enemy artillery targeting the army's communications, centred on the Arras-Cambrai road, remained very real.

Horne countered the threats in 2 main ways; by strengthening the organised defences facing the enemy and by large scale counter battery operations which persuaded the enemy to withdraw most of their artillery out of range of the Arras-Cambrai road. What remained continued to harass First Army's communications, but they were never seriously disrupted.

The activity that these measures entailed had the uncovenanted bonus of convincing the enemy that Horne was planning a turning movement from the south against their positions north of the Scarpe; they should therefore conserve the reserves they had available for a counter offensive to meet what was in fact a non-existent threat.[3] Horne was understandably keen to persuade the enemy that when his army renewed the offensive it would be north of the Scarpe and not south of the river, where the blow would actually fall. To this end, much of the 3 weeks available to him before the attack was actually launched was spent in efforts to persuade the enemy to keep, or move, their reserves away from the intended main scene of operations. Horne ordered his corps, cavalry, tank and RAF commanders north of the Scarpe to prepare for a large-scale attack. Tanks and infantry were to be trained in cooperation in localities where they could be observed by enemy aircraft; additional balloons were to be put up and artillery registration set in train; wire cutting and patrolling were to be stepped up; ammunition dumps and additional casualty clearing stations were to be established; Cavalry and Tank Corps officers were ordered to reconnoitre the whole front from the Scarpe north to the La Bassée Canal as conspicuously as possible.

The troops concerned soon realised that their efforts were part of a deception operation and to maintain plausibility Horne ordered a 'postponement' while at the same time instructing his corps commanders to carry out minor operations to continue the deception.[4] The outcome of 2 of these gave Horne particular pleasure. On 12 September the railway triangle opposite Givenchy, long considered almost impregnable, was captured along with about 50 prisoners. On the following day the mine with its accompanying slagheap known as Fosse 8 or 'the Dump', north of Loos and scene of much bitter fighting in 1915, was taken. Its seizure deprived the enemy of a valuable observation point which had been in their hands since the autumn of 1914, except briefly during the Battle of Loos.[5]

The Germans did not share the scepticism of the British troops about the purpose of the latters' activity north of the Scarpe. They showed their growing nervousness by stepping up their raids and patrolling and by drenching potential forming up points for an attack with mustard gas shells. More significantly, they reinforced their front north of the Scarpe by drafting in a further 3 divisions, while at the same time doing nothing to strengthen their defences south of the river.[6]

The growing perception that the Germans were increasingly on the back foot had not yet extended in Horne's case (along, it has to be said, with most of his fellow commanders) to a belief that Germany could be beaten in 1918. In mid September he wrote to his wife:

> I do not think [Germany] can be *defeated* till next year. She will make great efforts this year to get peace. She will endeavour to split the allies and her peace propaganda will be scattered broadcast, but it would be a peace which will not be a settlement. If a revolution broke out in Germany then we should have peace on proper terms, but unless something of that sort arrives I do not think the war can end this year. It would be a terrible calamity to have a peace which left Germany in a position to continue her operations against us in the east. I think that this is well understood by all the allies and that it will be next year before the war can end. However weary we may all be now, it would be a grave mistake to stop before we have accomplished sufficient to prevent a recurrence in a short time. For the sake of the peace of the world as well as the security of the British Empire, Germany must be beaten. It is sad, very sad, that all the misery and sadness must continue but I do not see how it can end just yet. We must struggle on bravely and not permit all that has been accomplished and all the suffering which has been borne to have been wasted.[7]

Horne also took the opportunity of a letter to his wife to comment disparagingly on the news that Sir Henry Wilson, the Chief of the Imperial General Staff, had been promoted substantive General, thus leapfrogging him. While expressing amusement and apparent indifference at the news, he reassured Lady Horne that the consensus of opinion was that it had been a bad move to overlook a general who had been in command of an army in the field for 2 years in favour of one who had never commanded troops in action at such a senior level.[8]

The enemy were given little respite in the days prior to the offensive. Raids continued, both to maintain the deception over the ultimate point of attack and to secure the best possible departure lines for it. The enemy felt a need to respond, sometimes with ephemeral success. During the night of 21/22 September 49th and 8th Divisions attacked north of Greenland Hill and east of Gavrelle and pushed their line forward 600 yards on a 2 mile front. A German counterattack pushed them back 300 yards and recaptured Square Wood. The next night the British resumed the attack and once more Square Wood changed hands. This time a German counterattack, preceded by a heavy bombardment, failed with heavy losses; the British remained in possession of the wood.[9]

On 19/20 September, in preparation for the attack, Horne's army's boundaries were adjusted slightly. The I Corps and the front held by them, from Loos to Violaines, were transferred to Fifth Army. To ensure that only First Army would be responsible for the capture of Bourlon Wood, the Canadian Corps took over from Third Army a stretch of the western bank of the Canal du Nord down to the northern edge of the village of Moeuvres. On the night of the 23rd/24th 2nd Canadian Division attacked southeast of Inchy and eliminated the last major enemy outposts west of the canal.[10]

Haig's initial orders for the offensive were issued to the 3 armies involved on 16 September. They called for them to establish themselves within striking distance of the enemy's main defences on the general line St Quentin-Cambrai. Detail was added on the 22nd. The First Army were instructed to attack on Z Day, capture the heights of Bourlon Wood and secure their left flank on the Sensée River. The Third Army would also attack on Z Day in cooperation with their neighbour so as to be in a position to cooperate with Fourth Army when they assaulted the Hindenburg Line on Z Day plus 2.[11]

Horne, fully aware of what was expected of his army, had issued his orders on the 18th after a meeting with the Commanders of the Canadian and XXII Corps.[12] The challenge was formidable. Before Bourlon Wood could be tackled there was the matter of crossing the Canal du Nord. Work on the unfinished canal had been brought to an end by the outbreak of war. But it still presented a daunting obstacle, made more so by the measures the Germans had taken to incorporate it into their defences. The canal was approximately 40 yards wide with a western bank 10–15 feet high and an eastern bank about 5 feet high. Its average depth of water was about 8 feet. Behind the canal itself was the German Canal du Nord Line bristling with machine guns and covered with dense belts of barbed wire. A mile to the east was the German Marquion Line, similarly well protected by barbed wire.

Between the Arras-Cambrai road and Sains-lès-Marquion the canal ran through naturally swampy ground. The Agache River, a sluggish, marshy stream lined with willows, which ran close to the eastern bank of the canal between Sains-lès-Marquion and Palluel, was a partial cause of the state of the ground, as was its deliberate flooding by the Germans. The whole area had thus been made virtually impossible for the bridging and road construction necessary to support an attack and had to be discounted. The attack would therefore need to be made over the drier area further south between Sains-lès-Marquion and Moeuvres, on the extreme right of the new First Army front. Here the canal itself was virtually dry except for occasional shallow pools. Infantry could feasibly cross without the need for bridging equipment. The approaches were also dry and offered good conceal-ment to attackers. The advantages of assaulting here were so manifest that it is the more surprising that the enemy allowed themselves to be persuaded that the attack would take place further north. (Horne's Chief of Staff somewhat wryly suggested that by now the enemy had an unshakeable belief in the BEF's fondness for frontal attacks on impassable obstacles to the exclusion of more practical alternatives.)[13]

There were however disadvantages to assaulting in this area. The main one was that, once over the canal, the attackers would have to cross areas of rising open ground between the canal and Quarry Wood and the Marquion Line, and between Bourlon village and Bourlon Wood. The enemy would, too, have the canal crossing points and subsequent progress by the attackers under continuous obser-vation from the latter wood.[14]

Horne's detailed orders thus called for the Canadian Corps to force crossings of the canal between Moeuvres and Lock 3 (500 yards south of Sains-lès-Marquion) before going on to attack and capture the Marquion Line and Bourlon village and Wood. They were to secure a general line running from the outskirts of Fontaine-Notre-Dame to the railway crossing over the canal 1,500 yards north of Marquion. If the Canadians were successful in achieving this advance it was to be exploited without delay with the object of securing the high ground about Sailly, Haynecourt, Epinoy and Oisy-le-Verger. Their eventual objective would be a line running from Morenchies to the Epinoy-Aubencheul-au-Bac road. The XXII Corps south of the Scarpe were given the supporting role of engaging the enemy holding the Canal du Nord between Sauchy Lestrée and Palluel to keep them guessing as to the main thrust of First Army's attack. They were also to push troops across the canal to work northwards along its eastern bank to assist the operations of the Canadian left flank.

North of the Scarpe VIII Corps and the rest of XXII Corps were instructed to carry out minor operations to tie down the Germans. The RAF were to prevent the enemy using the crossings over the Sensée Canal between Wasnes and Palluel and to assist generally the operations of the Canadians and XXII Corps.[15]

The spirited nature of the language in which Horne's orders, especially those concerning Canadian Corps, were drafted was a further indication that the complexion of the confrontation on the Western Front had changed. Haig had been quicker to recognise this than most. In late August he had told his army commanders that risks which a month previously would have been criminal to incur, ought from then on to be incurred as a duty. He had continued:

> It is no longer necessary to advance in regular lines and step by step. On the contrary, each division should be given a distant objective which must be reached independently of its neighbour, and even if one's flank is thereby exposed for the time being. Reinforcements must be directed on the points where our troops are gaining ground, not where they are checked ...[16]

It took a little time for this new doctrine to be fully embraced by Haig's subor-dinates. Old habits died hard and it was especially hard to contemplate the possi-bility of leaving flanks exposed to the threat of counterattack. But by the time that Horne was preparing his orders for the Canal du Nord, he was fully reflecting the

Commander-in-Chief's urgings of a month previously. The essence of the Canadian Corps' orders was to press on; while progress was possible it should be the first priority with mopping up, consolidation and the setting up of defensive flanks given secondary roles, or none at all.

Z Day was initially set by Horne for 25 September but on orders from GHQ, it was changed to the 27th. The 2 extra days saw the Canadian Corps, to which 11th British Division had been attached, complete their concentration south of the Arras-Cambrai road. The 24 tanks assigned to the corps moved up to their assembly positions. In total First Army would have elements of 9 divisions in the line, 1 in support and 4 in reserve. They would be facing 13 enemy divisions in the line with, in reserve, 5 divisions close by and 3 near Douai. Significantly however only 3 of the enemy front line divisions and 5 of those in reserve were immediately available to intervene in the area where the main assault would fall. The remaining 13 were deployed to meet an attack north of the Sensée Canal. The deception operation had worked.

The geographical and topographical constraints facing the attackers meant that although the overall frontage of the attack would ultimately expand to 15,000 yards, the crossing of the canal would take place on a frontage of only 2,700 yards. Once across the canal therefore, the attack would have to fan out to a width of 9,000 yards when it reached the line from Fontaine-Notre Dame to the railway crossing over the canal 1,500 yards north of Marquion. Thereafter, exploitation of success would result in the frontage of 15,000 yards. The Canadian Corps would initially attack using 4th Division on the right and 1st on the left to force the canal line between the northern end of Moeuvres and Lock 3. The former Division would then take Bourlon village and Wood before moving up to a line from the outskirts of Fontaine-Notre Dame north towards the Arras-Cambrai road. The latter Division would take Sains-lès-Marquion and extend the line north to Sauchicourt Farm.

The 3rd Canadian and 11th British Divisions would follow the first 2 Canadian divisions across the Canal and join them on the captured line where all 4 divisions would reorganise into a 4 divisional front to advance on and capture the Marcoing Line and the villages of Raillencourt, Haynecourt, Epinoy and Oisy-le-Verger.

The supportive role assigned to XXII Corps has already been outlined. The troops that would cross the canal north of the Arras-Cambrai road, once the enemy had been pushed back sufficiently by the Canadians to the south, would consist of 169th Brigade of 56th Division, a relatively weak brigade which by now could only muster 1,600 men. It was however deemed sufficient for the task of getting across the bridges which would have to be thrown across the canal, and then turning north to clear up the low lying marshy fields between the canal and the Marquion Line.

The artillery would play its customary crucial role. No fewer than 1,347 guns would be engaged, 60% in support of the Canadians and the remainder at the disposal of XXII Corps. The Canadian Corps would in addition be backed by a machine gun barrage. To ensure initial tactical surprise no bombardment would be fired prior to Zero Hour. In their supporting role, XXII Corps would fire 2 field artillery barrages on targets between Sauchy Lestrée and Oisy-le-Verger. Their

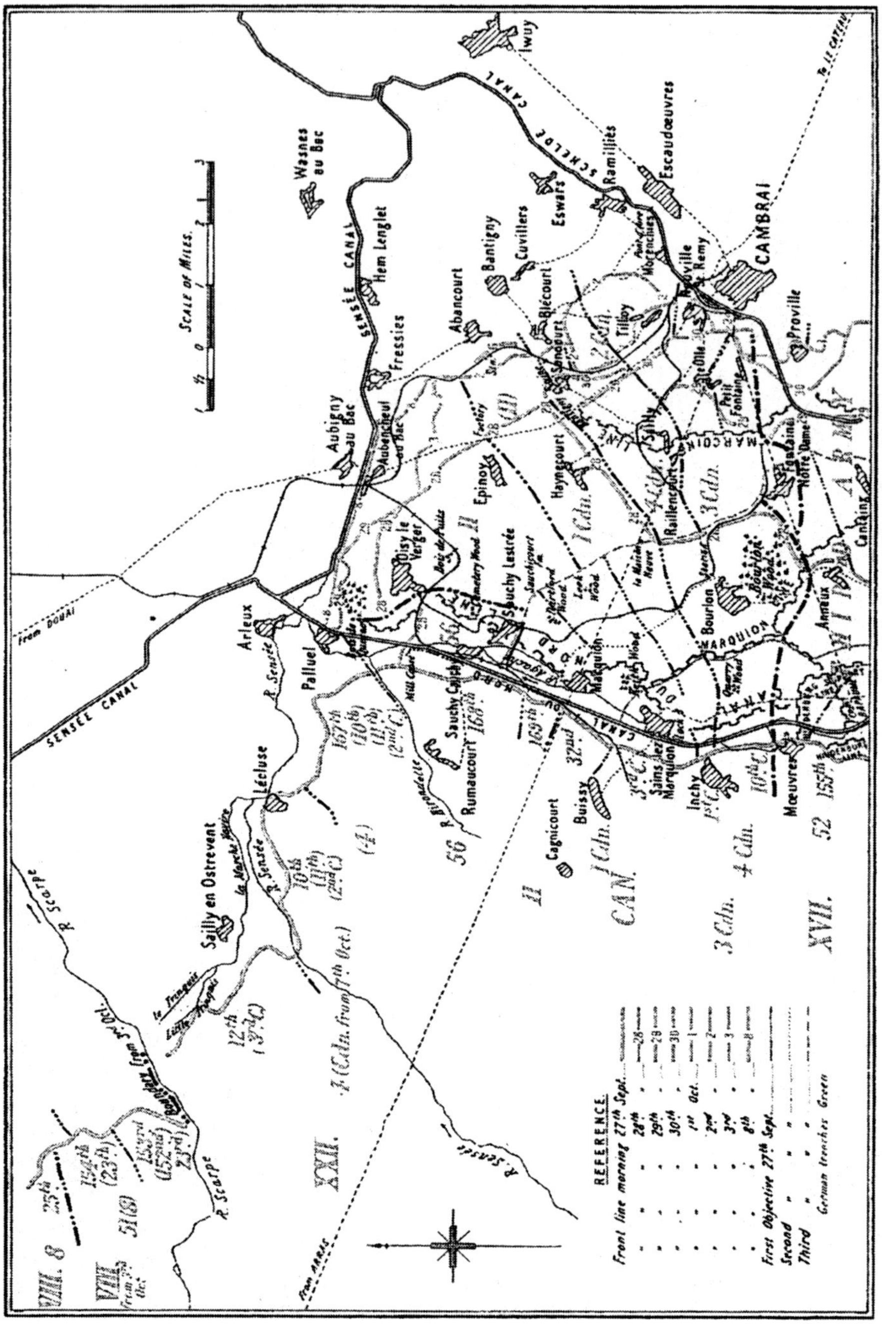

Map 17: Canal du Nord, Cambrai, Douai: September–October 1918 (I)

purpose would be to confuse the enemy as to whether they presaged an attack, to keep their heads down and to prevent them bringing up reinforcements. One round in 12 would be smoke to add to the enemy's uncertainty about what might be happening further south. The Corps' heavy artillery would bombard strongpoints on the Marquion Line and seek to neutralise hostile batteries attempting to intervene in the battle. To prevent their use by the enemy, crossings over the Sensée River would be kept under fire. Finally Palluel and the Bois de Quesnoy would be shelled with gas. In addition to carrying out similar roles to that of XXII Corps, the Canadian Corps artillery, using 18 pdrs, would support the assaulting divisions by firing a creeping barrage.

The last piece in the deception plan began at midnight on the night of 26/27 September when 8th and 20th Divisions of VIII Corps launched an assault on the town of Arleux. It succeeded both in diverting the enemy's attention from the area further south and in its own right, by capturing the town and creating a 500 yard deep indentation in the enemy's defences for a length of 2,000 yards north of Arleux.[17]

Zero Hour for the main attack was 05h20 on 27 September. At that hour all the guns available to First Army began the bombardment and 1st and 4th Canadian Divisions, which had formed up between 400 and 600 yards of the west bank of the canal, moved forward rapidly. They crossed the canal under cover of the creeping barrage and quickly carried the enemy trenches and rifle pits within 500 yards of its eastern bank. Within 33 minutes of Zero Hour 1st Canadian Division had turned north and forced themselves into Sains-lès-Marquion, completing its capture in a matter of minutes.

By this time the initial advantage of surprise had been lost. As 4th Canadian Division pressed on up exposed slopes towards the Marquion Line they were faced with determined pockets of resistance from enemy machine gun and rifle fire. These were mainly quickly overcome, but the fortified quarries in Quarry Wood checked the Canadian advance. They were finally cleared and the wood surrounded and captured with the help of the tanks which had followed hard on the heels of the infantry over the canal, having crossed the obstacle with little difficulty. With Quarry Wood in Canadian hands, the Marquion Line followed suit; by 07h30 the whole of the line from First Army's southern boundary to Keith Wood, northeast of Sains-lès-Marquion had been secured.

The initial Canadian assault had suffered very little interference from enemy artillery. Such activity as there was had at first concentrated on counter battery work, before shifting its targets to the line of the Canal du Nord. The German confusion over the main thrust of the attack became apparent at this stage as they focused on crossings at Marquion and further north, leaving the Canadian crossing area to the south virtually unscathed. By about 08h00 even this shelling was dying down, indicating that the Germans were beginning to withdraw their guns. It was during this period that the leading brigades of 3rd Canadian and 11th British Divisions moved up to the canal from their assembly positions preparatory to crossing.

With the Marquion Line secured, the 2 leading Canadian Divisions prepared for the second stage of their attack. The barrage moved forward and 4th Canadian Division began their assault on Bourlon village. The stubborn resistance they met from machine gun nests and groups of riflemen in house-to-house fighting, was once more overcome with the aid of the tanks. The attack moved on towards the western edge of Bourlon Wood. On the left 1st Canadian Division, setting off a little later than the 4th, and turning further left, captured a further stretch of the Marquion Line as far north as the village, and the village itself. Both divisions then paused for some 40 minutes at the foot of the final slope of the ridge running north northwest from Bourlon village to the east of Marquion. Meanwhile the 2 supporting divisions began crossing the canal and moving to the general line Quarry Wood – Keith Wood. They were sometimes harassed, but not delayed, by fire from enemy not mopped up by the leading divisions.

Shortly after 10h00 the 2 leading divisions resumed their advance. Because Bourlon Wood had been systematically shelled with mustard gas by Third Army (using captured German guns and ammunition) in the days leading up to the attack, there could be no question of entering it. Protected by a barrage, the bulk of 4th Canadian Division therefore passed north of the wood to reach its eastern edge. South of the wood were the trenches of the German Cantaing Line, an extension of the Marquion Line, and principally the objective of Third Army. The elements of 4th Canadian Division skirting the wood to the south synchronised their advance with that of 57th Division of Third Army's XVII Corps and materially assisted the latter in the capture of the village of Anneux and trenches of the German line. The 1st Canadian Division had little difficulty in clearing the crest of the ridge between Bourlon Wood and Sauchicourt Farm. This concluded the phase of the day's attack involving only 2 of Horne's divisions.

The attack frontage now widened to 9,000 yards with the introduction of 3rd Canadian Division on the right of 4th Canadian, and 11th British on the left of 1st Canadian. To make partial room, 1st and 4th Canadian Divisions narrowed their frontages. The 169th Brigade of XXII Corps' 56th Division had by now also crossed the canal, at Marquion, and had relieved the Canadians between the canal and Sauchicourt Farm, clearing out pockets of enemy left behind as they took over.

The success of the attack so far had, as foreseen, created an exposed left flank. This might have proved vulnerable to counterattack had it not been for the measures which had been, and were still being, taken to sow confusion in the minds of the Germans. The bombardments fired by XXII Corps, especially the use of smoke helped by favourable wind conditions, had proved very effective in screening what was happening from the German observation posts on the high ground north of the Sensée and around Oisy-le-Verger.

With his 4 divisions in position and with sufficient field artillery having crossed the canal to offer support, General Currie ordered the attack to be resumed at 15h00. Heavy artillery, still operating from positions west of the canal, was able to fire barrages, which lifted in accordance with prearranged timetables, in front of the advancing Canadians. On the extreme right 3rd Canadian Division were quickly pinned down by heavy fire from the village of Fontaine-Notre Dame, one of the objectives of Third Army's XVII Corps. Their 57th Division were still clearing out the Cantaing Line before moving on to Fontaine. It became clear that further attempts to advance by the Canadian Division before Fontaine was taken would involve unacceptable loss. To 3rd Division's left, 4th Canadian Division also found it difficult to make progress down the bare slopes leading to the village of Raillencourt and the German Marcoing Line in the face of heavy machine gun and rifle fire. What little forward momentum they could maintain was effectively stopped by a German counterattack by the Guards Reserve Division.

In contrast with their comrades' misfortunes to their right, Canadian 1st Division found little difficulty in advancing 3 miles despite heavy enemy wire entanglements. They took the village of Haynecourt and eventually established themselves on the Cambrai-Douai road, no less than 11,000 yards from their starting point that morning.

On the left flank of the Canadian Corps attack, 11th British Division were to fight 2 more or less separate actions, one of them in cooperation with 169th Brigade of 56th Division. The 11th Division's centre and right-hand brigades attacked northeast and north, forced their way through thick enemy wire running east-west between the Marquion and Marcoing Lines and captured the village of Epinoy, thus achieving an advance of 3 miles. The division's left hand brigade and 169th Brigade were ordered to capture the commanding German position of Oisy-le-Verger and the eponymous village. This entailed both brigades advancing northwards, the 169th between the canal and the Marquion Line and the 11th Division brigade to the east of the line. The artillery programmes fired in support of the 2 brigades allowed the latter to advance initially at twice the pace of the former. This had the effect of threatening to cut off the enemy garrisons in the Marquion Line and at Sauchy-Lestrée. The 169th Brigade found considerable numbers of enemy between the canal and the Marquion line who, although confused and disorientated from the artillery pounding they had suffered, were by no means all inclined to surrender. It required stiff fighting before the brigade were able to capture Sauchy-Lestrée, Sauchy-Cauchy and Cemetery Wood.

By this time once more in line and able to operate in tandem, the two brigades, after a further artillery bombardment of the area, were able to seize the Oisy-le-Verger position and village. As darkness fell the northern stretch of the Canadian Corps line ran 3 and a half miles from the Douai-Cambrai road east of Epinoy (where they were in touch with 1st Canadian Division) to the south of Aubencheul, and from there to the edge of the Bois de Quesnoy, close up to the banks of the Sensée Canal. The 11th Division and 169th Brigade had captured 1,200 prisoners and 40 guns during the day.

In peripheral actions on 27 September, the other two brigades of 56th Division pushed patrols forward to Palluel but were unable to enter the village in the face of heavy machine gun fire. Further to the west 4th Division, despite heavy opposition, established a small bridgehead across the Trinquis Brook west of Sailly-en-Ostravent.[18]

Horne could be hugely satisfied with his army's endeavours on 27 September. There was to be some criticism of the plan he had adopted to get his army across the Canal du Nord on the grounds that funnelling 6 divisions through a bottleneck only 2,700 yards wide had exposed them to an unacceptable risk of failure with heavy losses. Horne accepted that there had been an element of risk involved but that it had been minimised through thorough and painstaking planning and preparation. He paid due tribute for this to his staff led by Major General Hastings Anderson.

Horne had been fortunate in being allowed plenty of time to formulate his plans which were based on thorough reconnaissance of enemy dispositions and movements. His plan took the precaution of ensuring that the first 2 divisions across the canal were firmly established well to its east before the supporting divisions were moved across. All this was built into the timing of the second phase of the attack by the 4 divisions in line. The attackers were supported by elaborate and thorough artillery plans which were to work almost perfectly. The morale of the troops engaged was high, with officers, NCOs and men well-trained and fully conversant with their tasks, Horne singling out the Canadians for special praise. It had not been long before the initial bridgehead was widened sufficiently for the Royal Engineers to be able to construct a series of bridges and other crossings across the canal along a much greater length than that of the initial crossing. Last of all, the elaborate deception plan had succeeded in persuading the enemy that the attack would be made elsewhere, a fact which was confirmed by the thorough monitoring of enemy movements and other intelligence.[19]

Major General Anderson fully endorsed Horne's assessment of the reasons for the success of the attack. He added that the conformation of the ground had enabled direct observation of the battlefield by staffs and commanders thus enabling them to move forward reserves in full knowledge of the exact situation on the ground. Control of the artillery had also been much simplified. The successful passage of the tanks over the crossings had also played an essential part in the operation. Anderson too was full of praise for the magnificent fighting qualities of the young Canadian veterans, on whom the great weight of the fighting had devolved.[20]

The results of the day were sufficiently spectacular to justify the degree of risk involved. The First Army had forced the Canal du Nord from Moeuvres in the south to Palluel in the north. Its troops had captured 2 powerful systems of entrenchments, the Canal and Marquion Lines, and the important tactical positions of Bourlon Wood and Oisy-le-Verger and the ridge between them. The army's line had been advanced 5 miles on a front of nearly 9 miles. Favourable positions had been secured for future operations towards Cambrai and the Escaut river. A total of 4,000 prisoners and 100 guns had been captured. 3 German divisions had been routed and 2 severely damaged. On Horne's right, Byng's Third Army had also crossed the Canal du Nord and captured Flesquières Ridge and the Hindenburg Support Line.[21] Unsurprisingly, Horne was in an ebullient mood when he wrote to his wife after the day's events.

> Good news today. This morning I attacked the Canal du Nord position and all has gone very well. It was a difficult operation as the Canal itself is a very serious obstacle throughout a considerable portion of my front. From the Sensée River for some distance southwards it is full of water and dug deep. Then it becomes mud and water in a deep bed. This bed got gradually shallower as it approached Inchy and it is between Inchy and Moeuvres that we crossed. It was necessary to get the attacking troops across on a narrow front and then to deploy outwards like a fan. It was this that contributed the difficulty and some risk if the Boche recognised that we were advancing and put a heavy artillery fire on the portion of the Canal where we were crossing. By good artillery work we managed to make him think we were going to try and cross further north, and in addition we attracted attention to the Douai front further north by some minor operations there, so that we were able to confuse

him and the crossing took place without much trouble, whilst the Boche
shelled the Canal heavily elsewhere. Very satisfactory result. After that we got
on well and have taken a good number of prisoners and guns. A heavy defeat
for the Boche. South of me, Third Army have got on well also.[22]

There could be no question of Horne's army resting on the laurels of their
achievements of 27 September; the pressure on the enemy had to be maintained.
During the course of the night of the 27th/28th the Canadian Corps got nearly all
the remainder of their field artillery and the bulk of their heavy artillery across the
canal and into position to support further advances by the infantry. Horne's orders
for the 28th, issued at 18h50 the previous day, instructed the Canadian Corps to
aim to reach a line running from Morenchies to the Epinoy – Aubencheul-au-Bac
road, through the villages of Blécourt and Epinoy. Shortly afterwards, General
Currie ordered his troops to continue to gain ground during the night wherever
possible. The general advance would resume at 08h00 with the aim of securing the
objectives detailed by Horne.

At Zero Hour 3rd Canadian Division on the right, once again in cooperation
with Third Army's 57th Division advancing from the south, attacked Fontaine-
Notre Dame from the north. The enemy fought well but could not withstand the
joint assault and the village was taken. The Canadian Division pushed on and took
the front trenches of the Marcoing Line between the Bapaume-Cambrai and Arras-
Cambrai roads. On their left 4th Canadian Division took Raillencourt and Sailly
and also occupied front trenches of the Marcoing Line just to the south of the
Arras-Cambrai road. No further progress was possible in the face of stiffening
enemy resistance in the form of heavy machine gun fire. Next in line, 1st Canadian
Division, whose troops had found themselves well in advance of the divisions on
their right, stood pat for the day. On their left 11th Division did push forward.
Their right entered the outskirts of Aubencheul, their centre reached the Douai-
Cambrai road and their left worked down the Sensée Canal and linked up with
56th Division north of the Bois de Quesnoy. The latter had pushed through
Palluel and worked round the west of the wood to effect the linkup.

During the course of the day Third Army captured Cantaing, Noyelle and
Marcoing and secured a footing on the eastern bank of the Escaut river. There had
however been signs of a stiffening of enemy resistance with indications of increased
artillery activity. Horne described the day as one of getting on a bit, the slowness
compared with the previous day being due to the need to get the guns forward.

During the night of the 28th/29th elements of 56th Division crossed the
Sensée at Arleux in an attempt to establish a bridgehead on the northern side. A
determined German counterattack pushed them back over the river. The general
attack was resumed at 03h00 the same night. It was resisted strongly by enemy
artillery and machine gun fire, especially from the Marcoing Line south of the
Bapaume-Cambrai road. The machine guns were particularly troublesome. Nevertheless, by midday 3rd Canadian Division had captured La Petite Fontaine and
reached the western outskirts of St Olle. In the afternoon they completed the
capture of the village and the Marcoing Line between the Escaut and the Arras-
Cambrai road. Their advanced troops pushed on to reach the junction of the Arras-
Cambrai and Bapaume-Cambrai roads and the Cambrai suburb of Neuville-St
Rémy. To their north 1st and 4th Canadian Divisions also advanced rapidly at

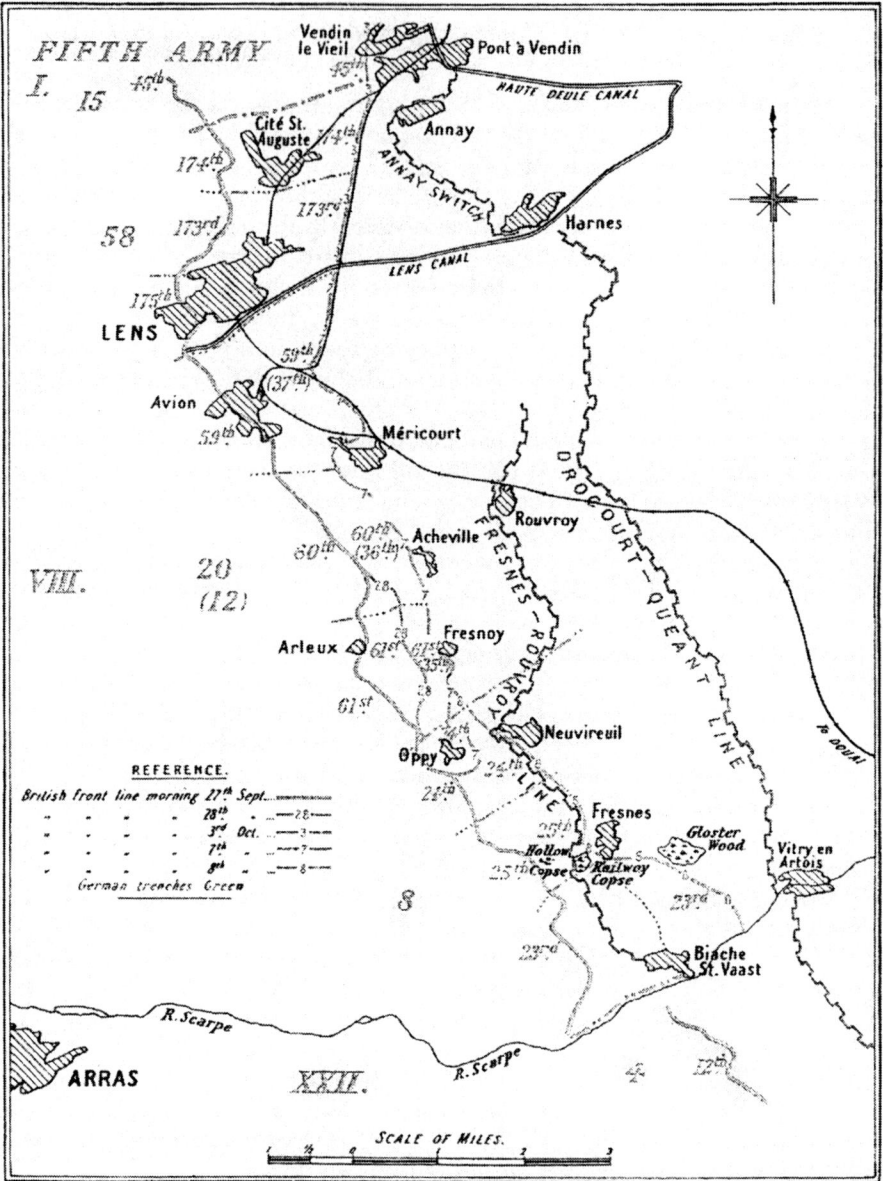

Map 18: Canal du Nord, Cambrai, Douai: September–October 1918 (II)

first, reaching the western edge of Tilloy, just north of Cambrai, and the railway line from there to Blécourt and Abancourt. Here their progress was dramatically halted by a German counterattack mounted from a sheltered approach from the Bantigny Ravine. The Canadians were forced back to Sancourt and the Douai road east of Epinoy. Further north still, 11th Division were also counterattacked and driven out of their outposts in Aubencheul.[23]

The severity of the day's fighting had indicated quite clearly that the enemy were not prepared to give up the high ground around Cuvillers and Abancourt without a struggle. The loss of this ground would inevitably entail their evacuation of Cambrai. Cuvillers, situated on a commanding spur on the plateau forming the watershed between the Escaut and the Sensée, constituted a very strong position. It could be reinforced along concealed lines of approach; it was protected on the north by the deep Bantigny Ravine to which the lower spur, on which Abancourt rests, acted as a flanking defence; to the southwest and south the ground fell gently down bare and exposed slopes.

Horne was pleased with the progress made by his troops during the day. He acknowledged that the German counterattacks, fuelled by fresh divisions from their reserves, had given problems and forced some retirements. But he was nevertheless satisfied with the progress made towards enveloping Cambrai, with his troops moving west and northwest of the town, and Third Army getting round the southwest against much lighter opposition. He anticipated the completion of the town's envelopment before long.

Horne also noted with pleasure the progress made in Flanders by the joint Belgian-Second Army attack which had by now reached places which had never previously been in Allied hands. He also noted the start of the Fourth Army's attack north of St Quentin. Early reports seemed very good. On this, the second anniversary of his assumption of command of the First Army, he paid private tribute to his staff and his troops by whom he had been well served. His army had been successful on the whole and had suffered no reverse except that of the Portuguese in April, 'which no man could have avoided, but which was soon stopped'.[24]

The 30 September was to see no decrease in the intensity of the fighting. The enemy were clearly operating under orders that any ground lost had to be regained through counterattacks, reflecting the importance they attached to retaining the high ground around Cuvillers. This ground alone protected their crossings over the Escaut between Cambrai and Estrun. When the Canadians resumed their attack at 06h00, they met with some initial success, capturing Tilloy and Blécourt and the road linking them. But a heavy enemy counterattack forced 4th Canadian Division back from Blécourt to the railway line between Sancourt and Tilloy. The Germans also regained the eastern part of Tilloy. On the right, 3rd Canadian Division, trying to push eastward along the Arras-Cambrai road and through Neuville-St Rémy towards the Escaut Canal, had become embroiled in house-to-house fighting. Progress was limited against determined opposition.

Horne's orders for the following day called for a continuation of the pressure being exerted on the enemy. The 3rd Canadian Division were to secure bridgeheads over the Escaut Canal at Pont d'Aire and Ramillies, 4th Canadian Division at Eswars. The 1st Canadian Division were given the highly challenging task of taking Blécourt, Cuvillers, Bantigny and Abancourt with 11th Division protecting their left flank. The 2nd Canadian Division, currently in reserve behind Bourlon Wood, were to form up just west of Raillencourt at Zero Hour and be prepared to pass through 3rd Canadian Division, should the latter succeed in crossing the canal.

Zero Hour was set for 05h00 on a day which was later described as perhaps the most severe day of fighting experienced by the Canadian Corps between Arras and the Armistice. The enemy remained determined to hold on to the Cuvillers position and progress was to be difficult and costly. On the corps' right, 3rd Canadian Division cleared Tilloy and reached a small wood east of the village of Morenchies. They also made ground along the spur running from Tilloy towards Ramillies. Their right flank completed the capture of Neuville-St Rémy and pushed on to the bank of the canal east of that suburb of Cambrai. To their north the 4th Canadians captured some old German practice trenches south of Cuvillers. Further north still, the 1st Canadians managed to take Blécourt and, continuing their advance, gained footholds in their remaining 3 objectives, Cuvillers, Bantigny and Abancourt, despite intense enemy rifle and machine gun fire. A German counterattack, launched at 10h00 up the Bantigny Ravine forced the Canadians out of Cuvillers and Abancourt and back to Blécourt and the line of the railway running northwest from the village towards Fressies. On this line they linked up with the 4th Canadians on their right, who had managed to keep hold of the old German practice trenches. On the corps' extreme left 11th Division's attempts to secure the spur running northeast from Epinoy towards Fressies had been frustrated by a deep belt of uncut enemy wire and the machine guns protected by it.

A day of heavy fighting ended with some progress having been made but by no means as much as had been hoped. On the plus side however, severe losses had been inflicted on the enemy, especially by artillery fire targeted on the Bantigny Ravine. 1,300 prisoners had been taken and positions had been secured from which attacks could be launched on the canal crossings at Pont d'Aire and Ramillies once Third Army were in a position to mount an operation for the capture of Cambrai from the south.[25] In his customary letter home Horne described the day.

> Hard fighting north of Cambrai, as the Boche has brought up all the reserves he can lay hands on and has counterattacked us there very heavily. Both yesterday and today he has counterattacked and he evidently is very much afraid of our getting round Cambrai in the north. We have beaten off the attacks and he must have suffered great losses. It has been hard fighting.

In the context of the news that Bulgaria had collapsed and was seeking an armistice, Horne wrote that the Allies must press on as hard as possible and try to force the Germans back still further.[26] More immediately, as a consequence of the severe fighting in which they had been engaged since 27 September, Canadian Corps were ordered to cease offensive operations and consolidate and reorganise. An exception was made for minor actions to make their positions on the Cuvillers and Abancourt spurs less vulnerable to counterattacks. Nor should any opportunity be lost to secure bridgeheads over the Canal de l'Escaut. Horne's orders made it clear that he was planning to relieve the Canadians by XXII Corps in the near future with a view to the latter resuming his army's offensive operations.

The first week in October on Horne's southern front was to be marked by a series of enemy counterattacks seeking to reverse First Army's recent gains. No fewer than 8 major assaults were mounted, all unsuccessful. By contrast, minor actions undertaken by Horne's divisions succeeded in their limited aims. On the night of 5/6 October, 11th Division attacked and captured Abancourt railway station. On the 7th this division and the 56th outflanked the enemy's strong wire entanglements on the south bank of the Sensée. They established outposts at the southern end of the bridges in Aubencheul-au-Bac and a line of posts running northwest towards the canal from the railway a mile north of Abancourt station. The woods east of Aubencheul were also captured after a sharp fight. Throughout this relatively quiet few days preparations were being made on the Cambrai front for a resumption of major operations in cooperation with an attack to be launched on 8 October by Third and Fourth Armies. Detailed orders for this were issued by GHQ on the 5th.[27]

Although somewhat overshadowed by events further south, Horne's north-ernmost VIII Corps were doing their part in maintaining pressure on the enemy on either side of the town of Lens, still in enemy possession. The successful crossing of the Canal du Nord and the growing pressure on Cambrai, together with the joint Belgian/Second Army advance in late September, had, as hoped, led the Germans to plan a withdrawal to the Haute Deule Canal of their troops in positions between the Scarpe River and Armentières. The First Army obtained confirmation from a prisoner that the withdrawal would take place on 2 October. The VIII Corps therefore pushed out strong patrols on either side of Lens on that date. South of the town, at Méricourt and Avion, the enemy were found to be holding on in strength with little indication that a withdrawal was planned. North of the town however, 50th Division found only weak rearguards and were able to move round its northern edge. On the First Army's extreme left 58th Division were able to enter Cité St Auguste, just northeast of Lens. Further north, Fifth Army found clearer indications of an enemy retirement and were able to take possession of Hulluch, Bénifontaine, Douvrin and La Bassée.

The following day, 58th Division maintained the pressure on the enemy by seizing the railway line linking Cité St Auguste to Lens and a wood on the northern side of the Cité. They were now east of Lens and working southwards. The encir-clement of the town was completed when they joined hands with 20th Division across the Souchez River. The latter Division had cleared German trenches east of Avion on their way east and north. When Horne's troops then entered Lens they found it empty of the enemy. The fall of the town was very much the end of a chapter for Horne for whom it had loomed very large for a very long time. When writing how glad he was to have taken it at last he recalled that he had very nearly taken it a year previously, only having been thwarted by priorities elsewhere.

With Lens secured, the main thrust of VIII Corps' activities moved further south. On 4 October 58th and 20th Divisions advanced to a line from north of Oppy to the railway line running north to Pont-à-Vendin through Fresnoy, Acheville and Méricourt. The speed of advance was dictated not so much by the level of enemy activity, by this time slight, but by the difficulty of the terrain being traversed; it was honeycombed by complicated trench systems that had to be checked and secured. Two days later 20th Division advanced its outposts to the

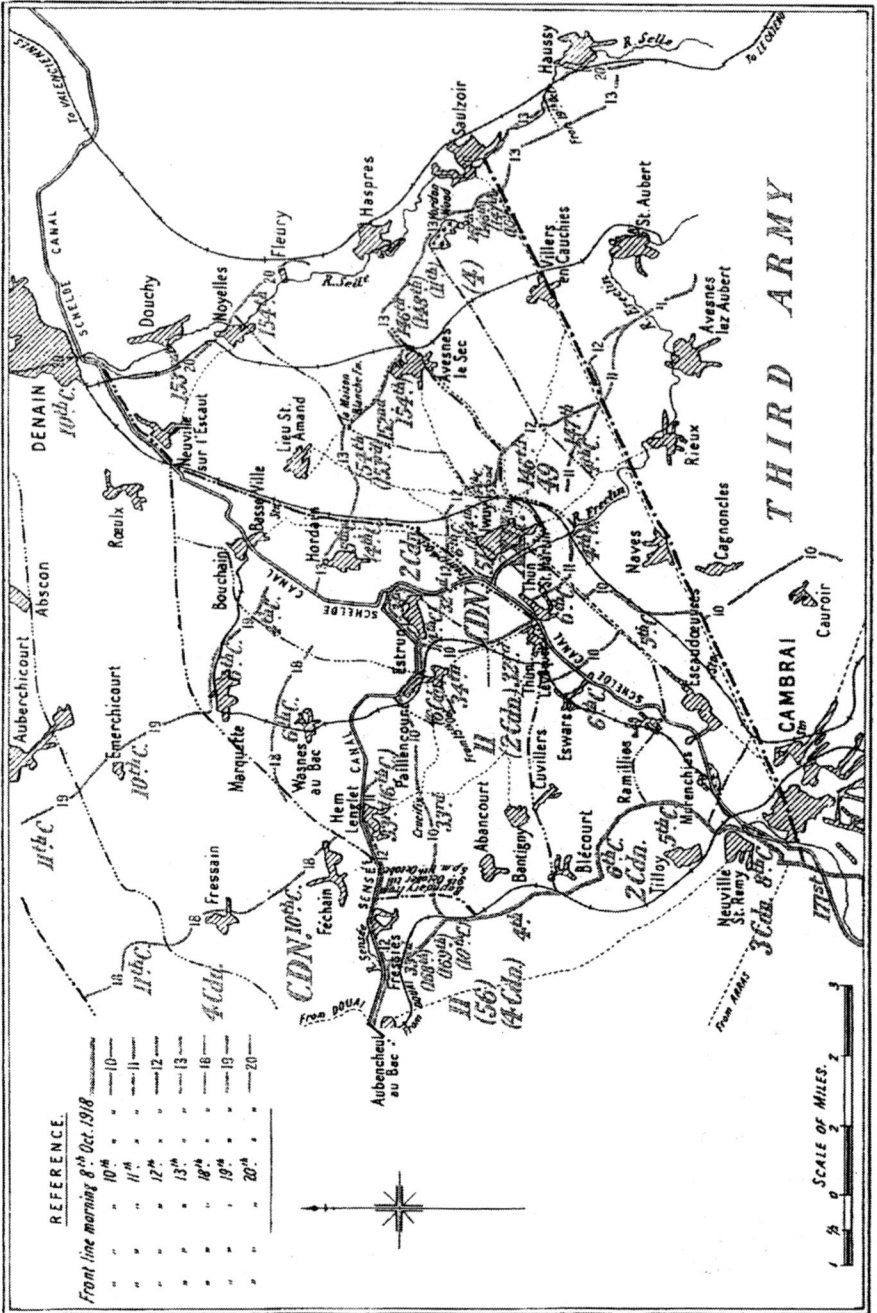

Map 19: Canal du Nord, Cambrai, Douai: September–October 1918 (III)

east of Fresnoy and thence north along Sallaumines Hill to the village of that name. On the same day 8th Division established posts south east of Oppy in preparation for an attack on the German Fresnes-Rouvroy Line the following day.

The attack duly went in on a 2 mile front immediately north of the Scarpe River between the Fresnes-Gavrelle road and Biache-St Vaast. By the evening the greater part of this powerful line of defences between Oppy and the Scarpe was in the hands of 8th Division despite the clear intention of the enemy not to give it up. The task was completed by daylight the following day by when 8th Division had established outposts on the western edge of Vitry-en-Artois and in Vitry marshes, and captured the village of Neuvireuil.[28]

On 8 October, Third, Fourth and First French Armies launched the attack which broke through the last defences of the Hindenburg Line between Cambrai and St Quentin. Horne's army was not due to join until the following day. But to assist the main attack on its first day XXII Corps carried out feint attacks against 3 crossings over the Sensée River and Trinquis Brook, using smoke and creeping barrages. The 1st Canadian Division, temporarily attached to XXII Corps, pushed out patrols which entered the western outskirts of Sailly-en-Ostrevent. North of the Scarpe, VIII Corps' 8th Division pushed patrols forward towards the northern stretch of the Drocourt-Quéant Line, a stretch which had not been attacked at the beginning of September and was still strongly held by the enemy. They were almost certainly planning its evacuation as part of a general move back to Douai and the Haute Deule Canal but had not yet had time to take away their stores and supplies and render the position useless to the attackers.

Horne was in no mood to allow the enemy the time they required and he and the GOC of XXII Corps considered options for capturing the line without resorting to a frontal assault. With increasing signs that enemy resistance was diminishing, 56th and 1st Canadian Divisions were ordered to reconnoitre the Sensée River and Trinquis Brook in order to take rapid advantage of any enemy withdrawal from their positions on the waterways. Patrols however found the enemy still firmly in position. Early on 10 October strong patrols of the 1st Canadian Division got into the Drocourt-Quéant Line north of Sailly-en-Ostrevent before being driven out by a strong counterattack. The 8th Division also found the enemy still holding the line in strength opposite them. Further north however Rouvroy and Loison were occupied by 12th and 58th Divisions respectively.

By the following day the anticipated lessening of enemy resolve began to show itself. Under protection of an artillery barrage 8th Division launched a dawn attack on a part of the Drocourt-Quéant line just north of the Scarpe. It met with immediate success with the attackers, once into the trench system, able to turn northwards, still under the protection of the barrage, and effectively roll up the enemy's defences. The attack ended with the line from Vitry-en-Artois to Izel-les-Equerchin firmly in British hands.

In the course of the same action a platoon of 2nd Bn the Middlesex Regiment succeeded in crossing the River Scarpe at Vitry and capturing the commanding position of Mont Métier. Here they were relieved by 1st Canadian Division which, earlier in the day, had occupied Sailly-en-Ostrevent without opposition and were to make further rapid progress. Crossing the Sensée at Lecluse, they drove the

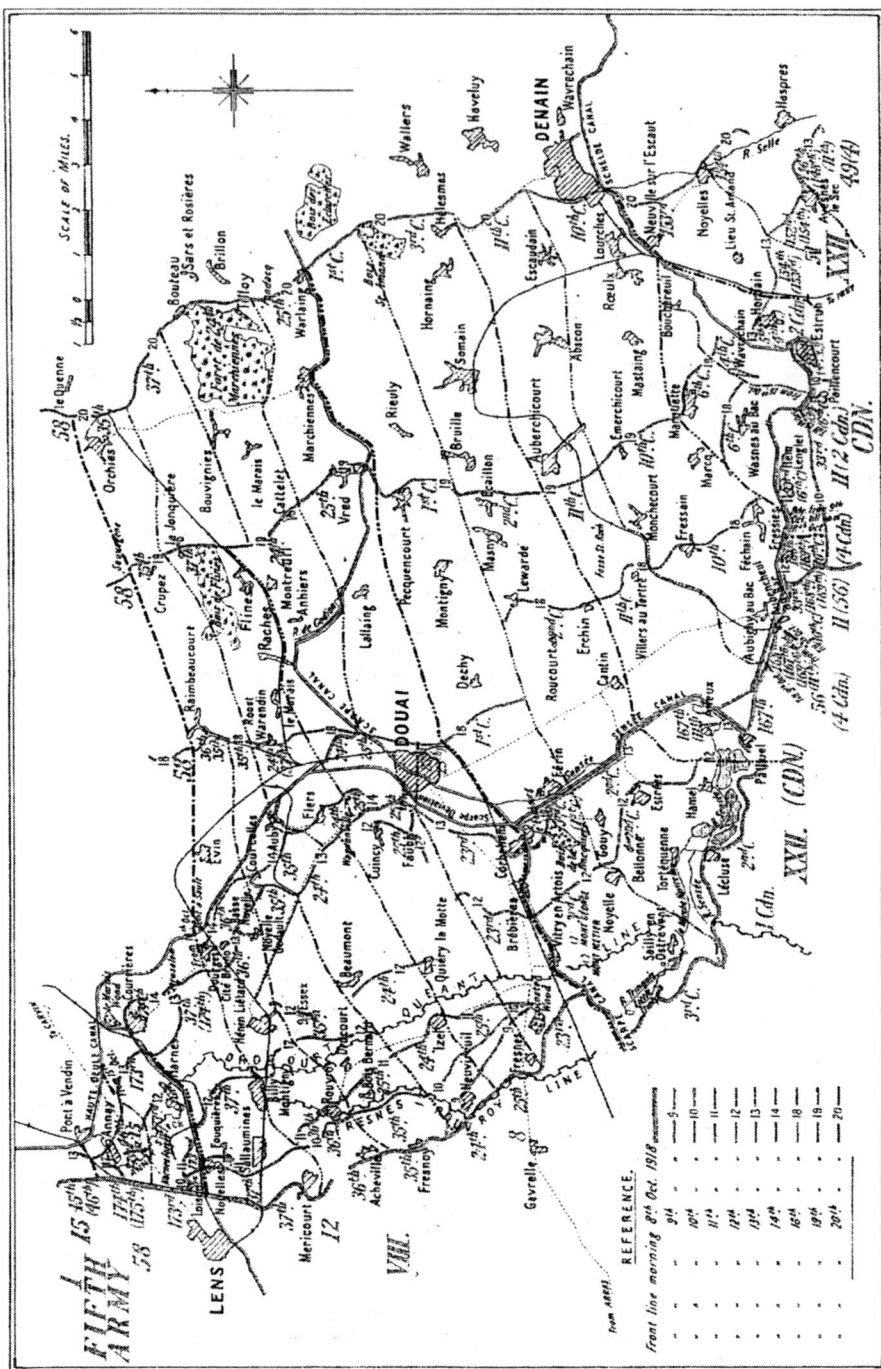

Map 20: Canal du Nord, Cambrai, Douai: September–October 1918 (IV)

enemy's rearguards out of Tortequesne and pushed on to Hamel, Bellonne and Noyelles-sous-Bellonne.

The whole of VIII Corps' front was by now moving forward rapidly against an enemy which was in retreat. By the evening 8th Division had captured Brebières and Petit Cuinchy to complete an advance of 5 miles during the day. The 12th Division captured Billy Montigny and 58th Division the collection of fosses immediately north of the canal opposite Noyelles.

For the next 5 days VIII Corps continued to press forward. Although not able to advance as rapidly as the progress being made further south, the consequent exposed flank was no longer under any serious threat from the retreating Germans. Indeed it was they who were most concerned by the development as it threatened their communications and the continuity of their line. Hence their decision to retire on 12 October to Douai and the line of the Haute Deule Canal. The advancing British troops nevertheless found themselves confronted by strong detachments of machine guns supported by artillery, land mines and booby traps. The troops were well aware of these latter dangers and their effectiveness was consequently minimised. But the need to neutralise their threat, and the general suitability of the country for determined rearguard action, meant that the advance was perforce cautious and less rapid than might have been wished. The area was covered by mining villages, mine workings, trenches and wire entanglements. A further difficulty was added to the advance when the enemy cut the canal banks south west of Douai. The resultant floods added to the problems presented by the naturally swampy ground adjoining the Haute Deule canal. Nevertheless a steady procession of villages fell to VIII Corps along their line of advance. By 16 October they had reached the canal along the whole of their front.[29]

Before returning to developments on the southern sector of Horne's front, it is worth recording Horne's views on the overall situation on the Western Front now that the Germans were clearly on the rack and making moves to secure peace. In letters to his wife in early October he wrote:

> The Boche is burning Douai and many other villages and mining centres and doing a very great deal of damage to the country for some distance eastwards which looks as if he meant to go further back. He is also flooding the country about Douai and the canal north of it. It seems to be the German intention to do as much damage as ever they can, in fact to devastate the country as they fall back through it. It is a *devilish* plan and I wish the people at home could realise more than they do what an inhuman nation they are. We must never make peace with them until they are utterly smashed and we must make them pay for the terrible damage they are doing. They cannot say that the fires and damage they are doing east of Douai is due to the British shellfire as we cannot range so far![30]

> ... The German is awfully put to it to find men to hold the length of line which he now occupies and he *must* shorten it, I feel sure. That means that he *must* give up the Channel ports, as otherwise he cannot shorten the line to any great extent, so I think we shall soon hear of his giving up Ostend and Zeebrugge and probably going back to Ghent or even Antwerp. He is evidently in a very bad way and that is why he is asking for peace, but I cannot think it is sincere. I fear he is only trying to gain time to carry out his retire-

ment unmolested. No one can believe a German nowadays. Also while he is asking for peace he is busy burning the mines east of Lens and devastating the country. They really are the limit. There is only one thing for them and that is "Force". I do hope the governments concerned will stand fast and reply that there can be no talk of peace until the Germans have withdrawn their troops to within their own frontiers. We can only dictate terms of peace on German soil. If this is not impressed upon the Germans they will think they have won the war.[31]

It was during this period, on 9 October precisely, that Field Marshal Haig received the final text of a message which Prime Minister Lloyd George had decided to send to the Commander-in-Chief in belated, and some might say begrudging, recognition of the recent achievements of the BEF. It read, as finally received and simultaneously published:

I have just heard from Marshal Foch of the brilliant victory won by the First, Third and Fourth Armies and I wish to express to yourself, Generals Horne, Byng and Rawlinson and all the officers and men under your command my sincerest congratulations on the great and significant success which the British Armies, with their American brothers in arms have gained during the past two days. The courage and tenacity with which the troops of the Empire, after withstanding the terrific enemy onslaught of the spring of this year, have again resumed the offensive with such decisive results is the greatest chapter in our military history. The smashing of the great defensive system erected by the enemy in the west and claimed by him to be impregnable is a feat of which we are all justly proud and for which the Empire will always be grateful.[32]

Haig was later to confide to his wife that it was only his intercession that secured a mention for Horne and his army in the message despite their significant contribution to the success of the events alluded to. It is not clear whether Horne was ever aware of his initial omission. If he were, he may well have been left wondering what one had to do to achieve recognition, even in a message as equivocal and unwholehearted as Lloyd George's was seen to be by its principal recipient, Haig.[33]

Orders issued by GHQ on 4 October called for Horne's army to cooperate with an attack by Third and Fourth Armies on a wide front between St Quentin and Cambrai, originally timed for the 7th but subsequently postponed to 8 October. Horne ordered the Canadian Corps to increase their artillery activity and patrolling north of the Escaut Canal to distract and confuse the enemy over the extent of the attack. They were also to secure crossings across the canal at Ramillies once it was clear that Third Army had secured the high ground about Awoingt, southeast of Cambrai. The 11th Division were ordered to clear the high ground between Abancourt and Aubencheul-au-Bac. The XXII Corps were instructed to carry out harassing fire along the Sensée River and Trinquis Brook and cooperate with 11th Division in their attack. Finally VIII Corps were to continue to press forward east of Lens.

The 24-hour postponement was not applied to 11th Division's attack which was successfully completed on the 7th.

Zero Hour for Third Army was 04h30 on 8 October, Fourth Army's an hour later. Both armies made good progress but the heavy fighting and resultant tiredness prevented Third Army from securing the Awoingt Heights on the first day. The Canadian Corps therefore made no move but were ordered to cooperate the following day in the capture of the heights and to attack Ramillies at an hour to be chosen by General Currie. Once they had taken the town and were over the Escaut they were to seek to join hands with Third Army on the high ground east and southeast of Escaudoeuvres. They should then move on towards the village of Cauroir and the Cambrai-Le Cateau road. As these later manoeuvres would expose his troops to traversing open ground between Tilloy and Ramillies, Currie decided to force the Escaut crossings by night so that his troops could cover the open ground before dawn. Zero Hour was accordingly set for 01h30.

The 2nd Canadian Division quickly found themselves in possession of Ramillies and a bridgehead across the Escaut at Pont d'Aire against only token opposition. Simultaneously 3rd Canadian Division were able to pass troops over the canal using a lock which, although destroyed, still allowed a passage for infantry. From there they were able to enter Cambrai which they found nearly empty of enemy. By 08h00 the town had been cleared and contact made with Third Army, whose troops were entering the town from the south. Two hours later the 2 armies were also in touch north of Awoingt near the Cambrai-Le Cateau road. With enemy resistance in front of them rapidly dissipating, 2nd Canadian Division were able to occupy Eswars, Cuvillers and Bantigny without difficulty as they began to clear the west bank of the Escaut in the angle between that canal and the Sensée Canal. The Division continued to enlarge their bridgehead east of the Escaut and by nightfall had captured Escaudoeuvres and the high ground east of the village.[34] Horne expressed his pleasure at the day's events in his letter home.

> Another great day today. The Fourth and Third Armies continued their attacks and have made great progress and I attacked the Canal d'Escaut north of Cambrai at 01h30, caught the Germans asleep and we got across the Canal and at the same time got through Cambrai. We took Cambrai from the north and the Third Army from the south and we have now joined hands east of it. I am well established across the Canal. The German is falling back and all I met was a rearguard. It is not very clear where he is going to fall back to, but he is holding on for the present to a line east of the Canal and east of Cambrai. It is a great thing getting him out of Cambrai but the brute has looted and destroyed a great deal of the town and has started many fires. He will say that it is the British who have destroyed the town, but that is not the case. We have not shelled it beyond a certain amount on the railway station.[35]

Late the same night Horne ordered the Canadians to continue their clearance of the angle between the two canals and to maintain their cover of the left flank of Third Army which was advancing towards Avesnes-les-Aubert. Progress was good in the morning with 11th Division capturing Estrun and 2nd Canadian Division completing the clearance of the angle between the 2 canals with the exception of 2 villages, Fressies and Hem Lenglet, where strong rearguards were to hold out until the following day. As the Canadians pushed forward in the afternoon they were held up on the approaches to the high ground southeast of Iwuy and could make no further progress.

The Canadian Corps resumed their attack the following day against stiffening resistance, notably from the enemy's artillery. But Iwuy was taken and German counterattacks, supported by 5 tanks and designed to drive a wedge between 2nd Canadian Division and 49th British Division, now attached to Canadian Corps, were successfully beaten off with little ground given. At 17h00 XXII and Canadian Corps changed places; the 51st Highland Division took over from 2nd Canadian Division. Two hours later, Horne's orders for the following day instructed XXII Corps to gain a general line running between Saulzoir and Lieu-St Amand through Avesnes-le-Sec, with both corps maintaining their cover of Third Army's flank.

The 12 October saw First Army's front remain static between Palluel and Estrun, but with considerable advances made to the east of the latter village. The 49th and 51st Divisions followed up enemy retirements reported by air reconnaissance and, despite strong rearguards, made good progress. In an advance of 3 miles 49th Division took Villers-en-Cauchies, the spur to the northeast of the village and the railway line running north to Avesnes-le-Sec station, before being stopped by high ground held in strength by the enemy. The 51st Division, starting from Iwuy, crossed the Iwuy-Lourches railway and made slow progress to Avesnes and Lieu-St Amand over bare slopes. Footholds were gained in Avesnes and on the spur to the northwest, but Lieu-St Amand remained unattainable. During the day Third Army reached the Selle River near Solesmes, where they found the enemy in considerable strength.

Horne's orders for the following day instructed XXII Corps to take Saulzoir and the ridge running from the village northwest by Lieu-St Amand to the Escaut Canal. At the same time the corps were to push advanced parties across the Selle River. The Canadians were told to take every opportunity that offered to seize bridgeheads across the Sensée east of Palluel so as to be in a position to exploit any enemy withdrawal in this sector. Overnight 49th Division patrols had reached the Selle south of Saulzoir but had been prevented from crossing by heavy machine gun fire.

Both Corps resumed the offensive at 09h00 against determined and well organised defences. On the right 49th Division succeeded in taking that part of Saulzoir to the west of the river, but effecting a crossing was out of the question. Indeed so tenuous was their hold that they were forced to make a partial withdrawal during the ensuing night to limit what were becoming unacceptably high casualties. They also pushed northwest along the ridge as far north as the Avesnes-le-Sec – Haspres road. But enemy fire from the high ground east of the river prevented any attempts to reach the western bank. An enemy counterattack supported by tanks was repulsed. Although severely hampered by heavy enemy fire from the dominant Lieu-St Amand, 51st Division cleared Avesnes-le-Sec and gained the high ground to the northwest. By evening they had reached the southern edge of Lieu-St Amand.

On 14 October First Army activity was largely limited to patrols seeking opportunities to cross the Selle. But the enemy were firmly in control of the eastern bank of the river as far north as Haspres, and of the high ground from that village to the Escaut at Lieu-St Amand. Horne and Byng realised that an organised joint attack of both their armies would probably be required to dislodge the Germans, and planning was put in hand. In the meantime further offensive operations were to be put on hold although opportunities to cross waterways were to be seized if they presented themselves. Nevertheless, on the 15th, 49th Division re-established their positions in the eastern part of Saulzoir, this time permanently.[36]

Events further north were however to ensure that there would be little time for Horne's troops to enjoy any sort of rest. On 14 October the Belgian and Second Armies had launched an offensive towards Courtrai which, within 3 days, had outflanked Lille, Tourcoing and Roubaix from the north. The salient thus created in the German defences not only threatened their hold on the Belgian North Sea ports, but also, when coupled with the salient established in their lines to the south, their entire position between Douai and Lille. In his letter home of 13 October Horne predicted that he would soon have Douai, a prediction which was fulfilled 4 days later, on a day when the Belgians also occupied Ostend and the Fifth Army, Lille.

The effects of events to the north had become apparent to Horne by the 17th with clear signs of an enemy withdrawal on his front. The 1st Canadian Division, opposed by only weak rearguards, were able to cross the Sensée Canal between Arleux and Corbehem and reach the Cantin-Douai road, south of the town. Their presence here had by noon diminished the enemy's previously stiff opposition to VIII Corps' approach to the town from the west. By early afternoon the Germans had abandoned Douai which was entered at 15h00 by 2nd Bn Rifle Brigade and 2nd Bn The Middlesex Regiment. Douai was empty and much of it was on fire. It had been comprehensively looted. The town centre was severely damaged before the fires were brought under control late the following day.[37] A day later Horne took the French Prime Minister, Georges Clemenceau, to see Douai and Lens. He commented, with unusual restraint for him when confronted with evidence of 'Hun beastliness':

> Douai is not much knocked about as regards the buildings but the Germans have stolen everything worth taking and smashed all they can lay hands on.[38]

Chapter XVIII

Army Commander: Valenciennes

The capture of Douai hardly caused Henry Horne's army to break stride as the enemy's retreat on the whole of the front north of the River Sensée seemed to gather momentum. During the night of 17/18 October 4th Canadian Division made unopposed crossings of the river at Fressies and Aubigny. By morning they had occupied the high ground about Fressain and Villers-au-Tertre. Further to the east the same division also crossed the river at Wasnes-au-Bac and occupied the ridge northwest of the village against slight resistance. At daybreak both the Canadians and VIII Corps resumed their advance against weak rearguards which made little attempt even to defend positions which offered good scope for defence. Both corps recorded advances of 6 to 7 miles during the day and during the night the Canadians occupied the villages of Emerchicourt and Pecquencourt, 10 kms east of Douai.

The advance continued on the 19th with little interference from the enemy. Such was its speed and the lightness of the resistance that cyclists and cavalry, who could easily handle such opposition as there was, were coming into their own. The VIII Corps' shortage of the latter was alleviated by the attachment to them of 4th Hussars from 3rd Cavalry Brigade. Once again the 2 corps recorded a day's advance of 6 miles. They had now reached a line from the western edge of the town of Denain northwest to Orchies by way of Hornaing and Marchiennes.

Further south XXII Corps, which had stood fast on the previous 2 days, noticed on the 19th that the Germans in front of them were showing signs of retiring. Patrols of 4th and 51st Divisions were able to take possession of Saulzoir and Lieu-St Amand. The enemy appeared determined to cling on to their bridge-head on the left bank of the River Selle at Haspres. But north of the village the 51st and 2nd Canadian Divisions were able to cross the river during the day and the same night with little trouble. They occupied Noyelles-sur-Selle and Douchy.

While the enthusiasm with which the advancing troops were being welcomed by the local population was very gratifying, the problem of feeding them when the Army was outrunning its own supplies was less so. The Germans had done their best to crater roads, and destroy bridges and railway lines, which might be of use to Horne's troops, now up to 35 miles in advance of their railheads. On the positive side, the newly liberated civilians proved invaluable in identifying bridges primed for demolition with delayed action fuses. The enemy too, in the haste of their departure, had frequently left behind valuable equipment and failed to set their usual booby traps. With the Germans clearly reeling from the blows they had suffered since early August, this was not the time to ease the pressure on them because of supply difficulties. Horne's staff made huge and largely successful efforts to keep the supplies to the army flowing and the civilian population fed.[1]

At 02h00 on 20 October 4th Division of XXII Corps launched an attack in cooperation with XVII Corps of Third Army on their right. The division crossed the Selle river between Saulzoir and Haspres and by noon had gained the high ground southeast of the latter village. With troops of 51st Division working down

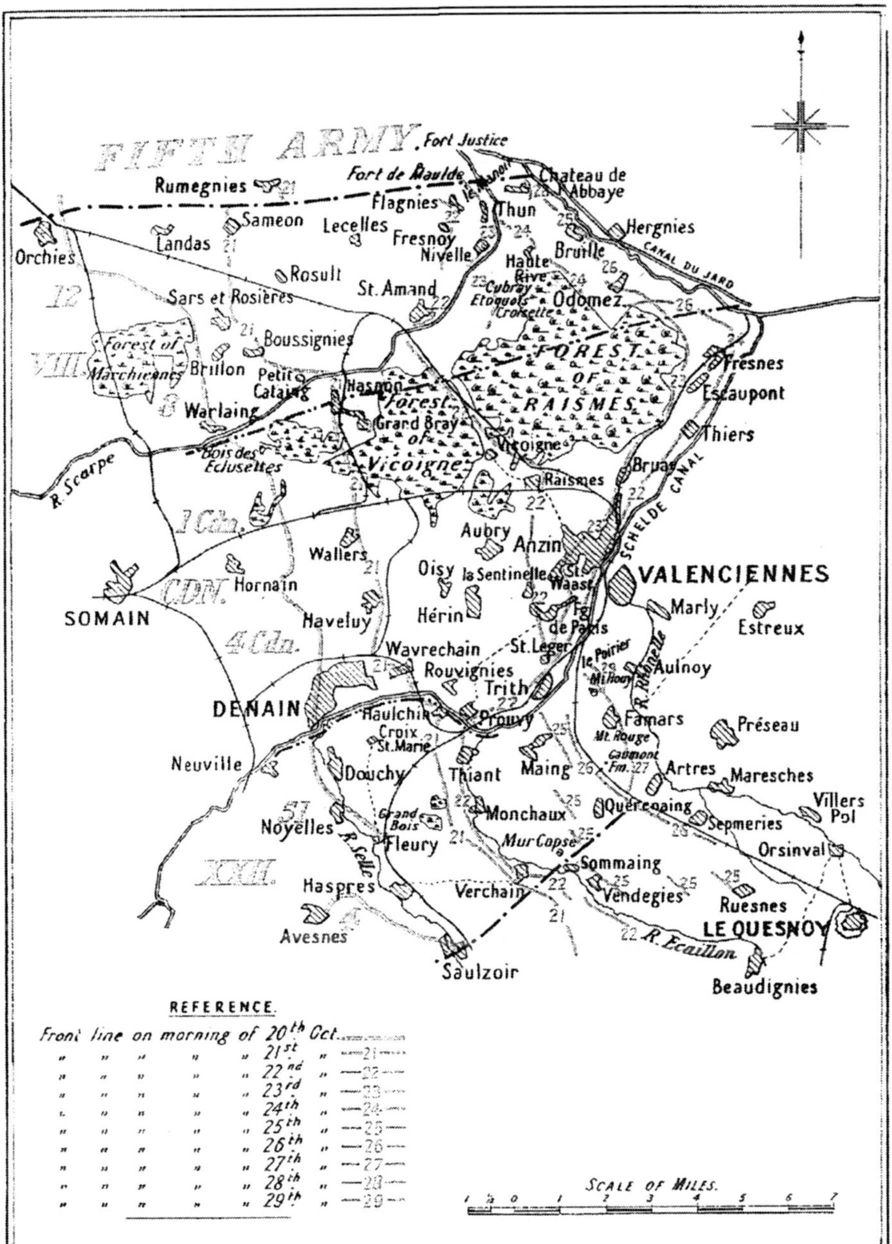

Map 21: Approach to Valenciennes: October 1918

the river from the north towards the village, the Germans began to evacuate their bridgehead and fall back. By evening Haspres was in British hands and the 2 British divisions were firmly established on the western crest of the ridge between the Rivers Selle and Ecaillon. Further north, cyclists of XXII Corps seized the village of Haulchin on the southern bank of the Escaut close to the point where the Ecaillon flowed into it. At this time Horne rejigged the boundary between XXII and Canadian Corps. It became the Escaut when 56th Division of XXII Corps relieved 2nd Canadian Division south of that river (more popularly known to the British by its German/Flemish names of the 'Scheldt' or 'Schelde').

North of the river during the course of the 20th, VIII and Canadian Corps both continued their advance, meeting different levels of resistance. The VIII Corps encountered little. By nightfall their cyclists and cavalry were still in touch with the enemy on a line from Bousignies to Saméon, with the infantry not far behind at Landas. The Canadians met stiffer and strengthening opposition but were able, early in the day, to occupy the town of Denain. They found it to be bursting with over 25,000 French civilians, many of whom had been brought in from outlying villages by the Germans. North of the town, the Canadians captured the villages of Haveluy, Wallers and Hasnon.

With Third Army also having had a successful day in which they had driven the enemy from the Selle and were pushing towards the Ecaillon, Horne issued his orders for the following day. The XXII Corps were to push on and gain the line of the Ecaillon river, maintaining touch with XVII Corps on their right. If the enemy were to retire they were to send forward advance parties with the aim of occupying the villages of Maing and Quérénaing. The Canadian and VIII Corps were also to advance, the former maintaining touch with XXII Corps on the other side of the Escaut and the latter establishing contact with I Corps of Fifth Army, also under orders to push forward.

During the night the enemy began a slight withdrawal south of the Escaut. The 51st Division were quick to follow up, sending out patrols to regain contact. By midday the division had occupied 2 woods overlooking the Ecaillon and entered the village of Thiant at the confluence of the Ecaillon and the Escaut. A strong German counterattack, with heavy artillery support, during the afternoon forced the Highlanders back over the river but not out of the western half of the village. The division reported that the high ground east of the Ecaillon between Thiant and Monchaux-sur-Ecaillon was still strongly held by the enemy, precluding an immediate crossing being made between the 2 villages.

The 2 divisions of the Canadian Corps engaged during the day had contrasting fortunes. The one on the right made little progress, but on the left 1st Canadian Division pressed forward briskly against minimal opposition, and passed through the Bois de Vicoigne. By the evening they had established outposts on a line running from Trith to the eastern edge of Bois de Vicoigne, through the villages of La Sentinelle and Aubry. Further north 4th Hussars of VIII Corps had captured St Amand by midday. They were subsequently held up by the Scarpe river, the bridges across which had been destroyed. Advanced guards of 8th and 12th Divisions reached a line from St Amand to Lecelles, close to the Belgian border, by the end of the day.

Horne's orders issued later that day were largely concerned with a planned joint attack with Third Army scheduled for 24 October. Its aim was essentially to get XVII and XXII Corps across the Ecaillon and onto the high ground east of the river. The XVII Corps would seize the hill south of Quérénaing in conjunction with the XXII, which would attempt to reach a line from there to the high ground northwest of the village, thence to Maing and finally to the Escaut south of St Trith, which was already in Canadian hands. Exploitation of success would be towards the Le Quesnoy-Valenciennes railway which curved northwest and then north from Le Quesnoy.

In the meantime pressure would be maintained on the enemy. During the night of 21/22 October, XXII Corps advanced their outposts close to the Ecaillon, from the western part of Thiant, south to Bouveneuil Farm and from there southwest to within 800 yards of the riverside village of Verchain-Maugre. During the day the right hand Canadian division continued their advance eastwards against progressively stronger opposition until they were held up at St Vaast, Anzin and Beuvrages. On the left the 3rd Canadian Division moved relatively easily through their sector of the Forêt de Raismes; by the evening they were on the edge of the forest west of Bruay. To their north VIII Corps attained a line running from La Croisette to Flagnies through Cubray and Nivelle.[2]

It was on this day that the Germans added to their reputation for beastliness in Horne's eyes. Having filled the spa town of St Amand-les-Eaux with the inhabitants of the surrounding villages and about 2,000 invalid and infirm people from the Douai area, they had withdrawn from the town as Horne's troops approached and, once the British troops were in possession, shelled it heavily. In justification they claimed the British had posted machine guns in one of the town's church towers. Horne indignantly rejected this. Quite apart from any moral considerations, it would have served no military purpose; at the only time the enemy would have been within machine gun range there had been a heavy mist limiting visibility to no more than 100 yards.[3]

On 23 October the Third and Fourth Armies attacked between Le Cateau and Solesmes, with complete success. Horne's army also participated. His northernmost corps, the VIII, had fallen somewhat behind the Canadian Corps on their right. They were ordered to push on and come up into line with the Canadians on the assumption that little resistance was to be expected until the River Escaut was reached. Although the corps' 8th Division had come under heavy machine gun fire from across the Scarpe during the night, they were able to cross the river with little difficulty in the morning. Passing through the northern part of the Forêt de Raismes, occupying several villages on their way, they were by evening in touch with the Canadians on their right south of the village of Odomez, which was still in enemy hands. North of the village, advanced guards of the corps reached the hamlet of Hauterive. There they found the enemy still in possession of strong bridgeheads covering the crossings over the Escaut at Hergnies. Horne's centre corps, the Canadians, had completed the capture of the Forêt de Raismes and had pushed on to reach the Escaut in the sector Thiers-Escaupont-Fresnes. Further south they had pushed into the extreme western suburbs of Valenciennes in their efforts to reach the river. His southernmost corps, the XXII, had stood fast all day on the Ecaillon. The day had seen Horne's troops reach and, in some places, get beyond their objectives.

The following day, most of VIII and Canadian Corps reached the Escaut, although the former corps' extreme left was still some way short. The XXII Corps, attacking with 4th and 51st Divisions in line, successfully crossed the Ecaillon, despite the enemy defences, a serious shortage of bridging material and the formidable nature of the river itself. It was 25 feet wide, with banks on either side that plunged 15 feet to the muddy river bottom, which contained 4 to 5 feet of water. It was heavily wired on both banks and more wire had been stretched from one bank to the other. Entrenched enemy outposts on the right bank and a trench line half way up the slope running eastwards had completed a formidable challenge. The dash with which these difficulties were rapidly overcome says much for the momentum which had been built up by First Army's recent rapid progress. Assisted by darkness, determination did the rest and at relatively light cost.

With the river successfully crossed, Monchaux and Maing were captured, the latter after prolonged and severe house-to-house fighting. By the end of the day the corps had established a new line running from Sommaing, 10 kms south of Valenciennes, to Trith-St Leger on the Escaut, 5 kms southwest of the city.

From 25 to 27 October Horne's 2 northernmost corps largely confined themselves to occupying ground vacated by the enemy and to local attacks to improve their positions. The 8th Division (VIII Corps) tried unsuccessfully to cross the Escaut in 3 places. The enemy mounted several strong counterattacks, some of which achieved limited success. In contrast to the 2 other corps, XXII Corps, Horne's southernmost, continued to attack vigorously along the full length of their front. Advancing northeast on the 26th, 4th Division rapidly captured the large village of Artres before pushing across the Rhonelle river to the heights beyond. To their left, 51st Division fought their way into Famars, less than 2 kilometres southeast of Mont Houy. Enemy resistance was fierce but, after a day of house-to-house fighting, the village was cleared. Heavy enemy fire from Mont Houy prevented any further progress northwards. On the 27th XXII Corps were kept busy bringing up guns and ammunition and fighting off a determined German counterattack on Famars which saw them well into the village before they were finally driven out.

By late October Haig could foresee the possibility of a complete German collapse on the Western Front. He thought this might be brought about by increasing the pressure on the Germans once the city of Valenciennes had been taken and the line of the River Escaut breached. Valenciennes was not just a convenient starting point for this latest evolution in Haig's strategy; it was an important military and psychological objective. Militarily, its capture would ease the forcing of the Scheldt Line; psychologically, the loss of the last major French conurbation in their hands would deal a further blow to German morale at a time when it was already deteriorating rapidly.[4]

Valenciennes stood firmly in the path of First Army and the task of its liberation, in an operation scheduled to be completed on 1 November, was given to Horne. On 27 October he called his corps commanders together at his newly established advanced headquarters at Auberchicourt, 11 miles west of Valenciennes. He put before them a 3 part plan designed to force an enemy evacuation of the city. Horne's plan had to take account of 2 important considerations. The known presence in the city of a large civilian population, as well as refugees, had led GHQ to rule out the bombardment of buildings in the city. Exempted from the ban were houses overlooking the Escaut canal which might be used by the enemy to inhibit the crossing of the waterway. (The course of the River Escaut in its passage through the centre of Valenciennes, had been diverted and canalised, hence the use of the term 'canal'.)

The second consideration was that any assault from the west or north of the city was effectively precluded because both banks of the Escaut had been heavily wired by the Germans. They had also fortified the east bank with a well-planned trench system. As an even greater deterrent, they had cut gaps in the canal dykes and opened sluice gates, thus flooding the country on both sides of the river to a width of several hundred yards. Horne was consequently forced to plan his army's approach and envelopment of the city from the south west and south. This brought into prominence a small area of partly wooded high ground, about 3 and a half kilometres south of the city centre, known as Mont Houy. Capture of this dominant position, nearly 290 feet high, would be a prerequisite to an entry into the city itself.

The first stage of Horne's plan was for XXII Corps to capture Mont Houy and the Aulnoy-Le Poirier road, just north of the high ground, on 28 October. On the night of the 28th/29th, assuming that XXII Corps had achieved all their objectives, the Canadian Corps would relieve them in the sector between the Rhonelle river, south of Aulnoy, and le Poirier.

The second stage would take place on the 30th when the 2 corps would capture Préseau and the Préseau-Marly road and from there occupy a line westward to the Escaut. The Third Army's XVII Corps would cooperate by covering the right flank of First Army and taking Maresches. On the night of the 30th/31st the Canadian Corps would take over more of the XXII Corps front, as far as the Famars-Estreux road.

The last stage of Horne's plan would see XXII and Canadian Corps completing the envelopment of Valenciennes from the south on 1 November, the former by capturing the high ground east of the city and the latter by pushing into the city from the west and south.[5]

As a defensive position Mont Houy enjoyed significant advantages. The thick undergrowth of a wood on its summit, which was honeycombed with deep trenches, would inhibit free movement. The Germans had also entrenched and wired the west and southwest crest of the hill. Their defensive preparations had clearly assumed that an attack would come from these directions. They had not prepared nearly as carefully against an attack from the south. Mont Houy's main disadvantage as a defensive position was, however, its vulnerability to concentrated artillery fire, a flaw which would ultimately prove its undoing. The task of seizing it, and thus implementing the first part of Horne's plan, was entrusted to 51st Highland Division.

The Highlanders launched their attack on Mont Houy at 05h15 on 28 October. It was made by a single battalion, the 4th Seaforth Highlanders, supported by 9 brigades of field artillery, five 6 inch howitzer and nine 60-pounder batteries. Despite strong opposition and heavy casualties (one company was reduced to 12 men) the whole of the position was taken. The leading troops of the battalion reached a line running from the Famars-Valenciennes road, about a kilometre north of Famars, westwards through the hamlet of Chemin Vert (now a suburb of Valenciennes) and along the Aulnoy-le Poirier road to le Poirier station. Unfortunately for the depleted 4th Seaforths, the configuration of the road offered them no protection from enemy fire across the 1,200 yard wide area of open ground to its north. An enemy counterattack launched at 14h30, with heavy artillery support, was thus able to force the centre of the Highlanders' line back over the summit of the hill and part way down its southern slope. The right of their line was pushed back to the northern edge of Famars. The left however maintained their hold on le Poirier station and a quarry at the southwest corner of the Mont Houy wood.[6]

The success of the enemy counterattack threw Horne's plan into some disarray. It had called for 51st Division, in full possession of Mont Houy and the Aulnoy-le Poirier road, to be relieved by a Canadian division immediately after dark on the 28th, as part of the relief of XXII Corps by the Canadian Corps during the course of the night. The 4th Canadian Division were in position to effect the relief by 16h00. Although it was not clear at that point whether the summit of Mont Houy was in British hands, it was manifestly clear that much of the Aulnoy-le Poirier road was not, and General Currie accordingly requested a postponement of the relief. Horne's response, issued at 17h00, was that if Mont Houy was held by 51st Division the Canadian Corps should take over the front as ordered. If, however, it was not, the relief was to be postponed. Horne left the final judgment on whether and when the relief should take place to the commanders of the troops on the spot. By nightfall it was apparent to the divisional commanders concerned that Mont Houy was not in British hands; the relief was accordingly postponed. Instead, the GOC of 51st Division relieved the 4th Seaforths with the 6th and part of the 7th Argyll and Sutherland Highlanders. Later that evening Horne issued an instruction that the Canadian relief of the 51st Division should take place the following night. The instruction also deferred the implementation of the second and third stages of Horne's overall plan by 24 hours.

There has been some controversy over Horne's handling of the setback to his plans caused by the partially successful German counterattack. His own Chief of Staff, Major General Hastings Anderson, was critical of the decision to defer the relief of 51st Division. His criticism appears to be threefold:

– that the plan itself was unduly rigid in setting down fixed objectives which the 51st Division had to achieve and consolidate before the relief would take place. Given that he would have had a major role in drawing up the plan this would seem to imply self-criticism as well as criticism of the Army Commander who signed off on it.

– that the Canadian Corps Commander was unduly inflexible in insisting that all the 51st Division's objectives had to have been achieved before the relief could take place, especially as the 4th Canadian Division's GOC was willing to make the changeover anyway.

– that the initial assault on Mont Houy should in any case never have been entrusted to the tired 51st Division. Far better if the Canadians, with the weight of artillery they could deploy, had been given the task from the outset.[7]

Whatever the merits of this last argument, and it could be equally argued that the Canadians had been heavily engaged in fighting since August and might also be tired, General Anderson claimed, quite correctly, that the delay in the relief of the

Highlanders was to cost the First Army 24 hours. But the Commander of the Canadian Heavy Artillery, Major General McNaughton, fully supported his Corps Commander's request for a postponement of the relief. The postponement, he claimed, gave the Canadian Heavy Artillery, 'a full and proper opportunity to do our work free from the hysteria of a suddenly improvised attack'. As it was the application of this heavy artillery that was to prove overwhelmingly decisive, General McNaughton's views deserve respect.[8]

During the course of 29 October, the Germans made 2 determined attempts to complete the total reversal of 51st Division's early gains of the day before. At 06h00 they launched an artillery and infantry assault on the left flank of the High-landers' positions between Mont Houy and le Poirier station. The attack was repulsed with heavy losses. At 16h00 the enemy put down a heavy artillery barrage along the whole of 51st Division's front as a preliminary to a further assault by infantry. The latter were, however, observed assembling and were dispersed before they could move off by heavy and field artillery firing from west of the Escaut. With the enemy's aggressive inclinations thus firmly blunted, the delayed relief of the Highlanders was carried out after dark. The 4th Canadian Division took over the line between Famars and the Escaut, and 49th Division the rest to the east of Famars.

At 22h00 on the 29th Horne issued the orders for the attack by the Canadian and XXII Corps on 1 November. Essentially these were a restatement of the second and third stages of his original plan except that the second stage now incorporated the reduction of Mont Houy before an advance to a line running from Préseau to the Escaut by way of the Marly steelworks and the railway between there and the river. This advance would bring the First Army well into the southern and south-eastern suburbs of Valenciennes. The success of the second stage was to be exploited by an advance to a line from Ferme de Wult, through Saultain to the southwest end of St Saulve. This would almost complete the envelopment of the city from the south and east. The XVII Corps of Third Army were to cooperate by capturing Maresches and St Hubert.[9]

The 2 days prior to the planned attack saw little fighting. The VIII Corps in the north withdrew some advanced posts back to the western side of the Escaut to avoid further unnecessary losses from heavy enemy trench mortar fire. The corps were told to restrict their operations to active patrolling.

Zero Hour on 1 November was 05h15. Precisely on time, and from right to left, 61st Division of XVII Corps, 4th and 49th Divisions of XXII Corps and 10th Infantry Brigade of the 4th Canadian Division assaulted. The 2 divisions of XXII Corps got across the Rhonelle river and gained the high ground south and north-west of Préseau. In attempting to capture the village itself 4th Division were coun-terattacked and forced back to the edge of the village where they were able to establish touch with 61st Division on the high ground between Maresches and Préseau. This was to be the limit of the day's advance on the British right.

Further north 49th Division had a day of mixed fortunes. Having gained the spur running between Préseau and Aulnoy, they successfully crossed open ground, despite heavy artillery and machine gun fire, and reached the Préseau-Marly road along their whole divisional front as far north as the railway immediately south of the Marly steelworks. Here they found themselves unable to advance further in the

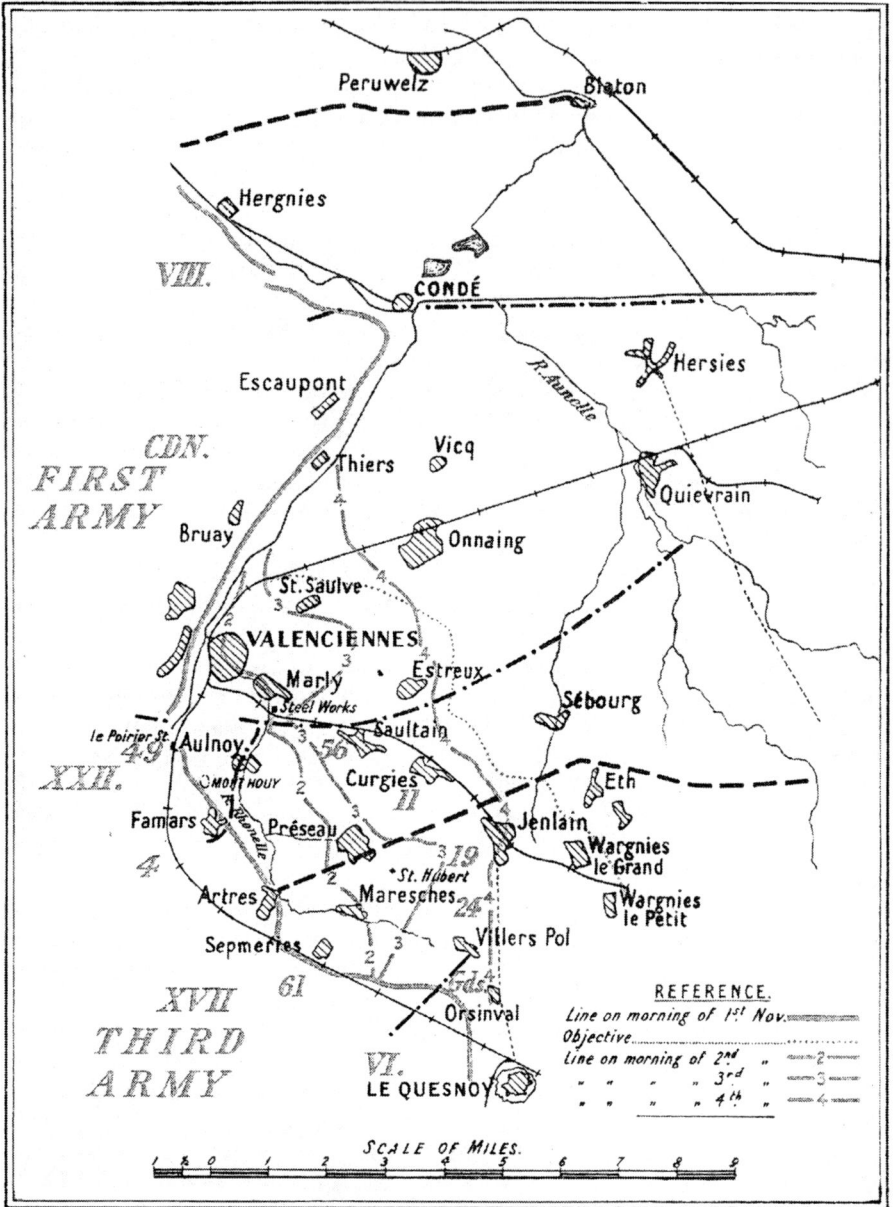

Map 22: Liberation of Valenciennes: 1–3 November 1918

face of heavy enemy fire. Their position worsened when the enemy counter-attacked their right flank with tanks. They were forced back about 1,000 yards to the line of the Préseau-Aulnoy road and, north of Aulnoy, to within a few hundred yards of the right bank of the Rhonelle river. Under less enemy pressure, their left flank was able to make contact with the right of the Canadians on the railway immediately south of the Marly steelworks.[10]

It was 10th Canadian Infantry Brigade which was to achieve the most striking success of the day. Two battalions (the 44th and 47th) were used initially, with the 46th leapfrogging through the 47th when the first objective had been secured. The 50th Bn were in reserve. All the battalions were by this time much under strength and could only muster 1,200 rifles for the attack, a total which included reserves. To achieve a degree of surprise no preliminary bombardment was fired; nor was there any target preregistration. But at Zero Hour a devastating, and probably unprecedented, concentration of artillery was unleashed which covered the infantry as they swept over Mont Houy and the open ground north of it.

Within 75 minutes of Zero Hour the brigade's advanced troops had secured the Aulnoy-le Poirier road on their line of advance. Without pausing they continued their advance and by 07h00 had cleared Aulnoy and captured intact the town's bridge over the Rhonelle river. Up to this point, the brigade had been harassed by heavy enemy artillery fire which was now steadily to decrease as the impact of the Canadian counter battery work became apparent. The infantry continued to press forward. By 12h00 they had gained the line of the railway west of the Marly steelworks and, on their left, occupied the Faubourg de Cambrai, less than 2 kms south of the city centre. They were prevented from making any significant further progress on their right by machine gun fire from the Marly steelworks. In the centre however, patrols were able to push on towards Marly and the southern outskirts of the city itself.

Once the extent of the success of 10th Brigade on the eastern side of the Escaut became clear, the Canadian 12th Brigade, holding the western bank, began passing troops across the river from the area of the Faubourg de Paris station and, further north, across the wrecked Valenciennes-St Amand bridge. Once across however, heavy enemy fire prevented any progress beyond the railway on the western outskirts of the city before nightfall. But under cover of darkness it became possible to infiltrate patrols into the city.[11]

Thus ended a day of almost undiluted success for Horne's army and especially for the Canadian Corps. The XXII Corps and the Canadians shared a bag of 2,750 prisoners and no fewer than 800 dead Germans were counted and buried in the Canadian 10th Brigade sector. The brigade had bought their success relatively cheaply, suffering a total of 501 casualties of whom 121 were killed or missing. The high German body count rekindled briefly the debate on the Canadian attitude to the taking of prisoners, but in this case it almost certainly reflected the terrifying effectiveness of the artillery bombardment. General Currie mentioned in his diary that it had not been the intention of his troops to take many prisoners as they had become more bitter than ever against the Germans, having seen at close hand how badly they had treated the French civilians during their occupation. It was probably fortunate for the Germans that they had usually surrendered in sufficiently large groups to obviate any means of dealing with them other than taking them prisoner.

Mention has been made of the effectiveness of the Canadian artillery in the events of the day. The First Army's possession of virtually all the area in their sector west of the Escaut as well as areas across the Escaut to the south and southeast of

Mont Houy had left that piece of high ground particularly vulnerable to artillery fire, which could converge on it from many points of the compass. The Canadian Corps had been quick to take advantage of this, being determined that German resistance would be crushed by weight of shells. Eight field and 6 heavy artillery brigades had been assigned to the support of 10th Brigade's attack, which initially debouched from a frontage of only 2,500 yards. Of the field artillery, 3 brigades had been positioned around Maing, south of the Escaut, to provide the frontal creeping barrage; one had been placed on the west bank of the Escaut at Trith-St Leger to add oblique fire to the barrage; 2 had been placed further north near La Sentinelle to deepen the barrage by enfilade fire. The creeping barrage had consisted entirely of 18-pr shrapnel shells and had moved at the rate of 100 yards in 4 minutes until the Aulnoy-le Poirier road was reached, after which it had slowed down to 100 yards in 5 minutes. Three batteries of 4.5" howitzers had also been employed to fire smoke to screen the attacking infantry from the enemy occupying rows of houses along their approach, and to bombard identified machine gun nests. Finally, 12 batteries of machine guns had been employed firing in close support or in enfilade from north of the Escaut.

The heavy artillery had been mostly sited west of the Escaut from where it could bring oblique, enfilade and even reverse fire to bear. Three and a half brigades had been assigned to counter-battery work. The remainder focussed on groups of houses believed to contain machine guns. A large number of 6" and 8" howitzers had fired a rolling barrage which moved along the rows of houses in the Rhonelle and Escaut valleys. The devastation wrought by this had had a quite disproportionate effect on the enemy's morale. There is little doubt that the Canadian 10th Infantry Brigade had enjoyed greater artillery support for their attack on 1 November than had ever previously been laid on in support of a single brigade action.[12] General McNaughton calculated that 2,149 tons of shells had been fired in support of the attack. He compared this with the 2,800 tons fired in the whole South African War by both sides.[13]

The enemy quickly recognised that the successful, if delayed, implementation of Horne's plan to envelop Valenciennes had made their continuing tenure of the city and the Scheldt Line impossible; an immediate withdrawal from both was ordered. That the Germans had recognised the danger to their overall position that the loss of the Scheldt Line would cause was evidenced by the resources they had employed, and the stubbornness and determination with which they had fought, to hold on to it. Elements of 8 German divisions were identified as having fought against the 3 divisions of First Army during the battle.[14]

Despite the German decision to withdraw, there was still to be some serious fighting before the liberation of Valenciennes was complete. Horne's orders for 2 November called for XXII Corps to capture Préseau, the line of the Préseau-Marly road and the Marly steelworks. The Canadians were to exploit eastwards through Valenciennes and take Marly. Both corps were to exploit success towards the general line Ferme de Wult-Saultain-St Saulve. Their attacks went in well before daylight. By daybreak 49th Division had established themselves on the Préseau-Marly road and taken the Marly steelworks. The right of the Canadian 4th Division were able to take Marly virtually unopposed, but the left made slow progress through Valenciennes against determined German rearguards. Nevertheless, by daybreak, the Canadian 12th Infantry Brigade had reached the eastern edge of the city and were pushing out patrols in the direction of St Saulve. By the evening they had taken the suburb and patrols had advanced 4 or 5 miles east of Valenciennes against slackening opposition. North of the city however, the enemy were showing little inclination to give up their positions on the eastern side of the Escaut and the Jard canal.

The 4th Division of XXII Corps, co-operating once again with XVII Corps of Third Army on their right, launched their attack at daybreak and were soon in possession of Préseau. They pushed on against heavy opposition to occupy the high ground east and north of the village. At the same time XVII Corps took Ferme de Wult. The advance of both divisions of XXII Corps was brought to a halt by the strength of the enemy resistance. They had taken nearly 1,000 prisoners during the day. Both divisions were relieved during the night, the 4th by the 11th and the 49th by the 56th.[15]

Horne's letters to his wife covering these momentous days reflect his intense satisfaction with the performance of his Army in the liberation of Valenciennes.

> We made an attack today south of Valenciennes and had a hard day's fighting – attacks and counterattacks. But we gained a good deal of ground ... and inflicted great loss on the Germans with artillery fire. I think by tomorrow we shall have the Boche out of Valenciennes. He has started a lot of fires in the town which he will probably attribute to our artillery, but that is not the case as we have not fired on the town, we have come round it to the south. We met with considerable resistance and the Germans were evidently trying to prevent our getting Valenciennes before they have got their stuff out of it.[16]

> We are now in possession of Valenciennes but the Boche has burnt and pillaged the town a great deal and is shelling it today. We got over 3,000 prisoners and inflicted very heavy loss on the Germans. In some cases they fought well, but in others they gave in without much resistance. Our own losses are very light I am thankful to say ...

> I have just received my evening reports and we have taken yesterday and today nearly 4,000 prisoners, at least 5 guns and 2 tanks. I have employed six brigades of infantry and have engaged and defeated 19 of the enemy belonging to 8 different divisions. A very successful battle.[17]

> Yesterday and the day before were great days. XXII and Canadian Corps of mine and one division of XVII Corps of Third Army inflicted heavy loss on the enemy. We got over 4,000 prisoners and XVII Corps got over 1,000. It cleared Valenciennes and the result is that the Boche has gone back in front of us last night and today we are now about 5 miles east of the town. I hear that the Boche has done a great deal of damage to it by burning and pillaging, but I have not yet seen – I shall go there tomorrow.[18]

The orders issued by Horne on the evening of 2 November reflected those he had received from Haig on 29 October instructing the First, Third and Fourth Armies, in conjunction with the French First Army, to launch a co-ordinated attack on 4 November. Horne's orders confirmed what he had already told the Commanders of XXII and Canadian Corps of the Commander-in-Chief's intentions, that Haig was looking for a general advance towards the line Avesnes-Maubeuge-Mons. The first part of this, as far as Horne's and Byng's armies were concerned, would be to attain a line from St Rémy Chaussée to the Montignies-Hensies road through Pont-sur-Sambre and Bavay. The Canadians and XXII Corps were to make a flying start to implementing their orders by setting off a day early after their patrols discovered they were only opposed by weak rearguards. The advance to Mons was on.[19]

As a footnote to the liberation of Valenciennes, Horne led his troops at a military parade in the city, in the presence of the Prince of Wales, on 7 November. The parade was followed by a civic reception offered by the Mayor and City Council at which the freedom of the city was conferred on Horne.[20] Later an avenue was to be named after him which bears his name to this day.

Chapter XIX

Army Commander: Mons

By 3 November the advance of Henry Horne's army was resembling a pursuit by advanced guards. The main problems were maintaining contact with a rapidly retreating enemy and, when achieved, to stop them settling into organised defensive positions. Horne's men were however to be disabused of any notion that the Germans were in headlong flight. On the day in question the enemy's retreat took them back as far as the Aunelle river, which marked the Franco-Belgian border on the First Army front. Following up closely, XXII and Canadian Corps had by evening established outposts on the high ground east of Curgies and Estreux and in the village of Onnaing. These successes meant they were already in possession of the first objectives allotted to First Army for the following day in an operation which would also involve the Third, Fourth and First French Armies. Horne therefore issued amended orders to the 2 corps calling for them to continue their advance towards the Bavay-Hensies road.[1]

The nature of the country over which First Army were now advancing was changing. East and south of the Escaut the ground had consisted of open, rolling downland which had been intersected at right angles to the axis of the Army's advance by the parallel Rivers Selle, Ecaillon and Rhonelle, all running north into the Escaut. The ground had been bare and exposed and only intruded on by the occasional village in the river valleys. East of the Aunelle however, Horne's troops would find themselves in much more broken country intersected by fast-flowing streams following tortuous courses. There would be deep valleys from which would rise steep slopes covered with woods, orchards and enclosed fields. The numerous villages would be densely populated, especially those on the Belgian side of the border, where the inhabitants had never felt the need, or been forced, to move away. The roads would be plentiful but narrow, usually with only room for one line of traffic and often cobbled (pavée).

Such topography presented obvious difficulties to troops trying to advance rapidly, especially when coupled with an ever increasing distance from the railheads through which their supplies had to be channelled. Fortunately for the supply situation the rapid retreat of the enemy meant it was generally no longer necessary to push forward heavy artillery, with its large tractors and ammunition requirements. All that was required was for 60 pounders and 6 inch howitzers to be kept available to be called up as necessary when the infantry encountered heavy resistance. The new conditions of mobile warfare left little scope for the rigid artillery plans of earlier days. Divisions were now being given general objectives which they were allowed full flexibility to achieve, provided only that they kept contact with the divisions on their flanks. Artillery support could now be called for, even down to battalion commander level.[2]

At first light on 4 November, the advanced guards of the Canadian and XXII Corps moved forward against enemy rearguards which continued to offer little resistance. The 11th and 56th Divisions of XXII Corps crossed the River Aunelle with little difficulty and took the villages of Le Triez, Sébourg and Sébourquiaux.

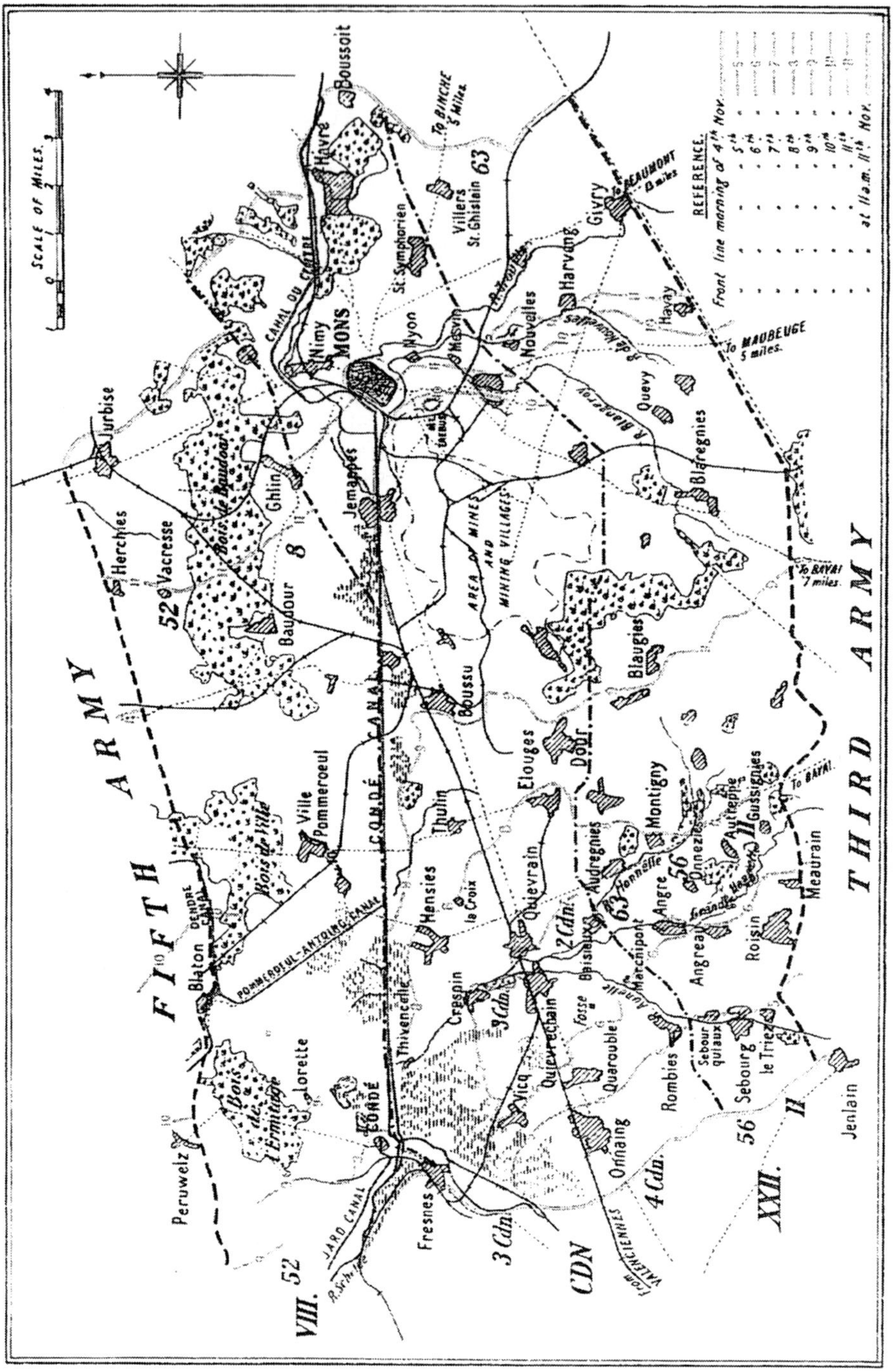

Map 23: Liberation of Mons: 4–11 November 1918

Advanced guards managed to gain a footing on the high ground east of the river. But the enemy were holding the ridge in strength and a counterattack forced the advanced guards back to the right bank of the river. Here the situation was stabilised, bridgeheads were established and bridges put in place. Supplies were brought up in anticipation of a resumption of the advance the following day.[3]

To XXII Corps' left, 4th Canadian Division reached the western outskirts of Rombies and Quarouble, still west of the Aunelle, despite strong enemy rearguards. On their left, and north of the Mons-Valenciennes railway, 3rd Canadian Division established outposts on a line between Onnaing and Escaupont. On the very left of Horne's Army, VIII Corps' attempts to get patrols across the Jard canal, north of Condé, were frustrated by heavy enemy machine gun fire.[4] To Horne's south, Third and Fourth Armies both enjoyed a good day. The 25th Division took Landrecies and the New Zealand Division, with a brilliant *coup de main*, Le Quesnoy. Much of the Forêt de Mormal, which had posed so many problems for the BEF during the retreat from Mons in 1914, was occupied.[5]

In commenting on the day in his diary, Field Marshal Haig wrote that the First Army had not reported much progress after midday. He noted that XXII Corps had had very hard fighting over the previous 3 days and that their consequent tiredness may have accounted for the slowness of their progress.[6] Horne was much more positive about his army's performance, writing that all was going well despite the difficulty of pinning the retreating Germans down, which often left his troops with no definite positions to attack.[7] The long sought after return of a war of movement was not proving to be an unmixed blessing.

Horne's orders for 5 November called for both XXII and Canadian Corps to continue to advance to the Bavay-Hensies road in cooperation with Third Army on XXII Corps' right. At Zero Hour, 05h30, both corps attacked. The 11th and 56th Divisions rapidly cleared the ridge east of the Aunelle river which had been so strongly held by the enemy the day before. Shortly afterwards they crossed the frontier into Belgium. Their next obstacles were the Rivers Angreau and Grande Honnelle. As they approached the first of these, capturing 5 ex-British tanks on the way, enemy resistance stiffened; they appeared determined to prevent any attempts to cross the second of the rivers.

By capturing the village of Roisin, 11th Division secured a passage across the Angreau from which they pressed on to seize the hamlet of Meaurain and the spur north of it overlooking the valley of the Grande Honnelle. But there could be no question of attempting a crossing of the river itself in the face of the heavy fire the enemy were pouring across it. The 56th Division also successfully achieved a crossing of the Angreau at the village of the same name, which had fallen to them. They were less successful in their attempts to cross the Grande Honnelle at Angre where the 2 rivers joined. The enemy had a strong bridgehead in place in the village covering possible crossing places and were not to be dislodged. In heavy fighting, which went on until late in the evening, all 56th Division could achieve was a foothold on the western edge of Angre.

The Canadian Corps also had a day of heavy fighting. The right hand brigade of 4th Canadian Division were held up all day at Marchipont, where fighting continued into the night until the enemy evacuated. The left brigade of the division cleared Quarouble. To their left, 3rd Canadian Division captured Vicq. The

Third Army reported that the Forêt de Mormal had been completely cleared during the day.[8]

The day's fighting had been conducted in wet and cold conditions, less than conducive to successful operations. Horne was becoming worried at the potential effects of mud on the roads he badly needed to keep his troops supplied and moving forward.[9] Nevertheless, his orders for the next day indicated that there would be no let up on the pressure being exerted on the enemy. The 2 corps were to continue their advance with their objective now being the line of the railway running between Mons and Aulnois to the south.[10]

Both corps resumed the attack at 05h30 but immediately ran into heavy German resistance. The 11th Division managed to reach the left bank of the Grande Honnelle but were prevented from crossing by heavy fire from the wooded slopes on the opposite bank. Elements of 56th Division did manage to cross just east of Angreau but were immediately driven back to the left bank of the river by a counterattack delivered from the Bois de Beaufort. Further downstream other elements of 56th Division twice managed to get across the Grande Honnelle at Angre and reach the high ground east and northeast of the village between Onnezies and Baisieux. But on both occasions they were driven back into Angre, although this time they were able to establish and maintain a bridgehead on the river's right bank.

The 4th Canadian Division found themselves called upon to advance across terrain which was much more favourable for the deployment of artillery than that further south. With the help of the guns they were able to capture the French border town of Quiévrechain and, having crossed the frontier, force a passage across the Grande Honnelle between Angre and Quiévrain. They then moved on to take Baisieux. Its loss posed a serious threat to the line of retreat of the Germans defending the line of the Grande Honnelle against XXII Corps further south. North of the Mons-Valenciennes railway, 3rd Canadian Division continued their advance along the southern edge of floods between the River Escaut and the Mons-Condé canal and reached the western outskirts of Crespin.[11]

While the events of the day had not been a total success for Horne's troops, the overall effect had been sufficiently favourable to leave withdrawal as virtually the only sensible option open to the enemy. Shortly after dark on the 6th, patrols detected the first signs of this along the whole front of XXII and Canadian Corps. Advanced guards were quickly deployed and found little opposition in front of them. The 56th Division rapidly crossed the Grande Honnelle during the night and occupied unopposed the high ground north of Onnezies, from which they had twice been expelled the previous day.

This success was to be the precursor of a day of rapid progress on the whole First Army front south of the Mons-Condé canal; only late in the afternoon did enemy rearguards offer up more than token resistance to Horne's advance. By dark 11th Division had reached the Bavay-Hensies road east of Gussignies and Autreppe, 56th Division were east of Montignies-sur-Roc and 63rd Division east of Audregnies. The 2nd Canadian Division had got even further ahead, their line running from Audregnies east to and beyond Elouges and from there north to the Mons-Valenciennes railway south of Thulin. The line of the 3rd Canadian Divi-sion, which had captured Hensies during the day, ran from the western outskirts of

Thulin through Montroeul-sur-Haine to the Mons-Condé canal at St Aybert. North of Condé the enemy were still maintaining their positions on the Jard and Escaut canals. Further south, the Germans had also spent the day retreating on the fronts of the Third, Fourth and First French Armies. The Third Army had captured Bavay. Rumours that the Germans would not stop their retreat until they reached Brussels were now gaining currency.[12]

By now the Germans could no longer disregard the imminent threat to Maubeuge and the effect its loss would have on the situation of their northern group of armies. If they were to maintain their current positions, they would be isolated, cut off and forced to surrender. Accordingly, on 8 November, the enemy began a retreat from their line on the Escaut between Condé and Audenarde, due north. The effect of this move was not immediately apparent on the First Army front along the Jard canal north of Condé. During the night of 7th/8th, First Army patrols were greeted with the heavy gunfire of an enemy seemingly determined to stay put. But the situation had changed by daylight. Patrols of VIII Corps were able to cross both the Escaut and Jard canals with no interference from machine guns, which had departed leaving only a light screen of riflemen to discourage the advancing British. Against such negligible opposition, the towns of Condé, Vieux Condé and Hergnies were quickly overrun and the advanced troops pushed on eastwards. The main problem now confronting them was not enemy resistance, but the flooding on either side of the canals, which made bridging operations difficult. It was not until late afternoon that cavalry and cyclists were able to get across.

South of the Mons-Condé canal, both Canadian and XXII Corps were able to advance throughout the day against virtually no opposition. By nightfall they had reached a line from le Camp Perdu northwards to the western edge of Boussu before turning northwest to the Mons-Condé canal at its junction with the Antoing-Pommeroeul canal, and thence westward along the former canal to a link-up with VIII Corps east of Condé. The Canadians also established bridgeheads north of the Mons-Condé canal near St Aybert.[13] Horne's letter that night expressed his satisfaction at developments.

> We continue to make progress along the road from Valenciennes to Mons and to the south of it. We are now 12 miles from Valenciennes and within 10 miles of Mons! I hope we get to Mons as it would be a great satisfaction to me to take Mons, as I commanded the rearguard of I Corps when we left it 4 years ago last August. The Boche is not offering any strong resistance. He places his machine guns and light artillery so as to delay our advance and as soon as we begin to press he moves off to the next suitable position. The machine gun well-placed and well-used is a formidable weapon and makes advance difficult as you have to find out where it is and bring fire to bear on it before you can advance. The German has also begun to give way on the Escaut Canal north of Condé this morning and my left Corps is beginning to get on there a bit also. It is wonderful the change that has come about and how easily we drive the Boche along now.[14]

Unsurprisingly, Horne's orders for 9 November called for a continuation of his troops' advance. The objective of the 2 corps south of the Mons-Condé canal would be the Maubeuge-Mons road, but they were to be ready to push advanced guards further east than this line should it be necessary in order to maintain contact with a withdrawing enemy. Additional orders were given to Canadian Corps that they should reconnoitre with a view to passing troops across the Mons-Condé canal east of its junction with the Antoing-Pommeroeul canal. From there they might advance northwards towards Pommeroeul and Ville-Pommeroeul and cut off any prospects of an enemy retreat by way of the Basècles-Tertre road.[15]

The 9th would prove to be another day of rapid progress for First Army. Resistance was light but, as Horne had written the previous evening, enemy machine gunners continued to pose a problem. His advanced guards were regularly forced to deploy to outflank them. As soon as they had done so, the machine guns withdrew to renew the battle further back. Despite this irritation, Horne's infantry recorded an average advance of 7 miles and his cavalry and cyclists no less than 13 miles. By evening, XXII Corps' infantry had reached their objective of the Maubeuge-Mons road, from southeast of Quévy to Asquillies; their cavalry were well to the east of the line.

Further north, the Canadian Corps had continued to close in on Mons, having spent the day manoeuvring skilfully through a mass of mining communities lying south of the Mons-Condé canal. By the end of the day they had established outposts on a line running from Genly to Jemappes through Frameries, with their cavalry in front of this line endeavouring to work round Mons, both north and south of the town. On the Canadian left flank, 3rd Canadian Division had crossed the Mons-Condé canal and occupied Ville-Pommeroeul. To their north, 32nd Division of VIII Corps had succeeded in crossing the Antoing-Pommeroeul canal, even though all the bridges were destroyed, by making use of passable locks. By nightfall all their infantry had got across and were advancing towards Hautrage, still some way to the west of the Canadians on their right. On this day, the Third Army completed the capture of the fortress city of Maubeuge and established outposts on the road linking the city with Mons.[16]

Horne's orders for 10 November called once again for a continuation of his army's advance. The XXII Corps were to establish themselves east of the Maubeuge-Mons road and ensure that they maintained touch with the enemy through their advanced guards and mounted troops. The Canadian Corps were to advance to the high ground east and northeast of Mons and also ensure that they remained in touch with the enemy south of the Canal du Centre to the east of Mons. The VIII Corps were to push forward their advanced guards and cavalry to reach the Mons-Jurbise road to the north of Mons.[17]

Here and there enemy rearguards were still standing fast and only retiring after they had forced their opponents to deploy. This was especially to be the case at Mons. The town might not have had for the Germans the huge emotional and symbolic significance it enjoyed in British eyes, but it was of great tactical importance to them. While it was in their possession, the important roads leading from it to Beaumont, Charleroi, Brussels and Ath could be protected. Hence their determination to make a fight for it.

But the First Army was not to be denied. On XXII Corps' front, 11th Division drove the enemy's rearguards through Havay, south of Mons, and occupied the high ground east and northeast of the village. The 56th Division reached Harveng and the 63rd Division, Nouvelles, both villages southeast of Mons. Well ahead, and slightly to the north of the infantry, the 16th Lancers reached the Mons-Givry road east of Spiennes.

On the Canadian Corps front, 2nd Canadian Division, advancing south of Mons, captured the villages of Mesvin and Hyon and the low but important hills overlooking the town from the south. Advancing on either side of the Mons-Condé canal, the 3rd Canadian Division found themselves held up outside Mons, south of the canal, by heavy machine gun fire. This was particularly difficult to suppress as the canal network made it very difficult to get to close quarters with the machine gunners. The Canadians therefore spent much of the daylight available to them working gradually and carefully up to the outer banks of the canals, both to the south and to the west of the town, with a view to crossing them under cover of darkness. North of the Mons-Condé canal the same division had some hard fighting, especially to the south of Ghlin. But by nightfall they had driven the enemy back beyond the Mons-Jurbise railway and established themselves on the northern arm of the canal.[18]

On what was to prove to be the last night of the war, there was to be no let up. The events of the previous day had rendered the enemy's hold on Mons precarious. Their line of retreat had become threatened by the overnight advance of 2nd Canadian Division towards St Symphorien and the high ground between that village and the town. The enemy decided to evacuate their main forces from the town but to leave behind numerous entrenched machine guns with orders to hold on as long as possible. These mounted a determined resistance to all attempts during the night by the 3rd Canadian Division to get across the canals and into the town. They were not finally overcome until the Canadians brought up trench mortars and mounted a bombardment of their positions. By 04h30, the Canadian infantry had successfully crossed the canals and were able to dispose rapidly of the remaining machine gun crews. By dawn on 11 November, 3rd Canadian Division had cleared the town of enemy. Their advanced guards had pushed on eastwards and joined hands with the 2nd Canadian Division on the Charleroi road.

The notification that the Armistice had been signed reached Horne's headquarters at 06h20 on 11 November. A message was immediately sent to all 3 corps that hostilities were to cease at 11h00 that morning. The Canadian Corps HQ reported that they were temporarily out of touch with their leading divisions, by now 5 miles east of Mons, as the telephone lines had been cut. But the message got through to the front line troops in sufficient time to ensure full observance of the end of the fighting.[19]

The cessation of hostilities not only brought to an end the most appalling war up to that point in the history of mankind, but also a most remarkable week for First Army. During it, XXII and Canadian Corps had advanced an average of 25 miles, distances which would have been inconceivable at earlier stages of the war. They had fought their way forward against resistance which might best be described as patchy. At times the German rearguards had given up or vanished very quickly. But on other occasions both corps had had to deal with determined opposition from forces much stronger than rearguards, who were not only ready to stand and fight, but also to deliver counterattacks. The country through which they had advanced had not been conducive to ease of movement. The XXII Corps had frequently been confronted with broken and enclosed ground. The Canadian

Corps had had to put up with marshy conditions on either side of the Mons-Condé canal as well as fighting through a succession of large mining villages and towns which offered ideal conditions for the enemy's defensive tactics.

The VIII Corps had covered a similar distance to the other 2 corps, but in only the last 4 days. They had met little resistance after the Germans had retreated from the Jard canal, but they had still had to cross the wide flooded areas on the eastern banks of the Jard and Antoing-Pommeroeul canals. Their line of advance had lain through low-lying wet country studded with woods which had inevitably put a brake on the pace of their pursuit.

Advances such as these had created huge problems for the supply services. Although, according to the map, the area had seemed to be well served with roads, these had seldom been fit for heavy traffic even in the most favourable conditions. These had rarely applied. The enemy had methodically and thoroughly destroyed both roads and railways as they retired. Hardly a bridge over a stream, river or canal had not been destroyed, and few crossroads had not been cratered and rendered unusable. By 11 November the nearest railheads had been about 30 miles behind Horne's leading troops. In addition to their difficulties in supplying the fighting troops with food and ammunition in these circumstances, the supply services had the further problem of feeding nearly a quarter of a million newly liberated Belgian civilians by the time hostilities ceased. It had been necessary for the road and railway construction troops and the labour gangs in effect to rebuild everything in their charge from Arras and Lens up to the forward areas. The most difficult task had been to replace the many heavy railway bridges. But even this was achieved to such effect that there had been no instance of the forward troops being left short of food or ammunition.

A further major contribution to the speed of advance of Horne's troops had been their morale. This had understandably risen as the realisation had grown that, after the dark and difficult days of spring, the tide had finally and irrevocably turned in the Allies' favour. It was boosted by the troops' reaction to the stories that they heard from the French and Belgian inhabitants of the areas occupied by the enemy since 1914, especially those relating to the ill-treatment that had sometimes been meted out to British prisoners of war. These had made them even more determined to continue to press forward and drive the enemy back to their own territory. It might have been expected that, as the prospect of an armistice being signed very soon looked like becoming a reality, a certain amount of circumspection would have begun to permeate throughout Horne's Army. But the apparently commonly shared view remained that the enemy should be driven back as far and as fast as possible before the armistice was signed, to leave as little doubt as possible in their minds that they were a defeated army. An additional incentive for Horne's army had been that they had had in their sights the town of Mons where it had all begun for the BEF more than 4 years previously. How gratifying it would be to conclude proceedings with the town wrested from the enemy and firmly back in First Army hands. In these circumstances, therefore, it is hardly surprising that there had been no relaxation of the vigour and determination of Horne's army's pursuit of what had by now become a manifestly beaten enemy.[20]

The accusation that generals had been insufficiently careful of their men's lives in their anxiety to press forward, when they could have in effect stood down and awaited an armistice, was to be resurrected and touch closely one of Horne's closest colleagues in First Army, the GOC-in-C of the Canadian Corps, Lt General Sir Arthur Currie. Probably more in pursuit of a personal vendetta than after a careful study of the facts, a former Canadian Defence Minister, Sam Hughes, accused Currie under the protection of Parliamentary privilege of putting his soldiers unnecessarily in harm's way in pursuit of his personal glory. The slander might have died with Hughes in 1921, but an Ontario newspaper chose to reprint his accusations later in the decade. Currie sued for libel and eventually won his case. But the stresses and strains of the long drawn out legal battle may have contributed to his premature death at the age of only 57.[21]

Problems such as those awaiting Currie were far from the thoughts of the Allied armies as they absorbed the reality that the war was at last over after over 4 years and 3 months of bitter struggle. Horne was delighted at the ending of the long ordeal and wrote that day:

> At 11h00 today hostilities ceased! ... We took Mons. We were well round it last night and early this morning we disposed of the Germans who made an attempt to hold it, and occupied the town. I am so pleased. I began at Mons and I end the fighting at Mons! The C-in-C was very pleased, I saw him today and told him.[22]

In words that, unusually for Henry Horne, matched the historical significance of the occasion, he also wrote:

> Now the mighty German nation is completely humbled and the great German Army, which regarded itself as the most powerful fighting machine in the world, is in retreat to its own frontiers, broken and defeated. It is marvellous and I realise that it is the hand of God and we can never be sufficiently thankful to Him for His mercy to us.[23]

Part Five

1918–1929

Chapter XX

The Post-War Years

When Henry Horne saw Haig on the day the Armistice was signed and came into effect, he learned that the First Army would not be participating in the military occupation of the Rhineland called for under its terms. Only 2 British armies were to go and the Second and Fourth had been selected on the basis of the seniority of their commanders, Generals Plumer and Rawlinson. Although clearly disappointed by Haig's decision, Horne loyally recognised that to go by seniority had been the only way to avoid much heart searching and criticism. To add a little bitterness to the pill that Horne had been obliged to swallow, he learned that he would be losing 8 of his divisions, including the whole Canadian Corps, to the occupying armies.[1]

The next few days would offer little time to dwell on disappointments as the victory celebrations got under way. A high point was Horne's official entry into Mons on 15 November. After a procession, parade and march past, Horne was guest of honour at a civic luncheon which was followed by a Te Deum in the cathedral. He was back in Mons for an audience with the King of the Belgians on the 27th. The next day, the Croix de Guerre was bestowed on him by the French government.[2]

In letters home he offered praise to both his Commander-in-Chief and the soldiers who had fought for him. He wrote:

DH has borne a heavy burden and borne it well and his decisions are vindicated by success.[3]

I have been holding an inspection of the 4th Division and saw a very fine body of troops who have fought splendidly for me. The men of the British Army are really the best soldiers in the world – there can be no doubt about that.[4]

By now, Horne was fully aware that his present command would soon come to an end. The First Army would shortly be disbanded as the repatriation, demobilisation and contraction of the army got underway. It was politically necessary to maintain a BEF in being of sufficient size to deter the Germans from having second thoughts about signing the peace treaty which was being drawn up, but this was considered achievable without retaining fully staffed headquarters for the 3 armies not participating in the occupation of the Rhineland. Accordingly, First Army was to be disbanded on 1 April 1919.[5]

Well before this deadline, Horne had begun to make soundings about his next job. He was 58 years of age and not in robust health but had no intention of retiring. The job he coveted was that of GOC-in-C Southern Command, perhaps one of the top 2 army commands in the United Kingdom. Horne clearly believed his seniority and record made him the prime candidate for the command, but he was to be disappointed. On 26 March the War Office offered him Eastern Command. He at once responded that he would prefer Southern Command[6] and sought an interview with the Secretary of State for War, Winston Churchill, which was granted on 1 April. Horne recorded the outcome.

> Interview with Secretary of State for War re want of consideration etc. extended to me in appointing me to Eastern Command when I wanted Southern Command. Churchill assured me it had not been represented to him. It is Henry Wilson's doing. He has purposely arranged to put Harper with Southern Command in preference to me! It is a "job" of the basest type. Similarly the appointment of Davies to succeed McCracken on grounds of "more recent war experience" is a very bad selection and causes great dissatisfaction.[7]

Horne's anger at being passed over in favour of General Harper was understandable. Although a distinguished and successful divisional and later corps commander on the Western Front, Harper had ended the war as a relatively junior Lieutenant General, well below Horne in seniority and experience. In blaming his misfortune on Chief of the Imperial General Staff Henry Wilson, Horne was making a judgement based on the long experience of himself and his fellow senior officers of Wilson's notorious propensity to intrigue. Wilson's explanations to Horne for the decision were blandness itself. But if he was aware, as he might well have been, that Horne held him in no high regard, then he might well have felt that he owed him no favours. He might also have resented Horne's rather dismissive attitude to Eastern Command as a job unworthy of him; Wilson had held the post for a few months in 1917. Whether or not Wilson's passing over of Horne was driven by military or personal considerations, or a mixture of both, the die was cast and Horne had no choice but to accept the Eastern Command appointment. He took over on 1 June 1919.[8] That he remained disenchanted with his East Anglian 'exile' is highlighted by the fact that when Henry Rawlinson was thought to be going to India in mid-1920, Horne formally applied to take over Aldershot Command It was not to be; Rawlinson went to India but Horne remained at Eastern Command.[9]

Although Horne's professional ambitions may have been disappointed, there was to be compensation in the numerous honours which were to be bestowed on him in the months following the end of the war. He received the first intimation of the most significant and gratifying of these in a letter from Lloyd George dated 5 August 1919. The Prime Minister told him that a Barony was to be conferred on him and Parliamentary sanction sought for him to receive an award of £30,000 in recognition of, and thanks for, his wartime services. He would, in addition, be elevated from KCB to GCB.

Horne was duly raised to the peerage on 8 October 1919. After considerable reflection, he decided to take the title Baron Horne of Stirkoke in the County of Caithness. He had hesitated to take the name of the family seat given that his elder brother, Colonel Edward William Horne, owned and resided at Stirkoke House. But his brother reassured him that he would count it a privilege if Stirkoke were part of his title. At the same time he warned Horne that the House might have to be put up for sale because of the heavy taxation now being levied as a result of the war.[10] Horne had also considered incorporating 'Vimy' into his title to commemorate his most famous victory, but decided against it. He was somewhat disconcerted to receive a letter from General Sir Julian Byng, who was being ennobled at the same time, saying that he was being pressed to incorporate 'Vimy' into his titles and, although personally indifferent, might do so unless Horne had any objections. Horne replied that he had decided against using the name but thought that if Byng did it might attract some adverse criticism. Byng clearly decided to live with this risk and, despite Horne's advice, went ahead with the incorporation of 'Vimy' into his titles.[11]

The new Lord Horne was worried that, as he had no male heir, and by now no discernible prospect of having one, his Barony would die with him. He accordingly made strenuous efforts to make it possible for his peerage to descend through the female line, citing as a precedent Field Marshal Lord Roberts of Kandahar, who had been granted this privilege in similar circumstances. Horne pressed his case with both the King and the Prime Minister. The former was the more sympathetic of the two but declined to act, despite a stated personal admiration for Lord Horne, on the grounds that it would set a difficult precedent. The case of Lord Roberts was different, Horne was told. He had been Commander-in-Chief of the whole British Army, and it was this designation which had led to an exception being made in his case. Horne could only reflect impotently that he had commanded many more men with the First Army than Lord Roberts ever had as C-in-C.[12]

What must have given him almost as much pleasure and pride as his elevation to the peerage, was his appointment as Colonel Commandant of the Royal Artillery in 1919.[13] When this was followed in 1926 by his appointment to the historic office of Master-Gunner, St James's Park, he could be content in the knowledge that he had reached the very pinnacle of his profession as a Gunner. These appointments not only reflected his pre-eminence in his profession but also his abiding love for the Royal Regiment of Artillery and his continuing involvement in its affairs.[14]

He received many other honours. In March 1920 he was appointed Aide-de-Camp General to the King. The previous year, Cambridge University had conferred on him an honorary degree which was to be followed by similar recognition from Edinburgh (1920) and Oxford (1927) Universities. Among foreign governments granting him awards were those of Belgium (Grand Officer of the Order of Leopold of Belgium), Japan (Order of the Rising Sun, First Class), the USA (Distinguished Service Medal), Portugal (Grand Cross of the Order of Christ) and France, from which nation he received the Légion d'Honneur to add to his Croix de Guerre.[15] He was granted the freedom of the City of London in 1921 and became a member of its Worshipful Company of Painter Stainers. Closer to home, he was made a Freeman of the Borough of Northampton and of the Town of Wick in Caithness.[16]

A beneficial effect of the Parliamentary grant of £30,000, and one that undoubtedly gave him great personal satisfaction, was that in 1921 he was able to purchase the family seat of the Stirkoke estate from his brother. Colonel Horne retained part of the estate for his own use but the bulk of it, including Stirkoke House, passed to Lord Horne. This was an outcome satisfactory to both brothers in that it relieved Colonel Horne of a burden he could no longer afford while, at the same time, keeping the property in the family. Lord Horne thereby became owner of a property commensurate with his prestige and title as well as being a place he knew well and loved deeply.[17] However, until his death, he continued to use Priestwell House in East Haddon, Northamptonshire, as his main residence, and largely confined his visits to Stirkoke House to fishing trips and the shooting season. He nevertheless did his best to replace his brother in the role of Laird of the district, taking a close interest in its doings. In particular he involved himself in the activities of his tenants and their families, who quickly came to hold him in very high regard. His links with the area of his birth and upbringing had been cemented by his appointment as Deputy Lieutenant of the County of Caithness in 1920.[18]

His links with Caithness were of necessity limited while he remained a full-time soldier with an appointment in the southern half of England. As GOC-in-C Eastern Command in the years immediately following the war, Horne found himself largely preoccupied with the issues arising from demobilisation as the army contracted from its wartime size and structures to a peacetime all-regular establishment. He also immersed himself in reorganising the administration and training arrangements of his command to meet the requirements of the return to a fully professional army. As a senior general, his views were sought on various issues arising out of the war as the military and civil authorities sought to absorb its lessons and chart the way forward.

In April 1920 the government agreed to set up a War Office Committee of Enquiry into Shell Shock under the chairmanship of Lord Southborough, which reported in 1922. Lord Horne intervened on 28 April 1920 in the debate in the House of Lords which led to the setting up of the committee. In his speech, he admitted it was possible that, in the early days of the war when shell shock was not understood, there may have been cases where men had suffered the death penalty under conditions of some injustice. He disclaimed direct knowledge of such instances which, he implied, had no longer been permitted to occur once the condition had been medically recognised. He defended the court-martial system in general, with the checks and balances involved, as fair and effective.[19] Seven years later, on 24 March 1927, he also intervened in the House of Lords' debate on the future of the Territorial Army.[20]

Horne's wartime experience also led him to conclude that the rank of Brigadier General served no useful purpose and should be abolished. In his view it would suffice for the command of a unit of 3 or 4 battalions, each commanded by a Lieutenant Colonel, to be entrusted to a full Colonel. The Brigadier rank should disappear leaving Major General as the lowest general officer rank. Horne claimed that the proliferation of Brigadier Generals in the BEF on the Western Front had led to much general ridicule and criticism by the French, justifiably he argued.[21]

Given his professional background and his very high position in the Royal Artillery hierarchy, it is no surprise at all that his major contribution to post-war debate was concerned with the reorganisation and reequipment of the regiment. He was strongly in favour of abolishing the separation of the Royal Garrison Artillery from the other 2 branches of the regiment, the Royal Field and the Royal Horse Artillery. He wanted to see the regiment's officers able to interchange between the branches, whatever equipment was being operated; amalgamation would achieve this. Officers should then spend a portion of their time in each rank with units operating light and heavy pieces. They should also spend 6 months in each rank with an infantry battalion, the better to appreciate the problems and requirements of the latter. Horne was also in favour of the regiment retaining responsibility for coastal defence and not handing it over to the Royal Navy; it should also be responsible for anti-aircraft defence.

As regards artillery organisation, Horne was justly proud of the system which had evolved in the First Army and urged that this should be adopted as the norm throughout the army with only minor modifications. He recommended that an infantry division's artillery should consist of 3 brigades each consisting of 3 batteries of 18 field guns and one battery of 18 field howitzers. In addition, there should be one brigade of medium mortars, consisting of 3 batteries of 6 mortars each, a divisional ammunition column and a divisional sub-park. Heavy artillery would not be included in the divisional organisation in accordance with British practice in the recent war. This had proved more effective than the German system of allotting it to divisions in that it allowed the heavy guns to be readily concentrated at a decisive point. Heavy artillery should thus continue to be allotted to armies, from where it could be reallocated as necessary to corps and, if desirable, divisions, as the situation demanded.[22]

A further activity connected with the regiment into which he threw himself with enormous enthusiasm was the commissioning and financing of a suitable commemoration of the Royal Artillery's contribution to the nation's war effort and sacrifice. He was still in France when he accepted an invitation to involve himself in the R.A. War Commemoration Fund. He eventually became its president, but from the outset set out to persuade all present and former members of the regiment, both officers and men, to contribute to the fund. His efforts, and those of others, were crowned with success when, on 1 May 1925, he laid a 'Roll of Honour' in the foundations of the Royal Artillery memorial being built at Hyde Park Corner in London. The memorial was unveiled on 25 October the same year by the Prince of Wales.[23] It proved to be a splendid design and remains a striking and evocative sight to this day.

Much of Horne's time, in the early post-war years, was spent in unveiling some of the war memorials which were sprouting up all over the country as virtually every community, school, commercial enterprise, etc. sought to honour their men who had paid the supreme sacrifice. Horne also responded positively to some of the charitable organisations which approached him to take up a figurehead position on their boards. If these organisations had military or Christian associations, or in some cases both, the greater was to be his enthusiasm and devotion to their interests. A particular favourite of his was the Church Lads' Brigade of which he became Governor and Commandant. He also became associated with The Army Scripture Readers and Soldiers' Friend Society, The Royal Army Temperance Association, the Corps of Commissionaires, the Ypres League, the Old Contemptibles Association, the British Legion, the National Association for Employment of Regular Sailors, Soldiers and Airman, the NAAFI, the Royal United Services Institute and the National Playing Fields Association, among others.[24] Another invitation which gave him particular pleasure was one to join the Board of Governors of his old school, Harrow. His appointment took effect from 24 June 1924 when he replaced Lord George Hamilton. He was to remain a governor until the end of his life.[25]

The year 1923 was to be a momentous one for Horne. On 1 February he had the happy duty of giving his beloved daughter Kate ('Kitten') away in marriage to a former ADC, Captain Arthur Hewson MC, RHA. One of the society weddings of the year, the marriage was celebrated at St Marks Church, North Audley Street, in London.[26] Horne must have been delighted with his daughter's choice for a husband, a fellow gunner who had won a Military Cross on the Somme. Just over a year later, the union was to be blessed with a granddaughter for Lord and Lady Horne. Mary Maive was born on 9 April 1924. A second granddaughter, Margaret Eve, was to follow on 10 May 1925. (A third, Deirdre Felicity, was to be born on 19 March, 1932, sadly after Lord Horne's death.)

Only a few weeks after his first granddaughter's birth, Horne's career as an active soldier came to an end. On 31 May 1923, he relinquished Eastern Command to a fellow Gunner, General Sir George Milne, and went on to half pay. He did this reluctantly, despite his advancing age and suspect health (his heart had for some years been a source of concern and was not improving). But the War Office was not able to offer him a position, commensurate with his rank, in the United Kingdom.[27] He was offered the Governorship of the Island of Malta in succession to his old comrade-in-arms, Field Marshal Lord Plumer, but this would have entailed moving there, something he was not prepared to contemplate at this stage of his life. So much that was pleasurable to him, hunting, fishing and shooting, as well as the prospect of watching grandchildren arrive and grow, could only be fully enjoyed while living in Britain. He did try to do a direct swap with General Milne which would have seen him continue on the active list as Lieutenant of the Tower of London. But this came to nothing.

Although on half pay Horne still found himself frequently donning military uniform as he fulfilled invitations to preside at events such as the unveiling of war memorials. But, for a time at least, he found himself with more time to ride to hounds with the Pytchley Hunt, close to his home at East Haddon. However his enjoyment of this pastime was to come to an end when Lady Horne was ordered to give up hunting on medical grounds. Lord Horne did not wish to continue without her, although his decision to give up may also have been influenced by the state of his own health.

Residence at East Haddon was also relatively convenient for the frequent visits he and Lady Horne paid to their daughter and son-in-law who were then living in Farnham, Surrey. He was also able to begin to establish his reputation as a good landlord with his tenants on the Stirkoke estate. He was fully supportive of a government scheme to give returning soldiers with the right background a croft with 10 to 15 acres to farm on land which would otherwise have not been farmed. He also encouraged his tenants to stock their farms with the North Country Cheviot breed of sheep which had been proved to flourish in the spartan conditions of northern Scotland.

Horne's period on half pay came to an end on 31 May 1926 when he finally retired from the army after 46 years and 13 days of commissioned service. He recorded that he felt sad but recognised the inevitable. 'I have had a happy life and have done my best for God, King and Country'. A few days prior to this landmark day in his life had seen Horne enrol as a Special Constable in Northampton as the country was wracked by the only General Strike in its history. Rather more enjoyably he and Lady Horne took advantage of their increased leisure time to make an ocean cruise to the West Indies. The experience was sufficiently pleasurable for them to make a further cruise, this time in the Mediterranean, in early 1929 only a few months before Lord Horne's death. He had the pleasure of bumping into his former close comrade, General Sir Arthur Currie, at the Semiramis Hotel in Cairo, during this cruise.

Perhaps one of the least enjoyable duties Lord Horne had found himself performing from time to time was acting as pallbearer at the funerals of some of his erstwhile senior comrades on the Western Front. In 1925 he carried out this melancholy role twice within a matter of weeks, first in April at the funeral of General Lord (Sir Henry) Rawlinson and the following month at the interment of Field Marshal the Earl of Ypres, formerly Sir John French. He must have been particularly sorrowful when he was called upon to perform the same function at the funeral of Field Marshal Earl Haig which took place on 3 February 1928. Haig and he were almost exactly of an age, Horne being the elder by only 4 months. The sudden and unexpected death of one who had played such a central role in his life must have come as a great shock and sadness to Horne. The sense that the captains and kings were departing must have been reinforced by the death the same year of Marshal Ferdinand Foch of France. It was not to be long before Lord Horne followed his illustrious colleagues.

Only 10 days before his death, in what was probably his last public act, Henry Horne represented the Imperial War Graves Commission at a ceremony at the Chapel of the French national shrine of Notre Dame de Lorette, at which he formally handed over the IWGC's gift to the French nation of commemorative stained glass windows. He also laid a wreath at the shrine's ossuary. In his short address during the ceremony, Lord Horne recalled his triumph at Vimy Ridge, so close to where he was speaking.[28]

On the afternoon of Wednesday 14 August 1929, Lord Horne was out shooting with dogs on the moorland of his Stirkoke estate in the company of 2 friends. Although shooting very well, he had become breathless on a few occasions and been obliged to rest for a minute or two. Suddenly he was seen to collapse and when his friends got to him he was unconscious. Within a couple of minutes he was dead, struck down by the heart weakness which had plagued his later years.

Over the weekend prior to his funeral, Lord Horne's body lay in state in the Stirkoke Recreation Hall with tenants and estate workers providing a guard of honour. The funeral was held on Monday 19 August and, in accordance with Lord Horne's wishes, had no military trappings whatsoever, apart from the covering of the coffin with the Union flag and the placing, on top, of his cap, sword and decorations. Early in the afternoon, the coffin was brought to the front of Stirkoke House and placed on trestles. The short funeral service was conducted there under a grey sky and drizzling rain. The coffin was then placed on a farm wagon drawn by 2 horses, which set off on the 3 mile journey to Wick, accompanied by a long procession of mourners. Notable among these was his former comrade-in-arms and Chief of Staff, Lieutenant General Sir Hastings Anderson, officially there as the representative of the Army Council, but also undoubtedly there as one who had shared, more closely than anyone else, the crises and triumphs of Henry Horne's First Army.

At the Wick Burgh boundary the cortege was met and joined by the Provost, Magistrates and Town Council of the Burgh and by many citizens. Many others lined the streets as the cortege moved on to Wick Cemetery led by pipers playing 'Flowers of the Forest'. At the cemetery, Lord Horne's body was laid to rest in the family plot, where he joined his parents, eldest brother and infant sister. A lone piper concluded proceedings with the lament 'Lochaber No More'. The simplicity of the event had matched Lord Horne's desire for it to be a farewell to a Highland laird, and not a military leader.[29]

The military establishment paid their own farewell to Lord Horne at a memorial service held at Woolwich at the same time as the funeral. The King was represented by General Sir Walter Braithwaite. Among the other notables present to pay their respects were Plumer, Allenby, Byng, Smith-Dorrien and Milne.[30]

Lord Horne's death was marked by an outpouring of press and other interest. Less ephemeral were memorials which were raised to him in the following months. The most touching of these was probably the memorial cairn surmounted by an Inverary cross, paid for and erected by the tenantry and staff of the Stirkoke estate, and placed on the spot where he died. The memorial still stands although it is now surrounded by trees and difficult to find. In Haster, the nearest village to the Stirkoke estate, there is a memorial well, again placed there at the behest of Lord Horne's tenantry and staff. In the 'English' Church in Moray Street, Wick, where Lord Horne worshipped when at Stirkoke, there are 2 memorial plaques to him. But his principal memorial is that accorded him by the Royal Regiment of Artillery, which he had risen to head. A Marble Pavement in St George's Royal Garrison Church, Woolwich, was unveiled and dedicated to Lord Horne on 21 November 1930 by Field Marshal Viscount Plumer.[31]

Following her husband's death, Lady Horne continued to divide her time between East Haddon and Stirkoke. But when their daughter's marriage unhappily ended in divorce in 1940, Lady Horne made Priestwell House over to her and made Stirkoke House her principal residence, which it remained until her death in 1947. Daughter Kate ('Kitten') remarried in 1940 a Captain (later Lt Colonel) Henry Hildreth of the Seaforth Highlanders who became a prisoner of war later that year, during the fall of France. Later on in the war, Kitten disposed of Priestwell House, which was subsequently to be torn down to make room for a residential development, and moved to Stirkoke to be with her mother. Here she was to die as the result of a riding accident in 1956. Colonel Hildreth remarried shortly thereafter and moved away from Stirkoke House, which passed into other hands and was left empty. In 1994 the house was badly damaged by fire in mysterious circumstances and now remains an uninhabitable and slowly declining ruin, a sad reminder of its days as the centre of a thriving community.

Lord Horne's death began that slow decline into obscurity which today means that his name and deeds are largely only remembered by his family and serious students of the First World War. His Barony has unavoidably disappeared, his homes have regrettably succumbed and his fame has undeservedly dimmed. His prominence and achievements as a senior British commander who made a significant contribution to victory in 1918 deserve much greater recognition and acknowledgement from posterity.

Chapter XXI

An Assessment

Once the immediate flurry of obituaries and career assessments had subsided, General Lord Horne's reputation seems to have begun its slow but steady descent from a pinnacle of ready recognition, respect and admiration to an obscurity deserving of the label of the forgotten General of the BEF. Such a fate is scarcely deserved. For over 2 years Henry Horne led an Army which at times consisted of half a million officers and men and over 1,300 guns, and which achieved major successes and suffered few setbacks under his command. His achievements were recognised officially by his ennoblement and the award of £30,000 by Parliament immediately after the Great War ended. He was one of only 10 senior army officers to be accorded this measure of Parliamentary approbation and one of only 7 to be raised to the peerage.[1]

Why has this contemporary recognition not been sustained since? His failure to publish memoirs or diaries has already been mentioned and may have played a part. But more likely perhaps are the assumptions that he did not quite measure up as an army commander; that he only got where he did because he was a favourite of Haig's; that he let his corps commanders, notably Lt General Currie of the Canadian Corps, fight his battles for him; that even his reputed technical expertise in the art of gunnery owed more to the endeavours of others than to himself. None of these assumptions tells the whole story; they are less than fair to Horne.

The guiding forces in Henry Horne's life were, in no particular order, his love of country, his profession of arms, his family, his passion for sport in general (and country sports in particular), and a deep and unquestioning religious faith which was to sustain him throughout his life.

The foundations of his lifelong steadfast Christianity would have been laid early in Horne's life through the example of his parents, stalwarts both of the Evangelical Church in Scotland; there is no indication of any subsequent wavering in his beliefs. There was nothing passive about his Christianity. When in France with the BEF, only the most urgent of operational reasons would prevent him attending at least one service on a Sunday. He listened carefully to the sermons and often reported them in some detail in his letters home to his wife. In these letters he also frequently invoked God, crediting Him when something good had happened and seeking His mercy and support when the reverse was the case.

In the early days of the war he clung to the hope that it would be fought with both sides observing as far as possible the norms of civilised Christian behaviour. He found it impossible to forgive the Germans when they departed from these norms and committed some unchristian act, such as waging war on civilians, and dropping bombs on the Sabbath. Horne clearly tried, largely successfully, to live his life in accordance with the precepts of his religion. His religious attitudes followed the accepted orthodoxy of the times. Although he had lived happily in predominantly Catholic Ireland and had many Catholic soldiers under his command, he could not countenance the prospect of an adherent of that religion as a son-in-law. If Horne was a bigot to hold such attitudes, then so was virtually everyone else in Britain at the time and for many years afterwards.

It is noticeable that many of the organisations and charities that Henry Horne supported after the war had a Christian basis. He was always ready to preside at meetings which concerned matters relevant to the army and the Church, such as those of the Royal Army Chaplain's Department. Horne always had a very great regard for the work of chaplains, rating them highly for their contribution to morale. After Horne's death, the Rev H Blackburn DSO, MC, who had been Assistant Chaplain General of the First Army, wrote to *The Times* as a follow up to the newspaper's obituary of Lord Horne.

> … At the close of these services he spoke a few words himself, and they were words that his hearers could not readily forget. There was nothing fanatical about his religion; he was just a broadminded Christian gentleman who had clear convictions as to the value of religion and its bearing on life. Many chaplains who served in the First Army, as well as myself. will be grateful if you will allow this tribute to one whom we all admired and loved to appear in your paper.[2]

Sporting pursuits played an important part in Horne's life. In his schooldays he enjoyed the team sports of cricket and football, demonstrating perhaps more enthusiasm than talent. But it was in equestrian sports, and especially hunting with the Pytchley, that he really flourished. Close to these in Horne's esteem were the other country pursuits of angling and shooting.

The letters Horne wrote to his wife from France make frequent references to the management of his stable at East Haddon, offering advice and instructions to her on the disposal and acquisition of horses. Horne did as much as was practicable of his moving around in France on horseback and the nearest he was to come to injury on active service was on the occasion when his horse stumbled and threw him on Vimy Ridge.

Their shared steadfast Christianity and delight in the pleasures of the hunt and angling must have been bedrocks of the very happy and loving union which Henry Horne and Kate Blacklock entered into in 1897. The newlyweds were soon to be separated for a long period by the South African War and were to be apart for long stretches when Henry Horne was on the Western Front and in the Middle East. They closed the gap and alleviated the pain of separation by exchanging letters, writing every day, and sometimes more often, even when, in Horne's case, there was the distraction of momentous events clamouring for his attention.

Their relationship followed the accepted norms of the time, with the man very much the master of the house and the wife the supportive spouse. Kate Horne took few decisions without consulting her absent husband, whose letters sometimes reflect this with a plethora of domestic trivia. He was also distracted by his wife's concerns about Dorothy, her daughter by her first marriage. Dorothy had taken on the management of a Church Army Hut (canteen) in Etaples and Lady Horne was clearly worried that she would not be able to cope. Horne found himself having to send ADCs regularly to Etaples in order to be able to reassure his wife that all was well. He paid the occasional visit himself.[3]

Even the most perfect marriage has its occasional downs and the Hornes' was no exception. In early 1918 Lady Horne became convinced that her husband was paying too close attention to the chatelaine of the chateau in which he was head-quartered. Horne strenuously protested his innocence but the fallout soured a subsequent brief leave Horne had in England. His troubles were further compli-cated a few weeks later by his objections to his daughter's Catholic boyfriend. In August 1918 he paid a quick visit to Folkestone which did little to alleviate matters. He recorded on his return that he had found an unhappy wife and a difficult daughter.[4] But these minor problems would soon blow over.

No assessment of Horne can ignore two crucial aspects of his military career; how he performed as a divisional, corps and army commander on the Western Front and how far, if at all, he owed his preferment less to his own abilities than to his personal relationship with Haig.

Whatever might be claimed about his military abilities, there can be no denying that Henry Horne very much looked the part. In appearance he was slim and erect, of medium height with hair and moustaches which had turned white relatively early in life. His features were fine and his gaze steady and unwavering. Impressive on foot, he was even more so in the saddle. Field Marshal Lord Milne's reference to the easy, graceful seat of his soldierly figure has already been alluded to.

In character Horne was a model of integrity and conscientiousness. His natu-rally austere manner and his sometimes perceived taciturnity did not hamper a capacity for getting on with both superiors and subordinates. Unsurprisingly, however, he seems to have inspired respect in them rather than affection. Nor did his general economy with words prevent him from being a prominent and persua-sive participant in meetings of army commanders, where he stood out among his sometimes inarticulate peers. No one has, or is likely to, claim that Horne was an intellectual or intuitive soldier. His approach was straightforward and efficient. Problems were addressed and solved sensibly and professionally. He was acutely aware that the least error on his part could be paid for in other men's lives, and did his level best to limit his mistakes.

An important and delicate aspect of Horne's exercise of command was the way in which he handled his relationships with Empire troops and Britain's French and Portuguese allies. Of these the least crucial in Horne's case were the French. While accepting that there were essential differences in approach, he demonstrated from the outset a great respect for them which put him on good terms with the French opposite numbers with whom he had to deal. Not for him the stereotypical atti-tudes of some British officers, only too ready to criticise the French at every turn. Horne recognised that it would be too much to expect French standards of trench maintenance and housekeeping to correspond with the British, and did not find fault when taking over part of the line from them. He made strenuous efforts to master French, but had to confess that it never got beyond an ability to conduct an everyday conversation.

As with the French, Horne's relationship with the Portuguese was very good on a personal level; he sympathised with the Commanding General's difficulties which he recognised were none of his making. But he and Haig quickly recognised that they were a major, and potentially disastrous, weakness. Horne and Haig did what they could to help the Portuguese surmount their problems. But there were limits on how far they could intrude. Their fears proved all too well-founded on the Lys. Following this disaster, the Portuguese presence on the Western Front was reduced to a token force which, Horne could not have been sorry to see, was transferred to Fifth Army.

Crucial to Horne's reputation and the success of his Army was his handling of the Canadian Corps which, apart from brief intervals with Second Army for Passchendaele and Fourth Army for Amiens, formed the backbone of First Army from late 1916 until the end of the war. Like most British generals of the time, Horne found Empire troops to be a bit of a conundrum. A comment he made in the last month of the war on the Australians, with whom he had had relatively little direct involvement, reflects this and, at the same time, perhaps indicates why his relationship with the Canadians was so harmonious.

> The Australians are fine men, peculiar in their manners sometimes, but all right and nice when you understand them.[5]

Horne deserves credit for maintaining close, and generally harmonious, relations with the Canadians in general and Lt General Sir Arthur Currie, their first Canadian-born commander, in particular. He well understood Canadian sensitivities and accommodated them as far as possible, despite occasional difficulties with Currie's assertiveness. Horne knew that the Canadians would resent any suggestion that they were being patronised or condescended to. It has been suggested that he was an untypical army commander in that he acquired the habit of giving all substantial offensive tasks to the Canadian Corps, leaving both planning and execution very largely to the Corps Commander and staff. Even if this is the whole story, it can be seen not as an abdication but of a playing to his Army's strengths. The Canadian Corps was, after all, an unusual type of corps with national sensibilities and ambitions to become an army in its own right (as was to be achieved in the Second World War).

Horne sensed he would get the best out of his Canadians if he gave them as free a rein as possible to come to their own decisions and make their own plans, which they were well equipped to do. If co-ordination with other corps and with other arms was called for, this would be done by Horne and his Army staff. The Canadians reciprocated with a willingness to serve under him when they would have been much less happy with an intrusive army commander and staff such as they believed they had suffered under General Gough in the Reserve Army on the Somme. Horne knew he had a highly able corps commander in Currie and was prepared to put up with a certain amount of posturing from him because he delivered the goods and, if treated tactfully, was prepared to commit his Corps to operation after operation, when many other corps commanders might have been crying foul.

There were times, however, when Horne's patience with Currie must have been sorely tried. Leaving aside Currie's nagging insistence that the Canadian divisions should fight only as a corps – an issue that clearly concerned Haig more than Horne – Horne found himself at odds with his Canadian subordinate on at least 3 well-documented occasions. The first of these derived from Horne's inference that Currie's insistence on keeping his corps together was an implicit criticism of the quality and fighting ability of some of the British divisions on the Western Front. Horne was incensed enough to call on Currie and tell him that he resented any reflection on the fighting ability of British divisions. While one of Currie's biographers suggests that his opinion was not a criticism of British fighting ability *per se*, but a reflection of the difficulties the divisions had found in coping with their reduction from 12 to 9 battalions, the Canadian Official History is less exculpatory and describes his opinions as ill-considered in taking little account of the reduction in size of divisions, and the overwhelming numerical superiority of the Germans at the time in question.[6]

The second occasion concerned the arrangements for the celebration of the liberation of Valenciennes. Horne insisted that XXII Corps should have equal billing with Canadian Corps in the ceremonies, including the march past. Currie was incensed at this perceived downplaying of his corps' leading role in the liberation and made his views clear, unavailingly, to an obdurate Horne.[7]

The third occasion arose with the publication by *The Times*, shortly after the Armistice, of *The Final Blow of the First Army in 1918*, by a certain 'W.I.' Currie considered this booklet to be a distortion of the truth of the events it purported to describe, especially in the way it diminished the role of the Canadian Corps. He wrote Horne a long letter detailing his criticisms and demanding that the record be put straight. Horne sent an emollient letter in reply which, while disclaiming all responsibility for the booklet's contents (the author was apparently a staff officer who had been temporarily attached to First Army from GHQ), candidly admitted that the typescript had been seen and cleared by the First Army staff. Nothing could be done to meet Currie's concerns.[8]

That none of these occasion led to a permanent souring of the personal relationship between Army and Corps Commander is demonstrated by the readiness with which Horne rallied to Currie's support during his libel action against an Ontario newspaper in the late twenties. Horne fully supported Currie in a written deposition to the court and would have been willing to testify in person had that been deemed necessary.

Horne's command of the First Army was in effect the distinguished climax of a military career which had begun four decades earlier. He never regretted that his choice of arm fell on the Royal Artillery. His progression in the early years was predictably steady and unspectacular even though he was seen as a coming man during his period in India. It was the South African War which gave him his first serious opportunity to shine and he seized it with both hands, fortuitously in full view of two officers, Kitchener and Haig, who were, or would soon be, in pivotal positions to influence his career just prior to and during the First World War. Horne was perceived by them, and others, as being thoroughly professional, competent and reliable – a safe pair of hands. In 1912 his close association with Haig was resumed at Aldershot Command where Horne, as Inspector of the RHA and RFA, was a frequent visitor. When war was declared, Horne was appointed Artillery Adviser to Haig's I Corps and he was on course for his subsequent spectacular rise to army command.

His prospects were enhanced when he performed well as Commander of 1st Corps' rearguard during the Retreat from Mons. That this potentially vital command was entrusted to an artillery officer says a great deal for the very high professional regard in which Haig held Horne. Promotion to Major General 'for services in the field' followed swiftly, and by the beginning of 1915 Horne was commanding the 2nd Division in the newly constituted First Army. The performance of the Division in the 10 months he was to spend in command can hardly be described as distinguished or successful. But little blame was to attach to Horne for this. No other unit of the BEF could be said to have performed outstandingly in 1915 which, in retrospect, can be seen as the first year of the steep learning curve the BEF would have to absorb in its search for the right mix of weaponry and tactics to enable them finally to defeat the German Army in the field so comprehensively in the last 100 days of the war. Despite the general disappointment of his experience of divisional command, Horne had shown a readiness to innovate, for example in mounting one of the BEF's first night attacks, at Festubert.

That Horne was still held in high regard by his superiors was demonstrated when, in November 1915, Kitchener selected him to accompany him to the eastern Mediterranean as his senior military adviser. Horne was none too happy to be moved away from the Western Front but, as it transpired, his relatively brief absence was to do him no harm at all. On the completion of his mission, Kitchener sent Horne to Egypt to reorganise the defences of the Suez Canal. Out of this came his promotion to Lieutenant General and, once it became clear that the Turks were in no position to launch a serious attack on the Canal, he found himself on his way back to the Western Front. This development had not been achieved without some energetic lobbying on his part and, Horne always assumed, the equally energetic advocacy of Haig.[9]

Horne's brief tenure in command of XV Corps of the Fourth Army on the Somme was, like his divisional command, hardly an unqualified success. There were nevertheless sufficient pluses in the corps' performance (its relatively successful first day, its success on Bazentin Ridge and its innovative use of artillery support) to offset its disappointments in the early failures at Mametz and High Woods. Horne's unfortunate experience with the 38th Welsh Division may have taught him a lesson that would stand him in good stead in his relationship with the Canadian Corps; not to interfere in matters best left to the subordinate commander on the spot.

Whatever disappointments there may have been in Horne's performance as a divisional and corps commander were put firmly behind him when, only a few weeks into the Somme campaign, he was notified that he would succeed to the command of the First Army as soon as he could be spared from XV Corps. Horne truly came into his own as an army commander. His performance was eminently creditable in both offensive and defensive operations. He was blessed with a highly competent staff, with the Canadian Corps and with some first class British divisions, such as the 51st Highland and the 55th West Lancs. He demonstrated a consistent readiness to take full advantage of the developments in the application of artillery power, not only because of its devastating effects on the enemy, but because it helped preserve the lives of his infantry. By the end of the war few would have questioned his right to be at the head of one of the BEF's 5 armies.

When doubts are expressed about Horne's right to have reached the rank of General it is usually in the context of his close association with Haig, with the implication that he owed everything to this and little to his own abilities. There can be no doubt that Horne's advancement owed a great deal to Haig. But this was surely because Haig was, from the South African War onwards, in a very good position to help one he genuinely believed, from the evidence of his own eyes, had what it took to hold down senior positions in active service conditions. Horne was not one to whom Haig would instinctively look for command potential. He was a Gunner and although there had been a number of instances of Gunners rising to the Army's highest ranks – Lord Roberts being a recent example – this would not have recommended him to Haig, whose instincts would point him towards the cavalry and the infantry as the main sources of the Army's leaders. Furthermore Horne had not attended Staff College, which was rapidly becoming the *sine qua non* for advancement to the highest ranks.

Haig's esteem for Horne derived from their campaigning together as members of the Cavalry Division in South Africa. The good opinion the former formed of the latter was reinforced in the 2 years prior to the outbreak of the Great War during Horne's frequent visits to Haig's Command at Aldershot. Haig was not alone in his high regard for Horne. His predecessor at Aldershot, Lt General Sir Horace Smith-Dorrien, in his valedictory confidential report on Horne, had described him as an officer fully capable of commanding all-arm units.[10] That this was a view in which Haig evidently concurred is confirmed by the readiness with which he entrusted Horne with command of I Corps' rearguard during the Retreat from Mons.

Horne did not let Haig down and he had no concern whatsoever when Horne was given command of an infantry division. The disappointments and vicissitudes of the fighting in the first half of 1915 did nothing to diminish Horne in Haig's eyes. When he entertained Prime Minister Asquith to lunch on 8 July of that year, he named Horne as one of four young and capable Major Generals who should be given command of armies. Mr Asquith took note.[11] Haig cannot have been too pleased when, a few weeks later, he received a peremptory order from Lord Kitchener that Horne should hand over his division and join him immediately in Paris for undisclosed reasons. Haig may have been reassured to some extent by the indication he was given that Horne would only be absent for a month. In the event it was to be over 6 months before Horne was back on the Western Front, convinced that he owed his reprieve from a Middle Eastern exile to Haig's lobbying on his behalf.[12]

There were sound military reasons for Horne's recall. Haig and Rawlinson, busy preparing the 'Big Push', had become concerned that XIII Corps, with 5 infantry divisions, would be too unwieldy for one corps headquarters to control, especially when the Corps Commander was Lt General Walter Congreve VC, reckoned by Rawlinson to be the weakest of his Lieutenant Generals. (In the event XIII Corps were to prove the only fully successful one on the first day of the Somme.) Haig decided on the creation of XV Corps, which would take over 3 of XIII Corps' divisions, and successfully sought Horne's return to command it.

The Somme campaign was a sad and tragic disappointment to Haig and his senior commanders who had launched it with such high hopes. In the midst of so much frustrated expectation it is perhaps not surprising that such successes as there were tended to be inflated, and failures played down. It can hardly be claimed that Horne had a brilliant Somme. His corps' first day was more successful than most. But thereafter there were to be lost opportunities and bloody attritional battles, only partially offset by the imaginative developments in gunnery which took place in parallel. But when it came to the search for a new commander for First Army there was no one whose performance on the Somme or elsewhere could be said to have outshone Horne's or to have established an automatic right to the elevation.

Nevertheless Horne's promotion was not cut and dried. Despite the innuendo about Haig's supposed favouritism, he was not the Commander-in-Chief's first choice. He wanted Lt General Haking to succeed, a choice that was vetoed by the War Office. Even then Horne might not have got the job if one or other of his rivals had been more readily available; none of the main contenders was. Horne was fortunately able to divest himself of XV Corps only a month or so after being told of his promotion.

Haig was to have no reason to regret that his choice for the First Army command had finally fallen on Horne. He was to prove to be the safe pair of hands Haig had perceived him to be so many years previously. The brilliant victory at Vimy Ridge in April 1917 was followed by the defensive battles of March and April 1918 where, despite some worrying moments, the enemy were stopped. It was during this anxious time that Haig found himself having to reassure the newly-appointed Allied Generalissimo, Marshal Foch, that the threat to France's major coalfield represented by the German offensive, could be left to the relatively inexperienced (in Foch's view) General Horne to deal with. When the BEF took the offensive in what was to prove to be the last 100 days of the war, Horne's Army was in the thick of the fighting and enjoyed some brilliant successes.

It has been suggested, most notably by Basil Liddell Hart, that Horne was an incompetent divisional, corps and army commander who should have been sacked during the Battle of the Somme by a Haig overcoming his endemic inability to sack corps commanders. Liddell Hart ascribed Horne's ability to overcome his alleged military incompetence and rise to army command to his sycophancy, a charge which does not bear close examination. Liddell Hart himself mentions one case, Bazentin Ridge, where Horne supported Rawlinson and opposed Haig, and there are several other instances when Horne told Haig things he would not have wanted to hear, for example at Mametz Wood and High Wood and also over Haig's ill-considered scheme to recapture Orange Hill.

A more likely reason for the close parallel in their careers is that Haig needed to have close subordinates he could trust, and his trust in Horne was total. What had helped to build this trust was the fact that they were from similar backgrounds, spoke the same language and shared similar interests. They were both Scots, even if from widely divergent parts of that country, and shared a similarly robust Christianity. Their wives were friends. Horne was steadfastly loyal to Haig. Early in the war he wrote that Haig was the best commander the BEF had on the Western Front and he never deviated from this belief throughout the trials to come.[13] Neither his letters home nor his diaries utter one word of criticism of Haig, although he was not above the occasional barbed remark directed at politicians (notably Lloyd George and Winston Churchill) and, much more rarely, at a fellow general (usually Henry Wilson). Their mutual trust was cemented by the fact that Haig never felt that his position was threatened by Horne. Henry Horne's ambition had been more than satisfied by his elevation to General and he neither sought nor considered himself suitable for any further advancement, certainly not at the expense of Haig.

No one would claim that Horne was one of the great captains of history. Nor even, as suggested by his First Army Chief of Staff, Sir Hastings Anderson, one of the outstanding soldier figures of the Great War.[14] But his achievements as an army commander were considerable, both in defence and on the offensive. They are deserving of the recognition and acclaim accorded them by his contemporaries in the immediate aftermath of the war, but which has sadly been withheld by subsequent generations through until the present day.

Illustrations

1. Major Henry Horne, South Africa 1900 (courtesy of Mrs Maive Impey)

2. Mrs (later Lady) Kate Horne: 1914
(courtesy of Mrs Pat Hall)

3. Lady Kate (Kitten) Horne
(courtesy of Mrs Pat Hall)

4. With Field Marshal Lord Kitchener at Sedd-el-Bahr, Gallipoli, 12 November 1915. Kitchener leads with French General Brulard. General Horne is fourth from the left. (Q13581. Photograph courtesy of the Imperial War Museum, London)

5. The King at Vimy Ridge escorted by General Horne and Lt Gen Currie (CO1612. Photograph courtesy of the Imperial War Museum, London)

6. General Horne greeting the King of the Belgians on the First Army front: 17 May 1917 (Q2175. Photograph courtesy of the Imperial War Museum, London)

7. General Horne and the judges at the First Army Horse Show, Château de la Haie: 25 June 1917 (Q2429. Photograph courtesy of the Imperial War Museum, London)

8. Generals Horne and Currie at the First Army Service commemorating the fourth
anniversary of the outbreak of the war, Ranchicourt: 5 August 1917
(Q5782. Photograph courtesy of the Imperial War Museum, London)

9. Generals Horne and Currie greeted by the Mayor of Valenciennes following the city's
liberation: 7 November 1918 (CO3614. Photograph courtesy of the Imperial War
Museum, London)

10. General Sir Henry Horne. Drawing by Francis Dodd, December 1917
(Courtesy of the Imperial War Museum, London)

11. General Horne takes the salute of the 7th Canadian Infantry Brigade, Mons: 15 November 1918 (CO3672. Photograph courtesy of the Imperial War Museum, London)

12. The King with his Generals at Buckingham Palace: 19 December 1918. Left to right: Birdwood, Rawlinson, Plumer, HM The King, Haig, Horne, Byng (Q56530. Photograph courtesy of the Imperial War Museum, London)

13. Oil painting of General Lord Horne at Harrow School (painted by the artist Sir Oswald Birley in 1933) Courtesy of Harrow School.

14. General Lord Horne's grave in Wick, Caithness.

15. The staff and tenants' memorial to Lord Horne on the Stirkoke estate (Courtesy of David More)

Stirkoke House, near Wick, then

Stirkoke House, near Wick, now

Notes

The three main sources used in the preparation of this book were:

1. The Official History of the Great War Military Operations (hereinafter 'OH') reprinted by the Imperial War Museum (IWM) Dept of Printed Books in association with The Battery Press Inc, Nashville 1995. Unless otherwise stated the volumes referred to will be those covering 'Military Operations France and Belgium'.

2. The papers of General Lord Horne of Stirkoke lodged with the Department of Documents of the Imperial War Museum (under references 62/54/1 to 17 and 73/ 60/1 and 2). The main sources quoted are Horne's letters to his wife 1914–18 (hereinafter 'Horne ls') and his diaries ('Horne d').

3. The diaries of Field Marshal Earl Haig consulted on microfilm at the Liddell Hart Centre for Military Archives, King's College, University of London. Hereinafter referred to as 'Haig d'.

Full details are provided in the Notes of all other sources cited.

Introduction

1. J.M. Bourne, *Who's Who in World War One*, pp. 133–4.

Chapter I

1. Horne Family Bibles. (See Acknowledgements.)
2. The OED describes Tacksman as, "One who holds a tack or lease of land; especially in the Highlands, a middleman who leases directly from the proprietor of the estate a large piece of land which he sublets in small farms."
3. Gunn, L., *Reverend Alexander Gunn, Watten. (1773–1836)*, <http:// www.geocities.com/cgherald/Archive/RevAlexGunn.html> (accessed 14 April 2006).
4. Source: Mrs. W.B. Ironside of Haster, Wick, Caithness. (See Acknowledgements.)
5. 'Deaths 1863', *Times of India, June to December 1863*.
6. J.B. Craven, *History of the Episcopal Church in the Diocese of Caithness*.
7. 'The Harrovian', 26.10.1929, p. 119. Harrow School Archive. (See Acknowledgements.)

Chapter II

1. R. Holmes (ed), 'Military Academies', *The Oxford Companion to Military History*, pp 3–4.
2. H. Uniacke, 'Lord Horne – the Gunner', *Journal of the Royal Artillery*, October 1929.
3. Ibid.
4. The 'gun-arc' consisted of a board about a yard long, graduated in half degrees, with, at each graduation, a hole for the reception of an acorn-shaped foresight. It was

intended to facilitate accurate aiming and firing from guns in covered or concealed positions. It was standard equipment during the South African War but had been replaced by the much more sophisticated 'dial sight' by the outbreak of the First World War. J. Headlam, *The History of the Royal Artillery from the Indian Mutiny to the Great War, Vol II*, pp. 97 and 105.

5. Uniacke, op. cit.
6. Mrs Kate Blacklock, '1891 Diary', *Horne Papers, IWM*.
7. Horne ls, 7.4.1895.
8. Ibid, 28.6.15.
9. Uniacke, op. cit.

Chapter III

1. *Horne Papers, IWM*.
2. H.S. Horne, *Reminiscences of the South African War*.
3. J. Terraine, *Douglas Haig the Educated Soldier*, p 22.
4. Ibid, p. 25.
5. Horne, op. cit.
6. Ibid, pp. 9–12.
7. Ibid, pp. 13–18.
8. H. Uniacke, 'Lord Horne – the Gunner', *Journal of the Royal Artillery*, October 1929.
9. Horne, op. cit., pp. 21–4.
10. Ibid, pp. 25–7.
11. Ibid, pp. 27–34.
12. Ibid, p. 32.
13. Ibid, pp. 35–6.
14. Ibid, pp. 38–43.
15. Ibid, pp. 44–50.
16. *Horne Papers, IWM*.
17. Uniacke, op.cit., p. 7.

Chapter IV

1. H. Uniacke, 'Lord Horne – the Gunner', *Journal of the Royal Artillery*, October 1929.
2. Ibid.
3. Ibid.
4. *Horne Papers, IWM*.
5. Ibid.
6. Uniacke, op. cit.

Chapter V

1. *OH 1914, Vol I*, p. 56.
2. W.S. Marble, *The Infantry Cannot Do with a Gun Less: the Place of the Artillery in the BEF 1914–18*.
3. Ibid.
4. Horne ls, 11.10.14.

5. *OH 1914, Vol I,* Appendix 9, p. 501.
6. The BEF did not adopt the 24-hour clock until 1st October 1918; until then am and pm were still used. Throughout the text I have taken the liberty of substituting 24-hour clock timings.
7. Ibid, p. 98.
8. Ibid, p. 105.
9. Ibid, p. 110.
10. Ibid, p. 226.
11. Ibid, p. 228.
12. Horne d., 10.9.14.
13. Horne ls, 10.9.14.
14. Horne d, 13.9.14.
15. Ibid, 18.9.14.
16. Marble, op. cit.
17. Horne d, 22 and 24.9.14.
18. Sir James Grierson might have rivalled Haig for the succession to Sir John French as Commander-in-Chief of the BEF. Given command of II Corps at the outbreak of war, however, he died of a heart attack on 17 August 1914, soon after arriving in France, and was replaced by Sir Horace Smith-Dorrien.
19. Marble, op. cit.
20. Horne ls, 5.10.14.
21. Haig d, 11 and 20.11.14.
22. Horne ls, 28.10.14.
23. Quoted in Horne ls, 6.12.14.
24. Horne ls, 27.10.14.
25. Ibid, 30.11.14.
26. Ibid, 16 and 17.12.14.
27. Ibid, 29.9.14.

Chapter VI

1. P. Warner, *The Battle of Loos,* p. 6.
2. OH 1915, Vol I, p. 70.
3. Haig d, 28.12.14.
4. Ibid, 18.12.14.
5. Horne ls, 1 and 2.1.15.
6. Haig d, 30.11.14.
7. Horne ls, 11 and 16.1.15.
8. Ibid, 4.1.15.
9. Ibid, 25.1.15.
10. OH 1915, Vol I, p. 30. Horne ls, 6.2.15.
11. Horne ls, 7.2.15.
12. OH 1915, Vol I, p. 72.
13. Ibid, p. 114 (footnote).
14. War Diary, 2nd Division, (WO 95/1284).
15. OH 1915, Vol I, p. 114.
16. A larger-than-life character, Major John Norton-Griffiths MP, whose nickname was "Empire Jack", used to travel round the battle area in his own adapted chocolate and black 2.5 ton Rolls-Royce. As an engineering contractor with South African mining

experience, Norton-Griffiths persuaded FM Kitchener to allow him to recruit men he had seen tunnelling a Manchester drainage system. Known as 'moles' or 'clay-kickers' these men sat in tunnels supported at an angle of 45 degrees by a wooden cross at their backs. They hacked out the clay with a light spade and passed it back with their feet for disposal behind, working very fast. They called it 'working on the cross' Norton-Griffiths' apotheosis came on 7 June 1917 with the devastatingly successful explosion of 19 mines below the German front line defending the Messines Ridge.

17. Horne d, 20 to 24.2.15.
18. Horne ls, 29.4.15.
19. OH 1915, Vol II, p. 80.
20. Ibid, pp. 7–8.
21. Ibid, pp. 19–39 passim.
22. Haig d., 12.5.15.
23. War Diary, 2nd Division, 15.5.15. E. Wyrall, *The History of the Second Division 1914–1918,* Vol I, p. 199.
24. OH 1915, Vol II, pp. 56–76 passim. Wyrall, op.cit., pp.203–13.
25. Horne ls, 18 and 19.5.15.
26. I. Cull, *The China Dragon's Tales: the 1st Battalion of the Royal Berkshire Regiment in the Great War.*
27. Horne ls, 1.6.15.
28. In mid-May 1915, Prime Minister H H Asquith replaced the Liberal government with a Coalition government of Liberals, Conservatives and Labour. He remained Prime Minister.
29. Ibid, 5.7.15.
30. Ibid, 24 and 25.6.15.
31. J. Terraine, *Haig the Educated Soldier,* pp. 153–6. Warner, op. cit., pp. 6–7.
32. OH 1915, Vol II, pp. 148–58.
33. Ibid, pp. 163–250 passim.
34. Ibid, pp. 259–261.
35. Ibid, pp. 251–3. War Diary, 2nd Division, Sept/Oct 1915. Wyrall, op. cit.,pp. 223–8.
36. OH 1915, Vol II, pp. 253–4. Wyrall, op.cit., pp. 228–230.
37. OH 1915, Vol II, p. 251.
38. Captain Sir Basil Liddell Hart (1895–1970) was a military historian and influential war theorist who enjoys a world-wide reputation. His output was prodigious. As a junior officer in 9th King's Own Yorkshire Light Infantry, 21st Division, he served in Horne's XV Corps during the Battle of the Somme.
39. OH 1915, Vol II, pp. 326–33.
40. B. Liddell Hart, *The Real War.*
41. Ibid, pp. 345–6.
42. Ibid, p. 392.
43. Haig d, 4.11.15.

Chapter VII

1. OH (Gallipoli) Vol II, p. 386.
2. Ibid, p. 402.
3. W.S. Churchill, *The World Crisis, Vol 2,* p. 516.

4. OH (Gallipoli), Vol II, pp. 405–6.
5. Ibid, pp. 398 and 405.
6. Horne d., 7 and 10.11.15.
7. Ibid, 12.11.15.
8. OH (Gallipoli), Vol II, p. 415.
9. Horne d, 13.11.15.
10. Ibid, 14.11.15.
11. OH (Gallipoli), Vol II, p. 415.
12. Horne d, 17.11.15.
13. Ibid, 20.11.15. OH (Gallipoli), Vol II, p. 420.
14. OH (Gallipoli), Vol II, p. 421.
15. Horne d, 22.11.15.
16. OH (Egypt and Palestine), Vol I, p. 85.
17. Ibid, pp. 83–4.
18. H.S. Horne, 'Report on Defensive Line East of Suez Canal', 8.12.15, Horne Papers IWM. OH (Egypt and Palestine), Vol I, p. 89.
19. OH (Egypt and Palestine), Vol I, pp. 89–90.
20. Ibid, p 90.
21. Horne ls, 1.1.16.
22. Ibid, 10.1.16.
23. Ibid, 4, 24 and 30.1.16.
24. Ibid, 5.2.16.
25. Ibid, 5 and 13.2.16.
26. Ibid, 13.2.16.
27. OH (Egypt and Palestine), Vol I, p. 161.
28. Enver Pasha was one of the leaders of the Young Turk revolution in 1908. He became Minister of War in early 1914 and, a Germanophile, played a major part in bringing Turkey into the war on Germany's side. He took command of Turkey's Third Army in the Caucasus where his military ineptitude led to a series of defeats at the hands of the Russians. His fixation with the Caucasus weakened the Turkish position on other fronts to the eventual benefit of Allenby in Palestine.
29. Horne ls, 13.3.16.
30. Ibid.
31. Ibid, 26.3.16.
32. Ibid, 28.2.16.
33. Ibid, 5.3.16.
34. Ibid, 11 and 13.4.16.

Chapter VIII

1. Horne d, 22.4.16.
2. OH 1916, Vol I, p. 26.
3. Ibid, p. 46.
4. Ibid, p. 38.
5. Sir W. Robertson, Papers, Liddell Hart Centre for Military Archives.
6. Horne d, 22.4.16.
7. OH 1916, Vol I, p. 289.
8. Ibid, p. 251.
9. Ibid.

10. Ibid, p. 308.
11. Ibid, p. 250.
12. Horne d, 16.6.16.
13. Horne ls, 7 and 13.6.16.
14. OH 1916, Vol I, p. 347.
15. Ibid, p. 349, and Appendix 23,(i) and (ii).
16. Ibid, p. 350 (footnote 1).
17. Ibid, pp. 348–9.
18. Ibid, pp. 351–5.
19. Ibid. p. 363.
20. Ibid, pp. 356–61.
21. Ibid, p. 362.
22. Ibid, pp. 362–4.
23. Ibid, pp. 367–8.
24. Ibid, p. 482.
25. OH 1916, Vol II, pp. 5–7.
26. Horne ls, 2.7.16.
27. Haig d, 2.7.16.
28. Horne ls, 6.7.16.
29. OH 1916, Vol II, p. 9.
30. Ibid, pp. 15–16.
31. Ibid, pp. 16–17.
32. Haig d, 4.7.16.
33. M. Renshaw, *Mametz Wood*, p. 31.
34. Relations between Pilcher and Fell were perhaps not all they might have been. Pilcher had told Fell the previous day that 51st Brigade should relieve 50th Brigade but that he wanted the 50th Brigade's Commanding Officer to take over Fell's Brigade because he was already familiar with the ground. It was only when 50th Brigade's Commander was seen to be deeply upset by his losses on the first day of the battle, that the order was countermanded and Brigadier General Fell reinstated.

Chapter IX

1. Haig d, 4.7.16.
2. C. Hughes, *Mametz*, pp. 73–4.
3. Horne ls, 4.7.16.
4. M. Renshaw, *Mametz Wood*, p. 33.
5. Ibid, p. 35.
6. Horne ls, 5.7.16.
7. Hughes, op. cit., pp.15–40 passim.
8. Haig, d, 16.1.16.
9. S. Sassoon, *Memoirs of an Infantry Officer*, p. 69.
10. Hughes, op. cit., p. 71.
11. Horne ls, 6.7.16.
12. OH 1916, Vol II, p. 29.
13. Ibid, p. 30.
14. Ibid, pp. 30–1.
15. Ibid, p. 31.

16. Ibid, p. 31–2. Hughes, op. cit., pp. 85–92.
17. OH 1916, Vol II, p. 31.
18. Horne ls, 7.7.16.
19. Ibid, 8.7.16.
20. Haig d, 7.7.16.
21. Ibid, 8.7.16.
22. Hughes, op. cit., pp. 94–5.
23. Haig d, 9.7.16.
24. Renshaw, op. cit., pp. 73–4.
25. Ibid, pp. 79–83.
26. Haig d, 9.7.16.
27. OH 1916, Vol II, p. 57.
28. Ibid, pp. 49–54. Hughes, op. cit., pp. 103–16.
29. OH 1916, Vol II, pp. 57–8.
30. Haig d, 10.7.16.
31. Horne ls, 10.7.16.
32. Hughes, op. cit., pp. 116–24.
33. OH 1916, Vol II, p. 54.
34. Horne ls, 12.7.16.
35. Renshaw, op. cit., p. 126. OH 1916, Vol II, p. 54 (footnote 1).
36. Sir H. Rawlinson, letter to Sir Wm Robertson, 14.7.16, Roberrtson Papers, LHCMA.
37. G.A.B. Dewar and J.H. Boraston, *Sir Douglas Haig's Command*, Vol I, pp. 113–6.
38. OH 1916, Vol II, p. 17.

Chapter X

1. OH 1916, Vol II, pp. 62–4.
2. B.H. Liddell Hart, *History of the First World War*, p. 322.
3. OH 1916, Vol II, p. 64.
4. Haig d, 10.7.16.
5. Ibid, 11.7.16.
6. OH 1916, Vol II, p. 65.
7. Ibid, pp. 65–6.
8. Horne ls, 13.7.16.
9. OH 1916, Vol II, pp. 66–7.
10. Liddell Hart Papers, Introduction, LHCMA.
11. Ibid.,Liddell Hart Notebook.
12. 'Great Generals of the War', *Daily Express*, 21.12.16.
13. Liddell Hart Papers, Transcription in Notebook, December 1916.
14. Liddell Hart Papers (LH/11/ND/70).
15. Liddell Hart, op. cit., p. 322.
16. OH 1916, Vol II, p. 67 and Note I, Chapter II, p. 59.
17. Ibid, pp. 75–8.
18. Ibid, pp. 80–2.
19. Ibid, p. 83.
20. Ibid, pp. 84–8.
21. Horne ls, 15.7.16.
22. Haig d, 15.7.16.

23. OH 1916, Vol II, p. 90.
24. Ibid, p. 92.
25. Ibid, pp. 94–5.
26. Horne ls, 16.7.16.
27. Haig d, 16.7.16.
28. OH 1916, Vol II, p. 99.
29. Ibid, pp. 99–104.
30. Haig d, 17.7.16.
31. OH 1916, Vol II, pp. 109–10.
32. Horne ls, 20.7.16.
33. Ibid, 21.7.16.
34. OH 1916, Vol II, p. 113.
35. Ibid, pp. 136–7.
36. Horne ls, 22.7.16.
37. Ibid, 23.7.16.
38. OH 1916, Vol II, p. 157.
39. Haig d, 28.7.16.
40. OH 1916, Vol II, pp. 158–61.
41. Ibid, pp 167–8. T. Norman, *The Hell They Called High Wood*, p. 180.
42. OH 1916, Vol II, pp. 193–5.
43. Haig d, 18 and 19.8.16.
44. OH 1916, Vol II, p. 204.
45. Horne ls, 30.8.16.
46. Ibid, 28.8.16.
47. Ibid, 1.9.16.
48. OH 1916, Vol II, pp. 205–7.
49. Ibid, pp. 262–5.
50. Horne ls, 4.9.16.
51. OH 1916, Vol II, pp. 274–5.

Chapter XI

1. OH 1916 Vol II, p. 241.
2. Ibid, Appendix 19.
3. Ibid, p. 242.
4. Ibid, Appendix 20.
5. Ibid, p. 299.
6. Ibid, Appendix 24.
7. Ibid, pp. 318–9.
8. Ibid, pp 319–31.
9. Ibid, pp. 306–18.
10. Ibid, pp. 331–8.
11. Ibid, pp. 338–43.
12. Ibid, pp. 343–4.
13. Horne ls, 16.9.16.
14. T. Pidgeon, *Flers and Gueudecourt*, p. 109.
15. OH 1916, Vol II, pp. 351–2.
16. Ibid, pp. 354, 357–9.
17. Ibid, pp. 377–80.

18. Horne ls, 25.9.16.
19. OH 1916, Vol II, pp. 384–6.
20. Haig d, 26.9.16.
21. OH 1916, Vol II, p. 389.
22. Haig d, 3.8.16.
23. Ibid, 11.8.16.
24. Sir Wm. Robertson, letter to Sir D. Haig, 10.8.16, Robertson Papers, LHCMA.
25. Haig d, 12.8.16.
26. Ibid, 20.8.16.
27. Ibid, 26.9.16.

Chapter XII

1. But see J. Terraine, *Haig the Educated Soldier*, p. 25.
2. T. Wilson, *The Myriad Faces of War*, p 203.
3. J. Headlam, *The History of the Royal Artillery from the Indian Mutiny to the Great War, Vol II*, pp. 97 and 105.
4. W.S. Marble, *The Infantry Cannot Do with a Gun Less.*
5. Liddell Hart Notebook, Transcription, December 1916, Liddell Hart Papers, LHCMA.
6. OH 1916, Vol II, Appendix 25.
7. Lord Alanbrooke, *Notes on My Life, Vol I 1883–1918*, (5/2/13–31),Alanbrooke.Papers, LHCMA.
8. Marble, op. cit.
9. A.F. Becke,'The Coming of the Creeping Barrage', *Journal of the Royal Artillery.*
10. Ibid.
11. Ibid.
12. OH 1916, Vol I, p. 349 and Appendix 23 (i) and (ii).
13. Alanbrooke, op. cit.
14. OH 1916, Vol I, Appendix 23 (i) and (ii).
15. Ibid, p. 349.
16. Ibid, p. 350.
17. Ibid.
18. Becke, op. cit.
19. OH 1916, Vol I, p. 350 (footnote 1).
20. OH 1916, Vol II, p. 50.
21. Ibid, p. 66.
22. Becke, op. cit.
23. Ibid.
24. T. Pidgeon, *Flers and Gueudecourt*, p. 40.
25. Marble, op. cit.

Chapter XIII

1. Horne ls, 30.9.16.
2. Horne d, 9 and 21.10.16.
3. Haig d, 1.10.16.
4. OH 1915, Vol II, p. 42.
5. Ibid, pp. 267–70.

6. OH 1917, Vol I, p. 27–9. But see Lord Alanbrooke, *Notes on My Life, Vol I 1883–1918*, (5/2/13–31), Alanbrooke Papers, LHCMA.
7. OH 1917, Vol I, pp. 55–7.
8. Ibid, p. 37.
9. Ibid, Appendix 6. Haig d, 22.12.16.
10. J. Williams, *Byng of Vimy: General and Governor-General*, p. 143.
11. OH 1917, Vol I, p. 302.
12. H. Anderson, 'Lord Horne as an Army Commander', *General the Lord Horne of Stirkoke.*
13. Haig d, 3.3.17.
14. OH 1916, Vol II, pp. 452 and 514–6.
15. Haig d, 5.10.17.
16. J. Nicholls, *Cheerful Sacrifice: the Battle of Arras 1917*, p. 51.
17. OH 1917, Vol I, p. 306. Williams, op. cit., pp. 144–9.
18. Williams, op. cit., p. 150.
19. OH 1917, Vol I, p. 304.
20. Ibid, p. 305.
21. Horne ls, 20 and 27.3.17.
22. OH 1917, Vol I, p. 312 and Appendix 15.
23. Ibid, p. 304.
24. Ibid, Appendix 27.
25. Ibid, pp. 321–39. Williams, op. cit., pp. 156–9.
26. OH 1917, Vol I, pp. 326–30 and 340–3.
27. Ibid, pp. 343–8.
28. Haig d, 12.2.17.
29. Sir Wm. Robertson, telegram to Sir D. Haig, 10.4.17, Robertson Papers, LHCMA.
30. G.W.L. Nicholson, *Official History of the Canadian Army in the First World War: Canadian Expeditionary Force 1914–1919*, p 265.
31. Haig d, 5.5.18.
32. Williams, op. cit., p. 168.
33. Anderson, op. cit.
34. OH 1917, Vol I, p. 352 (footnote 1).

Chapter XIV

1. OH 1917 Vol I, Appendix 22.
2. Ibid, p. 177.
3. Ibid, p. 236.
4. Ibid, pp. 113–5.
5. Ibid, p. 364.
6. Ibid, pp. 494–506.
7. Ibid, pp. 348–52.
8. Haig d, 16.4.17.
9. Ibid, 17.4.17.
10. Ibid, 21.4.17.
11. Horne ls, 22.4.17.
12. Haig d, 22.4.17.
13. OH 1917, Vol I, pp. 398–400.
14. Ibid, p. 405.

15. Horne ls, 23.4.17.
16. OH 1917, Vol I, pp. 404 and 406.
17. Ibid, pp. 383–98 and 400.
18. Ibid, pp. 414–8.
19. Ibid, pp 423–4.
20. Haig d, 28.4.17.
21. Ibid, 30.4.17.
22. Ibid, 2.5.17. OH1917, Vol I, pp. 431–3.
23. OH 1917, Vol I, pp. 445–51.
24. Horne ls, 4.5.17.
25. Ibid, 8.5.17.
26. OH 1917, Vol I, pp. 520–2. Horne ls, 8.5.17.
27. Horne ls, 23.4.17.
28. Ibid, 8.5.17.
29. Ibid, 3 and 4.6.17.
30. H. Anderson, 'Lord Horne as an Army Commander', *General the Lord Horne of Stirkoke*.
31. Haig d, 20.5.17.
32. Horne ls, 16.6.17. J. Williams, *Byng of Vimy: General and Governor-General*, p. 168–9.
33. G.W.L. Nicholson, *Official History of the Canadian Army in the First World War: Canadian Expeditionary Force 1914–1919*, pp., 283–4.
34. Haig d, 21.5.17.
35. Ibid, 3.6.17. Nicholson, op. cit., p. 281.
36. Horne ls, 17.6.17.
37. OH 1917, Vol II, pp. 112–3.
38. Anderson, op.cit.
39. OH 1917, Vol II, pp. 114–5.
40. Horne ls, 28.6.17.
41. Ibid, 29.6.17.
42. Haig d, 30.6.17.
43. Ibid, 3.7.17.
44. Ibid, 5.7.17.
45. Ibid, 8.7.17.
46. OH 1917, Vol II, pp. 219–20. Nicholson, op. cit., pp. 284–5.
47. OH 1917, Vol II, pp. 223–30. Nicholson, op. cit., pp. 287–92.
48. Horne ls, 15.8.17.
49. Ibid, 16.8.17.
50. Ibid, 19.8.17.
51. Nicholson, op. cit., p. 292.
52. Ibid, pp. 292–5.
53. Haig d, 27.8.17.
54. Ibid, 12.9.17.
55. Ibid, 2.10.17. Nicholson, op. cit., p.312.
56. Nicholson, op. cit., p. 327.
57. Haig d, 19.11.17.

Chapter XV

1. OH 1918, Vol I, pp. 51–5.
2. Ibid, p. 55.

296 THE SILENT GENERAL: HORNE OF THE FIRST ARMY

3. Haig d, 18.1.18.
4. Ibid, 5.2.18.
5. OH 1918, Vol I, p. 55.
6. G.W.L. Nicholson, *Official History of the Canadian Army in the First World War: Canadian Expeditionary Force 1914–1919*, pp. 352–3.
7. Horne ls, 12.11.17.
8. Ibid, 13.11.17.
9. Presumably General Sir Henry Wilson, appointed British Military Representative to the Supreme War Council. Wilson, a fluent French-speaking Francophile and a close friend of General Foch, might have been considered an ideal choice for the Council. But he was believed by nearly all his peers to be an arch-schemer and intriguer and was thoroughly distrusted by them. The main exception to this general disapprobation was General Sir Henry Rawlinson, a friend of Wilson's. But he was not much liked and trusted by some of his colleagues either, for similar reasons to Wilson.
10. Ibid, 14.11.17.
11. Haig d, 5.2.18.
12. Horne ls, 18.2.18.
13. Ibid, 20.2.18.
14. Haig d, 21,22 and 23.2.18.
15. Ibid, 28.2.18.
16. Ibid, 15.1.18.
17. Ibid, 1.3.18.
18. Ibid, 10.3.18.
19. Ibid, 11.3.18.
20. Ibid, 17.3.18.
21. Ibid, 21.3.18.
22. Ibid, 26.3.18.
23. Ibid, 3.4.18.
24. OH 1918, Vol II, pp. 62–4.
25. Ibid, pp. 67–72.
26. Haig d, 2.4.18.
27. OH 1918, Vol II, p. 138.
28. Haig d, 12.4.18.
29. Ibid, 2 and 6.4.18.
30. Horne ls, 1, 4 and 5.4.18.
31. Ibid, 4.4.18.
32. Ibid, 8.4.18.
33. OH 1918, Vol II, p. 141.
34. Ibid, pp. 148–9.
35. Haig d, 9.4.18.
36. B. Liddell Hart, *The Real War 1914–1918*.
37. OH 1918, Vol II, p. 149.
38. Ibid, p. 164.
39. Ibid, pp. 165–8.
40. Ibid, pp. 171–3.
41. J.O. Coop, *The Story of the 55th (West Lancashire) Division*.
42. OH 1917, Vol III, p. 169.
43. Ibid, pp. 176–185 passim.

44. OH 1918, Vol II, pp. 188–9.
45. Ibid, pp. 174–7.
46. Ibid, pp. 190–2.
47. Ibid, pp. 184–5.
48. Ibid, p. 187.
49. Horne ls, 9.4.18.
50. Ibid, 10.4.18.
51. OH 1918, Vol II, pp 193–215 passim. Haig d, 10.4.18.
52. Haig d, 10.4.18.
53. OH 1918, Vol II, p. 249 and Appendix 10.
54. Ibid, pp. 222–48 passim.
55. Horne ls, 11.4.18.
56. OH 1918, Vol II, pp. 256–7.
57. Horne ls, 12.4.18.
58. OH 1918, Vol II, pp. 257–69 passim.
59. Ibid, p. 285.
60. Horne ls, 13.4.18.
61. Haig d, 12.4.18.
62. OH 1918, Vol II, p. 300.
63. Ibid, pp. 323–5 and 330–9.
64. Ibid, pp. 357–63.
65. Horne ls, 17.4.18.
66. Ibid, 18.4.18.
67. Ibid, 19 and 21.4.18.
68. OH 1918, Vol II. p. 413. Haig d, 26.4.18.
69. OH 1918, Vol II, p. 442.
70. Haig d, 28.4.18.
71. Ibid, 18.4.18. Nicholson, op. cit., p. 380.
72. Ibid.
73. OH 1918, Vol II, p. 493.
74. H. Anderson, 'Lord Horne as an Army Commander', *General the Lord Horne of Stirkoke.*
75. B. Liddell Hart, Liddell Hart Collection, LH11/ND/70.
76. Anderson, op. cit.

Chapter XVI

1. OH 1918, Vol III, pp. 10–11.
2. Haig d, 13.5.18.
3. Ibid, 14.5.18.
4. J. Baynes, *Far From a Donkey: the Life of General Sir Ivor Maxse.* J.M. Bourne, *Who's Who in World War One.*
5. Bourne, op. cit.
6. Haig d., 5.5.18.
7. Ibid, 19.7.18.
8. Ibid, 14.5.18.
9. Ibid, 18.5.18.
10. OH 1918, Vol III, p. 157.
11. Horne ls, 4,5,7 and 8.6.18.

12. Haig d, 5,6 and 8.6.18.
13. Ibid, 11.6.18.
14. Horne ls, 14.6.18.
15. Haig d, 15.6.18. Horne ls, 15 and 16.6.18.
16. Haig d, 15.6.18.
17. OH 1918, Vol III, pp. 195–7.
18. Horne ls, 29.6.18.
19. Haig d, 23.6 and 21.7.18.
20. Ibid, 5.7.18.
21. Ibid, 15.7.18. OH 1918, Vol III, p. 312.
22. Haig d, 20.7.18.
23. Ibid, 15.7.18. OH 1918, Vol III, p. 313.
24. Horne ls, 15.7.18.
25. OH 1918, Vol III, pp. 313–4.
26. Haig d, 26.7.18.
27. OH 1918, Vol III, pp. 313–4.
28. OH 1918, Vol IV, pp. 20–1.
29. Ibid, p. 162.
30. Ibid, pp. 151–2.
31. Ibid, p. 167.
32. Ibid, p. 133.
33. Ibid, p. 169. Haig d, 15.8.18.
34. OH 1918, Vol IV, p. 173.
35. Ibid, pp. 263–94 passim, p. 345.
36. Horne ls, 23.8.18.
37. Haig d, 24.8.18.
38. Ibid.
39. OH 1918, Vol IV, p. 263.
40. Ibid, p. 258.
41. General Staff, First Army, *Report on First Army Operations 26 August–11 November 1918*, p. 3.
42. Haig d, 25.8.18.
43. OH 1918, Vol IV, pp. 305–6.
44. Ibid, pp. 307–310. G.W. Nicholson, *Official History of the Canadian Army in the First World War: Canadian Expeditionary Force 1914–1919*, pp. 428–9.
45. Haig d, 26.8.18.
46. OH 1918, Vol IV, p 327.
47. Ibid, pp. 327–9. General Staff, First Army, op. cit.
48. Horne ls, 28.8.18.
49. OH 1918, Vol IV, pp. 337–8.
50. Ibid, p. 347.
51. Ibid, pp. 364–6 and 381–3.
52. Ibid, pp. 396–7.
53. Horne ls, 31.8.18.
54. Haig d, 1.9.18.
55. OH 1918, Vol IV, p. 397.
56. Ibid pp. 399–403. General Staff, First Army, op. cit.
57. General Staff, First Army, op. cit., p. 14, hand written marginal note by Horne.
58. OH 1918, Vol IV, p. 413.

59. Ibid, pp. 415–7.
60. General Staff, First Army, op. cit., p.13.
61. Horne ls, 3.9.18.
62. Ibid, 6.9.18.

Chapter XVII

1. Horne ls, 28.8.18.
2. General Staff, First Army, *Report on First Army Operations 26 August–11 November 1918*, p. 13.
3. Ibid, pp. 14–5.
4. Ibid, pp. 18–9.
5. Horne ls, 12 and 13.9.18.
6. General Staff, First Army, op. cit., p. 20.
7. Horne ls, 12.9.18.
8. Ibid, 7.9.18.
9. General Staff, First Army, op. cit., pp. 19–20.
10. Ibid, p. 20.
11. OH 1918, Vol V, pp. 14–5.
12. Ibid, pp. 17–9.
13. OH 1918, Vol IV, p. 424, Vol V, p19 (footnote 2). H. Anderson, *The Crossing of the Canal du Nord – 27th September 1918.*
14. Anderson, op. cit.
15. Ibid. OH 1918. Vol V, pp. 17–19.
16. C-in-C's telegram to Army Commanders of 22.8.18. OH 1918, Vol IV, Appendix XX, pp. 587–8.
17. OH 1918, Vol V, pp. 17–21. Anderson, op. cit.
18. OH 1918, Vol V, pp. 21–9 passsim. Anderson, op. cit.
19. Anderson, op. cit., (text of Horne's presiding comments).
20. Anderson, op. cit.
21. General Staff, First Army, op. cit., p. 31.
22. Horne ls, 27.9.18.
23. General Staff, First Army, op. cit., p. 33.
24. Horne ls, 29.9.18.
25. General Staff, First Army, op. cit., pp. 34–5.
26. Horne ls, 1.10.18.
27. General Staff, First Army, op. cit., pp. 37 and 44.
28. Ibid, pp. 39–40.
29. Ibid, p. 43.
30. Horne ls, 5.10.18.
31. Ibid, 7.10.18.
32. J. Terraine, *To Win a War*, pp. 200–1.
33. Ibid, p. 201.
34. General Staff, First Army, op. cit., pp. 44–5.
35. Horne ls, 9.10.18.
36. General Staff, First Army, op. cit., pp. 47–50.
37. Ibid, p. 51.
38. Horne ls, 19.10.18.

Chapter XVIII

1. General Staff, First Army, *Report on First Army Operations 26 August–11 November 1918*, p. 52.
2. Ibid, pp. 52–4.
3. Ibid, p. 54.
4. Ibid, pp. 55–7.
5. OH 1918, Vol V, p. 395.
6. General Staff, First Army, op. cit., p. 59.
7. Ibid, p. 60.
8. A.G.L. McNaughton,'The Capture of Valenciennes:A Study in Co-ordination', *Canadian Defence Quarterly, 1933*, p. 281.
9. General Staff, First Army, op. cit., p. 61.
10. Ibid, pp. 61–2.
11. Ibid, p. 62.
12. Ibid, p. 63.
13. McNaughton, op. cit., p. 293.
14. General Staff, First Army, op. cit., p. 65.
15. Ibid, pp. 64–5.
16. Horne ls, 1.11.18.
17. Ibid, 2.11.18.
18. Ibid, 3.11.18.
19. General Staff, First Army, op. cit., p. 65.
20. Horne ls, 7.11.18.

Chapter XIX

1. OH 1918, Vol V, p. 488.
2. General Staff, First Army, *Report on First Army Operations 26 August–11 November 1918*, pp. 67–8.
3. OH 1918, Vol V, p. 488.
4. General Staff, First Army, op. cit., p. 68.
5. Ibid.
6. Haig d, 4.11.18.
7. Horne ls, 4.11.18.
8. General Staff, First Army, op. cit., p. 69.
9. Horne ls, 5.11.18.
10. General Staff, First Army, op. cit., p. 69.
11. Ibid, pp. 68–9.
12. Ibid, p. 70.
13. Ibid, pp. 70–1.
14. Horne ls, 8.11.18.
15. General Staff, First Army, op. cit., p. 71.
16. Ibid, p. 71.
17. Ibid, p. 72.
18. Ibid.
19. Ibid, p. 73.
20. Ibid, p. 74.
21. R Neillands, *The Great War Generals on the Western Front 1914–1918*, p. 519.

22. Horne ls, 11.11.18.
23. Ibid.

Chapter XX

1. Horne ls, 11.11.18.
2. Ibid, 15, 27 and 28.11.18.
3. Ibid, 12.11.18.
4. Ibid, 28.11.18.
5. H. Uniacke, 'Lord Horne – the Gunner', *General the Lord Horne of Stirkoke*, p. 15.
6. Horne ls, 26.3.19.
7. Horne d, 1.4.19.
8. Horne Papers, IWM (62/54/11).
9. Ibid.
10. Letter of 10.8.19 from Col E.W. Horne, Horne Papers, IWM (62/54/9).
11. Horne Papers, IWM (62/54/11).
12. Ibid.
13. Ibid.
14. Uniacke, op. cit., p. 18.
15. Horne Papers, IWM (62/54/11).
16. Ibid.
17. Ibid, (62/54/12).
18. Ibid, (62/54/11).
19. Hansard (House of Lords) of 28.4.20 (Vol 39, No. 29), Horne Papers, IWM (62/54/1).
20. Horne Papers, IWM (62/54/12).
21. Ibid, (62/54/2).
22. Ibid.
23. Ibid.
24. Ibid, (62/54/1).
25. Governors' Minutes of 24.6.24, Harrow School Archive.
26. Horne Papers, IWM (62/54/6).
27. Horne d, 1.6.23. War Office letter of 11.5.23, Horne Papers, IWM (62/54/1).
28. Horne Papers, IWM (62/54/3).
29. Ibid, (62/54/8).
30. Ibid.
31. Ibid, (62/54/3).

Chapter XXI

1. *Morning Post*, 6.8.19. Horne Papers, IWM (62/54/11).
2. *The Times*, 22.8.29.
3. Horne Papers, IWM (62/54/7).
4. Horne d, 14.8.18.
5. Horne ls, 12.10.18.
6. A.M.J. Hyatt, *General Sir Arthur Currie*, pp.104–6. G.W.L. Nicholson, *Official History of the Canadian Army in the First World War: Canadian Expeditionary Force 1914–1919*, p. 380.
7. D.G. Dancocks, *Sir Arthur Currie. A Biography*, p.171.

8. Horne Papers, IWM (73/60/2).
9. Horne ls, 11.4.16.
10. Horne Papers, IWM (62/54/3).
11. Haig d, 8.7.15.
12. Horne ls, 11.4.16.
13. Ibid, 30.12.14.
14. H. Anderson, 'Lord Horne as an Army Commander', *General the Lord Horne of Stirkoke.*

Bibliography

Alanbrooke, Field Marshal Viscount, *Notes on my Life, Vol I 1883–1918 (Typescript)*, Liddell Hart Centre for Military Archives (ALANBROOKE 5/2/13–31).

Anderson, Lt General Sir H., 'Lord Horne as an Army Commander', *Journal of the Royal Artillery, Vol 56*, 1930.

Anderson, Major General H., *The Crossing of the Canal du Nord – 27th September 1918 (Typescript)*, Lecture to Royal United Services Institute on 25 January 1922, Horne Papers IWM (62/54/1).

Baynes, J., *Far from a Donkey: the Life of General Sir Ivor Maxse*, London, Brassey's, 1995.

Becke, Major A. F., 'The Coming of the Creeping Barrage', *Journal of the Royal Artillery, Vol 58*, 1931–2.

Beckett, I.F.W. and Corvi, S.J. (eds), *Haig's Generals*, Barnsley, Pen & Sword, 2006.

Berton, P., *Vimy*, Barnsley, Pen & Sword, 2003.

Bewsher, Major F.W., *The History of the 51st (Highland) Division 1914–1918*, Edinburgh, William Blackwood,1921.

Blake, R. (ed), *The Private Papers of Douglas Haig 1914–19*, London, Eyre and Spottiswoode,1952.

Bond, B., 'Liddell Hart and the First World War', *Look to your Front (Studies on the First World War)*, British Commission for Military History, Staplehurst, Spellmount, 1999.

Bonham Carter, V., *Soldier True. The Life and Times of Field Marshal Sir William Robertson*, London, Frederick Muller,1963.

Bourne, Dr J.M., *Who's Who in World War One*, London, Routledge, 2001.

Bristow, A., *A Serious Disappointment: the Battle of Aubers Ridge and the Munitions Scandal*, London, Leo Cooper,1995.

Brooke, Lt Col A.F., 'The Evolution of Artillery in the Great War': Parts 1–4, *The Journal of the Royal Artillery, Vols 51–53*, 1924–6.

Cave, N., *Vimy Ridge: Arras*, London, Leo Cooper,1996.

Charteris, Brigadier General J., *At GHQ*, London, Cassell,1931.

Charteris, Brigadier General J., *Field Marshal Earl Haig*, London, Cassell, 1929.

Cherry, N. *Most Unfavourable Ground: The Battle of Loos 1915*, Solihull, Helion, 2005.

Churchill, W.S., *The World Crisis, Vol 2*, London, Thornton Butterworth, 1923.

Clark, A., *The Donkeys*, London, Hutchinson,1961.

Coop, Rev. J.O., *The Story of the 55th (West Lancashire) Division*, Liverpool 'Daily Post' Printers, 1919.

Corrigan, G., *Mud, Blood and Poppycock*, London, Cassell, 2003.

Craven, Rev. J.B., *History of the Episcopal Church in the Diocese of Caithness*, Kirkwall, 1908.

Cull, I. (with J. Chapman, M. McIntyre, and L. Webb), *The China Dragon's Tales: the 1st Battalion of the Royal Berkshire Regiment in the Great War*,

Royal Gloucestershire, Berkshire and Wiltshire Regiment Museum Trust, 2004.

Dancocks, D.G., *Sir Arthur Currie. A Biography*, Toronto, Methuen, 1985.

Edmonds, Brigadier General Sir J.E (ed), *History of the Great War Based on Official Documents: Military Operations. France and Belgium: 1914, Vols I and II; 1915, Vols I and II; 1916, Vols I and II; 1917, Vols I and II; 1918, Vols I to V: Gallipoli: Vol II: Egypt and Palestine: Vol I*, Nashville, Imperial War Museum Dept of Printed Books in association with The Battery Press Inc, 1995.

Ellis, J. and Cox, M., *The World War I Databook*, London, Aurum Press, 1993.

Farrar-Hockley, A.H., *The Somme*, London, Batsford, 1964.

Fraser, D., *Alanbrooke*, London, Harper-Collins, 1982.

General Staff, First Army, *Report on First Army Operations, 26 August–11 November 1918*, March 1919, Horne Papers, IWM (62/54/2).

Gliddon, G., *The Battle of the Somme: a Topographical History*, Stroud, Sutton, 1994.

Gough, General Sir H., *The Fifth Army*, London, Hodder & Stoughton, 1931.

Harris, J.P., *Amiens to the Armistice*, London, Brassey's, 1998.

Headlam, Major General Sir J., *The History of the Royal Artillery from the Indian Mutiny to the Great War, Volume II, 1899–1914*, Woolwich, Royal Artillery Institution, 1937.

Holmes, R. (ed), *The Oxford Companion to Military History*, Oxford University Press, 2001.

Horne, Major H.S., *Reminiscences of the South African War*, privately printed, 1900.

Hughes, C., *Mametz – Lloyd George's 'Welsh Army' at the Battle of the Somme*, Gliddon Books, 1990.

Hyatt, A.M.J., *General Sir Arthur Currie*, Toronto, University of Toronto Press, 1987.

Liddell Hart, B., *The Real War 1914–1918*, London, Faber and Faber, 1930.

Liddell Hart, B., *Reputations Ten Years After*, Little Brown & Company, 1928.

Liddell Hart, B., *History of the First World War*, London, Cassell, 1970.

Loomis, Major General F.O.W., *Narrative of 3rd Canadian Division Operations from 10th October to 11th November 1918*, Horne Papers, IWM.

McCarthy, C., *The Somme: the Day-by-Day Account*, London, Brockhampton Press, 1998.

McNaughton, Major General A.G.L., 'The Capture of Valenciennes: a Study in Co-ordination', *Canadian Defence Quarterly, Vol 10, No 3 (4/1933)*.

Marble, W. S., 'The Infantry Cannot Do with a Gun Less': the Place of the Artillery in the BEF, 1914–1918*, King's College, University of London (Doctoral Thesis).

Middlebrook, M., *The First Day on the Somme: 1 July 1916*, London, Allen Lane, 1971.

Moore, W., *The Thin Yellow Line*, Ware, Wordsworth Editions, 1999.

Neillands, R., *The Great War Generals on the Western Front 1914–1918*, London, Robinson Publishing, 1999.

Nicholson, Colonel G.W.L., *Official History of the Canadian Army in the First World War: Canadian Expeditionary Force 1914–1919,* Ottawa, Queen's Printer, 1962.

Norman, T., *The Hell They Called High Wood: the Somme 1916,* London, Leo Cooper, 2003.

Passingham, I., *Pillars of Fire: the Battle of Messines Ridge June 1917,* Stroud, Sutton, 1998.

Pidgeon, T., *Flers & Gueudecourt: Somme,* Barnsley, Leo Cooper, 2002.

Pitt, B., *1918:The Last Act,* London, Cassell, 1962.

Renshaw, M., *Mametz Wood: Somme,* Barnsley, Leo Cooper, 1999.

Powell, G., *Plumer: the Soldiers' General,* Barnsley, Pen & Sword, 2004.

Sassoon, S., *Memoirs of an Infantry Officer,* London, Faber and Faber, 1930.

Sheffield, G. & Bourne, J. (eds), *Douglas Haig: War Diaries and Letters 1914–1918,* London, Weidenfeld & Nicholson, 2005.

Sheffield, G., *Forgotten Victory; The First World War Myths and Realities,* London, Headline Book Publishing, 2001.

Sixsmith, Major General E.K.G., *British Generalship in the Twentieth Century,* Arms and Armour, 1970.

Stedman, M., *Fricourt-Mametz: Somme,* Barnsley, Leo Cooper, 1997.

Stewart, Colonel H., *The New Zealand Division 1916–1919: A Popular History Based on Official Records,* Auckland, Whitcombe & Tombs, 1921.

Terraine, J., *1914–1918 Essays on Leadership & War,* The Western Front Association, 1998.

Terraine, J., *Haig: the Educated Soldier,* London, Hutchinson, 1963.

Terraine, J., *Mons: the Retreat to Victory,* London, Leo Cooper, 1991.

Terraine, J., *To Win a War: 1918 the Year of Victory,* London, Cassell, 1978.

Uniacke, Lt General Sir H., 'Lord Horne – the Gunner', *General the Lord Horne of Stirkoke,* Woolwich, Royal Artillery Institution, 1929.

Warner, P., *The Battle of Loos,* Ware, Wordsworth Editions, 2000.

'W.I.', *The Final Blow of the First Army in 1918,* London, Times Publishing Co, 1919. Horne Papers IWM (62/54/7).

Williams, J., *Byng of Vimy: General and Governor-General,* London, Leo Cooper/Secker & Warburg, 1983.

Wilson, T., *The Myriad Faces of War,* Cambridge, Polity Press, 1986.

Winter, D., *Haig's Command: A Reassessment,* London, Viking, 1991.

Wood, H.F., *Vimy,* London, MacDonald, 1967.

Wyrall, E., *The History of the Second Division 1914–1918: Vol I 1914–1916,* London, Nelson, c1921.

Private Papers

Imperial War Musuem. Dept of Documents.
General Lord Horne of Stirkoke.

Liddell Hart Centre for Military Archives.
Alanbrooke, Field Marshal Viscount
Allenby, Field Marshal Viscount
Haig, Field Marshal Earl

Kiggell, Lt General Sir s Edward
Liddell Hart, Captain Sir Basil
Robertson, Field Marshal Sir William Robert

War Diaries

National Archive, Kew
Canadian Corps, WO 95 1049–1054
Fifth Infantry Brigade, WO 95 1344
First Battalion, Royal Berkshire Regiment, WO 95 1361
Fourth Guards Brigade, WO 95 1341
Second Battalion, Royal Sussex Regiment, WO 95 1269
Second Division, 1915, WO 95 1284–1287
Sixth Infantry Brigade, WO 95 1352–1353s

Index

Related titles published by Helion & Company
A selection of forthcoming titles

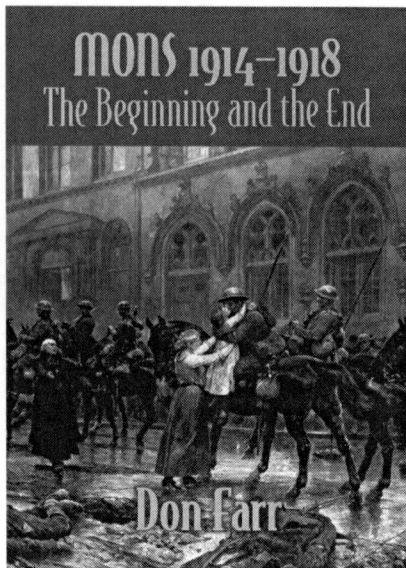

The Whole Armour of God:
Anglican Army Chaplains in the
Great War
Linda Parker
96pp   Paperback
ISBN 978-1-906033-42-2

Mons 1914–1918:
The Beginning and the End
Don Farr
256pp   Hardback
ISBN 978-1-906033-28-6

Landrecies to Cambrai. Case studies of German offensive and defensive operations
on the Western Front 1914–17
Duncan Rogers (ed.)   ISBN 978-1-906033-76-7

The Other Side of the Wire Volume 1.
With the German XIV Reserve Corps on the Somme, September 1914–June 1916
Ralph J. Whitehead   ISBN 978-1-906033-29-3

Sniping in France 1914–18. With notes on the scientific training of scouts, observers and snipers
Major H. Hesketh-Prichard DSO MC   ISBN 978-1-906033-49-1

HELION & COMPANY
26 Willow Road, Solihull, West Midlands, B91 1UE, England
Tel 0121 705 3393   Fax 0121 711 4075
Website: http://www.helion.co.uk

Lightning Source UK Ltd.
Milton Keynes UK
UKOW030614151112

202192UK00003B/7/P

9 781906 033477